Grid Computing
Achievements and Prospects

Grid Computing
Achievements and Prospects

Edited by

Sergei Gorlatch
University of Münster
Germany

Paraskevi Fragopoulou
FORTH-ICS
Heraklion, Crete, Greece

Thierry Priol
IRISA/INRIA
Rennes, France

 Springer

Editors:
Sergei Gorlatch
Institut fuer Informatik
University of Münster
Einsteinstr. 62
48149 Münster
Germany
gorlatch@math.uni-muenster.de

Paraskevi Fragopoulou
Foundation for Research and Technology - Hellas
(FORTH)
Institute of Computer Science N. Plastira 100 Vassilika
Vouton, GR-700 13 Heraklion, Crete, Greece
  With the Department of Applied Informatics and
Multimedia, Technological Educational Institute of Crete
Greece
fragopou@ics.forth.gr

Thierry Priol
IRISA / INRIA Rennes
Campus de Beaulieu
35042 Rennes CX
France
thierry.priol@irisa.fr

ISBN-13: 978-1-4419-3482-6   e-ISBN-13: 978-0-387-09457-1

Printed on acid-free paper

9 8 7 6 5 4 3 2 1

springer.com

Contents

Foreword

This volume is a selection of best papers presented at the CoreGRID Integration Workshop 2008 (CGIW'2008), which took place on 2–4 April 2008 in Hersonissos, Crete, Greece.

The workshop was organised by the Network of Excellence CoreGRID funded by the European Commission under the sixth Framework Programme IST-2003-2.3.2.8 starting September 1st, 2004 for a duration of four years. CoreGRID aims at strengthening and advancing scientific and technological excellence of Europe in the area of Grid and Peer-to-Peer technologies. To achieve this objective, the network brings together a critical mass of well-established researchers from forty institutions who have constructed an ambitious joint programme of activities.

The goal of this regular workshop is to promote the integration of the Core-GRID network and of the European research community in the area of Grid and P2P technologies, in order to overcome the current fragmentation and duplication of efforts in this area.

The list of topics of Grid research covered at the workshop included but was not limited to:

- knowledge and data management;
- programming models;
- system architecture;
- Grid information, resource and workflow monitoring services;
- resource management and scheduling;
- systems, tools and environments;
- trust and security issues on the Grid.

Priority at the workshop was given to work conducted in collaboration between partners from different research institutions and to promising research proposals that can foster such collaboration in the future.

The workshop was open to the members of the CoreGRID network and also to the parties interested in cooperating with the network and/or, possibly joining the network in the future.

The Programme Committee who made the selection of papers included:

Sergei Gorlatch, University of Münster, Chair, UMUE
Paraskevi Fragopoulou, Institute of Computer Science - Hellas, FORTH
Marco Danelutto, University of Pisa, UNIPI
Vladimir Getov, University of Westminster, UOW
Pierre Guisset, CETIC
Domenico Laforenza, ISTI-CNR
Norbert Meyer, Poznan Supercomputing and Networking Center, PSNC
Ron Perrot, Queen's University Belfast, QUB
Thierry Priol, INRIA/IRISA
Uwe Schwiegelshohn, University of Dortmund, UNIDO
Domenico Talia, Universita della Calabria, UNICAL
Ramin Yahyapour, University of Dortmund, UNIDO
Wolfgang Ziegler, Fraunhofer-Institute SCAI

All papers in this volume were reviewed by the following reviewers whose help
we gratefully acknowledge:

Alessandro Basso
Artie Basukoski
Alexander Bolotov
Maciej Brzezniak
Marco Danelutto
Patrizio Dazzi
Jan Dünnweber
Paraskevi Fragopoulou
Stefan Freitag
Vladimir Getov
Sergei Gorlatch
Christian Grimme
Pierre Guisset
Terry Harmer
Stavros Isaiadis
Peter Kilpatrick
Tamas Kiss
Domenico Laforenza
Joachim Lepping
Norbert Meyer
Stéphane Mouton
Jens Müller-Iden
Alexander Papaspyrou
Ron Perrot
Marcin Plociennik

Alexander Ploss
Thierry Priol
Maraike Schellmann
Lars Schley
Uwe Schwiegelshohn
Fabrizio Silvestri
Alan Stewart
Domenico Talia
Gabor Terstyanszky
Jeyarajan Thiyagalingam
Nicola Tonellotto
Pawel Wolniewicz
Ramin Yahyapour
Wolfgang Ziegler

We gratefully acknowledge the support from the members of the Scientific Advisory Board and Industrial Advisory Board of CoreGRID, and especially the invited speakers Ewa Deelman (USC Information Sciences Institute, USA), Christos N. Nikolaou (Department of Computer Science, Crete, Greece) and Yannis Ioannidis (University Of Athens, Greece). Special thanks are due to the authors of all submitted papers, the members of the Programme Committee and the Organising Committee, and to all reviewers, for their contribution to the success of this event. We are grateful to ICS FORTH for hosting the Workshop and publishing its preliminary proceedings. Many thanks go to Jürgen Vörding and Waldemar Gorus who helped a lot with organizing the Workshop and preparing this volume.

Muenster and Hersonissos, April 2008

Sergei Gorlatch, Paraskevi Fragopoulou and Thierry Priol

Contributing Authors

Marco Aldinucci Computer Science Department, University of Pisa, Largo Bruno Pontecorvo 3, 56127 Pisa, Italy (marco.aldinucci@di.unipi.it)

Filipe Araujo CISUC, Department of Informatics Engineering, University of Coimbra, Portugal (filipius@dei.uc.pt)

Rosa M. Badia Univ. Politècnica de Catalunya, C/ Jordi Girona, 1-3, E-08034 Barcelona, Spain (rosab@ac.upc.edu)

Zoltan Balaton Computer and Automation Research Institute, Hungarian Acadamy of Sciences (MTA-SZTAKI), Budapest, Hungary (balaton@sztaki.hu)

Ranieri Baraglia ISTI - Institute of the Italian National Research Council, Via Moruzzi 1, Pisa, Italy (ranieri.baraglia@isti.cnr.it)

Daniela Barbalace DEIS, University of Calabria, Rende (CS), Italy (barbalace@si.deis.unical.it)

Alessandro Bassi Hitachi Sophia Antipolis Laboratory, Immeuble Le Thélème, 1503 Route de Dolines, 06560 Valbonne, France (alessandro.bassi@hitachi-eu.com)

Nicolas Bersano Escuela de Ingenieria Informatica. Universidad Diego Portales Av. Ejercito 441, Santiago, Chile (nbersano@al.udp.cl)

Angelos Bilas   Institute of Computer Science, Foundation for Research and Technology-Hellas, P.O. Box 1385, 71110 Heraklion-Crete, Greece (bilas@ics.forth.gr)

Marian Bubak   Institute of Computer Science, AGH, al. Mickiewicza 30, 30-059 Kraków, Poland
Academic Computer Centre – CYFRONET, Nawojki 11, 30-950 Kraków, Poland (bubak@agh.edu.pl)

Javier Bustos-Jimenez   Escuela de Ingenieria Informatica. Universidad Diego Portales Av. Ejercito 441, Santiago, Chile (javier.bustos@inf.udp.cl)

Louis-Claude Canon   LORIA, INRIA, Nancy University, CNRS Campus Scientifique – BP 239, 54506 Vandoeuvre-lès-Nancy Cedex, France (louis-claude.canon@loria.fr)

Gabriele Capannini   ISTI - Institute of the Italian National Research Council, Via Moruzzi 1, Pisa, Italy (gabriele.capannini@isti.cnr.it)

Miguel Cardenas-Montes   Extermadura Advanced Research Center (CETA-CIEMAT), Trujillo, Spain (miguel.cardenas@ciemat.es)

Michael Classen   University of Passau, 94030 Passau, Germany (classenm@fim.uni-passau.de)

Philipp Classen   University of Passau, 94030 Passau, Germany (classen@fim.uni-passau.de)

Augusto Ciuffoletti   INFN-CNAF, Viale Berti Pichat 6/2, 40126 Bologna, Italy (augusto@di.unipi.it)

Pasquale Cozza   DEIS, University of Calabria, Rende (CS), Italy (pcozza@deis.unical.it)

Marco Danelutto   Computer Science Department, University of Pisa, Largo Bruno Pontecorvo 3, 56127 Pisa, Italy (marco.danelutto@di.unipi.it)

Patrizio Dazzi IMT (Lucca Institute for Advanced Studies), Lucca, Italy ISTI/CNR, Pisa, Italy (patrizio.dazzi@isti.cnr.it)

Marios Dikaiakos Department of Computer Science, University of Cyprus, P.O. Box 1678, Nicosia, Cyprus (mdd@ucy.ac.cy)

Patricio Domingues School of Technology and Management, Polytechnic Institute of Leiria, Portugal (patricio@estg.ipleiria.pt)

Jan Dünnweber Mathematics and Computer Science Department, University of Muenster, Einsteinstrasse 62, Muenster, Germany (duennweb@uni-muenster.de)

Ad Emmen AlmereGrid, Almere, Netherlands (ad@almeregrid.nl)

Thomas Fahringer Institute of Computer Science, University of Innsbruck, Technikerstrasse 21a, A-6020 Innsbruck, Austria (tf@dps.uibk.ac.at)

Zoltan Farkas Computer and Automation Research Institute, Hungarian Acadamy of Sciences (MTA-SZTAKI), Budapest, Hungary (zfarkas@sztaki.hu)

Gilles Fedak INRIA Saclay, Grand-Large, Orsay, France (fedak@lri.fr)

Evangelos Floros National and Kapodistrian University of Athens, Department of Informatics and Telecommunications, Athens, Greece (floros@di.uoa.gr)

Michail Flouris Institute of Computer Science, Foundation for Research and Technology-Hellas, P.O. Box 1385, 71110 Heraklion-Crete, Greece (flouris@ics.forth.gr)

Agostino Forestiero CNR-ICAR, Rende (CS), Italy (forestiero@icar.cnr.it)

Paraskevi Fragopoulou Institute of Computer Science, Foundation for Research and Technology-Hellas, P.O. Box 1385, 71110 Heraklion-Crete, Greece (fragopou@ics.forth.gr)

Wlodzimierz Funika   Institute of Computer Science, AGH, al. Mickiewicza 30, 30-059 Kraków, Poland (funika@uci.agh.edu.pl)

Joaquim Gabarró   Universitat Politècnica de Catalunya, ALBCOM Research Group Edifici Ω, Campus Nord Jordi Girona, 1-3, Barcelona 08034, Spain (gabarro@lsi.upc.edu)

Alina García   Universitat Politècnica de Catalunya, ALBCOM Research Group Edifici Ω, Campus Nord Jordi Girona, 1-3, Barcelona 08034, Spain (agarcia@lsi.upc.edu)

Vladimir Getov   Harrow School of Computer Science, University of Westminster, London, UK (v.s.getov@wmin.ac.uk)

Ali Ghodsi   Swedish Institute of Computer Science P.O. Box 1263, 164 29 Kista, Sweden (ali@sics.se)

Pierpaolo Giacomin   Hitachi Sophia Antipolis Laboratory, Immeuble Le Thélème, 1503 Route de Dolines, 06560 Valbonne, France (giacomin@few.vu.nl)

Harald Gjermundrod   Department of Computer Science, University of Cyprus, P.O. Box 1678, Nicosia, Cyprus (harald@cs.ucy.ac.cy)

Frank Glinka   Mathematics and Computer Science Department, University of Muenster, Einsteinstrasse 62, Muenster, Germany (glinkaf@uni-muenster.de)

Gabor Gombas Computer and Automation Research Institute, Hungarian Acadamy of Sciences (MTA-SZTAKI), Budapest, Hungary (gombasg@sztaki.hu)

Sergei Gorlatch   Mathematics and Computer Science Department, University of Muenster, Einsteinstrasse 62, Muenster, Germany (gorlatch@uni-muenster.de)

Christian Grimme   Dortmund University of Technology, IRF & ITMC 44221 Dortmund, Germany (christian.grimme@udo.edu)

Ralf Gruber   École Polytechnique Fédérale de Lausanne, 1015 Lausanne, Switzerland (ralf.gruber@epfl.ch)

Seif Haridi   Swedish Institute of Computer Science P.O. Box 1263, 164 29 Kista, Sweden (seif@sics.se)

Yannis Ioannidis   National and Kapodistrian University of Athens, Department of Informatics and Telecommunications, Athens, Greece (yannis@di.uoa.gr)

Alexandru Iosup   Faculty of Electrical Engineering, Mathematics, and Computer Science, Delft University of Technology, Delft, Netherlands (A.Iosup@tudelft.nl)

Stavros Isaiadis   Harrow School of Computer Science, University of Westminster, London, UK (s.isaiadis@wmin.ac.uk)

Emmanuel Jeannot   LORIA, INRIA, Nancy University, CNRS Campus Scientifique – BP 239, 54506 Vandoeuvre-lès-Nancy Cedex, France (emmanuel.jeannot@loria.fr)

Peter Kacsuk   Computer and Automation Research Institute, Hungarian Acadamy of Sciences (MTA-SZTAKI), Budapest, Hungary (kacsuk@sztaki.hu)

George Kakaletris   National and Kapodistrian University of Athens, Department of Informatics and Telecommunications, Athens, Greece (gkakas@di.uoa.gr)

Vincent Keller   École Polytechnique Fédérale de Lausanne, 1015 Lausanne, Switzerland (vincent.keller@epfl.ch)

Ian Kelley   Cardiff University, Cardiff, UK (i.r.kelley@cs.cardiff.ac.uk)

Thilo Kielmann   Vrije Universiteit, Computer Systems Group, Dept. of Computer Science, Vrije Universiteit, Amsterdam, Netherlands (kielmann@cs.vu.nl)

Peter Kilpatrick   School of Computer Science, Queen's University of Belfast, Belfast BT7 1NN, Northern Ireland (p.kilpatrick@qub.ac.uk)

Tamas Kiss University of Westminster, London, UK (t.kiss@westminster.ac.uk)

Dalibor Klusáček Faculty of Informatics, Masaryk University, Botanická 68a, 60200 Brno, Czech Republic (xklusac@fi.muni.cz)

Derrick Kondo Laboratoire d'Informatique de Grenoble INRIA, France (dkondo@imag.fr)

Marcin Krystek Poznan Supercomputing and Networking Center, Noskowskiego 10, 61-704 Poznan, Poland (mkrystek@man.poznan.pl)

Pierre Kuonen École d'Ingénieurs et d'Architectes, 1705 Fribourg, Switzerland (pierre.kuonen@eif.ch)

Krzysztof Kurowski Poznan Supercomputing and Networking Center, Noskowskiego 10, 61-704 Poznan, Poland (krzysztof.kurowski@man.poznan.pl)

Theodoros Kyprianou Intensive Care Unit, Nicosia General Hospital, Nicosia, Cyprus (drtheo@cytanet.com.cy)

Jesús Labarta Univ. Politècnica de Catalunya, C/ Jordi Girona, 1-3, E-08034 Barcelona, Spain (jesus@cepba.upc.es)

Christian Lengauer University of Passau, 94030 Passau, Germany (lengauer@fim.uni-passau.de)

Joachim Lepping Dortmund University of Technology, IRF & ITMC 44221 Dortmund, Germany (joachim.lepping@udo.edu)

Oleg Lodygensky LAL Universite Paris Sud, CNRS, IN2P3, France (lodygens@lal.in2p3.fr)

Robert Lovas Computer and Automation Research Institute, Hungarian Acadamy of Sciences (MTA-SZTAKI), Budapest, Hungary (rlovas@sztaki.hu)

Jesus Luna Institute of Computer Science, Foundation for Research and Technology-Hellas, P.O. Box 1385, 71110 Heraklion-Crete, Greece (jluna@ics.forth.gr)

Manolis Marazakis Institute of Computer Science, Foundation for Research and Technology-Hellas, P.O. Box 1385, 71110 Heraklion-Crete, Greece (maraz@ics.forth.gr)

Yari Marchetti INFN-CNAF, Viale Berti Pichat 6/2, 40126 Bologna, Italy (yari.marchetti@cnaf.infn.it)

Attila Csaba Marosi Computer and Automation Research Institute, Hungarian Acadamy of Sciences (MTA-SZTAKI), Budapest, Hungary (atisu@sztaki.hu)

Carlo Mastroianni CNR-ICAR, Rende (CS), Italy (mastroianni@icar.cnr.it)

Jens Müller-Iden Mathematics and Computer Science Department, University of Muenster, Einsteinstrasse 62, Muenster, Germany (jmueller@uni-muenster.de)

Monika Moser Zuse Institut Berlin, Berlin, Germany (moser@zib.de)

Farrukh Nadeem Institute of Computer Science, University of Innsbruck, Technikerstrasse 21a, A-6020 Innsbruck, Austria (farrukh@dps.uibk.ac.at)

Vlad Nae Institute of Computer Science, University of Innsbruck, Technikerstrasse 21a, A-6020 Innsbruck, Austria (vlad@dps.uibk.ac.at)

Ariel Oleksiak Poznan Supercomputing and Networking Center, Noskowskiego 10, 61-704 Poznan, Poland (ariel@man.poznan.pl)

Harris Papadakis Institute of Computer Science, Foundation for Research and Technology-Hellas, P.O. Box 1385, 71110 Heraklion-Crete, Greece (adanar@ics.forth.gr)

Antonis Papadogiannakis Institute of Computer Science, Foundation for Research and Technology-Hellas, P.O. Box 1385, 71110 Heraklion-Crete, Greece (papadog@ics.forth.gr)

Alexander Papaspyrou Dortmund University of Technology, IRF & ITMC 44221 Dortmund, Germany (alexander.papaspyrou@udo.edu)

Marco Pasquali ISTI - Institute of the Italian National Research Council, Via Moruzzi 1, Pisa, Italy (marco.pasquali@isti.cnr.it)

Jose Miguel Piquer Departamento de Ciencias de la Computacion (DCC). Universidad de Chile, Blanco Encalada 2120, Santiago, Chile (jpiquer@dcc.uchile.cl)

Alexander Ploss Mathematics and Computer Science Department, University of Muenster, Einsteinstrasse 62, Muenster, Germany (ploss@uni-muenster.de)

Michalis Polychronakis Institute of Computer Science, Foundation for Research and Technology-Hellas, P.O. Box 1385, 71110 Heraklion-Crete, Greece (mikepo@ics.forth.gr)

Paul Polydoras National and Kapodistrian University of Athens, Department of Informatics and Telecommunications, Athens, Greece (p.polydoras@di.uoa.gr)

Radu Prodan Institute of Computer Science, University of Innsbruck, Technikerstrasse 21a, A-6020 Innsbruck, Austria (radu@dps.uibk.ac.at)

Hassan Rasheed École Polytechnique Fédérale de Lausanne, 1015 Lausanne, Switzerland (hassan.rasheed@epfl.ch)

Alexander Reinefeld Zuse Institut Berlin, Berlin, Germany (ar@zib.de)

Hana Rudová Faculty of Informatics, Masaryk University, Botanická 68a, 60200 Brno, Czech Republic (hanka@fi.muni.cz)

Krzysztof Rzadca   LIG, Grenoble University, avenue Jean Kuntzmann 51, 38330 Montbonnot Saint Martin, France
Polish-Japanese Institute of Information Technology, Koszykowa 86, 02-008 Warsaw, Poland (rzadca@imag.fr)

Rizos Sakellariou   School of Computer Science, University of Manchester, Manchester M13 9PL, UK (rizos@cs.man.ac.uk)

Satu Elisa Schaeffer   Universidad Autonoma de Nuevo Leon, FIME - Posgrado en Ingenieria de Sistemas, AP 126-F. Ciudad Universitaria, San Nicolas de los Garza, NL 66450, Mexico (elisa@yalma.fime.uanl.mx)

Thorsten Schütt   Zuse Institut Berlin, Berlin, Germany (schuett@zib.de)

Frank J. Seinstra   Vrije Universiteit, Computer Systems Group, Dept. of Computer Science, Vrije Universiteit, Amsterdam, Netherlands (fjseins@cs.vu.nl)

Maria Serna   Universitat Politècnica de Catalunya, ALBCOM Research Group Edifici Ω, Campus Nord Jordi Girona, 1-3, Barcelona 08034, Spain (mjserna@lsi.upc.edu)

Tallat M. Shafaat   Royal Institute of Technology (KTH), Stockholm, Sweden (tallat@kth.se)

Luis Moura Silva   CISUC, Department of Informatics Engineering, University of Coimbra, Portugal
Dep. Engenharia Informática, University of Coimbra, Polo II, 3030–Coimbra, Portugal (luis@dei.uc.pt)

Alan Stewart   School of Computer Science, Queen's University of Belfast, Belfast BT7 1NN, Northern Ireland (a.stewart@qub.ac.uk)

Domenico Talia   DEIS, University of Calabria, Via P. Bucci 41C, 87036 Rende (CS), Italy (talia@deis.unical.it)

Ian Taylor   Cardiff University, Cardiff, UK (ian.j.taylor@cs.cardiff.ac.uk)

Gabor Terstyanszky   University of Westminster, London, UK
(g.z.terstyanszky@westminster.ac.uk)

Johannes Tomasoni   Mathematics and Computer Science Department,
University of Muenster, Einsteinstrasse 62, Muenster, Germany
(jtomasoni@uni-muenster.de)

Alberto Troisi   Department of Engineering, University of Sannio, Benevento,
Italy (altroisi@unisannio.it)

Paolo Trunfio   DEIS, University of Calabria, Via P. Bucci 41C, 87036 Rende
(CS), Italy (trunfio@deis.unical.it)

Oliver Wäldrich   Department of Bioinformatics, Fraunhofer Institute SCAI,
53754 Sankt Augustin, Germany (oliver.waeldrich@scai.fraunhofer.de)

Philipp Wieder   Central Institute for Applied Mathematics, Research Centre
Jülich, 52425 Jülich, Germany
Dortmund University of Technology, IRF & ITMC
44221 Dortmund, Germany (ph.wieder@fz-juelich.de)

Ramin Yahyapour   Dortmund University of Technology, IRF & ITMC
44221 Dortmund, Germany (ramin.yahyapour@udo.edu)

Wei Zheng   School of Computer Science, University of Manchester, Manchester M13 9PL, UK (zhengw@cs.man.ac.uk)

Wolfgang Ziegler   Department of Bioinformatics, Fraunhofer Institute SCAI,
53754 Sankt Augustin, Germany (wolfgang.ziegler@scai.fraunhofer.de)

Maciej Zientarski   Institute of Computer Science, AGH, al. Mickiewicza 30,
30-059 Kraków, Poland (maciej.zientarski@gmail.com)

Eugenio Zimeo   Department of Engineering, University of Sannio, Benevento, Italy (zimeo@unisannio.it)

QUERY PROCESSING OVER THE GRID: THE ROLE OF WORKFLOW MANAGEMENT

E. Floros, G. Kakaletris, P. Polydoras and Y. Ioannidis
National and Kapodistrian University of Athens
Department of Informatics and Telecommunications,
Athens, GREECE
floros, gkakas, p.polydoras, yannis@di.uoa.gr

Abstract   gCube Information Retrieval Engine differentiates from federated search. Data and services are scattered over the infrastructure instead of being contained in confined sub-sections, made accessible via narrow interfaces. Grid, where gCube runs, is not meant for interactive work, but offers a vast pool of resources for processing large amounts of information. In such domain it comes as natural consequence the preference of machinery that can employ the afforementioned resources for offering a different range of services, over a traditional search facility.

Keywords: Optimisation, Process Scheduling, Information Retrieval, Grid Computing, Workflow Execution

1.   Introduction

In traditional *Information Retrieval (IR)*, managed or federated, systems exploit domain-specific constructs targeting the needs of a particular application scenario. Query execution on these systems generally assumes that the way to exploit resources is predefined, while the optimal roadmap to obtain results is roughly known a-priori to the system (in contrast to RDBMSs), with minimal potential deviations driven from cardinalities and resource availability - in face of failures and load.

These, otherwise stable assumptions, do not hold in case of *Virtual Research Environments (VREs)* [2]. In these environments, the size and type of information managed and the ways it can be exploited, might vary significantly due to different user / application needs, a challenge which grows under the perspective of hosting them on a dynamic, uncontrolled vast environment, such as a computational grid.

Under the herein described *gCube* framework [1], the aforementioned challenges are handled through the innovative approach of dynamic composition and execution of workflows of services that, step-by-step, carry out the individual tasks implied by an information retrieval request, in a near optimal manner.

The rest of this paper is structured as follows: in section 2 we present the rationale behind the complex Information Retrieval mechanism of gCube and background information on the framework's fundamental concepts and technologies. We describe in more details the gCube framework, in section 3, and we unveil the details of how a simple user query is transformed into a standard-based graph of service invocations and subsequently gets executed. The system evaluation is presented in section 4 along with intentions for future work and system enhancements.

2. Background Information

2.1 gCube

gCube is a middleware for the realisation of Virtual Research Environments on top of a grid-enabled infrastructure. Being multidisciplinary in nature, spreads over domains which, among others include: Knowledge Management / Information Retrieval, Data Management / Data Processing, Distributed Computing, Resource Management, Service Semantics Definition and Service Orchestration. In the context of this paper we introduce Workflows as a mechanism that enables Information Retrieval on the Grid Computing domain:

In **Grid Computing**, a Computational Grid [4] represents a vast pool of resources, interconnected via networks and protocols, that form the substrate where storage and computational demands can be satisfied at large, in a cross-organisational scope. The enabling software (middleware) that brings the infrastructure together and its capabilities can vary significantly, yet, it is generally expected that it offers mechanisms to allow infrastructure and security management, such as information services, authentication mechanisms etc.

Information Retrieval is an empowering concept [5], of Knowledge Management, satisfied nowadays mainly through two architectural models: autonomous systems and federated ones, the latter being a model which fits the SOA paradigm and leaves space for independent realisations of local services. Despite the hard to beat performance of dedicated systems, be it autonomous, federated, network (web) or desktop based, bringing Information Retrieval to the Grid is quite attractive because, on this new joint-domain, VREs can exploit:

- shared, generic resources, with significant lower cost than dedicated infrastructures, for hosting their Knowledge Banks

- large capacities for on demand processing of information beyond the typical mechanisms of the IR domain

- opportunities for exploiting highly demanding IR techniques over the hosted content, such as, but not limited to, Feature Extraction and Query By Example over multimedia content

Under these assumptions, the provision of a standards-based, open system that allows arbitrary realisation of Information Processing scenarios, utilising resources not known a-priori, seems to be fundamental for exposing the benefits of IR over the Grid.

gCube middleware attempts to capture the above-mentioned requirements via a set of specifications and an entire mechanism that transforms user-queries into workflows of service invocations and subsequently manages all the details of communication and execution. It builds on top of OGSA, WS-* and WSRF specifications and exploits the Globus Toolkit 4 provided WS-Core implementation of WSRF. It offers the means for building, managing and running an infrastructure that hosts VREs and a complete set of tools for hosting data and information and exploiting them efficiently in the Knowledge Management domain [3].

Among its core constructs and contents, the Information System, is the glue that keeps the infrastructure together by offering the system-wide registry of gCube and the machinery to interact with it. The *gHN (gCube Hosting Node)*, corresponds to the storage / computing resource of the infrastructure, being correspondent to a container in a physical machine. Registring, exploring, monitoring and running elements on the infrastructure, all pass through these two tightly collaborating elements.

On top of gHNs live the Resources, which can be fairly diverse in nature. Services, Web Service Resources, software components, or even "files" can be resources that may be published and consumed. Every publishable entity exposes a profile in the IS, which renders the set of information upon which it is discovered by its potential consumers. Due to the aforementioned heterogeneity of resources in this infrastructure, the profiles are classified in several subclasses, while more generic ones exist for arbitrary usage. Among these profiles we distinguish the Running Instance and the WebResource profiles, which describe entities that contain "executable logic", i.e. web services, under the WS Resource perspective.

2.2   Services and Resources

gCube is inherently Service Oriented. Service Oriented Architecture (SOA) [6]) is a model ideal for the realisation of large scale systems, essentially distributed. Composing individual entities (services) that encapsulate state, physical resources and logic behind narrow interfaces, is achieved via the numerous protocols on which service interaction is based. The publisher / subscriber model, for declaring the availability and the requests for consumption of Services, is essential for rendering a Service Oriented System able to modify its internal flow of information and control and take advantage of the composition in a manner other than statically binding pieces of logic together.

Service Oriented conceptualisation has received wide acceptance and a wide proliferation after the emergence of XML based technologies of Web Services / HTTP / SOAP stack ([8]). The grid computing community, through its official standardisation body, the *Open Grid Forum* (OGF), having early recognised that computational grids should be build on service oriented foundations, has proposed the *Open Grid Services Architecture* (OGSA) [10] as the blueprint for building and deploying grid tools and infrastructures. The cornerstone of this architecture is the Web Services Resource Framework (WSRF) [9].

Web Services in principle are stateless. They avoid formalising the handling of state among interactions, letting the designer apply home-grown techniques for offering feature rich systems, in a similar way this is handled in the stateless HTTP world. This gap in specification is filled by the WSRF, a set of concepts ([7]), specifications, practices and tools, which do not specify just a formal way for stateful service interactions but defines the Web Service Resource entity as an undividable, identifiable, discoverable and utilisable composition of logic, soft-state and physical resources with a life-time. WSRF builds upon Web Service specifications, like WSDL, WS-Notifications , WS-Addressing , and adds new ones consequence of its new concepts (XML infoset , WS-ResourceProperties , WS-Resource Lifetime, ERP etc) ([8], [9]). These are currently incarnated in reference implementations such as WS-Core (included with the Globus Toolkit 4 [11]) that provides the basic tooling for building Web Service grids. WS Resources are integral part of the gCube architecture and raise a number of challenges for the workflow composition and execution engine.

2.3   Workflows on Grids

As will be shortly shown, IR queries in gCube are transformed into workflows for execution on the Grid. Naturally Workflow management and processing have attracted tremendous interest in the context of computational grids and scientific computing [14], being employed by almost every non-trivial computation / data-intensive application. Under this observation, reuse is quite desirable, thus tools and abstractions are needed to define, execute and monitor such workflows.

In the business world, WS-BPEL (Business Process Execution Language for WebServices) [12] has become the standard notation for defining workflows (or "processes") of web services. The standard is supported by many commercial and open-source platforms providing tooling for programming, deploying and executing BPEL processes. Yet, in the context of scientific computing and computational grids, BPEL has witnessed limited proliferation till now. This is mainly due to the fact that the standard unit of execution currently on the large grid infrastructures, remains the job, rather than the service.

A job encapsulates an application and its dependencies, that is autonomously being executed on a cloud of physical grid resources. The execution of such workflows typically is based in the implicit flow of data between jobs, which can have sequential or parallel control dependencies.

This model of workflow definition is provided by almost all of the popular workflow tools. For instance Condor [13], one of the most well known middleware for setting up campus-wide and corporate-wide grids, provides DAGMan (Directed Acyclic Graph Manager). The same approach has been adopted by gLite middleware [18] developed in the context of EGEE project [17], and by P-Grade which builds above the previous tools and provides a portal and workflow execution engine for inter-grid workflows.

On the other hand there exist high level tools that break the barriers of DAGs and go beyond jobs, either by supporting pure web service integration or hybrid solutions, where web services wrap local applications, remote applications or complete jobs. Nevertheless, the majority of these tools don't use any standardised workflow representation and provide capabilities for defining and running only static workflows. Two good examples of generic engines are the *Taverna* and *MOTEUR* which both use *SCUFL* (Simple Conceptual Unified Flow Language) as the workflow description language. Other examples of traditional scientific workflow tools, with web service extensions, include *Triana*, *Kepler* and *Karajan*. For more details on the above tools/activities see [14].*K-Wf* [15] uses stateful WSRF services as the main unit of execution and supports knowledge based execution in which the workflow enactment is based on stored ontologies of the subsystems involved. It also uses its own workflow definition language based on Petri-nets.

OGSA-DAI (OGSA-Data Access and Integration) [16], can be also considered as data-centric workflow execution framework. It captures three aspects of distributed data-management: acquisition / delivery, processing (transformations) and transportation. Beside the built-in constructs, extending the framework allows custom application logic to be invoked in all sections of the workflow.

2.4 Service Composability

The composability of the various web services into a meaningful workflow is an essential yet not easily tackled, multifaceted issue:

Service semantics: The roles to be undertaken by an entity in a workflow is an integral property of the entity. In typical SOA, consumers of services are a-priori explicit on their requirements. Yet dynamic service composition sce-

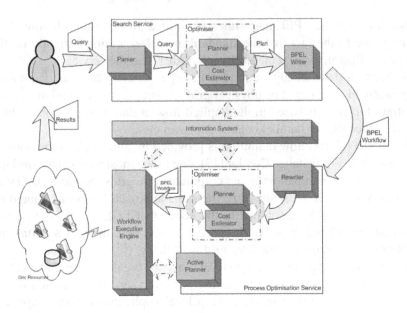

Figure 1.   gCube Workflow Composition and Execution Architecture

narios require sufficient flexibility in their selection mechanisms, which can be achieved by describing the entities at a higher level of abstraction. Service Semantics capture not only the internal operation of an entity, but also its interfacing (parameters / results).

Communication mechanism: The various entities of a workflow communicate via technologies that are determined by their nature. For instance, in Web Services, communication is based upon W3C specifications, which, unfortunately do not supply sufficient support for managing large data sets or streams, which pushes towards proprietary implementations.

Data integration: Normalising the data for exchange among the various stake-holders is prerequisite of composition. Ontologies can be employed for resolving schema mappings, yet in several cases simpler solutions (direct mapping) can be applied. Data integration can be conceived as a sub case of service semantics, yet in applied systems it is often realised separately with simpler mechanisms (transformations).

3.   Query Processing in gCube

In Figure 1 we render the main operational blocks of gCube workflow composition and execution mechanism, which us being s in the following paragraphs.

3.1 From query to workflow

gCube search engine exposes its capabilities via a functional, relational-algebra-like, well-formed query language. By the term "functional" we mean that every query operation acts as a function that applies to a given set of input arguments and produces a certain output. In this way, query operations can be put together, with one consuming the output of the other, forming an operation tree. Schematically, it resembles lisp function calls, in a pipelined manner. All traditional relational operations are supported (sort, project, join, etc.) along with several others stemming from the IR domain, such as full-text , geospatial, and content based search. The functional nature of the query language, offers true extensibility, allowing developers to add their own custom-made operations, while conditional execution allows true/false branching.

Behind this language, the framework follows a three step procedure for carrying out its operation, roughly assimilating the operation of modern RDBMSs, with several modifications in order to fit in the distributed nature of wide area networks and more specifically the Grid:

Query Parsing.   User-defined queries are fed to the query parser, which processes the requests, validates the queries and forms the corresponding internal query representations as strongly-typed graphs. The validation process includes checks against data source definition, argument incompatibilities and obviously the necessary syntactic conformance.

Query Planning.   The query planner is responsible for producing an execution plan that computes the original query expression. This plan is actually a web service workflow. Its nodes represent invocations of service instantiations and its edges communication channels between pairs of instantiations, in other words, producer-consumer relations. The input data stream of the producer service instance are being transported to the consumer instance for further processing via a transportation leveraging mechanism called gRS (gCube Result Set) [3].

The planner exploits registered service semantic descriptions [1], in order to decide which service instances can compute given query operations. Through the same mechanism the instance invocation parameters are generated, in accordance with the user query expression. Finally, data incompatibilities are resolved based on (data) source descriptions registered in the infrastructure.

As a result the planner creates an initial (non-optimal) execution plan. Although optimisation and service scheduling are left for subsequent stages, pre-

---

[1]metadata descriptions of service capabilities and instantiation procedures, expressed in XML Schema format [XSD]

liminary query optimisation is also applied here, based on heuristics and pre-defined cost estimations that take advantage of IR domain-specific knowledge.

The execution plan, which is still in an internal representation form, goes through the BPELBuilder component which produces the BPEL process, which along with some supplementary information, specific to each BPEL implementation, can be redirected to any BPEL engine. Due to the Workflow creation cost a caching mechanism is employed which, in the case of identical queries, requires the minor cost of validating against potential stale instances.

3.2   Process Optimisation

The gCube Process Optimisation Services (POS) implement core functionality in the form of libraries and web services for Process scheduling and execution planning. POS is comprised by a core optimisation library (POSLib) and two Web Services (RewriterService and PlannerService) that expose part of the library's functionality. POSLib implements three core components of process optimisation. POS is an integral part of query execution in gCube, since it is responsible for the optimised scheduling of workflows produced by the query planner and consequently is a key player in alleviating the grid overhead in query execution

Rewriter Provides structural optimisation of a process. It receives as input a BPEL process, analyses the structure, identifies independent invocations and formulates them in parallel constructs (BPEL *flow* elements) in order to accelerate the overall process execution. It is the first step of optimisation that takes place before the process arrives at the execution engine.

Planner Performs the pre-planning of the process execution. Receives an abstract BPEL process and generates various scheduling plans for execution. The generation of an executable plan implies that all references to abstract services are replaced by invocations to concrete, instantiated services in a gCube infrastructure. The Planner uses information provided by the gIS which keeps up-to-date metrics for resources employed in the grid (physical machines, services, etc). This information is input to various cost functions (applied by the paired Cost Estimator) that calculate the individual execution cost of a candidate plan.

The selection of best plans is performed by a custom implementation of the Simulated Annealing algorithm. The outcome of the planning is a set of executable BPEL processes that are passed to the workflow execution engine. Cost calculation can be guided by various weighted optimisation policies passed by the author (human or application) of the BPEL process inside the BPEL description.

ActivePlanner Provides run-time optimised scheduling of a gCube process. It is invoked during the process execution before any invocation activity to ensure that the plan generated by the Planner (during pre-planning) is still valid (e.g. the selected service end-point is still reachable) and optimal (according to the user-defined optimisation policies). If any of the former criteria has been violated the ActivePlanner re-evaluates a optimal service instance for the current process invocation. It can also work without pre-planning being available.

3.2.1 Optimisation Policies. The Planner and ActivePlanner components perform optimised scheduling of abstract BPEL processes based on user defined policies. Optimisation policies are declared within the BPEL document and can apply to individual *partnerLinkTypes* or to the whole process.

The selection of a specific Web Service instance to be used in a particular process invocation is driven by the optimisation policy applied either on the process level or on a partnerLink level. Currently POS supports six different optimisation policies:

Host load: Hosts with the lowest system load take precedence.

Fastest CPU: Hosts are ranked based on their CPU capabilities and the best is selected.

Memory Utilisation: Hosts are ranked according to the percentage of available memory as reported by the Java VM. The one with the highest percentage is selected.

Storage Utilisation: Hosts are ranked according to their total available disk space. The one with the larger available space is preferred.

Reliability: Hosts are ranked based on their total uptime. Precedence is given to hosts which have been running without interruption for longer time.

Network Utilisation: When the Planner evaluates multiple possible scheduling plans it will show preference to those plans where the web services are located close to each other (based on the reported host locality information). The Planner will avoid co-scheduling invocations to the same host in order not to overload it.

3.2.2 BPEL Optimisation Extensions. gCube POS functionality heavily depends on the BPEL standard (notation based on BPEL4WS v1.1). BPEL XML schema has been extended to include optimisation information such as process policy information per partnerLinks, the definition of abstract or concrete services, allocation relationship between invocations etc.

To define process wide optimisation policies we introduce the *optimisation-Policy* attribute at the BPEL process element. For example the process defined by the BPEL excerpt in Figure 2 will be scheduled according to the *fastest_cpu* policy (with higher weight) and the *storage_utilization* policy (lower weight).

If no policy is defined the default used is the *host_load* policy.

The policies defined on process-wide level pertain the planning of all partnerLinks included in the process unless a specific policy is defined on the part-

```
<process optimisationPolicy="fastest_cpu storage_utilization" xmlns:... >
    <partnerLinkTypes>
        <partnerLinkType name="BPELD4SProcess">
            <role name="BPELD4SProcessProvider">
                <portType serviceType="concreteGCubeService" name="tns:BPELD
            </role>
        </partnerLinkType>
        <partnerLinkType name="fulltextindexlookupserviceLT">
            <role name="fulltextindexlookupserviceRole">
                <portType xmlns:fulltextindexlookupservice="http://diligentp
            </role>
        </partnerLinkType>
        <partnerLinkType name="sortoperatorserviceLT">
            <role name="sortoperatorserviceRole">
                <portType xmlns:sortoperatorservice="http://diligentproject.
```

Figure 2.   Process wide optimisation policy definition in BPEL

nerLink element. To define such policy we use the *partnerLinkPolicyType* attribute of the BPEL partnerLink element. This attribute is used similarly to the above example, except that the network_utilization policy, if defined, is ignored, since this policy makes sense only for the whole process and not for a particular web service.

3.3   Execution Stage

Apart from the execution engine, which does not fall within the scope of this paper and can be mostly outsourced, two important aspects of the Execution Stage are the services themselves and the data transport mechanism. Although potentially any Web Service can be employed in such a workflow as long as it gets sufficiently described for the framework, gCube comes with a rich set of components that implement core logic of structured and semi-structured data processing and information retrieval. Furthermore, as already mentioned, gRS is the special mechanism employed for data transports, that overcomes conceptual limitations and performance issues of Web Services and actually is the means via which data are streamed back to their requester.

4.   Evaluation - Future Work

One inherent problem of Web Services based interactions is that they are not designed for low-latency, high-speed data transfers, while the SOAP processing stack, in practice proves to be quite a bottleneck for High Performance Computing.

The gCube framework has been exposing its facilities to selected user communities, through a Web Based user interface, which has given valuable feedback to the implementation team. Although the performance for interactive use cannot yet compete with the well known search facilities, the results are quite encouraging. Several optimisations, at various levels, allow for an acceptable response of the system to the interactive user even in non-optimally allocated resource schemes. The benefits of the system are materialised when the infrastructure is automatically reorganised and when data / computing intensive operations take place, such as the on-the-fly production of thumbnails of 100MB-sized images, or the extraction of the features of 1000s of images, without the employment of a pre-allocated infrastructure.

Practical issues rise with caching mechanisms, due to the size of the information they target and partially the insufficient support by underlying systems, which upon departs and arrivals of resources might become stale for short periods.

Today, gCube framework has reached a mature stage and is currently under way to production environments [19]. In this operational context, beyond the primary objective of maximum robustness, the aspects of optimisation and openness will be further elaborated. Optimisation techniques currently under development will exploit intermediate size estimations methods (via statistics, curve fitting etc). Steps considered for the future include rate-based optimisation methods for streamed flows and ontological matching of services. A low-level step towards performance will be the ability to dynamically combine executables (jars) under the encapsulation of a hosting web service.

Finally, driven from user requirements and system evolution, the Query Language will be revised in order to allow seamless integration of fundamentally different data sources.

Acknowledgments

This work is currently partially funded by the European Commission in the context of the D4Science project [19], under the 1st call of FP7 IST priority. Original work was partially funded in the context of DILIGENT project [20].

References

[1] gCube system, *http://www.gcube-system.org/*

[2] L. Candela, D. Castelli, P. Pagano, *gCube: A Service-Oriented Application Framework on the Grid*, ERCIM News, 48-49, Jan 2008

[3] Simeoni, Candela, Kakaletris, Sibeko, Pagano, Papanikos, Polydoras, Ioannidis, Aarvaag, Crestani, et al. *A Grid-based Infrastructure for Distributed Retrieval*, ECDL 2007, Proc. 11th European Conference on Research and Advanced Technology for Digital Libraries, Sept. 2007.

[4] Ian Foster, Carl Kesselman, Steven Tuecke. *The Anatomy of the Grid: Enabling Scalable Virtual Organizations*, Lecture Notes in Computer Science (v2150), 2001

[5] Ricardo Baeza-Yates, Berthier Ribeiro-Neto, *Modern information retrieval*, ACM Press, ISBN 0-201-39829-X, 1999

[6] E. Newcomer, G. Lomow, *Understanding SOA with Web Services*, Addison Wesley, ISBN 0-321-18086-0, 2005

[7] Foster et Al, *Modeling Stateful Resources with Web Services* whitepaper, IBM, 2004

[8] World Wide Web Consortium (W3C), *http://www.w3.org/*

[9] Organization for the Advancement of Structured Information Standards (OASIS), *http://www.oasis-open.org/*

[10] I. Foster, C. Kesselman, J. Nick, S. Tuecke, *The Physiology of the Grid: An Open Grid Services Architecture for Distributed Systems Integration*, Globus Project, 2002

[11] Globus Toolkit 4, *http://www.globus.org/toolkit/*

[12] *Business Process Execution Language for Web Services version 1.1*, IBM, BEA Systems, Microsoft, SAP AG, Siebel Systems, 2002-2007

[13] Condor Project HomePage, *http://www.cs.wisc.edu/condor/*

[14] I. J. Taylor, E. Deelman, D. Gannon and M. S. Shields (eds.), *Workflows for e-Science: Scientific Workflows for Grids*, ISBN 978-1-84628-519-6, Springer London, 2007

[15] KWf Grid Project Web Site, *http://www.kwfgrid.eu/*

[16] OGSA Data Access and Integration (OGSA-DAI), *http://www.ogsadai.org.uk/*

[17] The EGEE Project, *http://www.eu-egee.org/*.

[18] gLite, *http://glite.web.cern.ch/*.

[19] The D4Science Project, *http://d4science.research-infrastructures.eu/*.

[20] The DILIGENT Project, *http://www.diligent-project.org/*.

FROM ORC MODELS TO DISTRIBUTED GRID JAVA CODE*

Marco Aldinucci and Marco Danelutto
Dept. of Computer Science – University of Pisa – Italy
Marco.Aldinucci@di.unipi.it, Marco.Danelutto@di.unipi.it

Peter Kilpatrick
Dept. of Computer Science – Queen's University Belfast – UK
p.kilpatrick@qub.ac.uk

Patrizio Dazzi
ISTI/CNR – Pisa, Italy
patrizio.dazzi@isti.cnr.it

Abstract   We present O2J, a Java library that allows implementation of Orc programs on distributed architectures including grids and clusters/networks of workstations. With minimal programming effort the grid programmer may implement Orc programs, as he/she is not required to write any low level code relating to distributed orchestration of the computation but only that required to implement Orc expressions. Using the prototype O2J implementation, grid application developers can reason about abstract grid orchestration code described in Orc. Once the required orchestration has been determined and its properties analysed, a grid application prototype can be simply, efficiently and quickly implemented by taking the Orc code, rewriting it into corresponding Java/O2J syntax and finally providing the functional code implementing the sites and processes involved. The proposed *modus operandi* brings a Model Driven Engineering approach to grid application development.

Keywords: Grid, orchestration, model-driven engineering, distributed computing.

---

*This research is carried out under the FP6 Network of Excellence CoreGRID and the FP6 GridCOMP project funded by the European Commission (Contract IST-2002-004265 and FP6-034442).

1.   Introduction

In recent years Model-Driven Engineering (MDE) [11, 6] has emerged as a means of employing abstraction to allow exploration of properties of a system free of implementation detail. MDE advocates building models of systems to be implemented, reasoning informally about these models (for example, comparing alternative designs, identifying bottlenecks, etc.) and then developing code from these models, ideally automatically or semi-automatically.

In many ways MDE is similar in intent, if not in style, to Formal Methods (such as B [4], VDM [7]). A formal method requires a developer to provide a specification of a system written in a mathematically precise (i.e. formal) notation. The developer may then prove properties of the specification before committing to implementation. The implementation may proceed through a series of refinement steps, which can be proven consistent. The requirement for such (expensive) mathematical precision may have been a contributory factor to the limited uptake of Formal Methods.

In earlier work [1–3] we presented a semi-formal approach to the development of grid software. The approach draws upon ideas from both Formal Methods and MDE: we use a formal notation (Orc [8]) to describe different designs of grid software, together with an informal style of reasoning about the properties of the designs. Orc is suitable for the description of such software [12] as it has been designed explicitly as an orchestration language for distributed services. Orc has the benefit of being a formal notation in the sense that it is a small abstract notation (like traditional process algebras) amenable to reasoning, while at the same time (unlike traditional process algebras) it has a syntax which is appealing to the programmer and thus allows the description of highly readable designs and the development of informal arguments which reference code extracts.

Here we extend our earlier work, again in the spirit of MDE, by addressing the issue of generation of implementations from models. We describe O2J, a Java library that supports the semi-automated development of grid implementations from Orc models. The idea of such a system was introduced briefly in [3] where we described a preliminary version of O2J. Here we present a detailed description of the O2J library together with sample translations and a step-by-step guide indicating how the developer may use O2J to support the development of grid software.

2.   Orc specification of distributed (grid) applications

In this section we present a simple example to motivate the approach and provide an orchestration expression to illustrate the use of O2J. First we briefly summarise the Orc notation.

2.1 The Orc notation

Orc is a "programming language and system for orchestrating distributed services " [9]. Its focus is on the *orchestration* of what might be termed "services" (web site calls, grid site calls, method calls, etc.) which provide core functionality. The notion of service is captured by the *site* primitive and the orchestration of site calls is described using three operators plus recursion. (See [8] for a very readable introduction to Orc.)

Site A site call may return a *single* value or remain silent (not respond). A site represents the simplest form of Orc expression.

Sequential composition In $E_1 > x > E_2(x)$, expression E_1 is evaluated and may produce zero or more results. For each result generated, the result is labelled x and a new instance of expression E_2 is executed with parameter x. If evaluation of E_2 is independent of x the expression may be written $E_1 \gg E_2$.

Parallel Composition In $E_1 \mid E_2$ both E_1 and E_2 are evaluated in parallel. The output is the interleaved outputs of the constituent expressions.

Asymmetric Parallel Composition In E_1 where $x :\in E_2$ both E_1 and E_2 are evaluated in parallel. If E_1 names x in some of its site calls, its evaluation halts at the point of dependency. Evaluation of E_2 proceeds until it delivers a value for x at which point its evaluation is terminated. E_2 may now continue its evaluation with a binding for x.

Finally, the notation $(\mid i : 1 \leq i \leq 3 : W_i)$ is used as an abbreviation for $(W_1 \mid W_2 \mid W_3)$.

2.2 Example

Consider a straightforward but common distributed application: data items in an input stream are processed independently and the results written to a shared state (for simplicity assume that the update function is associative and commutative). In [3] we presented two alternative designs for this application and it was shown there how detailed analysis of the Orc designs allowed comparison of their expected performances. Here we present the simpler design (see Fig. 1) as a vehicle to illustrate the use of O2J.

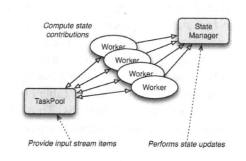

Figure 1. Master/worker implementation of state update (grey boxes represent sites, white ovals represent processes)

This design is based on the classical master/worker implementation where centralized entities provide the items of the input stream and collate the resulting computations in a single state. The *system* comprises a taskpool (modelling the input stream), *TP*, a state manager, *SM* and a set of workers, W_i. The workers repeatedly take tasks from the taskpool, process them and send the results to the state manager. The taskpool and state manager are represented by Orc sites; the workers are represented by processes (expressions). This specification corresponds to the diagram in Fig. 1 and can be formulated as follows:

$$system(TP, SM) \triangleq workers(TP, SM)$$
$$workers(TP, SM) \triangleq | \, i : 1 \leq i \leq N : W_i(TP, SM)$$
$$W_i(TP, SM) \triangleq$$
$$\quad TP.get > tk > compute(tk) > r > SM.update(r) \gg W_i(TP, SM)$$

3.   Generating a distributed Java framework from Orc orchestration code

As discussed above, Orc fully supports distributed program orchestration design and refinement. Its conciseness and operational style allows one to construct compact implementation-oriented models of distributed system orchestrations unobscured by superfluous detail. The main focus here is to bridge the gap between the abstract (and therefore powerful) modelling and the actual (and therefore error prone and cumbersome) distributed programming practice by providing automatic translation from Orc code to Java implementation.

We present and discuss here a run time support (the O2J Java library, **Orc to J**ava) allowing Orc "programmers" to write simple and concise Java programs that can be run on a collection of processing elements implementing the distributed orchestration modelled by a given Orc expression/program. This is the first step in a process that will eventually be completed by a compiler taking as input Orc programs and generating in an automatic way the Java code implementing that particular Orc program. At the moment we concentrate on providing a suitable Java run time library allowing programmers to write Orc code in a "Java friendly" syntax. Table 1 presents Orc constructs and their corresponding library implementations. Thus, for example, the call `OrcSeqVar(f, x, g)` provides a Java implementation of the Orc sequential composition (with parameter passing) $f > x > g(x)$.

3.1   Library usage example

Consider again the example outlined in 2.2. Using O2J, the Orc program can be implemented by the Java code shown in Figure 2 (IW08Sample.java editor window) provided that suitable classes implementing the TP and SM sites as well as the WP process are provided by the user. Any site can be provided by subclassing `OrcSite` class and implementing an `OrcMessage`

body(OrcMessage call) method. This method handles a single call message
(the call) to produce a single answer to the call. For example, the TP site can
be provided by programming an OrcSite subclass implementing the body
method as follows:

```
public OrcMessage body(OrcMessage dummy) {
  // upon any request, send the next integer in the list, up to MAXTASK
  System.out.println("TaskPool "+getName()+" got request "+dummy);
  if(task < MAXTASK) {
    System.out.println("TaskPool "+getName()+" sending task "+task);
    return(new OrcMessage(new Integer(task++)));
  } else {
    System.out.println("TaskPool "+getName()+" returning a null");
    return null; // this implies blocking the answer ...
  }
}
```

The Manager object declared at the beginning of the main is the manager
handling all the non-functional features related to execution of the Orc program.
In particular, the Manager starts the run time processes needed to support the
execution of the Orc program and manages the processing elements available
according to the allocation strategies required by the programmer.

3.2 Deriving Java code from Orc: the formal steps

Formally, in order to implement an Orc program using O2J, the programmer
must follow a precise procedure:

1 Write one class for each of the sites used in the program. Each class
subclasses OrcSite and provides (in addition to constructors needed to
store site specific parameters) the method handling a single call, i.e. an
OrcMessage body(OrcMessage call).

2 Write one class for each of the processes used in the program. As
for sites, each class subclasses OrcSite and provides (in addition to
constructors needed to store site specific parameters) an OrcMessage
body(OrcMessage call) method hosting the code implementing the
process body. The code may use send, receive and call methods
provided by OrcSite to implement process actions.

3 Write a Java main which involves:

  (a) declaring a Manager (the Orc runtime) and possibly calling Manager
  methods to set up non-functional parameters for program execution;

  (b) declaring the sites used by calling the constructors defined in the
  classes extending OrcSite that represent the user defined sites;

    (c) implementing the program expression, using the appropriate library objects implementing the Orc parallel, asymmetric parallel and sequential operators (OrcPar modelling the | operator, OrcSeq modeling the > operator and OrcAsymm modeling the **where x:∈** operator); and

    (d) starting the execution of the program by issuing a startSite() call on the main expression object.

It is worth pointing out that, at the moment, the Orc program modelled in the main corresponds to the *full inlining* of the actual Orc program in that all the expression calls are substituted by the corresponding expression bodies. In particular, the code presented at the beginning of section 3.1 is actually implemented as expressed in the Orc expression

$$E \triangleq | \ i : 1 \le i \le N :$$
$$(TP.get > tk > compute(tk) > r > SM.update(r) \gg E)$$

Also, tail recursion is to be programmed as infinite loops, and therefore the actual code implemented in the Java main corresponds to

$$| \ i : 1 \le i \le N :$$
$$\texttt{while(true)}\{ \ TP.get > tk > compute(tk) > r > SM.update(r) \ \}$$

This will change in the near future, as we are currently designing a Java based compiler accepting as input Orc expressions and producing as output the skeleton of the Java code of the main program.

The whole process achieves a clear separation of concerns between programmers and O2J library code (that is, between programmers and system designers): programmers must concentrate on the Orc code and they must of course also provide the functional code – for sites, the code handling a single call; for processes, the process body code. The O2J code then handles all the details one usually has to take into account when running distributed code, that is process/thread decomposition, mapping and scheduling, communication implementation, etc.

To support our claim, let us consider the code the programmer must supply to implement the WP process in the example discussed above. This code consists in class subclassing OrcSite and implementing[1] the method:

```
public OrcMessage body(OrcMessage dummy) {
  while(true) { // get a task (TP.get > tk )
    OrcMessage taskMessage = call(taskPoolName,OrcMessage.nullMessage());
    Object tk = taskMessage.getValue();
    // then process it (tk > compute(tk) > r)
    Object r = compute(tk);
    // eventually send new contrib. to the SM (SM.update(r) >> )
```

---

[1] overwriting, actually: OrcSite by default implements a site that just echoes call messages

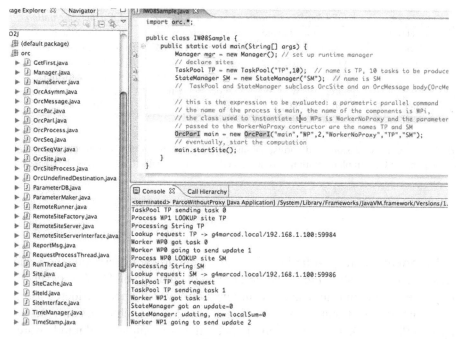

Figure 2. O2J at work in Eclipse

```
      call(stateManagerName,new OrcMessage(r));
   } // then recur (recursive call => loop) (>> Wi(TP,SM) )
}
```

where the call message received at the beginning is just a dummy call initiating
the computation and the recursive structure of the worker is implemented by an
infinite loop. This is more or less what the programmer writes in the (inlined)
Orc code. In particular, no code is needed to take care of explicit communications synchronization, handling of the mechanisms used to implement the Orc
runtime (e.g. sockets, processes), etc., that is, those things that require extensive
distributed/parallel architecture knowledge in order to be used efficiently.

3.3   Implementation

The Orc runtime implemented by O2J is completely OO and quite straightforward. Sites and processes are implemented by objects distributed on the
available processing nodes by using features of ProActive [10] active objects.
In turn, site and process objects communicate with other sites and processes
using plain TCP/IP sockets and OrcMessages. We could have used any other
mechanism suitable for instantiating and running an object on a remote processing element. In fact, we are considering using plain RMI (possibly wrapped
through ssh) instead of the ProActive migrateTo mechanism that requires the

Orc term	O2J implementation
O2J RTS start	mgr=new Manager()
$f \gg g$	OrcSeq(f,g)
$f > x > g(x)$	OrcSeqVar(f,"x",g)
$f \mid g$	OrcPar(f,g)
$\mid i : 1 \leq i \leq k : W_i$	OrcParI("W",k,W)
$f(x)$ where $x :\in g$	OrcAsymm(f,g,"x")

Orc mechanism	O2J implementation
site call	call(sitename,message)
channel send	send(dest,message)
channel receive	m = receive(source)
process start	process.startSite()
process/site naming	setName(name)
formal param access	x=getParam("x")

Table 1. Orc expressions and corresponding O2J constructors (left), Orc mechanisms and corresponding O2J implementations (right; procedure calls are calls to methods of the OrcSite class).

full ProActive library to be installed on the employed nodes. For the same reason (clean OO structure of the library and plain usage of TCP/IP sockets to implement communication and synchronization), we have not considered using more elaborate distributed programming environments such as the ones developed in Pisa (muskel [5] and ASSIST) or even more complex grid middleware.

A centralized name server, started by the Manager constructor, takes care of all the port numbers and IP addresses needed to communicate with sites and processes. When a site/process object is created, it publishes a ServerSocket to accept calls/messages and communicates the IP address, port number and site/process name to the centralized name server. The first time a call or a send is performed at a given site/process, the runtime communicates with the centralized name server to get the IP address and port number of the destination site/process. These values are stored in a local cache and all future communications involving that site/process are handled by looking up the addresses in the local cache.

When a new site or a new process is declared in the user defined main it is allocated on one of the available machines according to an allocation strategy established with the manager. To this end, users can call a Manager setAllocationStrategy(OrcRTSAllocStrategy s) method to establish an OrcManager.SPECULATIVE or an OrcManager.CONSERVATIVE allocation strategy such as the ones discussed in [2]. In the former case, sites and processes are always placed on new processing elements, if available. In the latter, sites and processes are preferably placed on the processing element where the parent site or process expression has already been placed. The list of available processing elements is provided by an external XML file which is consulted when the Manager is started. We are considering also the possibility of having a distinct and autonomous "discovery thread" in the Manager that constantly keeps the list up to date by querying the networked processing elements and discovering their capabilities to run O2J processes[2]. In both cases (in the conservative and in the speculative strategy) the OrcSite invokes Manager methods (services) to determine which processing element is to be used to run the site (process).

O2J also provides a very basic logging facility. Every site or process can issue a log(String eventName) call to register an event in a trace that can be consulted offline after (or during) program execution. The trace is maintained by a centralized process and each event is registered in the trace with its name, the local timestamp (i.e. the time value obtained on the machine where the event was generated) and a global timestamp (i.e. the time value taken at the central-ized server when the logging message was received). Despite the fact that local timestamps may be generated on processing elements with non-synchronized timers and the global timestamp counts also the communication overhead in-curred in the logging process, the logging mechanism has proven effective at measuring coarse grain computations. With such computations the overhead involved in logging message transmission to the centralized log manager is negligible w.r.t. the times we wish to measure and therefore global timestamps may be used to determine the actual behaviour of distributed computations.

4. Experiments

The feasibility of the O2J approach was first tested with O2J 1.0, an imple-mentation realized by Antonio Palladino, for his graduation thesis at the Dept. of Computer Science in Pisa, under the supervision of the authors. Once the feasibility was demonstrated we carried out a complete re-engineering of the library to obtain O2J 2.0. This required substantially new code, although the structure of sites, processes and manager did not change significantly. Here we present results achieved with O2J 2.0.

With O2J 2.0, the programmer may directly translate to O2J objects any part of a given Orc program. Table 1 summarizes the main correspondences between Orc constructs and O2J code. A *Manager* object is used to handle those aspects concerned with distributed implementation of the Orc code. After establishing the *Manager* object and the sites of the Orc program, the programmer must set up the O2J objects modelling the Orc expression to be evaluated in the program (as depicted in Figure 2). Then the program computation is started by issuing a startSite() method call on the main object representing the Orc program.

Using O2J 2.0, we implemented several Orc programs and successfully ran these programs with the expected modest programming effort: the program-mer was required to write only the functional code (the routines to represent site calls and the bodies of the processes in the program) and all the rest was handled by the library. The messages output by running the sample code dis-

---

[2]A similar mechanism is successfully used in muskel [5].

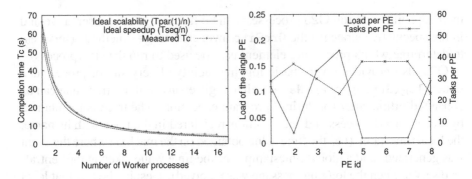

Figure 3.   Sample experimental results: scalability (left) and load balancing (right)

cussed in Section 3 are shown in the lower window in Figure 2 (the Console window here shows only an initial portion of the messages printed by the sample code). It is worth pointing out that, in this case, both worker WP0 and WP1 were placed on the same machine. As a result, the first time a worker tried to call site SM, a lookup call was issued to the centralized manager which replied with the IP/port of site SM (this is the Lookup request: SM -> g4marcod.local/192.168.1.100:54882 line in the dump). After some time, process WP1 attempted to send an update to SM but this time the address was resolved using the local cache (line Process WP1 LOOKUP site SM).

Figure 3 shows examples of results achieved with O2J 2.0. All the experiments have been run on a set of Linux workstations running kernel 2.4, Java 1.5 and interconnected via a Fast Ethernet network. The left half of the figure plots completion time for a run of the O2J implementation of the code described in Section 2 and whose process structure is shown in Figure 1. Using the program, we computed 256 tasks using a number of worker processes ranging from 1 to 16. The figure shows that good scalability is achieved up to 16 workers, despite the bottlenecks represented by the taskpool and by the state manager sites. The right part of the figure, plots average load (taken with the Linux command uptime) and number of tasks executed relative to a single processing element hosting a worker process. As the code shown in Section 2 clearly implements a self-scheduling policy (worker i calls the taskpool site to have a new task to compute as soon it completes the previous one), we expect that a sound implementation will achieve load balancing for either variable size tasks or heterogeneous processing elements. The right half of Figure 3 corresponds to a single run of the farm program of Section 2 with 8 workers. Nodes with a higher average load executed fewer tasks, as expected. It is worth noting that the variance in load (due to the concurrent run of a full compilation of *mpich*) is very small, but the auto scheduling reacted appropriately by running more tasks on the machines without the additional load (PEs 2, 5, 6 and 7, in this case).

We ran the program several times, using different loads to make the processing elements heterogeneous and each time we obtained results comparable to the ones in Figure 3.

The completion times used to compile Figure 3 (left) have been taken without considering the deployment time, i.e. from the moment the objects representing Orc sites and processes have been deployed onto their "home" remote nodes and initialized. As the code eventually run uses plain TCP/IP socket wrapped into Object streams, we did not measure any significant overhead with respect to hand written code modelling the same Orc program. In particular, the grain needed to achieve good scalability on the 16 nodes in the experiment of Figure 3 is of the same order of magnitude as that needed to make a `muskel` task farm scale (`muskel` uses only RMI and `ssh` to run applications).

Finally, we compared the amount of code needed to implement a simple site with O2J, with the amount of code needed to implement it in the library, representing a rough measure of the code needed to implement the same site from scratch. The Worker process of the program of Section 2 represents about 65 lines of Java code. The library classes used to implement the Site (of which Process is a sub-class) account for 10 times as many lines of code, without taking into account the `Manager` and deployment code.

Overall, the experimental data obtained has demonstrated reasonable efficiency in the O2J implementation of Orc programs, and the small amount of code needed to implement sites, processes and the Orc expressions to be evaluated illustrates the expressive power of using O2J.

5. Conclusions

We have discussed O2J, a Java library supporting distributed application development based on the Orc formal orchestration language. O2J allows Orc programmers to write Java code implementing Orc programs and to run these programs on distributed architectures hosting Java and ProActive enabled processing elements. Grid targeting comes as a consequence of the usage of ProActive as the "distributed/grid middleware". We presented a simple example that notably requires considerable programming effort if implemented directly using standard middleware mechanisms and we showed that the amount of Java/O2J code needed is small and mostly a direct translation from the high level specification of the problem in Orc. We also discussed some preliminary experimental results demonstrating the feasibility of the approach. Currently, to the best of our knowledge, there are no other "distributed" implementations of Orc (the Orc system available at [9] is not a distributed implementation). Our approach allows application programmers to reason about their distributed application structure in terms of an abstract Orc model and then obtain support from the O2J tools to produce the actual distributed implementation. Thus it brings grid application development under the umbrella of Model Driven Engineering techniques, and, as such, represents a significant step toward freeing the developer from the burden of detailed middleware knowledge.

Acknowledgments The authors wish to thank Antonio Palladino who implemented O2J 1.0 demonstrating the feasibility of the approach. They thank also the anonymous referees for their careful reading of the original submission and their constructive suggestions.

References

[1] M. Aldinucci, M. Danelutto, P. Kilpatrick, Management in distributed systems: a semi-formal approach. in: A.-M. Kermarrec, L. Bougé, and T. Priol, eds., *Proc. of 13th Intl. Euro-Par 2007 Parallel Processing*, vol. 4641 of LNCS, pp. 651–661, Rennes (F), Aug. 2007. Springer.

[2] M. Aldinucci, M. Danelutto, P. Kilpatrick, Adding metadata to Orc to support reasoning about grid programs, in: T. Priol and M. Vanneschi, eds., *Proc. of the CoreGRID Symposium 2007*, pp. 205–214, Rennes (F), Aug. 2007, Springer.

[3] M. Aldinucci, M. Danelutto, P. Kilpatrick, A framework for prototyping and reasoning about grid systems, in: C. Bischof, M. Bücker, P. Gibbon, G. R. Joubert, T. Lippert, B. Mohr, and F. J. Peters, eds., *Parallel Computing: Architectures, Algorithms and Applications (Proc. of PARCO 2007, Jülich (G))*, vol. 38 of NIC, pp. 355–362, Dec. 2007.

[4] B home page (2007). http://www-lsr.imag.fr/B/

[5] M. Danelutto, P. Dazzi, Joint structured/non structured parallelism exploitation through data flow, in: V. Alexandrov, D. van Albada, P. M. A. Sloot, J. Dongarra (Eds.), *Proc. of ICCS: Intl. Conference on Computational Science, Workshop on Practical Aspects of High-level Parallel Programming*, vol. 3992 of LNCS, Springer, Reading (UK), 2006.

[6] OMG Model Driven Architecture (2007). http://www.omg.org/mda/

[7] J. S. Fitzgerald, P. G. Larsen, P. Mukherjee, N. Plat, M. Verhoef, Validated Designs for Object-oriented Systems, Springer, 2005. ISBN: 1-85233-881-4.

[8] J. Misra, W.R. Cook, Computation Orchestration: A basis for a wide-area computing, *Software and Systems Modeling*, 6(1):83–110, Mar. 2006. DOI 10.1007/s10270-006-0012-1.

[9] Orc home page (2007). http://www.cs.utexas.edu/users/wcook/projects/orc/

[10] ProActive home page (2007). http://www-sop.inria.fr/oasis/proactive/

[11] D.C. Schmidt, Model-Driven Engineering, *Computer*, 39(2):25–31, Feb. 2006.

[12] A. Stewart, J. Gabarró, M. Clint, T. Harmer, P. Kilpatrick, R. Perrott, Managing Grid Computations: An ORC-Based Approach, in: M. Guo et al, eds., *Parallel and Distributed Processing and Applications (ISPA)*, vol. 4330 of LNCS, Springer, pp. 278-291, 2006.

USING CLIQUES OF NODES TO STORE DESKTOP GRID CHECKPOINTS

Filipe Araujo
CISUC, Department of Informatics Engineering, University of Coimbra, Portugal
filipius@dei.uc.pt

Patricio Domingues
School of Technology and Management, Polytechnic Institute of Leiria, Portugal
patricio@estg.ipleiria.pt

Derrick Kondo
Laboratoire d'Informatique de Grenoble INRIA Rhône-Alpes, France
dkondo@imag.fr

Luis Moura Silva
CISUC, Department of Informatics Engineering, University of Coimbra, Portugal
luis@dei.uc.pt

Abstract

Checkpoints that store intermediate results of computation have a fundamental impact on the computing throughput of Desktop Grid systems, like BOINC. Currently, BOINC workers store their checkpoints locally. A major limitation of this approach is that whenever a worker leaves unfinished computation, no other worker can proceed from the last stable checkpoint. This forces tasks to be restarted from scratch when the original machine is no longer available.

To overcome this limitation, we propose to share checkpoints between nodes. To organize this mechanism, we arrange nodes to form complete graphs (cliques), where nodes share all the checkpoints they compute. Cliques function as survivable units, where checkpoints and tasks are not lost as long as one of the nodes of the clique remains alive. To simplify construction and maintenance of the cliques, we take advantage of the central supervisor of BOINC. To evaluate our solution, we combine simulation with some real data to answer the most fundamental question: what do we need to pay for increased throughput?

Keywords: Desktop grid, checkpointing, clique

1.   Introduction

The enormous success of BOINC [1] , fueled by projects like SETI@home or climateprediction.net, turned Desktop Grid (DG) communities into some of the most powerful computing platforms on Earth. This trend mounts on the motivation of volunteers eager to contribute with idle resources for causes of their interest. With an average utilization of CPU as low as 5% [6] and with new CPUs shipping with increasing number of cores, more and more resources should be available for grid computing in the near future.

Although bearing enormous potential, volatility of workers poses a great challenge to DG. To mitigate volatility, at certain points in the computation, the worker computes a checkpoint and stores it locally. This enables the *same* worker to resume computation from the last checkpoint, when it resumes computation. Unfortunately a worker can be interrupted by a single key stroke and can also depart from the project at any time. In this case computation of the worker in the task is simply lost.

One obvious limitation of storing checkpoints locally is that they become unavailable whenever the node leaves the project. Martin et al. [11] reported that climateprediction.net would greatly benefit form a mechanism to share checkpoint files among worker nodes, thus allowing the recovery of tasks in different machines. Storing the checkpoints in the central supervisor is clearly unfeasible, because this would considerably increase network traffic, storage space and, consequently, management costs of the central supervisor. Another option could be to use a peer-to-peer (P2P) distributed storage (refer to Section 4). We exclude this option for a number of reasons. First, P2P storage systems would typically require a global addressing scheme to locate checkpoints, thus imposing an unnecessarily high burden for storing replicas of a checkpoint. Unlike this, we can store all replicas of a checkpoint in nearby nodes, because we can afford to lose checkpoints and recompute respective tasks from scratch. This way, we trade computation time for simplicity. Moreover, in a P2P file system, replicas of a checkpoint are stored in arbitrary peers. We follow the approach of storing checkpoints in nodes that might use them. This is simpler, involves fewer exchanges of checkpoints and can allow nodes to use checkpoints they store to earn credits.

In this context, we present *CliqueChkpt*, which follows from our previous approach in [5] , where we used dedicated storage nodes to keep checkpoints of tasks. To make these checkpoints available to the community, workers self-organized into a DHT where they stored pointers to the checkpoints. In *Clique-Chkpt*, we try to improve this system. First, we address the requirement of using dedicated storage nodes to hold the checkpoints. Second, we address the requirement for storing pointers to the checkpoints in the DHT, which raised the complexity of the system. To achieve this, we connect nodes in complete graphs (i.e., graphs where all the vertices are connected to each other, also know as cliques). These cliques form small and independent unstructured P2P networks, where workers share all their checkpoints. This enables *Clique-Chkpt* to easily achieve a replication factor that ensures checkpoint survivability despite frequent node departures. Unlike some P2P systems that are fully distributed and thus require considerable effort to find clique peers [10] , we simply use the central supervisor for this purpose. We show that *CliqueChkpt* can achieve consistent throughput gains over the original BOINC scheme and we assess the bandwidth and disk costs that we need to pay for this gain.

The rest of the paper is organized as follows: Section 2 overviews *Clique-Chkpt*. In Section 3 we do some preliminary evaluation of *CliqueChkpt*. Section 4 presents related work and Section 5 concludes the paper.

2. Overview of *CliqueChkpt*

In *CliqueChkpt*, upon request from a worker, the central supervisor assigns it one or more tasks. The worker then computes the tasks, sending back the results when it is done. We only consider sequential tasks, which can be individually broken into multiple temporal segments $(S_{t_1}, \ldots, S_{t_i}, \ldots, S_{t_n})$ and whose intermediate computational states can be saved in a checkpoint when a transition between temporal segments occurs. Whenever a task is interrupted, its execution can be resumed from the last stable checkpoint, either by the same node (if it recovers) or by some other worker. Our main goal is to increase throughput of the entire computation. In all that follows we consider single-replica computation. Extending this to scenarios where multiple replicas exist is straightforward.

2.1 *Chkpt2Chkpt*

CliqueChkpt follows from our previous work in a system called *Chkpt2-Chkpt* [5] . In *Chkpt2Chkpt*, we had the following components: the central supervisor, the workers (including one particular type of worker, called the Guardian) and Storage Points. The workers self-organized into a DHT that served to store two kinds of information: indication of the current state of a task (owner and number of the checkpoint being computed) and pointers to previous checkpoints. This worked as follows (see Figure 1): i) worker requests task from server and gets its data; ii) worker registers task in the Guardian (which in fact is just a standard worker); iii) worker finishes a checkpoint and uploads it to a storage point; iv) client stores the pointer to the checkpoint, updates the Guardian (not shown) and v) sends results to the central supervisor.

The advantage of *Chkpt2Chkpt* over standard BOINC happens when there is some worker that departs leaving some computation unfinished. In this case, the cycle above changes slightly. Instead of restarting the task from the

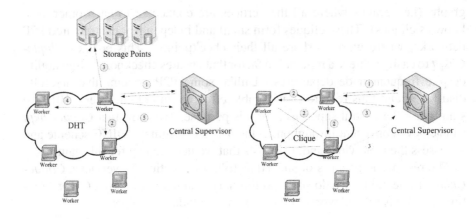

Figure 1. Overview of *Chkpt2Chkpt*   *Figure 2.* Overview of *CliqueChkpt*

beginning, the worker can look for a recent checkpoint using the DHT. We showed in [5] , that under certain scenarios our system could considerably decrease the turnaround time of tasks, for checkpoint availabilities starting at 40%.

2.2 *CliqueChkpt*

In *CliqueChkpt*, we tackle the following shortcomings of our previous approach. *Chkpt2Chkpt* required the use of special dedicated nodes for storage and it depended on pointers stored in volatile nodes. To overcome the first problem, we store checkpoints in standard workers. Any node that stores a checkpoint can use it to get extra credits in the task, when the original worker fails. This gives nodes the motivation to increase storage space for checkpoins. To handle volatile nodes, we increase redundancy. Redundancy was harder to increase in *Chkpt2Chkpt*, because we used several pointers to handle tasks and checkpoint information. To replicate we would need to also replicate these pointers. This would raise complexity and, at the same time, it could fail to work, because pointers themselves are also highly volatile.

We now use a simple *ad hoc* peer-to-peer network, where nodes form independent and completely connected graphs — a clique (Figure 2). Each node of the clique requests tasks from the central supervisor (step 1). After reaching a checkpoint, the worker fully replicates the checkpoint inside its clique (step 2). Finally, the worker submits results to the central supervisor (step 3). If the worker fails any other worker from the clique can use the checkpoint to finish computation and submit the results (dashed step 3). We take advantage of the central supervisor role to handle the workers that belong to each clique. Since the central supervisor needs to know all the workers that exist in the system, we use it to set clique membership. Management of the group itself, like node failure detection, reliable group communication, checkpoint download, upload and so on, is up to the workers in the clique and does not involve the central supervisor.

Workers have a system-wide variable, which tells the number of members in each clique. Whenever they boot or if they find at some moment that their clique is too small they request a new group from the central supervisor. To reduce the load in the central point, in some cases, specially when operational cliques still exist, workers should postpone this request until they really need to communicate with the central supervisor (for instance, for delivering results or requesting new tasks). The central supervisor keeps information of all the cliques that exist in the system.

Whenever a node requests a new clique, the central supervisor looks for an appropriate clique for the node and replies. This can involve three distinct situations: i) the client should join a new clique, ii) or the client already has a clique and this clique should be merged with some other, iii) or the clique should remain unchanged. Only the two first cases are of interest to us. A node can join a new clique or can request another clique to merge by sending a messages to some node of the clique (which can redistribute the message inside the clique afterward). One very important detail here is that some nodes can be inactive very often. For instance, in some configurations, if users interact with the system, BOINC middleware hands the CPU back to the user. We do a clear distinction between the communication group of the clique and the clique itself: the former is a subgroup of the latter (possibly the same). Workers should only consider their peers as missing from the clique (and thus form new cliques) after relatively large periods. For instance, simple heartbeats or disconnection if nodes keep TCP connections alive can serve to identify departing nodes.

At least one of the nodes in a clique should have a public accessible IP address[1]. This node must receive incoming connections from unreachable NAT peers to keep open ports at routers. This will make these nodes responsible for routing messages inside the clique. To pay for this effort, these nodes could be allowed to belong to several different cliques to raise their chance of resuming stalled computations and earn credits.

2.3 Definition of the Cliques

The central supervisor needs to have fast access to the size of the cliques. It can store this in a simple array ordered by clique size, starting from 1 and ending in the largest possible cliques (this array has necessarily a small number of entries, because cliques cannot be big). In a first approach the elements

---

[1]This is not strictly necessary as we could use a node outside the clique to serve as communication broker.

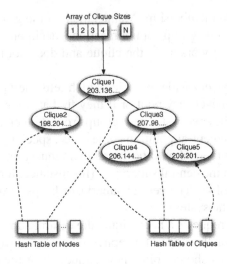

Figure 3.   Internal structure of the central supervisor

of this array could point to a simple linked list with cliques of the same size. When needed, the central supervisor would just pick the first clique in the list and remove it from there (either to add an element or to merge with some other clique). However, to conserve bandwidth and reduce latency a simple approach would be to make cliques of nearby IP addresses, as these will often (but not always) reflect topological proximity. In this way, we can organize the cliques into ordered trees. To do this, we can compute the "average" IP address of a node in the clique or picking the address of one of the nodes. By keeping these trees balanced, searching a clique can have a time cost of $O(\log n)$, where n is the number of nodes. Additionally, this requires, $O(n)$ space, which is reasonable if we consider that the server already uses this space to keep information of nodes. Correlated failures of nodes of the same clique pose little problem to *CliqueChkpt*, because tasks can be recomputed.

The former structure makes cliques accessible by their size and by their IP addresses. We also need some data structure that makes cliques accessible by their identification and also by their nodes. To access a particular clique in $O(1)$ time, both these structures could be hash tables. Deletion of old cliques occurs when new ones are formed from merging operations. To remove other cliques made of nodes that become inactive, the central supervisor must remove the workers first, one at a time. We show the entire structure in Figure 3.

Workers inside a clique control the activity of each other, such that they can tell whenever a clique peer is not computing its task anymore. In this case, active nodes can request the central supervisor to acquire the task. However, the central supervisor needs to have some mechanism to prevent faster nodes from stealing checkpoints from slower ones. A related problem is to prevent nodes from getting undeserved credits that could be earned from checkpoints. To prevent these situations, we force nodes to periodically claim ownership of a task. If a worker fails to do so, it can be overrun by another worker. This can be combined with a Trickle mechanism [3] to give the appropriate credits to the right worker, when it reaches certain points in the computation. In this way, nodes can claim their credits as they go, they do not allow other nodes to steal their tasks, while at the same time, they can also claim ownership on a stalled task. Like in the standard BOINC case, the central supervisor must use replication to get some confidence that workers have done, in fact, real work.

3.   Experimental Results

To evaluate the capabilities of our system, we built a simple event-based simulator. This simulator includes workers and a central supervisor. All workers are similar in CPU performance, all have public IP adresses and follow a fail-stop approach. In practical terms this means that all the nodes abandon the project at some random point in time. In Section 3.3, we evaluate such assumption against known figures for node attrition of climateprediction.net. Workers start in a sleeping state and wake up at random moments. Then, they request a task and compute it, repeating these two steps as many times as they can before thy leave. After another random period of time (with the same average length), new nodes enter the network in a fresh state (no task and no checkpoints). All the (pseudo) random times that govern the states of nodes follow an exponential distribution. We used 35 nodes in the simulation, 200 different tasks and 20 checkpoints per task. Simulation time is set as the end of the 150th task (whatever task it is) to exclude waiting times in the end. Currently in the simulator, we still do not take into consideration the time that it takes to create and transfer the checkpoints.

3.1   Evaluation of Clique Size

We first try to determine the ideal clique size. It turns out that this value depends heavily on nodes lifetimes. In Figures 4 and 5, we fixed node average lifetime and varied the size of the clique. The former figure shows throughput relative to the throughput achieved by (standard) nodes with private checkpoints. Figure 5 refers to the costs: we measure storage space as the average number of checkpoints that each active node stores on disk; and we measure bandwidth as the average number of times that each checkpoint is exchanged in the network[2].

---

[2]Computed as $\frac{E_{checkpoints}}{T_{checkpoints}}$, where $E_{checkpoints}$ is the total number of checkpoints exchanged in the entire simulation and $T_{checkpoints}$ is the total number of checkpoints that exist in the simulation.

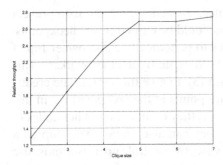   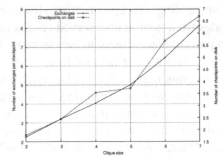

Figure 4.   Relative throughput   *Figure 5.*   Chkpt. exchanges and space in disk

We can see that throughput goes up with clique sizes until it reaches a plateau. To conserve space we omit plots for different average lifetimes. If nodes live longer, we have little gain in increasing clique sizes and we get an approximately horizontal line in the throughput (with values below 1.5). If nodes live shorter, there is a consistent gain in throughput with clique size. This suggests that for a given node lifetime there is an ideal clique size. We have rapid gains in throughput as we reach that size and no gains after that point.

Unlike throughput, bandwidth and disk space seem to grow linearly with clique size. This makes it difficult to pick the right size for the clique, as, in general, the designer may not know exactly the lifetime of nodes. Depending on the available resources, a conservative approach points to small cliques, as they promise improvements at controlled costs in bandwidth and disk space.

3.2   Comparison of Performance

In Figures 6, 7 and 8, we plot throughput, bandwidth consumption and occupied disk space, for varying worker average lifetimes. We consider cliques with 3, 5 and 7 nodes as well as a setting where nodes can upload and download all the checkpoints from storage points (as in *Chkpt2Chkpt*, except that in Figures 6, 7 and 8 nodes always succeed to download the checkpoints). This shows that an ideal storage point is unbeat by cliques, which, on the other hand, can achieve much higher throughputs than nodes with only private checkpoints. This gap widens as the failure rate of nodes goes up (this rate is computed as task duration divided by the average lifetime of a node).

3.3   A Simple Estimation of Trade-offs

In this paper, we basically propose to get more throughput in exchange of disk space and bandwidth. In this section we roughly quantify these trade-offs using figures from climateprediction [3] . Machine attrition should be around 2/3, which means that around 2/3 of the machines drop computation before

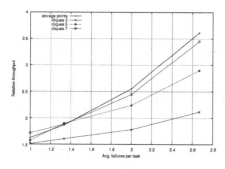

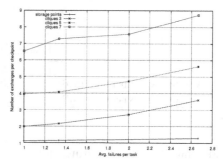

Figure 6. Rel. throughput for fail. rate   *Figure 7.* Avg. exchanges of each checkpoint

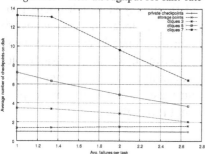

Figure 8. Average number of checkpoints on disk per active node

finishing an entire task. This means that our fail-stop model only applies to $2/3$ of the machines, while in $1/3$ of the machines we might not gain much from using cliques. Assume that due to their failures, these $2/3$ of the machines take n times more to compute a task in average. Assume also that failure-free workers compute T_{ff} tasks per time unit. This means that failure-prone machines will compute $2T_{ff}/n$ tasks per time unit, as they are twice as much, but n times slower. We roughly evaluate throughput with all machines, T_{all}, and the gain in throughput, G, as:

$$T_{all} = T_{ff} + \frac{2T_{ff}}{n} = \frac{n+2}{n}T_{ff}$$

$$G = \frac{T_{all}}{T_{ff}} = \frac{\frac{n+2}{n}T_{ff}}{T_{ff}} = \frac{n+2}{n}$$

The gain G is very sensitive to n and tends to 1 (no gain) as n grows. In Table 1, we show the gains in throughput and the costs of using cliques in the computation of a task. We assume the following data (taken from our previous experiments and from [3]): 20 checkpoints of 20MB for task; 40-day computation (so we have a checkpoint on every two days on average); and failure-prone

Table 1.   Analysis of trade-offs

Parameter	Storage Point	Clique 3	Clique 5	Clique 7
Days saved	18.6	13.2	17.7	17.8
Avg. disk space per node (MB)	31.8	41	73.8	128.8
Avg. exchanges per node (MB)	515.8	1439.8	2250.6	3492.6

nodes fail 2.66 times during those 40 days (this number matches Figure 4). It should be noticed that the frequency at which we publish checkpoints can be made totally independent from the actual frequency at which nodes produce local checkpoints. climateprediction.net creates local checkpoints every 15 minutes, but we can distribute a checkpoint only once in every two days. Table 1 shows that although the potential to save time in a task is considerable, bandwidth required might be beyond what is available for most computers today, if we think of a 20-30 day span to compute a task (after the improvements). On the contrary, disk space requirements are not too high.

4.   Related Work

The idea of using cliques in distributed systems is not new. However, to our best knowledge, these have been used in different contexts and for different purposes. For example in LARK [10] , nodes form ad hoc cliques with peers. The purpose of LARK is to do multicast at the application level. To multicast a message, nodes just send it to all the peers they know in different cliques. Most complexity of LARK comes from the need to create and maintain the cliques in a way that is, at the same time, efficient and tolerant to failures. Unlike LARK, we can greatly benefit from the central supervisor to discard all this complexity from the system. CliqueNet [9] also uses cliques, but for the sake of ensuring communication anonymity.

CliqueChkpt directly follows our previous work in *Chkpt2Chkpt*, where we used a DHT to store checkpoints and to manage some data related to the BOINC tasks [5] . Here, we try to remove some of the constraints existing in *Chkpt2-Chkpt* and shift all the storage back to the volunteer nodes. Interestingly, there is one project called Clique [13] , which targeted a lightweight distributed file system, where nodes self-organize into cliques. Clique also offered the possibility of disconnected operation because it includes a reconciliation protocol. Unlike this project, our cliques are logical and do not need to correspond to some topological division. Besides Clique there are many other systems that provide distributed storage. These often use DHTs to store either the files or pointer to files. Consider the case of PAST [8] , Venti-DHash [14] , Shark [2] or OceanStore [12] , just to name a very small set. Most of these systems reach far beyond what we really need for sharing checkpoints as they are fully fledged file systems, while all we need is to store some checkpoints in a purely best-effort basis.

With respect to storage requirements our system is closer to Condor [15] and Condor-G [4] (Condor for multi-institutional Grids), which have powerful mechanisms to generate checkpoints and migrate jobs. However, the specificities of these systems cannot be reproduced in DG systems. They push tasks to available computers (inside LAN or accessible to Globus in Condor and Condor-G, respectively) that share some sort of administrative ties. Unlike this, volunteers of a DG system are very loosely coupled and the only central entity is often over-utilized, under-financed and cannot be used to store checkpoints. In a previous work, we also analyzed the effects of sharing checkpoints in local area environments, resorting to a centralized checkpoint server [7] .

5. Conclusions and Future Work

In this paper we proposed a system called *CliqueChkpt*, where we organize workers of BOINC into complete graphs (cliques) to share checkpoints of tasks. This involves the central supervisor to manage the groups, but does not use neither this central component, nor any other dedicated machines to store checkpoints. Additionally, nodes storing checkpoints can potentially use them to earn CPU credits, which serves as motivation for volunteers to donate resources. Our simulations suggest that *CliqueChkpt* can bring considerable advantage over private checkpoints when tasks are very long, as in projects like climateprediction.net. To demonstrate the feasibility of our scheme, we used some figures from climateprediction.net to produce a rough estimate of advantages, as well as some costs involved. This analysis showed that while there is a huge potential for these schemes, bandwidth can be a major hurdle.

As we referred before, our work has some limitations that we intend to tackle in the future, namely in the simulator, as we are not considering the times needed to produce and exchange a checkpoint. Concerning the use of cliques, we believe that there is considerable room for reducing the costs involved in exchanging the checkpoints. In fact, we use a very straightforward scheme that always downloads all the checkpoints missing from a node when there is a change in the clique of that node. Just to name one possibility, we could reduce the number of checkpoint replicas in each clique and use short timeouts to detect worker failures.

Acknowledgments

This work was supported by the CoreGRID Network of Excellence, funded by the European Commission under the Sixth F.P. Project no. FP6-004265.

References

[1] D. Anderson. BOINC: A system for public-resource computing and storage. In *5th IEEE/ACM International Workshop on Grid Computing*, Pittsburgh, USA, 2004.

[2] S. Annapureddy, M. Freedman, and D. Mazieres. Shark: Scaling File Servers via Cooperative Caching. *Proceedings of the 2nd USENIX/ACM Symposium on Networked Systems Design and Implementation (NSDI), Boston, USA, May,* 2005.

[3] C. Christensen, T. Aina, and D. Stainforth. The challenge of volunteer computing with lengthy climate model simulations. In *1st IEEE International Conference on e-Science and Grid Computing*, pages 8–15, Melbourne, Australia, 2005. IEEE Computer Society.

[4] Condor-g. http://www.cs.wisc.edu/condor/condorg/.

[5] P. Domingues, F. Araujo, and L. M. Silva. A DHT-based infrastructure for sharing checkpoints in desktop grid computing. In *2nd IEEE International Conference on e-Science and Grid Computing (eScience '06)*, Amsterdam, The Netherlands, December 2006.

[6] P. Domingues, P. Marques, and L. Silva. Resource usage of windows computer laboratories. In *International Conference Parallel Processing (ICPP 2005)/Workshop PEN-PCGCS*, pages 469–476, Oslo, Norway, 2005.

[7] P. Domingues, J. G. Silva, and L. Silva. Sharing checkpoints to improve turnaround time in desktop grid. In *20th IEEE International Conference on Advanced Information Networking and Applications (AINA 2006), 18-20 April 2006, Vienna, Austria*, pages 301–306. IEEE Computer Society, April 2006.

[8] P. Druschel and A. Rowstron. Past: A large-scale, persistent peer-to-peer storage utility. In *HotOS VIII*, Schoss Elmau, Germany, May 2001.

[9] S. Goel, M. Robson, M. Polte, and E. G. Sirer. Herbivore: A scalable and efficient protocol for anonymous communication. Technical Report TR2003-1890, Cornell University Computing and Information Science Technical, February 2003.

[10] S. Kandula, J. K. Lee, and J. C. Hou. LARK: a light-weight, resilient application-level multicast protocol. In *IEEE 18th Annual Workshop on computer Communications (CCW 2003)*. IEEE, October 2003.

[11] A. Martin, T. Aina, C. Christensen, J. Kettleborough, and D. Stainforth. On two kinds of public-resource distributed computing. In *Fourth UK e-Science All Hands Meeting*, Nottingham, UK, 2005.

[12] S. Rhea, C. Wells, P. Eaton, D. Geels, B. Zhao, H. Weatherspoon, and J. Kubiatowicz. Maintenance-free global data storage. *IEEE Internet Computing*, 5(5):40–49, 2001.

[13] B. Richard, D. Nioclais Mac, and D. Chalon. Clique: A transparent, peer-to-peer collaborative file sharing system. Technical Report HPL-2002-307, HP Laboratories Grenoble, 2002.

[14] E. Sit, J. Cates, and R. Cox. A DHT-based backup system, 2003.

[15] D. Thain, T. Tannenbaum, and M. Livny. Distributed computing in practice: the Condor experience. *Concurrency and Computation Practice and Experience*, 17(2-4):323–356, 2005.

EDGES: THE COMMON BOUNDARY BETWEEN SERVICE AND DESKTOP GRIDS

Zoltan Balaton, Zoltan Farkas, Gabor Gombas,
Peter Kacsuk, Robert Lovas, Attila Csaba Marosi
MTA SZTAKI, Budapest, Hungary,
CoreGrid Institute on Architectural Issues
{balaton, zfarkas, gombasg, kacsuk, rlovas, atisu}@sztaki.hu

Ad Emmen
AlmereGrid, Almere,
The Netherlands
ad@almeregrid.nl

Gabor Terstyanszky, Tamas Kiss
University of Westminster, London, UK,
CoreGrid Institute on Grid Systems,
Tools and Environments
{G.Z.Terstyanszky, T.Kiss}@westminster.ac.uk

Ian Kelley, Ian Taylor
Cardiff University, Cardiff, UK,
CoreGrid Institute on Grid Systems,
Tools and Environments
{I.R.Kelley, Ian.J.Taylor}@cs.cardiff.ac.uk

Oleg Lodygensky
LAL Universite Paris Sud, CNRS, IN2P3, France,
CoreGrid Institute on Resource
Management and Scheduling
lodygens@lal.in2p3.fr

Miguel Cardenas-Montes
Extermadura Advanced Research
Center (CETA-CIEMAT), Trujillo, Spain
miguel.cardenas@ciemat.es

Gilles Fedak
INRIA Saclay, Grand-Large, Orsay, France,
CoreGrid Institute on Architectural Issues
fedak@lri.fr

Filipe Araujo
University of Coimbra, Coimbra, Portugal,
CoreGrid Institute on Architectural Issues
filipius@dei.uc.pt

Abstract   Service grids and desktop grids are both promoted by their supportive communities as great solutions for solving the available compute power problem and helping to balance loads across network systems. Little work, however, has been undertaken to blend these two technologies together. In this paper we introduce a new EU project, that is building technological bridges to facilitate service and desktop grid interoperability. We provide a taxonomy and background into service grids, such as EGEE and desktop grids or volunteer computing platforms, such as BOINC and XtremWeb. We then describe our approach for identifying translation technologies between service and desktop grids. The individual themes discuss the actual bridging technologies employed and the distributed data issues surrounding deployment.

Keywords: Desktop Grids, BOINC, EGEE, XtremWeb, Distributed Data, Peer to Peer

1.   Introduction

There is a growing interest among scientific communities to use Grid computing infrastructures to solve their grand-challenge problems and to further enhance their applications with extended parameter sets and greater complexity. Such enhancements were often limited or unattainable in compute systems prior to the era of Grid computing due to increased resource requirements. However, even existing grids are often smaller than many new scientific communities and their complex applications would like to use.

E-infrastructures play a distinguished role in enabling large-scale innovative scientific research. In order to establish such e-infrastructures, various grids have been created and run as a service for the scientific community. Originally, the aim of Grid systems was that anyone (donors) could offer resources for a given Grid, and anyone (users) could claim resources dynamically, according to their actual needs, in order to solve a computational or data intensive task. This twofold aim has however not fully been achieved, and we can today observe two different trends in the development of Grid systems: Service Grids and Desktop Grids.

Researchers and developers in Service Grids (SGs) first create a Grid service that can be accessed by a large number of users. A resource can become part of the Grid by installing a predefined software set, or middleware. However, the middleware is usually so complex that it often requires extensive expert effort to maintain. It is therefore natural, that individuals do not often offer their resources in this manner, and SGs are generally restricted to larger institutions, where professional system administrators take care of the hardware/middleware/software environment and ensure high-availability of the Grid. Examples of such infrastructures are EGEE, the NorduGrid, or the NGS (National Grid Service) in the UK. Even though the original aim of enabling anyone to join the Grid with one's resources has not been fulfilled, the largest Grid in the world (EGEE) contains around forty thousand processors. Anyone who obtains a valid certificate from a Certificate Authority (CA) can access those Grid resources that trust that CA. This is often simplified by Virtual Organization (VO) or community authorization services that centralize the management of trust relationships and access rights.

Desktop Grids (DGs) on the other hand are commonly known as *volunteer computing systems* or *Public-Resource Computing*, because they often rely upon the general public to donate resources. i.e. "spare cycles" or storage space. Unlike Service Grids, which are based on complex architectures, volunteer computing has a simple architecture and has demonstrated the ability to integrate dispersed, heterogeneous computing resources with ease, successfully scavenging cycles from tens of thousands of idle desktop computers. This paradigm represents a complementary trend concerning the original aims of

Grid computing. In Desktop Grid systems, anyone can bring resources into the Grid, installation and maintenance of the software is intuitive, requiring no special expertise, thus enabling a large number of donors to contribute into the pool of shared resources. On the downside, only a very limited user community (i.e., target applications) can effectively use Desktop Grid resources for computation. The most well-known DG example is the SETI@HOME [2] project, in which approximately four million PCs have been involved.

DGs However, cannot work as services nor be used by anyone who has not already setup their project to function in this environment. Additionally, unlike most Service Grids, which have reciprocal agreements for resource utilization among partners, participants in DG systems, cannot use the system for their own goals. Because of this limitation, the Grid research community considers DGs only as particular and limited solutions. Until now, these two kinds of Grid systems have been completely separated and hence there has not been a mechanism to be able exploit their individual advantageous features in a unified environment. However, with the objective to support new scientific communities that need extremely large numbers of resources, the solution could be to interconnect these two kinds of Grid systems into an integrated Service Grid–Desktop Grid (SG–DG) infrastructure.

In this paper, we described research on how such an integrated SG–DG infrastructure can be established, how applications can be adapted and developed for such an infrastructure, and how the execution of these applications can be controlled and managed. The formulation of these questions and research collaboration to answer them has already been started within the Core-Grid Institute on Architectural Issues. More recently a new European project, called EDGeS (Enabling Desktop Grids for e-Science) has been accepted by the European Commission in order to build this architecture and provide it as a service for the European research community. This paper gives an overview on the research perspectives and proposed solutions within EDGeS. In the next section, we provide a taxonomy of existing systems. We then describe the related work and core technologies we are working with in service and desktop grids in Section 3. In Section 4, we provide an outline of the three main areas of research within the EDGeS project, in providing a SG–DG bridge, application development and user access, and the distributed data access concerns between such systems. In Section 5, we present our concluding remarks.

2. Taxonomy of Existing Desktop and Service Grids

The main distinguishing feature between SGs and DGs is the way computations are initiated at the resources of the grid. In Service Grids a job submission or a service invocation is used to initiate activity on a grid resource. Both can be considered as a specific form of the *push model* where the service requester pushes jobs, tasks, service invocations on the passive resources. Once such a request is pushed on the resource, it becomes active and executes the requested activity. Desktop Grids work according to the *pull model*. Resources that have got spare cycles pull tasks from the application repository which is typically placed on the DG server. In this way resources play an active role in the DG system, they initiate their own activity based on the task pulled from the server.

Both SGs and DGs can be public (global) and non-public (local). A public (or global) grid refers to a grid that connects resources from different administrative domains, which are typically interconnected by wide-area network. Non-public (or local) grids, on the other hand, connect resources within the same administrative domain by using a local-area network or a VPN. Typical public service grids are EGEE, OSG [11], TeraGrid [13], etc. Non-public service grids are typically interconnected local clusters (for example university wide local Grids like the Oxford Campus Grid [12]). Both public and local desktop grids can be further divided as volunteer and non-volunteer DGs. Resources of volunteer DGs are collected from individual desktop owners as their volunteer contribution to the Desktop Grid. Typical public, volunteer DGs are the BOINC-based DG systems like SETI@HOME, Einstein@HOME [5], SZTAKI Desktop Grid [4], etc. AlmereGrid [6] and XtremWeb [7] are also volunteer, public DG systems.

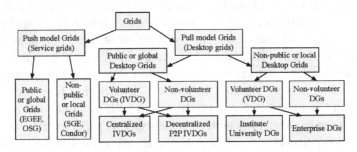

Figure 1.   Taxonomy of grid systems from the Desktop Grid point of view.

In a non-volunteer DG individual desktop owners are instructed to contribute their resources to the DG. Examples for such non-volunteer DGs are the Extremadura School DG and the Westminster DG. The Extremadura School DG is a public non-volunteer DG where the regional government instructed the schools of the region to contribute their desktops to the DG system. The Westminster DG is also a non-volunteer DG but this is a local DG working inside the University of Westminster. Public volunteer DG systems can be realized as centralized DG systems having one centralized server or as decentralized DG systems where several DG servers are used and connected by a P2P network. All the previously mentioned DG systems are centralized DGs. An example for a P2P DG system is the OurGrid DG infrastructure from Brazil [3].

In the next section, we introduce the most important technologies that form the basis of the integrated SG–DG platform.

3. Core Technologies and Related Work

EGEE (*Enabling Grids for E-sciencE*) makes grids available to scientists and engineers, the second phase of the European Commission funded project (EGEE-II) has started in April 2006. The infrastructure is an ideal platform for any scientific research area, especially for high energy physics and life sciences whose computing demand is high. EGEE offers 40000 CPUs and about 5PB of storage space, with a throughput of around 100000 jobs a day.

EGEE is built on the gLite middleware, a middleware for building a grid that pulls together contributions from many other projects, including LCG and VDT. gLite supports different services, namely resource brokers, computing elements, storage elements, security services, information systems, worker nodes and user interfaces. All the services are deployed on a Scientific Linux installation. The basic building blocks of the gLite middleware are the *Worker Nodes* (WN). These machines are responsible for the actual execution of applications in gLite. Users can assume that their application is run within a well-defined environment when executing on a worker node. Worker nodes are similar to the nodes of a cluster and a group of worker nodes is attached to a *Computing Element* (CE). Computing elements provide a gateway to the worker nodes and therefore essentially CEs provide the grid resources.

Condor [8] also allows EGEE resources to temporarily join a Condor pool using the Condor Glidein [14] mechanism. This works by submitting Condor itself to a grid resource and then this Condor instance can run jobs submitted to the original Condor pool on the EGEE resource. However this has to be configured manually and cannot be done automatically when the number of jobs would justify it. Also, if there are currently not enough jobs in the Condor pool to utilize the grid resource, then it may be wasted.

Another approach followed in [9] is to configure a DG Client (in this case an XtremWeb client) as a backfill job for Condor. Whenever there are unused resources available, Condor starts the backfill job (in this case a desktop grid client) on the available computers. This approach has disadvantages: first, it requires explicit support from the local job scheduler. Second, the administrator of the EGEE computing element must statically configure the desktop grid client, meaning this solution is not available for regular EGEE users. So this approach helps computing element administrators who want to increase the utilization of their resources, but it does not help regular users who already have desktop grid applications and want to use more resources for them.

A good example for Desktop Grids is BOINC [1] (*Berkeley Open Infrastructure for Network Computing*). Desktop grids generally maintain a single central service and allow users to offer their computers' CPU cycles for free. As such, they are referred to as volunteer computing and generally the more exciting the problem is, the more users will volunteer to offer resources.

BOINC builds on two main components: the desktop grid server and the user's machines. Users can join machines to a BOINC DG by installing a client-side application, which measures the performance of the machine and then communicates with the BOINC server, sending it performance specifications and a request for work. The server replies by sending application executables and the requested work. The client processes the downloaded data and upon completion uploads the results back to the server and then requests more work. The BOINC server is the key part of a BOINC-based desktop grid. It provides an entry point for the users, stores applications, their related work units and user information, and deals with requests from BOINC clients. BOINC servers use a web server (Apache) for the project users, which exposes a simple web page offering basic functionalities: user registration, statistics, query, BOINC client download, etc. The BOINC server also operate as user forums related to the project where users can ask questions and report their problems. BOINC uses a relational database (MySQL) for storage of applications, their related work units, client and user information, and so on.

4.   SG and DG Bridging Technologies

EDGeS is attempting to close the gap between DG and SG computing. In particular, we would like to run SG jobs in a DG and vice versa in a seamless way. The bridge between a SG and a DG must work in either direction, but the different directions have different issues and requirements and therefore they need different solutions. A SG$\Rightarrow$DG bridge means that jobs submitted to a SG system (for example the EGEE) should be executed using DG resources while a DG$\Rightarrow$SG bridge allows resources from a SG to be used in a DG.

4.1   The SG–DG Bridge

Creating the connection between SGs and DGs will enable the interoperability of EGEE and Volunteer Computing systems. Jobs originating from EGEE should be allowed to run on Desktop Grids, and Desktop Grids should be able to use EGEE Computing Elements as donors within a Desktop Grid project. Right now, Desktop Grids running BOINC or XtremWeb can only use traditional donors, and no other valuable computing power, like those EGEE provides. On the other hand, as DG systems are very easy to set up and maintain, using them in EGEE adds notable computing power to already existing VOs.

Bridging from DGs to EGEE The DG to EGEE bridging can be achieved in two ways. The first approach is creating a modified version of the Desktop Grid client software that represents itself as a very powerful computer (with hundreds or thousands of processors) toward the desktop grid server. The modified client does not run the work units received from the desktop grid server itself but instead transfers the input data and executables to an EGEE VO and executes the job on an EGEE resource, using the APIs provided by the EGEE gLite middleware. This is most easily realized by launching a wrapper in place of the real application that does the conversion and job submission and acts as a proxy for the real application. The output of the job is also collected by this wrapper and then sent back to the Desktop Grid server. Figure 2 depicts a prototype version of this solution.

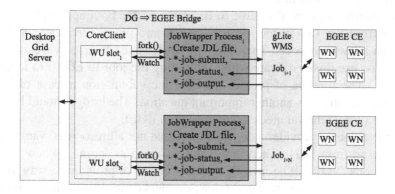

Figure 2.   Structure of the DG⇒EGEE bridge.

This approach is very similar to the Cluster Client developed by SZTAKI to utilize Condor clusters in a BOINC based DG which is described in [10]. The advantage of this solution is that submission is done via the interface provided by the SG middleware, meaning it is using a well defined interface and not relying on the internal structure of the SG. Basically the SG is a black-box for the client and the WNs do not need to have in-/outbound network connection or any direct communication with the Bridge or the Desktop Grid server.

The difficulty in this approach is to harmonize the internal scheduler of the desktop grid client with the EGEE gLite WMS. The internal scheduler of the client decides how much work the desktop grid client asks from the server. In order to make a good decision, the internal scheduler has to know how loaded the EGEE resources are and must dynamically adapt itself to the level of resources available. This will require implementing more advanced scheduling strategies in the desktop grid client than currently available.

The second approach is to build an "overlay DG" on top of EGEE resources by submitting agents wrapped as grid jobs. This solution was pioneered by

Condor Glide-in and is also prototyped in XtremWeb. The agents are desktop grid clients configured appropriately, so after landing at a WN and being started by the SG middleware they connect to the Desktop Grid server to obtain work and start processing it as a normal client. The agents are continue getting work from the DG and processing it as long as their time, allocated by the SG middleware, is up or there is no more work to get. The purpose of the Bridge in this solution is not to convert DG work units to SG jobs but to keep the overlay DG running by submitting and managing the agents. The advantage of this approach is that it can be easily implemented using existing components without modifying the internal scheduler of the DG client but the drawback is that the SG middleware is not utilized as intended but rather circumvented. This can be a problem e.g. for sites using internal network for WNs that do not allow network communication.

The security aspects also have to be observed for both approaches. Jobs arriving from the DG system do not have secure proxy certificates that the EGEE middleware expects. Therefore, the Bridge must have its own certificate and it must use this certificate when submitting the jobs to EGEE to identify DG jobs. The lifetime of proxies used for job submission in case of long-running applications is another important question. The bridge should be able to use the proxy renewal mechanism present in EGEE.

On the resource provider side, we expect that not all resources want to run jobs arriving from DGs. Therefore, solutions such as setting up new virtual organizations (VO) will be investigated as a means of providing a way to differentiate the jobs and allow the service providers control over what is run and where. Jobs arriving from desktop grids will then be sent only to resources that are part of this desktop grid VO.

Bridging from EGEE grids to Desktop Grids   EGEE users require transparent access to DG resources: they want to get information about the DG, submit jobs to the DG, and get job status information and results back from the DG using EGEE tools. Users should also be able to run jobs that make full use of the EGEE infrastructure, for example accessing files located on EGEE Storage Elements (SE). In order to achieve this, the DG must behave like an EGEE Computing Element (CE) belonging to the VO the user wants to use. Let us overview the most important aspects of achieving this goal.

In order to make the bridge capable of transferring jobs to the DG, the bridge must provide a GRAM interface. Using this interface, the EGEE VO's Resource Broker (RB) can talk to the DG.

Every job submitted from EGEE to DG will generate a single work unit. This ensures the same behavior for the DG resource that is expected from an EGEE CE. Direct mapping between the EGEE job and the Desktop Grid work unit allows verifying that the submitted job has all parameters set for the exe-

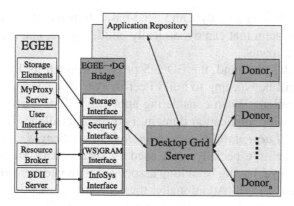

Figure 3. Structure of the EGEE⇒DG bridge.

cution. Input files need to be retrieved, if not stored locally. These files are then mapped to the input files of the Desktop Grid application and a ready-to-submit work unit is created.

Since the DG clients are outside EGEE they have no access to Storage Elements. Therefore, remote files required for work unit creation must be retrieved before execution. Work units are created on the DG server. Before the executable is sent to clients, the bridge must ensure that all input files are present on the DG server.

Security is a key challenge in this case as well. DGs are typically single user systems and do not apply user certificates for authentication and authorization. This means, that some kind of mapping from EGEE user certificates to DG projects needs to be implemented.

4.2   SG–DG Data Access

One key component to EDGeS is the ability to satisfactorily handle the data requirements that arise when transferring jobs between service and desktop grids. The easiest solution to this problem would be to directly expose the service grid data layer to the desktop grid environment. This would closely mimic the functionality that is currently employed by most BOINC projects, where data is centrally distributed to all Desktop Grid participants through a set of known, trusted, and centralized servers. This simple solution, however, has many potentially limiting drawbacks that make it an unattractive solution for EDGeS, for example: Service Grids might not be able to cope with the increased bandwidth requirements imposed by this solution; there are significant security implications in exposing these data systems to direct outside semi-anonymous access; and, unlike traditional BOINC projects, which are relatively static in their data inputs and code requirements, the jobs being migrated by EDGeS would be dynamic need-based transfers that would rely on an underlying system that can dynamically build, expose, and propagate data to network participants.

With these ideas in mind, the EDGeS project, through its JRA3 Data Access activity, will be working to build Peer-to-Peer data sharing mechanisms for data propagation. When considering applying P2P data access technologies to the scientific application domain, two broad challenge areas must be addressed: *social acceptability* and *technological challenges*. Socially, Peer-to-Peer technologies, especially when used for sharing data, are often viewed with a skeptical eye, having been long associated with widespread file sharing of copyrighted material. Additionally, there is also substantial concern that mixing Peer-to-Peer with volunteer computing could, in the event of malicious attacks on the network, cause irreparable damage to the volunteers' trust in the network and thereby adversely effect their willingness to continue donating resources. During the EDGeS project, these social concerns are ongoing and take on a very important role during the current design process, in which we are seeking to identify solutions that not only move forward Desktop Grid utilization, but also to introduce Peer-to-Peer networks and P2P file sharing as both valid and legitimate options for scientific computing.

Within the technical area, security and scalability are the main issues that are being considered. Scalability for large P2P networks has evolved into two general categories: Distributed Hash Tables (DHTs) and super-peer topologies. Both of these approaches are valid and have their unique advantages and disadvantages depending on the problem one is trying to solve, generally with a trade-off between speed, accuracy, and flexibility — finding the correct balance for each individual situation is the important factor. With this in mind, scalability research in EDGeS is focusing on designing an adaptable network that can automatically change its topology to optimally balance network load, an especially useful trait in the case of super-peer technologies, where effective algorithms can help promote an efficient and scalable design.

Security is a much larger issue. Due to the sensitive and vulnerable nature of Desktop Grids, it is critical that not only are peer nodes secure from malicious attacks, but also that data integrity and reliability is ensured. The easiest solution, and perhaps the most susceptible to attacks is a pure P2P network, in which any node is allowed to receive and share information with any other node on the network. This allows for the most network flexibility and client resource usability, however, since in this scenario any node has the capability to promote information, it also has the ability to flood the network with false information. Even though safeguards and hashing can be put in place to mitigate these effects, there is still the potential for malicious network utilization. In a more restricted network, where only "trusted" peers are allowed to act as data cachers and rendezvous nodes the probability that this will happen is diminished, however usability and flexibility are reduced as a result.

The EDGeS project is currently working to pursue a balance between a free forming and a restricted network. Current security infrastructure is being based upon the idea of secure super-peer data centers. In this type of system, every network peer is allowed to receive data, however, only those that meet certain security restricts are allowed to propagate the data to other network partici- pants. Although these security constraints could be based upon any number of configurable factors, in its initial iteration, we envision it to be something as simple as a dynamic set of trusted peers that are identified through being signed by a common X509 root certificate. In future iterations of the security infrastructure, the feasibility of more interesting and fine-tuned scenarios will be investigated, such as making use of a users' "BOINC credit" standing to certify them as a "trusted party" that can safely relay messages and store data.

EDGeS's data access research is broken down into three distinct tasks that, when completed, should provide a complete data access solution for the EGEE- DG Bridge as well as a useful data access layer for generic Desktop Grids. The tasks involved are as follows: *(i)* data migration from Service Grids to Desktop Grids; *(ii)* data distribution in Desktop Grids; and, *(iii)* data access inside Desktop Grids.

5. Conclusion

The EDGeS project started in January 2008 but collaboration between con- sortium partners started earlier within the Scalability for Desktop Grids Re- search Group of the CoreGrid Institute on Architectural Issues. The work pre- sented here describes the main research themes for the project for enabling bridging technologies between service and desktop Grids that were identified during collaboration within CoreGrid. The main issues discussed in this pa- per include security and bridging techniques for translating SG primitives into their DG counterparts and vice versa, as well as proposed distributed data ac- cess and scalability solutions. The bridging solutions discussed in this pa- per were already prototyped to evaluate their advantages and disadvantages of possible approaches in order to select the ones that will be elaborated by the project. These prototypes and preliminary results of the evaluation were also presented. The duration of the EDGeS project is two years and it will end in December 2009. However, by not starting from scratch but basing our work on results achieved earlier and existing collaboration induced by CoreGrid we are confident that we can meet the ambitious goals in this short timeframe.

Acknowledgments

The EDGeS (Enabling Desktop Grids for e-Science) project receives Community funding from the European Commission within Research Infrastructures initiative of FP7 (grant agreement Number 211727). The work presented here was partly funded by FP6 CoreGrid Network of Excellence (contract number IST-2002-004265).

References

[1] D. P. Anderson. Boinc: A system for public-resource computing and storage. In R. Buyya, editor, *GRID*, pages 4–10. IEEE Computer Society, 2004.

[2] D. P. Anderson, J. Cobb, E. Korpela, M. Lebofsky, and D. Werthimer. Seti@home: an experiment in public-resource computing. *Commun. ACM*, 45(11):56–61, 2002.

[3] N. Andrade, L. Costa, G. Germoglio, and W. Cirne. Peer-to-peer grid computing with the OurGrid Community. In *Proc. of the 23rd Brazilian Symposium on Computer Networks*, 2005.

[4] Z. Balaton, G. Gombas, P. Kacsuk, A. Kornafeld, J. Kovacs, A. C. Marosi, G. Vida, N. Podhorszki, and T. Kiss. Sztaki desktop grid: a modular and scalable way of building large computing grids. In *Proc. of the 21th International Parallel and Distributed Processing Symposium, 26-30 March 2007, Long Beach, California, USA*. IEEE, 2007.

[5] Einstein@Home Project. http://www.physics2005.org/events/einsteinathome/.

[6] A. Emmen. Almeregrid, the world's first city supercomputer, is taking shape, October 2004. http://www.hoise.com/primeur/04/articles/monthly/AE-PR-10-04-69.html.

[7] G. Fedak, C. Germain, V. Neri, and F. Cappello. Xtremweb: A generic global computing platform. In *Proceedings of CCGRID'2001 Special Session Global Computing on Personal Devices*, Brisbane, Australia, May 2001. IEEE/ACM, IEEE Press.

[8] M. Litzkow, M. Livny, and M. Mutka. Condor: A Hunter of Idle Workstations. In 104-111, editor, *Proceedings of 8th International Conference of Distributed Computing Systems,*, June 1988.

[9] O. Lodygensky, G. Fedak, F. Cappello, V. Neri, M. Livny, and D. Thain. Xtremweb & condor : Sharing resources between internet connected condor pools. In *Proceedings of CCGRID'2003 Special Session Global Computing on Personal Devices*, number 2003, Tokyo, Japan. IEEE/ACM.

[10] A. C. Marosi, Z. Balaton, P. Kacsuk, and D. Drotos. SZTAKI Desktop Grid: Adapt Clusters for Desktop Grids. Technical report, MTA SZTAKI, 2008. Submitted to the 3rd International Workshop on Distributed Cooperative Laboratories: Instrumenting the Grid (INGRID 2008), Lacco Ameno, Island of Ischia, Italy.

[11] OSG Executive Board. The open science grid. Submitted to SciDAC PI Meeting, 2007.

[12] Oxgrid, a campus grid for the university of oxford. http://www.ict.ox.ac.uk/strategy/events/wallom/.

[13] The Teragrid Project. http://www.teragrid.org.

[14] D. Thain, T. Tannenbaum, and M. Livny. Distributed Computing in Practice: The Condor Experience. *Concurrency and Computation: Practice and Experience*, 17, 2005.

P2P-BASED JOB ASSIGNMENT FOR PUBLIC RESOURCE COMPUTING

Daniela Barbalace, Pasquale Cozza
DEIS University of Calabria, Rende (CS), Italy
barbalace@si.deis.unical.it, pcozza@deis.unical.it

Carlo Mastroianni
CNR-ICAR, Rende (CS), Italy
mastroianni@icar.cnr.it

Domenico Talia
DEIS University of Calabria, Rende (CS), Italy
talia@deis.unical.it

Abstract   Complex applications often require the execution of a large number of jobs in a distributed environment. One highly successful and low cost mechanism for acquiring the necessary compute power is the "public resource computing" paradigm, which exploits the computational power of private computers. However, applications that are based on this paradigm currently rely upon centralized job assignment mechanisms that can hinder the achievement of performance requirements in terms of overall execution time, load balancing, fault-tolerance, reliability of execution results, scalability and so on. This paper extends a super-peer protocol, proposed earlier by this group, for the execution of jobs based upon the volunteer requests of workers. The paper introduces a distributed algorithm that aims to achieve a more efficient and fair distribution of jobs to workers. This is obtained by the definition of different roles that can be assumed by super-peers and ordinary nodes on the basis of their characteristics. A simulation study is carried out to analyze the performance of the super-peer protocol and demonstrate the advantage of distributing the job assignment process.

Keywords: data caching, Grid computing, job execution, job assignment, public resource computing, super-peer.

1.   Introduction

The term "public resource computing" [1] is used for applications in which jobs are executed by privately-owned and often donated computers that use their idle CPU time to support a given (normally scientific) computing project. The pioneer project in this realm is SETI@HOME [3], which has attracted millions of participants wishing to contribute to the digital processing of radio tele-scope data in the search for extra-terrestrial intelligence. A number of similar projects are supported today by the BOINC (Berkeley Open Infrastructure for Network Computing [2]) software infrastructure. The range of scientific objec-tives amongst these projects is very different, ranging from Climate@HOME's [5], which focuses on long-term climate prediction, to Einstein@HOME's [9], aiming at the detection of certain types of gravitational waves.

This paper enhances a P2P-based distributed model, firstly proposed by this group in [8], that supports applications requiring the distributed execution of a large number of jobs with similar properties to current public-resource com-puting systems like BOINC. In such systems, a "super-peer" node can act as a centralized resource for a limited number of regular nodes, in a fashion similar to a current Grid system. At the same time, super- peers can make interconnec-tions with other super-peers to form a P2P overlay network at a higher level, thereby enabling distributed computing on much larger scales.

Unlike BOINC, the model presented here does not rely on any centralized mechanisms for job and data distribution, but exploits decentralizes techniques which are enabled by the super-peer paradigm. The jobs to execute are assigned to workers by means of "job adverts" which are produced by a job manager. A job advert is an XML document that describes the properties of a job to execute.

In the enhanced version discussed here, a distributed approach is used not only for job execution and data caching but also for job assignment. Job adverts are disseminated to a number of "job assigners" that are available on the network, and then assigned by these to worker nodes. Assignment is made in two phases: (i) first the job manager searches the network to discover job assigners and distribute job adverts among them, then (ii) workers, which are available for job executions, issue query messages to find job assigners and retrieve job adverts.

The super-peers play two fundamental roles: they route messages in a peer-to-peer fashion and also act as rendezvous to *match* queries issued by job as-signers and workers with compatible job adverts.

The objective of this work is to evaluate and point out the benefits that derive from this decentralized approach for job assignment. This approach is profitably combined with a decentralized data caching scheme, already described in [7], through which workers retrieve input data, needed for the execution of jobs, from "data centers", i.e., from nodes specialized for the storage of such data.

Simulation analysis performed with an event-driven simulator shows that the simultaneous use of these decentralized mechanisms for job assignment and data download can actually improve performance of public computing.

The remainder of the paper is organized as follows. Section 2 discusses related work in the field and shows how the implemented architecture presented here goes beyond currently supported models. Section 3 presents the super-peer model and the related protocol. Performance is analyzed in Section 4, and conclusions are discussed in Section 5.

2. Related Work

Volunteer computing systems have become extremely popular as a means to garnish many resources for a low cost in terms of both hardware and manpower. The most popular volunteer computing platform currently available, the BOINC infrastructure [2] is composed of a scheduling server and a number of clients installed on users' machines. The client software periodically contacts the scheduling server to report its hardware and availability, and then receives a given set of instructions for downloading and executing a job. After a client completes the given task, it then uploads resulting output files to the scheduling server and requests more work. The BOINC middleware is especially well suited for CPU-intensive applications but is somewhat inappropriate for data-intensive tasks due to its centralized approaches for job assignment and data distribution.

The job assignment/scheduling problem consists in the assignment of a set of n jobs to a set of m machines such that some overall measure of efficiency is maximized, e.g., the time required to complete all tasks. This is a NP-hard problem [4], which is generally solved with centralized or hierarchical approaches [11]. Recently, distributed algorithms have been proposed for adaptation to P2P and Grid environments, for example, in [12] and [13]. However, to the best of our knowledge, distributed algorithms have never been applied to public resource computing applications.

The P2P paradigm has proven to be effective also for distributed data caching. Recently, BitTorrent [6] has become the most widely used and accepted protocol for P2P data distribution, relying on a centralized tracking mechanism to monitor and coordinate file sharing.

However, P2P protocols might not be appropriate to scientific volunteer computing platforms due to their "tit for tat" requirement that necessitates a ratio between upload and download bandwidth, thus requiring peers to share data if they are recipients of it on the network. Further, it is difficult to establish trust for nodes that act as job assigners or data providers in the network; that is, it is difficult to stop these nodes acting as rogue providers and serve false data across the network or disrupt the network in some way.

The approach proposed in [8] and [7] , and enhanced in this paper, attempts to combine the strengths of both a volunteer distributed computing approach like BOINC with decentralized, yet secure and customizable, P2P data sharing practices. It differs from the centralized BOINC architecture, in that it seeks to integrate P2P networking directly into the system, as job descriptions and input data is provided to a P2P network instead of directly to the client.

3. A Super-Peer Protocol for Job Submission

A data-intensive Grid application can require the distributed execution of a large number of jobs with the goal to analyze a set of data files. One representative application scenario defined for the GridOneD project [10] shows how one might conduct a massively distributed search for gravitational waveforms produced by orbiting neutron stars. In this scenario, a data file of about 7.2 MB of data is produced every 15 minutes and it must be compared with a large number of templates (between 5,000 and 10,000) by performing fast correlation. It is estimated that such computations take approximately 500 seconds. Data can be analyzed in parallel by a number of Grid nodes to speed up computation and keep the pace with data production. A single job consists of the comparison of the input data file with a number of templates, and in general it must be executed multiple times in order to assure a given statistical accuracy or minimize the effect of malicious executions.

Currently, this kind of application is usually managed through a centralized framework, in which one server assigns jobs to workers, sends them input data, and then collects results; however this approach clearly limits scalability. Conversely, we propose a decentralized protocol that exploits the presence of super-peer overlays, which are more and more widely adopted to deploy interconnections among nodes of distributed systems and specifically of Grids.

In the super-peer overlay, the simple nodes, or *workers*, are responsible for the execution of jobs, whereas the *super-peers* constitute the backbone of the super-peer overlay. A worker or super-peer node can play different *roles*, as detailed in the following:

- *job manager*: a node that plays this role produces *job adverts*, i.e., files that describe the characteristics of the jobs that must be executed, and distributes these adverts to job assigners, which in turn assigns jobs directly to workers. The job manager is also responsible for the collection of output results.

- *job assigner*: it receives a number of job adverts from the job manager and is responsible for the assignment of the corresponding jobs to workers.

- *data source*: it receives data from an external sensor, and provides this data as input for the execution of jobs. Each data file is associated to a *data advert*, i.e. a metadata document which describes the characteristics of this file.

- *data cacher*: it has the ability to cache data (and associated data adverts) retrieved from a data source or another data cacher, and can directly provide such data to workers.

In the following, *data sources* and *data cachers* are collectively referred to as *data centers*, since both are able to provide data to workers, although at different phases of the process: data sources from the beginning, data cachers after retrieving data from data sources or other data cachers. When a worker is available for a job execution, it first issues a *job query* to obtain a job advert and then a *data query* to retrieve input data. A worker can disconnect at any time; if this occurs during the downloading of a data file or the execution of a job, that one will not be completed. Super-peers play the role of both *routing* and *rendezvous* nodes, since they compare job and data description documents (*job* and *data adverts*) with *queries* issued to discover these documents, thereby acting as a meeting place for job or data providers and consumers.

3.1 Job Assignment and Data Download

The objective of the job assignment protocol is the distribution of jobs among workers. To decentralize the assignment of jobs, the protocol exploits the presence of multiple *job assigners* on the network. After producing a number of job adverts, the job manager distributes them to the job assigners, which then assign them to workers.

Figure 1 depicts the sequence of messages exchanged among the job manager, the job assigners and the workers. A sample topology is shown, with 6 super-peers, among which 2 assume also the role of job assigner.

After producing a number of job adverts, which describe the job to execute, the job manager JM issues an "assigner query" to search for available job assigners on the network. This query is replicated and forwarded by super-peers (step 1). As job assigners, in this case the nodes JA_1 and JA_2, receive an assigner query, they respond to the job manager by directly sending it an "assigner advert" (step 2). The job manager collects assigner adverts for a given interval of time, than it distributes the job adverts among the discovered job assigners (step 3).

Subsequently, Figure 1 describes the behavior of the protocol when a job query is issued by the workers W_A and W_B (step 4). A job query is expressed by an XML document and typically contains hardware and software features of the requesting node as well as CPU time and memory amount that the node offers. A job query matches a job advert when it is compatible with the information contained in the job advert, e.g., the parameters of the job and the characteristics of the platforms on which it must be executed. A job query is forwarded through the super-peer network until it is delivered to a job assigner. If the job assigner has not assigned all the matching job adverts received by the job manager, one of these job adverts is sent to the worker (step 5) that will execute the corresponding job.

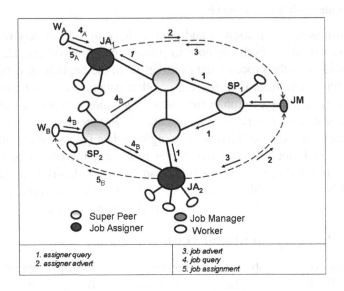

Figure 1.   Super-peer job assignment protocol: sample network topology and sequence of exchanged messages to distribute job adverts among job assigners (messages 1, 2, 3) and assign them to workers (messages 4, 5).

The job advert also contains information about the data file which is required for the job execution and must be retrieved by the worker. Download of input data is performed in the *data-download* phase, which is not described in Figure 1 and is better detailed in [7]. In a similar fashion to the job assignment phase, the worker sends a *data query* message, which travels the super-peer network searching for a matching input data file stored by a data center. Since the same file can be maintained by different data centers, a data center that successfully matches a data query does not send data directly to the worker, in order to avoid multiple transmissions of the same file. Conversely, the data center sends only a small *data advert* to the worker. In general, a worker can receive many data adverts from different data centers. Then it chooses a data center, according to policies that can rely on the distance of data centers, their available bandwidth etc. After making the choice, the worker initiates the download operation from the selected data center. When the super-peer connected to the worker acts also as a data cacher, data is first retrieved from the data cacher and then forwarded to the worker. This enables the dynamic caching functionality, which allows for the replication of data files on multiple data cachers and leads to well known advantages such as increased degree of *data availability* and improved *fault tolerance*. Dynamic caching also allows for a significant improvement of performances, as shown in Section 4.

Upon receiving the input data, the worker executes the job, reports the results to the job manager and possibly issues another *job query*, so restarting the protocol. Each job must be executed a specified number of times, as mentioned in Section 3. As a job manager receives the result of a job execution, it checks if the required number of executions has been reached for that job. In this case, the job manager informs the job assigners, that will no longer assign this specific job to workers.

4.   Performance Evaluation

A simulation analysis was performed by means of event-based simulation, in order to evaluate the performance of the super-peer protocol described in the previous section. The simulation scenario, and the related network and protocol parameters, are set to assess the representative astronomy application mentioned in Section 3.

The number of workers is set to 1000 and it is assumed that an average of 10 workers are connected to a super-peer. Each super-peer is connected to at most 4 neighbor super-peers. Workers can disconnect and reconnect to the network at any time: average connection and disconnection time intervals are set, respectively, to 4 hours and 1 hour. A data download or job execution fails upon the disconnection of the corresponding worker. The number of jobs N_{job} varies from 50 to 500. In our application scenario, each job corresponds to the analysis of a portion of the gravitational waveforms received from the detector. The parameter N_{exec} is defined as the minimum number of executions that must be performed for each job, either to enhance statistical accuracy or minimize the effect of malicious executions. To achieve this objective, redundant job assignment is exploited: each job advert can be matched and assigned to workers up to a number of times equal to the parameter MTL, or *Matches To Live*, whose value must be not lower than N_{exec}. A job is assigned to workers until either the MTL parameter is decremented to 0 or the job manager receives the results for at least N_{exec} executions of this job. A proper choice of MTL can compensate for possible disconnections of workers and consequent job failures.

It is assumed that local connections (i.e., between a super-peer and a local simple node) have a larger bandwidth and a shorter latency than remote connections. Specifically, the bandwidth values of local and remote connections are set to 10 Mbps and 1 Mbps, respectively, whereas transmission delays are set to 10 ms and 100 ms. A TTL parameter is used to limit the traffic load: this corresponds to the maximum number of hops that can be performed by a job query issued by a worker. In our test, this parameter is set to 3.

Simulations have been performed to analyze the overall execution time, i.e. the time needed to execute all the jobs at least N_{exec} times. The overall execution time, T_{exec}, is crucial to determine the rate at which data files can be retrieved from the detector and sent to the network, so as to guarantee that the workers are able to keep the pace with data production. We also evaluated the balancing of jobs among workers and the average utilization of data centers.

4.1   Performance of Distributed Job Assignment

The first set of simulations was performed to verify the advantage of having multiple job assigners in a network. The number of data sources is set to 2, whereas the overall number of data centers is 50, which is half the number of super-peers. The values of T_{exec} and MTL are set, respectively, to 10 and 20. This value of MTL is sufficient to compensate for possible disconnections of workers, while larger values would be ineffective. This kind of analysis is discussed in [7].

Figure 2 shows the overall execution time and the network load vs. the number of job assigners, with different values of N_{job}. In Figure 2(a), a significant reduction of T_{exec} is perceived as the number of job assigners increases. This can be explained as follows. If only one or few job assigners are available, most jobs will be assigned to the workers which are close to job assigners, because their job queries will succeed with a higher probability and in a shorter time. Therefore a small percentage of workers will issue a high percentage of data queries, which will be likely served by the data centers close to such workers. Two main drawbacks derive from this scenario: (i) many jobs will be served by a few workers and (ii) many download operations will be served by a small set of data centers. A larger overall execution time is the obvious consequence. A wider availability of job assigners can limit both the mentioned drawbacks. Furthermore, the reduction of T_{exec} is more evident when the computational load, i.e., the number of jobs, is higher. It is noted, however, that as the number of job assigners increases, the execution time first decreases then tends to get stable: therefore the optimum number of job assigners can be set depending on the minimum incremental improvement (i.e., the improvement obtained by adding one more data center) that is considered acceptable.

Figure 2(b) reports the overall number of query messages that are forwarded on the network to complete the required number of job executions. As the number of job assigners increases, fewer hops are necessary to discover a job assigner, therefore the traffic load correspondingly decreases.

Further simulation results prove that the maximum number of jobs assigned to a single worker remarkably decreases as the number of job assigners increases.

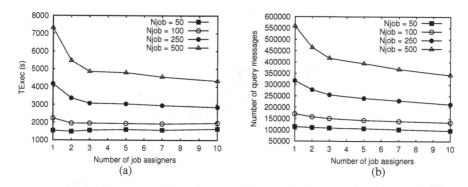

Figure 2. Performance results vs. the number of job managers, for different numbers of jobs: (a) overall execution time; (b) network load.

A reduction in this index corresponds to a better load balancing among workers, which is another obvious objective of public scientific applications. The trend of this index, not reported here, is qualitatively very similar to that of execution time.

4.2 Performance of Distributed Data Caching

A second set of experiments was performed to evaluate the effectiveness of the distributed caching approach, enabled by the availability of multiple data centers, when combined with distributed job assignment. The examined network is analogous to that examined in Section 4.1, except that the number of jobs to execute is fixed to 500 and the number of available data centers is varied from 2 (which is the number of data sources) to 50, i.e., half the number of super-peers. Moreover, results are reported for a number of job assigners ranging from 1 to 5, since this is the interval for which a significant impact on performance indices can be perceived, as shown in Section 4.1.

Figure 3 shows the values of the overall execution time calculated for this scenario. The time decreases as more data centers are made available in the network, for two main reasons: (i) data centers are less heavily loaded and therefore data download time decreases, (ii) workers can exploit a higher parallelism both in the downloading phase and during the execution of jobs.

Figure 3 does not report results for some combinations of the number of data centers and the number of job assigners, because the disconnections of workers do not allow for the completion of all the required job executions. Specifically, if the number of job assigner is 2 or larger, the number of data centers should be at least 15, while, if only one job assigner is available, at least 10 data centers are needed. In fact, if only a few data centers are available, each of these is likely to be overloaded by a large number of workers' requests; as a consequence, the

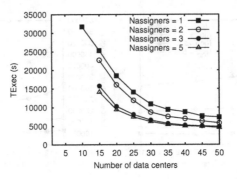

Figure 3.   Overall execution time vs. the number of data centers, for different numbers of job assigners.

download time increases and the disconnection of a worker during the download phase becomes a more probable event.

Figure 4 shows the average utilization of data centers for the same scenario. This is defined as the fraction of time that a data center is actually utilized, i.e., the fraction of time in which at least one download connection, from a worker or a data cacher, is active with this data center. The value of this index is averaged on all the data centers and is an important efficiency index that helps to evaluate the convenience of adding more data centers to the network.

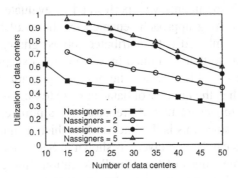

Figure 4.   Average utilization of data centers vs. their number, for different numbers of job assigners.

The average utilization decreases as the number of data centers increases but, in contrast with the execution time, curves do not get to a relatively stable value. This is a useful indication for setting a proper number of data centers. To illustrate this, consider the results obtained with 3 job assigners. While the overall execution time can be decreased until the number of data centers is increased to about 40, the average utilization continues to decrease as more data centers are made available. As an example, if the number of data centers were increased from 40 to 50, there would be a worse exploitation of data centers but no significative reduction in the execution time, from which it can be concluded that an appropriate number of data centers is indeed 40.

5. Conclusions

In this paper we have reported on the analysis and performance evaluation of a super-peer protocol for the execution of scientific applications according to the "public resource computing" paradigm. Use of super-peer overlays allowed us to define distributed protocols both for the assignment of jobs and for the retrieval of input data. Specifically, these two phases exploit the availability of super-peer nodes that, in addition to play the role of routing and rendezvous nodes, are also configured to act as job assigners and data centers, respectively.

Simulation results showed that the combined application of distributed job assignment and distributed data download leads to considerable performance improvements, in terms of the amount of time required to execute the jobs, the network load, the balancing of load among workers and the utilization of data centers.

Acknowledgments

This work is carried out under the FP6 CoreGRID Network of Excellence funded by the European Commission (Contract IST-2002-004265). We would like to thank Ian Taylor and his colleagues at the Cardiff University for their help in defining the protocol presented here.

References

[1] David P. Anderson. Public computing: Reconnecting people to science. In *Proceedings of Conference on Shared Knowledge and the Web*, pages 17–19, Madrid, Spain, November 2003.

[2] David P. Anderson. Boinc: A system for public-resource computing and storage. In *GRID '04: Proceedings of the Fifth IEEE/ACM International Workshop on Grid Computing (GRID'04)*, pages 4–10, 2004.

[3] David P. Anderson, Jeff Cobb, Eric Korpela, Matt Lebofsky, and Dan Werthimer. Seti@home: an experiment in public-resource computing. *Communications of the ACM*, 45(11), 2002.

[4] Peter Brucker. *Scheduling Algorithms*. Springer-Verlag New York, Inc., Secaucus, NJ, USA, 2001.

[5] Climateprediction.net. See web site at http://climateprediction.net/.

[6] B. Cohen. Incentives Build Robustness in BitTorrent. In *Proceedings of the First Workshop on Economics of Peer-to-Peer Systems*, June 2003.

[7] Pasquale Cozza, Ian Kelley, Carlo Mastroianni, Domenico Talia, and Ian Taylor. Cache-enabled super-peer overlays for multiple job submission on grids. In *Proceedings of the CoreGRID Workshop on Grid Middleware*, Dresden, Germany, June 2007.

[8] Pasquale Cozza, Carlo Mastroianni, Domenico Talia, and Ian Taylor. A super-peer protocol for multiple job submission on a grid. In *Euro-Par 2006 Workshops*, volume 4375 of *Springer-Verlag LNCS*, Dresden, Germany, 2007.

[9] Einstein@home. See web site at http://einstein.phys.uwm.edu/.

[10] GridOneD. See web site at http://www.gridoned.org/.

[11] Klaus Krauter, Rajkumar Buyya, and Muthucumaru Maheswaran. A taxonomy and survey of grid resource management systems for distributed computing. *Software-Practice and Experience*, 32(2).

[12] Vijay Subramani, Rajkumar Kettimuthu, Srividya Srinivasan, and P. Sadayappan. Distributed job scheduling on computational grids using multiple simultaneous requests. In *Proceedings of the 11th IEEE Symposium on High Performance Distributed Computing*, Edinburgh, UK, 2002.

[13] Norihiro Umeda, Hidemoto Nakada, and Satoshi Matsuoka. Peer-to-peer scheduling system with scalable information sharing protocol. In *Proceedings of the 2007 International Symposium on Applications and the Internet Workshops SAINT-W '07*, 2007.

ESTIMATING THE SIZE OF PEER-TO-PEER NETWORKS USING LAMBERT'S W FUNCTION.

Javier Bustos-Jimenez, Nicolas Bersano
Escuela de Ingenieria Informatica. Universidad Diego Portales
Av. Ejercito 441, Santiago, Chile.
javier.bustos@inf.udp.cl, nbersano@al.udp.cl

Satu Elisa Schaeffer
Universidad Autonoma de Nuevo Leon. FIME - Posgrado en Ingenieria de Sistemas.
AP 126-F. Ciudad Universitaria, San Nicolas de los Garza, NL 66450. Mexico.
elisa@yalma.fime.uanl.mx

Jose Miguel Piquer
Departamento de Ciencias de la Computacion (DCC). Universidad de Chile.
Blanco Encalada 2120, Santiago, Chile.
jpiquer@dcc.uchile.cl

Alexandru Iosup
Parallel and Distributed Systems Group,
Faculty of Engineering, Mathematics and Computer Science, Delft University of Technology,
Mekelweg 4, 2628 CD, Delft, The Netherlands
A.Iosup@tudelft.nl

Augusto Ciuffoletti
Department of Computer Science. University of Pisa
Corso Italia 40, 56125 Pisa - Italy.
augusto@di.unipi.it

Abstract   In this work, we address the problem of locally estimating the size of a Peer-to-Peer (P2P) network using local information. We present a novel approach for estimating the size of a peer-to-peer (P2P) network, fitting the sum of new neighbors discovered at each iteration of a breadth-first search (BFS) with a logarithmic function, and then using Lambert's W function to solve a root of $a \ln(n) + b - n = 0$, where n is the network size. With rather little computation, we reach an estimation error of at most 10 percent, only allowing the BFS to iterate to the third level.

Keywords: Peer-to-Peer, Network size, Estimation

1.   Introduction

In this work, we address the problem of locally estimating the size of a Peer-to-Peer (P2P) network using local information. Our approach is based on a *breadth-first search* (BFS) rooted in the node that wants to discover the size of the system. It is easy to design an algorithm that eventually counts all the nodes in the system, by recursively acquiring the neighbors of the discovered nodes. We however seek to limit the depth to which the BFS explores the network to avoid generating more traffic in the network, computing an estimate instead of the exact network size.

The rest of this article is organized as follows: in Section 2 we present the algorithm for P2P network-size estimation. In Section 3 we evaluate of our algorithm in terms of the estimation error (in percentages of the real network size). Finally, conclusions and future work are presented in Section 4.

1.1   Motivation

The potential applications of accurate estimates of network size are various. One broad class of applications are the numerous algorithms that either require knowledge of the network size or greatly benefit from such information, which is the case in some routing tasks. Essentially, in many distributed protocols the knowledge of the network size is implicitly assumed.

For example, when estimating the information spread or the gossiping coverage [1], knowing the network size helps. These algorithms have direct applications in the field of P2P recommendation schemes. Knowing the network size is also useful in estimating the latency of gossip based broadcast, especially in setting up a time-to-live (TTL) mechanism for gossips.

Secondly, many parameters that control the provisioning of resources in commercial P2P applications (such as data or video on demand) should be based on the network size [2]. To give a concrete example, the performance of BitTorrent can be improved by selecting the choking/unchoking count and rate dynamically, which eliminates a a potential source of poor performance [3].

We observe that none of the above examples is overly sensitive to the precision of the evaluation of network size: for instance, the time needed to visit all nodes (or *cover time*) in a randomly configured network of n nodes using a random walk has complexity $\mathcal{O}(n \log(n))$. Therefore, an error in the estimate of n reflects almost linearly in the estimate of the cover time. Such consideration justifies the interest for a distributed algorithm that returns a sufficiently precise estimate of the size of the system, but without incurring in the the cost of an exhaustive computation.

Starting from this concept, Horowitz and Malkhi [4] propose a scheme for dynamically estimating network size at each node of the network as the network evolves (that is, while nodes join and leave the network), by maintaining an estimate of the logarithm of network size. Their algorithm exhibits three limits, that may be critical in a Grid environment:

(i) the presence of a directory of the nodes is not excluded,

(ii) the system is extremely unstable, since the precision of a new estimate depends on the precision of the previous one, and

(iii) an error on in the estimate of a logarithm reflects exponentially on the network size.

In this paper we propose a new method that, with similar purposes, does *not* require the presence of a centralized directory, is memoryless, and substantially improves the precision of the estimate. As a counterpart, our methodology is more expensive, since we require a bounded flooding of the network. However, the nodes involved in the flooding will finally obtain an estimate of network size. As an additional feature, the size of the system is obtained on demand, whenever a node happens to need that information, without maintaining activity at all nodes as all times, as in Horowitz and Malkhi scheme.

In essence our methodology consists of launching a Breadth First flooding, which stops whenever a certain criteria, based on a mathematical modeling of the number of hosts reached by the flood, is satisfied. The criteria guarantees that a significant approximation of the network size is obtained well before the flooding reaches each node, and in this sense we speak of an *early stopping* flooding.

1.2 Data Validity

For modeling Peer-to-Peer networks, we used the Delft BitTorrent DataSet 2[1], which is the outcome of a large-scale measurement of the BitTorrent network during one week in May 2005 [5]. The data set tracks over 450,000 BitTorrent users coming from PiratesBay, the largest BitTorrent community at the time of the measurements.

The measurement tracked peers participating in any swarm of size 40 or above. By tracking peers interested in a broad range of file types and sizes, the measurement captured the characteristics of a world-wide community of users.

There are over 35 million BitTorrent peer events recorded in the data set, making it the largest publicly available P2P data set. The measurement also included the Internet routes used by peers to exchange information. This information was gathered through multi-sourced traceroutes and spanned about 20 million IP addresses.

---

[1]The Delft BitTorrent DataSet 2 is available online at http://multiprobe.ewi.tudelft.nl/

2.   Peer-to-Peer network size

Three seminal papers, i.e., Watts and Strogatz [6] on the small-world networks, Faloutsos et al. [7] on the structure of the Internet, and Barabasi and Albert [8] on scale-free networks, gave rise to research on the models and the properties of *nonuniform networks* (cf. for example [9]). Nonuniform networks are graph models of real-world systems where the edges are *not* placed uniformly at random among the vertices. In such systems, the structure of the network is typically nontrivial and the network behavior is complex. Most of the P2P systems used in practice, and all the major P2P file-sharing systems, are forms of nonuniform networks.

There have been numerous studies on the size and shape of the P2P file-sharing systems. Using BFS (crawling), Saroiu et al. [10], Ripeanu et al. [11], and more recently Stutzbach and Rejaie [12] measure the properties of Napster and Gnutella. Also using BFS, Pouwelse et al. [13] and Iosup et al. [5] measure the properties of BitTorrent. However, the use of BFS as in these works may bias the results, especially for P2P systems of hundreds of thousands to millions of peers. The BFS throughput is at most (usually) 20 kpeers/minute per crawler (machine), which means that for a network of 100,000 peers the crawling time would be 5 (100) minutes in the optimal (average) case. However, the faster version [12] does not cover firewalled and overloaded peers. In P2P systems, the number of firewalled peers varies between 25-60% [5, 12, 13, 14], with higher values for the most popular networks, e.g., BitTorrent [5]. If many peers in a P2P system use BFS to find the size and the properties of the network, contacted peers become overloaded. For the slower version of the BFS, we note tha many peers stay in the network in the order of (tens of) minutes [15], and that even more peers quit soon after obtaining content from the network [10, 13], which may render long BFS measurements inaccurate. We conclude that using an unmodified. full-scale BFS for measuring the network size does not scale with the size of today's P2P networks.

Alternatively to using BFS, Sen and Wang [15] measure using router flow information the properties of Gnutella, FastTrack (KaZaA), and DirectConnect. However, this method requires access to routers across the ISP's network over the world, which is not possible for a wide majority of the peers inside the P2P network.

We propose in this work an alternative to the full-scale BFS, which combines a limited BFS with mathematical analysis to achieve a good network size estimation (i.e., above 90% accuracy). The mathematical analysis is based on the observation that plotting the the number of new nodes discovered upon visiting each vertex during a BFS, depicts a fuzzy, hard-to-model function, but when instead the contributions of the neighbors are summed.

Let us model the network as a graph $G = (V, E)$, with $|V| = n$ being the total number of nodes. We denote the set of neighbors of a node $v \in V$ by

$$\Gamma(v) = \Gamma_1(v) = \{w \mid (u, w) \in E\}, \tag{1}$$

we define the second-neighborhood of v as

$$\Gamma_2(v) = \bigcup_{w \in \Gamma(v)} \Gamma(w) \tag{2}$$

and recursively from thereon the k-distance neighborhood of v as

$$\Gamma_k(v) = \bigcup w \in \Gamma_{k-1}(v)\Gamma(w). \tag{3}$$

One can compute iteratively for a starting node $v \in V$ the following value for $i = 1, 2, 3, \ldots$ until the value drops to zero:

$$\Lambda_i(v) = \Gamma_k(v) \setminus \bigcup_{j=1}^{k-1} \Gamma_j(v), \tag{4}$$

that is, the number of new nodes reached at step i of the BFS.

The function,

$$S_i(v) = \sum_{j=1}^{i} |\Lambda_i(v)| \tag{5}$$

obtained summing the contributions has a quite smooth plot, as you can see in Figure 2.

In the rest of this paper, we first define the functions used and then present the results obtained by studying the function $\Lambda_i(v)$ varying the starting node v. Eventually $S_i(v)$ levels off as $\Lambda_i(v)$ falls to zero, meaning that the entire network has been traversed and new nodes can no longer be found.

In BFS, nodes "pass on messages" to their neighbors, who then pass messages on to their neighbors – the messages being in a sense recursive procedure calls. This process resembles that of how a *rumor* spreads in a population, although in BFS the nodes pass the information or the request onto *all* of their neighbors, whereas rumors tend to spread less efficiently. Supposing that each node was to pass the message to just one random neighbor, the process of spreading would effectively be a random walk. Pittel [16] studies the coverage that a rumor achieves given the number of "rounds" of gossip-passing. Another good analogy comes from *epidemic spreading*, where it is of interest to estimate the number of infected individuals at a given time [17]. Analogies to epidemic spreading have been applied in data-base system design [18].

We use the *Lambert's W function* [19], which is the inverse function of $f(w) = we^w$ and cannot be directly expressed in terms of elementary functions, to *estimate* the network size based on the form of plots of accumulated sums of $|\Lambda_i(v)|$ for different nodes v.

The details on how this is done are presented in Section 2, where we justify the application of the W function in estimating the network size based on the shape of the plot of the accumulated sums for fixed v, which has the shape of $f(i) = a \log(i) + b$. Our choice of the W function bases on the work of Corless et al. [20], where a recurrence relation is used to calculate W, providing fast convergence to the desired result in less than 100 iterations.

In a P2P network, technically every node could explicitly calculate the network size by running a BFS (see pseudo-code in Figure 1).

```
procedure BFS(node s, graph G)

queue q;

// put the starting node s into the queue
put(q, s);

N = 1; // initial known network size

// while the queue is not empty
while (!empty(q)) {

    // retrieve the first element of the queue
    v = get(q);

    // mark the node v to have been visited
    mark_visited(v);

    // retrieve the list of neighboring nodes to v
    list = neighbours(v);

    // remove from the list all previously visited nodes
    list = remove_visited(list);

    // add to the known network size the newly encountered nodes
    n = n + size(list);

    // add the elements of list to the end of the queue
    put(q, list);
}
```

Figure 1.   The BFS algorithm that would need to be executed to determine the size of the network n given the network as a graph G and a starting node s.

In large networks, this is a long and communication-intensive procedure, as each edge of the network must be traversed. The size of list at each iteration is the number of new nodes discovered, $|\Lambda_i(v)|$. We found that the shape of the curve of $S_i(v)$ (Equation 5) can be approximated by

$$S_i(v) \approx y = a \ln(i) + b \qquad (6)$$

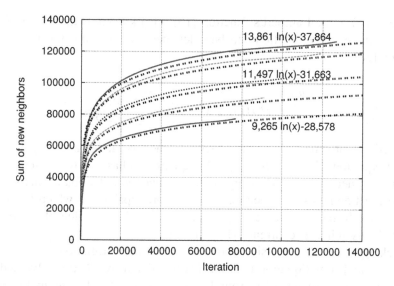

Figure 2.   Accumulated sum of new neighbor (in color) along with their representative function (drawn black)

as is shown in Figure 2. We found an even better fit with a function with an additional term with $\ln(\ln(i))$, but we could only work with such a function using numerical methods. Nevertheless, the simpler form of Equation 6 serves our purposes and gives a reasonable fit, we saw no need to complicate the fitted function further.

The value of $S_i(v)$ as it levels off is exactly n, as the maximum value of $S_i(v)$ is the size of the whole network. Hence, the points that interest us are those with $S_i(v) = n$, which is necessarily the case for $S_n(v) = n$, although the leveling off can occur much earlier, depending on the network structure[2].

The point $S_n(v) = n$ corresponds in the fitted function (Equation 6) to the solution of this equation:

$$n = a \ln(n) + b. \tag{7}$$

Equation (8) in itself is solved by

$$n = -a \cdot W\left(-\frac{e^{-b/a}}{a}\right), \tag{8}$$

---

[2]When i reaches diam(G), the diameter of G, which is the maximum distance in terms of number of edges on the shortest paths between any two nodes, necessarily the BFS has reached the entire network regardless of the starting vertex v. Typically diam$(G) \ll n$, although in the worst case diam$(G) = n - 1$.

where $W(z)$ is the Lambert's function [19] (also known as the *Omega function*). Lambert's W function can be calculated by the following recurrence relation [20],

$$w_{j+1} = w_j - \frac{w_j e^{w_j} - z}{e^{w_j}(w_j + 1) - \dfrac{(w_j + 2)(w_j e^{w_j} - z)}{2w_j + 2}}, \tag{9}$$

included in mathematical software packages such as Matlab and Maple.

Our equation $a\ln(n) + b - n = 0$ (Equation 7) has two roots (see Figure 3), and the network size is given by the *second root*. To obtain this second root using Lambert's W function, is its non-principal value which has to be calculated. In our case, as $z \in [-1/e, -0.1]$, an initial value of $w_0 = -2$ should be used in the recurrence (Equation 9).

Seeking to simplify the situation, we studied the correlations of the coefficients a and b of Equation 6 in the fits to the real-world data obtained by computing the values of $S_i(v)$ from different nodes of the data set up to $i = n$. As a positive surprise, we found a strong, stable correlation:

$$b = c_1 a + c_2, \tag{10}$$

where c_1 and c_2 are constants that do not appear to depend strongly on the starting node v and could be obtained numerically from a small data set of the P2P network. From our data set, we estimated the values of $c_1 = -2.0552$ and

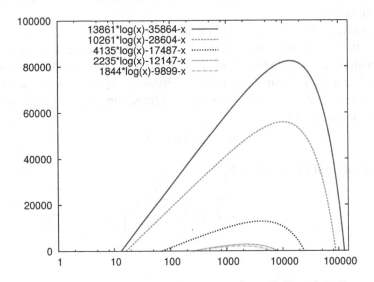

Figure 3.   The two roots of $a\ln(n) + b - n = 0$.

$c_2 = -7840$ that turned out to be well-behaving. We can therefore replace the constant a by the following substitution (from Equation 6):

$$a = \frac{y - c_2}{\ln(n) + c_1}. \tag{11}$$

The precision of our estimate of n will depend on the correctness of the estimation of a. Once the estimation algorithm reaches a stable value for a, the estimate of n can be computed. The estimation of a is done by starting a BFS at a node v, setting a_0 at an initial guess (we used $5,000$), computing at each iteration i the value

$$a' = \frac{S_i(v) - c_2}{\ln(i) + c_1}, \tag{12}$$

based on which a_i is computed as

$$a_i = \frac{1}{i}\big((i-1)a_{i-1} + a'\big). \tag{13}$$

The BFS is cut off when $a_i \approx a_{i-1}$, that is, when the estimate of a no longer significantly changes. In the next section, we study at which number of iterations i the estimate of a, and hence the estimate of n, typically stabilizes.

Should this iteration count be significantly smaller than the diameter of the P2P network (around 14 in our data set), the estimation method would provide an estimate on the network size with less communication overhead than the straightforward method. Another option would be to simply give a TTL for the BFS to explicitly cut it off after a fixed number of iterations.

3. Evaluation of the estimation method

We evaluate our algorithm by computing the estimation error, defined as

$$\epsilon = \frac{100 \,|\text{real size} - \text{estimated size}|}{\text{real size}}\% \tag{14}$$

by each new neighbor visited and by the depth-level i of the BFS. Figure 4 shows that, for small networks (with less than $80,000$ nodes), running $5,000$ iterations (10% of whole network) is sufficient to reach an estimation error of 10 percent, and around $26,000$ iterations suffice for larger networks (with over $100,000$ nodes) to achieve same estimation error.

Using a fixed TTL to control the depth to which to perform the BFS, our experiments show that for all networks, finishing the *third* level of BFS, the estimation error is at most 10 percent of the real network size (see Figure 5). This is a promising result for quickly estimating the size of a P2P network.

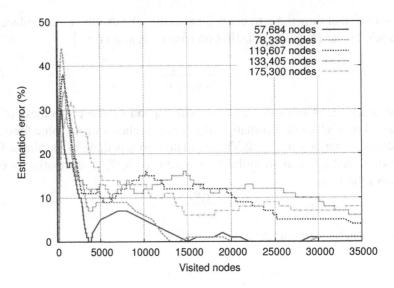

Figure 4. Estimation error (as a percentage of the network real size, Equation 14) by iteration.

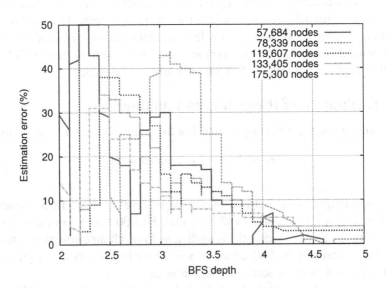

Figure 5. Estimation error (as a percentage of the real network size, Equation 14) for different values of BFS depth.

4.   Conclusions and Future Work

We presented a novel approach for estimating the size of a peer-to-peer (P2P) network, fitting the sum of new neighbors discovered at each iteration of a breadth-first search (BFS) with a logarithmic function, and then using Lambert's W function to solve a root of $a \ln(n) + b - n = 0$, where n is the network size. With rather little computation, we reached an estimation error of at most 10 percent, only allowing the BFS to iterate to the third level.

As future work, we plan to study the effect of fitting instead a function $d \ln(\ln(x))$ that have a better fit to the real data. This function is more difficult to manage analytically, but could enable us to fine-tune of the parameters of the proposed method. Additionally, possible effects of network structure, such as the presence of clustering, on the values of c_1 and c_2 (of Equation 10) are of interest. We also plan to implement our estimation algorithm in real systems, where it can be of direct practical use.

Acknowledgments

This work was partially funded by CoreGrid NoE and NIC Labs. The work of Dr. Schaeffer is partially funded by PROMEP.

References

[1] Mark Jelasity, Spyros Voulgaris, Rachid Guerraoui, Anne-Marie Kermarrec, and Maarten van Steen. "Gossip-based peer sampling." *In ACM Transactions on Computer Systems, vol. 25, no. 3, 2007.*

[2] Alexandru Iosup, Pawel Garbacki, and Dick Epema. "Provisioning and Scheduling Resources for World-Wide Data-Sharing Services." *In Proceedings of IEEE e-Science , p. 84, 2006.*

[3] Arnaud Legout, Nikitas Liogkas, Eddie Kohler, and Lixia Zhang. "Clustering and sharing incentives in BitTorrent systems." *In Proceedings of ACM SIGMETRICS, pp. 301–312, 2007.*

[4] Keren Horowitz and Dahlia Malkhi. "Estimating network size from local information." *In Information Processing Letters, vol. 88, no. 5, pp. 237–243, 2003.*

[5] Alexandru Iosup, Pawel Garbacki, Johan Pouwelse, and Dick Epema. "Correlating Topology and Path Characteristics of Overlay Networks and the Internet." *In Proceedings of CCGrid, p. 10, 2006.*

[6] Duncan J. Watts and Steven H. Strogatz. "Collective Dynamics of 'Small World' Networks." *In Nature, vol. 393, no. 6684, pp. 440–442, 1998.*

[7] Michalis Faloutsos, Petros Faloutsos, and Christos Faloutsos. "On Power-law Relationships of the Internet Topology." *In Proceedings of ACM SIGCOMM, pp. 251–262, 1999.*

[8] Albert-Laszlo Barabasi and Reka Albert. "Emergence of scaling in random networks." *In Science, vol. 268, pp. 509–512, 1999.*

[9] Satu Elisa Schaeffer. "Algorithms for nonuniform networks." *Technical Report HUT-TCS-A102, Helsinki University of Technology, Finland, 2006.*

[10] Stefan Saroiu, P. Krishna Gummadi, and Steven D. Gribble, "Measuring and analyzing the characteristics of napster and gnutella hosts." *In Multimedia Systems, vol. 9, no. 2, pp. 170–184, 2003.*

[11] Matei Ripeanu, Adriana Iamnitchi, and Ian T. Foster, "Mapping the gnutella network." *In IEEE Internet Computing, vol. 6, no. 1, pp. 50–57, 2002.*

[12] Daniel Stutzbach and Reza Rejaie, "Capturing accurate snapshots of the gnutella network." *In Proceedings of IEEE INFOCOM, vol. 4, pp. 2825–2830, 2006.*

[13] Johan A. Pouwelse, Pawel Garbacki, Dick H. J. Epema, and Henk J. Sips, "The BitTorrent P2P file-sharing system: Measurements and analysis." *In Proceedings of IPTPS, vol. 3640 of LNCS, pp. 205–216, 2005.*

[14] Wenjie Wang, Hyunseok Chang, Amgad Zeitoun, and Sugih Jamin, "Characterizing guarded hosts in peer-to-peer file sharing systems." *In Proceedings of IEEE GLOBE-COM, vol. 3, pp. 1539–1543, 2004.*

[15] Subhabrata Sen and Jia Wang, "Analyzing peer-to-peer traffic across large networks." *In IEEE/ACM Transactions on Networking, vol. 12, no. 2, pp. 219–232, 2004.*

[16] Boris Pittel. "On Spreading a Rumor.." *In SIAM Journal on Applied Mathematics, vol. 47, no. 1, pp. 213–223, 1987.*

[17] Romualdo Pastor-Satorras and Alessandro Vespignani. "Epidemic spreading in scale-free networks." *In Physical Review Letters, vol. 86, no. 14, pp. 3200–3203, 2001.*

[18] Alan Demers, Dan Greene, Carl Hauser, Wes Irish, John Larson, Scott Shenker, Howard Sturgis, Dan Swinehart, and Doug Terry. "Epidemic algorithms for replicated database maintenance." *In Proceedings of ACM PODC, pp. 1–12, 1987.*

[19] Leonhard Euler. "De serie Lambertina Plurimisque eius insignibus proprietatibus." *Acta Acad. Scient. Petropol. 2, pp. 29–51, 1783.* Reprinted in *Euler, L. Opera Omnia, Series Prima, Vol. 6: Commentationes Algebraicae. Leipzig, Germany: Teubner, pp. 350–369, 1921.*

[20] Robert M. Corless, Gaston H. Gonnet, David E. G. Hare, David J. Jeffrey, and Donald E. Knuth. "On the Lambert W function." *In Advanced Computational Mathematics, vol. 5, pp. 329–359, 1996.*

COMPARATIVE EVALUATION OF THE ROBUSTNESS OF DAG SCHEDULING HEURISTICS

Louis-Claude Canon and Emmanuel Jeannot
LORIA, INRIA, Nancy University, CNRS
Campus Scientifique – BP 239
54506 Vandoeuvre-lès-Nancy Cedex, France
louis-claude.canon@loria.fr
emmanuel.jeannot@loria.fr

Rizos Sakellariou and Wei Zheng
School of Computer Science,
The University of Manchester,
Oxford Road, Manchester M13 9PL, U.K.
rizos@cs.man.ac.uk
zhengw@cs.man.ac.uk

Abstract   In this paper, we analyze the robustness of 20 static, makespan-centric, DAG scheduling heuristics of the literature. We also study if dynamically changing the order of the tasks on their assigned processor improves the robustness. Based on experimental results we investigate how robustness and makespan are correlated. Finally, the heuristics are experimentally evaluated and ranked according to their performance in terms of both robustness and makespan.

Keywords: DAG scheduling heuristics, robustness, makespan, stochastic.

1.   Introduction

With the emergence of distributed heterogeneous systems, such as grids, and the demand to run complex applications such as workflows, the problem of choosing *robust* schedules becomes more and more important. Indeed, in such environments, a carefully crafted schedule based on deterministic, statically-known, estimates for the execution time of the different tasks that compose a given application, may prove to be grossly inefficient, as a result of various unpredictable situations that may occur at run-time. Still, the existence of a good schedule is an important factor affecting the overall performance of an application. Thus, to mitigate the impact of uncertainties, it is necessary to choose a schedule that guarantees *robustness*, that is, a schedule that is affected as little as possible by various run-time changes.

There are several ways to achieve robustness. A first approach is to overesti-mate the execution time of individual tasks. This results in a waste of resources as it induces a lot of idle time during the execution, if the task duration is much shorter than the estimation. Another solution is to reschedule tasks dynamically allocating them to an idle processor in order to take into account information that has been made available during the execution. However, rescheduling a task is costly as it implies some extra communication and synchronization costs. Relevant studies [19] indicate that, in addition to rescheduling, it is important to have a static schedule with good properties before the start of the execution. Therefore, even if a dynamic strategy is used, a good initial placement would reduce the possibility of making a (later to be proved) bad decision and, hence, would reduce the extra costs of resorting to a dynamic strategy.

A significant amount of work in the literature has focused on proposing static directed acyclic graph (DAG) scheduling heuristics that minimize the overall application execution time (known as the *makespan*). However, to the best of our knowledge, so far, no study has tried to evaluate these heuristics with respect to the robustness of the schedule they produce. In this paper, we assess the robustness of twenty DAG scheduling heuristics from the literature designed to minimize the makespan.

In the remainder of this paper, Section 2 reviews related work on robustness and provides the definition used in this paper. Section 3 presents the model used to assess heuristics in terms of robustness. Section 4 describes the methodology of the experiments, Section 5 presents the experimental results and Section 6 concludes the paper.

2.   Related work

The literature is abundant of makespan-centric, static DAG scheduling heuris-tics. For our evaluation, we chose 20 of these heuristics, which include some of the most widely used and cited. Due to lack of space, we refer the reader to the relevant publications for the description of the heuristics. The 20 heuristics, in alphabetical order, are: BIL [16], CPOP [4], DPS [1], Duplex [8], FCP [17], FLB [17], GDL [22], HBMCT [18], HCPT [12], HEFT [23], k-DLA [24], LMT [13], MaxMin [8], MCT [8], MET [8], MinMin [6], MSBC [10], OLB [8], PCT [15], WBA [6].

Some work in the literature has attempted to define and model robustness; no widely accepted metric exists. In [2], the authors propose a general method to define a metric for robustness. First, a performance metric is chosen (this is the metric that needs to be robust). In our case, this performance metric is the makespan as we want the execution time of an application to be as stable as possible. Second, one has to identify the parameters that make the performance metric uncertain. In our case, it is the duration of the individual tasks and their communications. Third, one needs to find how a modification of these parameters changes the value of the performance metric. In our case, the answer is fairly simple, as an increase of the task or communication duration generally implies an increase of the execution time (even though, in some cases, a task may have a longer duration than expected and due to the structure of the schedule, such modification may not impact the overall makespan). Lastly, one has to identify the smallest variation of a parameter that makes the performance metric exceed an acceptable bound. A schedule A is said to be more robust than a schedule B if this variation is larger for A than for B. However, estimating this variation is the most difficult part as it requires to analyze deeply the structure of the problem and its inputs.

In order to simplify this framework, research in the context of evaluating the robustness of the makespan has proposed several other metrics, such as: the slack [7, 21, 19]; the probability that an execution exceed some expected bounds [20] (called the probabilistic metric); measures based on the Kolmogorov-Smirnov (KS) distance between the cumulative distribution (CDF) of the performance metric under normal operating conditions and the CDF of the same performance metric when perturbation applies [11]; or the differential entropy of the makespan [7]. In [9], we have studied the differences between these metrics and have concluded that the makespan standard deviation, the probabilistic metric and the differential entropy are highly correlated. This correlation was possibly due to the quasi-normality of the makespan distribution. Intuitively, the standard deviation of the makespan distribution indicates how narrow this distribution is. The narrower the distribution, the smaller the standard deviation is. This metric is related to the robustness because when two schedules are given the one for which the standard deviation is smallest is the one for which actual executions are more likely to have a makespan close to the average value. Mathematically, over several different values of the makespan, the standard deviation is given by $\sigma_M = \sqrt{avg(M^2) - avg(M)^2}$, where $avg(M)$ is the average value of all makespan values available. The standard deviation will be used as a metric to assess robustness in this paper.

3.   A Stochastic Model to Assess Robustness

We are given an application that is modeled by a stochastic task graph. This graph is a DAG, where vertices represent computational tasks and edges represent task dependencies (often due to communication). To model the uncertainty, task and communication cost are given by a random variable that follows a specific law (which can be different for all the tasks and communications). Hence, for each execution of the graph these costs may be different.

The task graph is executed on a set of heterogeneous resources. We assume that the topology of this infrastructure is complete (every machine can communicate to every one). We use the *related model* [14] concerning CPU capabilities: each CPU i is given a value τ_i, the time to execute one instruction. This means that if the cost of a task drawn from its random variable is c the execution time of this task on processor i is c_i. Concerning communication, we model each link by its latency (α) and its bandwidth (β). The time to send m bytes on link i is then $\alpha + \beta \times m$.

As we use static makespan-centric scheduling heuristics to map tasks onto the processors, we need to adapt the model to compute the schedule. We also need to compute the distribution of the makespan to determine its mean (average makespan) and its standard deviation (robustness).

To solve the above issues, we have proceeded as follows. Given a stochastic task graph, we transform it to a deterministic task graph by using only the mean value of the communication and task duration. With this deterministic task graph, we compute a schedule using one of our 20 heuristics. To compute the distribution of the makespan, we simulated, a large number of times, the execution of the schedule on the (heterogeneous) resources. This is a Monte-Carlo (MC) method, which means that each time a value for the duration of a task or communication is needed, this value is generated using the random variable that described it in the stochastic task graph. This allows us to compute the empirical distribution function (EDF), which converges to the true law of the makespan as the number of simulations increases, as stated by the Glivenko-Cantelli theorem. The precision achievable with a given number of MC simulations is given by the confidence intervals of the calculated approximations of the makespan mean and standard deviation. Since we consider the makespan distribution to be approximately normal, we use the Student's t and the chi-square distributions to compute these intervals and choose the number of simulations needed (see below).

Another issue that needs to be taken into account is the following. When doing a MC simulation of a deterministic schedule using a stochastic task graph, it is not always possible, at runtime, to respect the start and end times of each task (that is, the times that were computed using static estimates). To address this problem, we propose (and use) two solutions. The first solution is that on each processor, we fully respect the order of the tasks, as it was produced by the schedule. A task is scheduled for execution only when all the tasks that, according to this schedule, must be executed before a given task have finished. We call this strategy *sequence*, because on a given processor, all tasks are executed in the same order than in the static schedule. The second solution is to respect processor assignments of tasks onto processors, but schedule ready tasks (that is, tasks whose parents have finished execution and all necessary data has been transmitted to these tasks) as soon as they become ready. This means that, sometimes, the order of the tasks, as given by the schedule for a single processor, may not be respected. We call this strategy *assignment*, because only the processor assignments in the schedule are respected, not the order as well.

4.   Methodology

There are two phases in our experiments: a *deterministic* phase and a *stochastic* phase. In the first phase (deterministic), a specific DAG with static performance estimates is the input for each of the 20 static scheduling heuristics to generate a schedule. These schedules are further evaluated in the stochastic phase.

Two types of DAG are considered in our experiments. One type is derived from the Montage astronomy application [5]. The other is a random DAG, instances of which are randomly generated based on the following approach: (1) specify the number of nodes; (2) specify the number of levels; (3) randomly allocate the number of nodes at each level; (4) for each node except the exit, randomly appoint children nodes (at least one) in its lower neighbor level; (5) for each isolated node (non-entry node without parent), randomly appoint parent nodes in its upper neighbour level. In our experiments, we consider both Random and Montage DAGs with the following numbers of nodes: 58, 100, 500, 740, 1000, and 1186. In random DAGs, the number of levels is equal to the square root of the number of nodes. By combining each type of DAG with each different number of nodes, we generate 12 different DAGs.

We adopted the approach used in [3] to model task duration heterogeneity. A uniform random number R_{res} ranging from 1 to 10 is generated to describe resource heterogeneity, and another random number R_{task} following the same distribution is generated to describe task heterogeneity. Thus, the duration to run task i on resource j is determined by $T_{i,j} = R_{res} \times R_{task}$. In addition, the communication cost is modeled to satisfy that the ratio between mean task duration and mean communication duration is 1.0.

All DAGs can make use of 10 heterogeneous resources. Using this information, for each DAG generated as described above and for each of the 20 heuristics mentioned in Section 2, a static schedule is obtained, which will be assessed in the stochastic phase.

In the second phase of our experiments, once the deterministic graphs (and their schedules) have been produced, task durations are replaced by a random variable (RV) having as a mean the values described above. The distribution of these RV follows a Beta distribution with parameters $\alpha = 2$ and $\beta = 5$ (see [9] for a justification). In order to fully specify this, we also need to define the ratio between the maximum and the minimum bounds. We call this parameter the uncertainty level (UL) and set it to 1.1 on average with a very low dispersion (the UL is thus almost constant).

Finally, we need to settle the number of MC simulations in order to have a relevant precision for the calculated approximations of the makespan mean and standard deviation. To this end, we suppose that the makespan distribution is normal (as hinted in [9]). We can then easily measure the confidence intervals of these approximations. We see that for low variations of the makespan (as in our case), the variation of the standard deviation is preponderant and only depends on the number of MC simulations. To have less than 5% of precision with a confidence level of 99% we need 20,000 MC simulations. This amount increases quickly for better precision (750,000 for 1% of precision, for example).

5.   Experiments

5.1   Normality

Our study is based on the hypothesis that the makespan of a stochastic graph is normal (it follows a Gaussian distribution). We validated this experimental hypothesis here by doing the Anderson-Darling (AD) test, which is one of the best EDF omnibus tests for normality. Intuitively, the statistic obtained corresponds to the distance of the EDF with a normal distribution. We observe that 96% of the schedules in the sequence case and 54% in the assignment case have an AD statistic smaller than 30 (the same as a Student distribution with 8 degrees of freedom). As these AD tests corroborate the normality assumption, we can reduce the simulation values to only 2 measures (average makespan and standard deviation) almost without loss of information in most cases.

5.2   Comparison of the sequence and assignment strategies

For each type of DAG, we have represented the performance of all the heuristics in Figures 1 and 2. Each heuristic has a different symbol. The x-axis represents the average makespan of the schedule produced by the heuristic. The

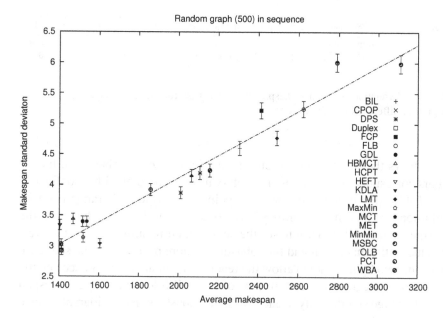

Figure 1. Mean vs. standard deviation of the makespan of different heuristics with the sequence strategy.

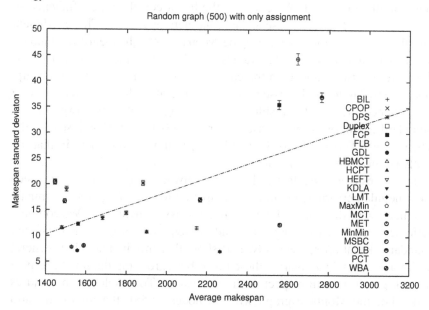

Figure 2. Mean vs. standard deviation of the makespan of different heuristics with the assignment strategy.

strategy	m58	m100	m500	m740	m1000	m1186	r58	r100	r500	r740	r1000	r1186
assignment	0.55	0.20	-0.19	0.76	0.66	0.60	0.73	0.05	0.59	0.44	0.60	0.36
sequence	0.81	0.85	0.62	0.71	0.73	0.62	0.47	0.87	0.97	0.91	0.97	0.89

Table 1. Correlation between makespan and robustness for the assignment and sequence strategies for different kind of graphs.

y-axis shows the standard deviation, the metric we use for robustness; the error bars correspond to the confidence intervals of each point with a confidence level of 99% (the probability for every point to be inside this range is 0.99). In addition, we plot the best fitting linear function for the points based on the least squares method. It helps to see the degree of correlation between the average value of the makespan and the robustness (more profound in the sequence case). The two figures shown allow the reader to compare the sequence and the assignment strategies for a certain type of DAG. While the average makespan does not change significantly in each case, the robustness is considerably worse with the second strategy.

As observed in the above example, the makespan mean and standard deviation are highly correlated. We compute the linear correlation coefficients (or Pearson coefficient) for each case and exhibit them in Table 1. This coefficient denotes the linear relationship existing between two RV (the mean and standard deviation estimators here). It takes values between -1, in the case of a decreasing linear relationship, and 1, in the case of an increasing linear relationship. Values close to 0 indicate the absence of a linear relationship. When restricting to the sequence strategy, the results show a strong correlation between mean and standard deviation in most cases (more than 0.7 in 75% of cases for the sequence case). This confirms the results in [9] and extends them in that the currently studied schedules are near-optimal.

We now investigate the effect of the choice between assignment and sequence on the schedule performance. In the example above, the most notable impact was an increase of the standard deviation in the assignment case. We compute the ratio between the assignment case and the sequence case for the mean and the standard deviation respectively, and show that this increase is a general trend. Tables 2 and 3 summarize these ratios by regrouping them with respect to the task graph or with respect to the heuristics. This table can be read as follows. For the Montage graph with 58 nodes (m58), the minimum ratio is 0.92 and the maximum ratio is 1.08, for the average makespan. For the standard deviation, 75% of the cases (from the 20 heuristics) have a ratio lower than 1.05. The first five columns indicate that, in most cases, the makespan remains extremely stable (with only a few extra-cases having more than 10% of difference). However, when there is a difference, the assignment strategy

Graph	Mean					Standard deviation				
	Min	25%	Med	75%	Max	Min	25%	Med	75%	Max
m58	0.92	1.00	1.00	1.00	1.08	0.79	1.00	1.00	1.25˙	13.8
m100	0.91	1.00	1.01	1.05	1.10	0.95	1.81	4.33	5.85	10.5
m500	0.88	1.00	1.00	1.00	1.00	0.94	1.00	1.00	1.25	4.90
m740	0.86	1.00	1.00	1.00	1.00	0.89	1.00	1.00	1.00	1.13
m1000	0.85	0.98	1.00	1.00	1.00	0.96	1.00	1.00	1.01	1.22
m1186	0.87	0.99	1.00	1.00	1.00	0.94	1.00	1.00	1.00	1.18
r58	0.92	1.00	1.00	1.01	1.06	0.99	1.00	1.00	2.55	11.3
r100	0.87	0.99	1.00	1.02	1.05	0.81	1.00	1.32	2.58	5.72
r500	0.82	0.91	1.01	1.03	1.07	1.48	2.50	3.88	5.93	8.46
r740	0.84	0.99	1.04	1.10	1.17	3.14	4.58	6.53	8.32	11.1
r1000	0.81	0.90	1.00	1.05	1.08	2.34	3.20	3.72	4.57	6.99
r1186	0.78	0.97	1.01	1.10	1.16	3.72	6.09	7.45	9.33	14.0

Table 2. Tukey's five number summary (quartiles) of ratio between the assignment case and sequence case for makespan and robustness; task graph view.

Heuristics	Mean					Standard deviation				
	Min	25%	Med	75%	Max	Min	25%	Med	75%	Max
BIL	0.93	0.99	1.00	1.04	1.13	0.98	1.00	2.10	4.16	11.0
CPOP	0.87	0.90	0.91	0.99	1.10	0.79	1.01	1.11	4.52	10.5
DPS	0.78	0.85	0.88	0.92	1.03	0.89	1.01	3.24	5.40	9.59
Duplex	1.00	1.00	1.02	1.03	1.06	1.00	1.00	2.40	4.07	6.98
FCP	1.00	1.00	1.01	1.06	1.06	1.00	1.00	1.50	5.62	6.80
FLB	0.94	0.99	1.00	1.00	1.03	0.96	1.00	1.93	3.68	8.46
GDL	1.00	1.00	1.01	1.04	1.16	0.99	1.00	2.24	5.91	11.1
HBMCT	1.00	1.00	1.02	1.06	1.10	0.98	1.00	3.41	7.31	9.72
HCPT	0.86	0.88	0.92	0.98	1.08	0.94	1.08	3.30	5.45	13.8
HEFT	1.00	1.00	1.00	1.07	1.16	1.00	1.00	1.57	6.48	14.0
KDLA	1.00	1.00	1.02	1.05	1.17	0.99	1.00	2.79	5.55	8.94
LMT	0.91	0.96	0.98	1.00	1.03	0.83	0.99	1.00	2.16	8.04
MaxMin	0.98	1.00	1.00	1.01	1.02	0.81	1.00	1.68	2.56	6.20
MCT	1.00	1.00	1.01	1.02	1.05	1.00	1.00	2.72	4.67	8.50
MET	0.85	0.87	0.94	1.00	1.00	0.92	1.00	1.56	6.99	11.3
MinMin	1.00	1.00	1.01	1.03	1.06	1.00	1.00	1.65	4.07	6.98
MSBC	0.82	0.87	0.98	1.00	1.00	1.00	1.04	1.20	2.53	4.46
OLB	0.98	1.00	1.00	1.00	1.02	1.00	1.00	1.00	5.11	8.52
PCT	1.00	1.00	1.00	1.07	1.16	0.84	1.00	1.19	6.25	11.1
WBA	0.99	1.00	1.00	1.00	1.05	1.00	1.00	1.03	3.70	8.01

Table 3. Tukey's five number summary (quartiles) ratio between the assignment case and sequence case for makespan and robustness; heuristics view.

Rank	Montage		Random	
	mean	std dev	mean	std dev
1	GDL [1.7]	GDL [2.0]	HEFT [2.7]	HEFT [3.7]
2	HBMCT [3.7]	HEFT [2.8]	PCT [3.3]	PCT [4.2]
3	BIL [4.2]	KDLA [3.3]	Duplex [3.7]	HBMCT [4.8]
4	HEFT [4.5]	PCT [3.5]	GDL [4.8]	Duplex [5.7]
5	PCT [4.5]	BIL [5.7]	MinMin [5.5]	GDL [6.3]
6	KDLA [6.3]	HBMCT [6.8]	MCT [7.2]	KDLA [6.3]
7	Duplex [7.0]	FCP [9.0]	KDLA [7.3]	MaxMin [6.7]
8	MCT [8.5]	Duplex [10.7]	MaxMin [7.5]	MinMin [7.0]
9	MinMin [9.2]	MSBC [10.8]	HBMCT [7.8]	MCT [9.5]
10	MaxMin [9.8]	MaxMin [11.0]	BIL [12.0]	WBA [11.0]
11	FCP [11.0]	CPOP [11.3]	FCP [12.5]	BIL [12.3]
12	WBA [11.7]	MCT [12.3]	WBA [13.0]	DPS [12.3]
13	MSBC [13.7]	WBA [13.0]	LMT [14.2]	HCPT [12.7]
14	OLB [13.8]	MinMin [13.5]	CPOP [14.3]	LMT [13.7]
15	CPOP [14.2]	LMT [13.8]	FLB [14.3]	CPOP [14.0]
16	FLB [15.0]	OLB [14.5]	HCPT [14.3]	FCP [14.8]
17	LMT [16.0]	FLB [14.7]	DPS [14.8]	FLB [15.2]
18	MET [18.3]	DPS [15.7]	MET [15.5]	MET [15.2]
19	DPS [18.5]	HCPT [16.5]	OLB [16.8]	OLB [17.0]
20	HCPT [18.5]	MET [19.0]	MSBC [18.3]	MSBC [17.7]

Table 4. Makespan and robustness ranking of the heuristics for the montage and random task graph cases.

allows more gain than the sequence strategy. Regarding the robustness metric, in most cases the assignment strategy is at least two times worse than the sequence strategy and in extreme cases, it can be up to one order of magnitude worse. This signifies that the assignment strategy is inferior in term of robustness but almost equal in terms of average makespan performance. In Table 3, this comparison can also be thought as a kind of sensitivity analysis of the stability of the schedule generated by a given heuristic. Even though the quantity of schedules is too low to draw any conclusion with respect to this point, it appears that heuristics such as LMT, MaxMin, MSBC are among the most stable. Similarly, the montage graph seems to be in general less sensitive than random graphs.

5.3   Heuristic comparison

In this last part, we rank every heuristic with the sequence strategy as this strategy has been shown superior in the previous section. Table 4 features the best heuristics in term of both the mean and the standard deviation of the makespan, and for the two types of task graph (random and montage). While the precision for the makespan mean is always below 0.1%, the precision for the standard deviation is only 5%. We observe that the best heuristic for the montage graphs is GDL and for the random graphs, HEFT (in term of both average makespan and robustness).

6. Conclusion

In this paper we have studied the robustness of 20 static makespan-centric DAG scheduling heuristics from the literature, using as a metric for robustness the standard deviation of the makespan over a large number of measurements.

Our results are three-fold. First, we have shown that it is better to respect the static order of the tasks on the processors than to change this order dynamically. Second, we have shown that robustness and makespan are somehow correlated: as it has been suggested elsewhere [19], schedules that perform well statically tend to be the most robust. Third, we have shown that, for the cases we have studied, heuristics such as HEFT, HBMCT, GDL, PCT, are among the best for both makespan and robustness.

Future work can be directed to the study of robustness-centric heuristics like slack-based or convex clustering strategies. Another direction is to develop multi-criteria strategies (that both optimize robustness and makespan). Lastly, it would be interesting to see how to deal with stochastic information inside a deterministic heuristic, instead of only using the mean, as in this present work.

References

[1] I. Ahmad, M.K. Dhodhi, and R. Ul-Mustafa. DPS: Dynamic Priority Scheduling Heuristic for Heterogeneous Computing Systems. *IEE Proceedings – Computers & Digital Techniques*, 145(6), pp. 411-418, 1998.

[2] S. Ali, A. A. Maciejewski, H. J. Siegel, and J.-K. Kim. Measuring the Robustness of a resource Allocation. *IEEE Transactions on Parallel and Distributed Systems*, 15(7), pp. 630-641, July 2004.

[3] S. Ali, H.J. Siegel, M. Maheswaran, D. Hensgen and S. Ali. Task Execution Time Modeling for Heterogeneous Computing Systems. *Proceedings of the 9th Heterogeneous Computing Workshop*, pp. 185-199, 2000.

[4] O. Beaumont, V. Boudet, and Y. Robert. The Iso-Level Scheduling Heuristic for Heterogeneous Processors. *Proceedings of the 10th Euromicro Workshop on Parallel, Distributed and Network-Based Processing (PDP2002)*, 2002.

[5] G.B. Berriman, J.C. Good, A.C. Laity, A. Bergou, J. Jacob, D.S. Katz, E. Deelman, C. Kesselman, G. Singh, M. Su and R. Williams. Montage: a Grid Enabled Image Mosaic Service for the National Virtual Observatory. *Astronomical Data Analysis Software and Systems XIII (ADASS XIII)*, Vol. 314, 2004.

[6] J. Blythe, S. Jain, E. Deelman, Y. Gil, K. Vahi, A. Mandal, and K. Kennedy. Task Scheduling Strategies for Workflow-Based Applications in Grids. *CCGrid 2005*, 2005.

[7] L. Bölöni and D. C. Marinescu. Robust scheduling of metaprograms. *Journal of Scheduling*, 5(5), pp. 395-412, September 2002.

[8] T.D. Braun, H.J. Siegel, N. Beck, et al. A Comparison of Eleven Static Heuristic for Mapping a Class of Independent Tasks onto Heterogeneous Distributed Computing Systems. *Journal of Parallel and Distributed Computing*, 61, pp. 810-837, 2001.

[9] L.-C. Canon and E. Jeannot. A Comparison of Robustness Metrics for Scheduling DAGs on Heterogeneous Systems. In *HeteroPar'07*, Sept. 2007.

[10] H. Chen. On the Design of Task Scheduling in the Heterogeneous Computing Environments. *IEEE Pacific Rim Conference on Communications, Computers and Signal Processing*, 2005.

[11] D. England, J. Weissman, and J. Sadagopan. A New Metric for Robustness with Application to Job Scheduling. *Proceedings of the 14th IEEE International Symposium on High Performance Distributed Computing*, pp. 135-143, July 2005.

[12] T. Hagras and J. Janecek. A Simple Scheduling Heuristic for Heterogeneous Computing Environments. *Proceedings of the 2nd International Symposium on Parallel and Distributed Computing*, pp. 104-110, 2003.

[13] M. Iverson, F. Ozguner, and G. Follen. Parallelizing Existing Applications in a Distributed Heterogeneous Environment. *Proceedings of the 4th Heterogeneous Computing Workshop (HCW'95)*, 1995.

[14] J.W.S. Liu and C.L. Liu. Bounds on scheduling algorithms for heterogeneous computing systems. *Proceedings of IFIP Congress 74*, pp. 349-353, 1974.

[15] S. Manoharan and N. P. Topham. An Assessment of Assignment Schemes for Dependency Graphs. *Parallel Computing*, 21(1), pp. 85-107, 1995.

[16] H. Oh and S. Ha. A Static Scheduling Heuristic for Heterogeneous Processors. *Proceedings of the 2nd International Euro-Par Conference*, vol. 2, pp. 573-577, 1996.

[17] A. Radulescu and A. Van Gemund. Fast and Effective Task Scheduling in Heterogeneous Systems. *Proceedings of the 9th Heterogeneous Computing Workshop (HCW)*, pp. 229-238, 2000.

[18] R. Sakellariou and H. Zhao. A Hybrid Heuristic for DAG Scheduling on Heterogeneous Systems. *Proceedings of the 13th Heterogeneous Computing Workshop (HCW)*, IEEE Computer Society Press, 2004.

[19] R. Sakellariou and H. Zhao. A low-cost rescheduling policy for efficient mapping of workflows on grid systems. *Scientific Programming*, 12(4), December 2004, pp. 253-262.

[20] V. Shestak, J. Smith, H. J. Siegel, and A. A. Maciejewski. A Stochastic Approach to Measuring the Robustness of Resource Allocations in Distributed Systems. *2006 International Conference on Parallel Processing*, August 2006.

[21] Z. Shi, E. Jeannot, and J. J. Dongarra. Robust Task Scheduling in Non-Deterministic Heterogeneous Computing Systems. *Proceedings of IEEE International Conference on Cluster Computing*, September 2006.

[22] G.C. Sih and E.A. Lee. A Compile-Time Scheduling Heuristic for Interconnection-Constrained Heterogeneous Processor Architecture. *IEEE Transactions on Parallel and Distributed Systems*, 4(2), pp. 175-187, 1993.

[23] H. Topcuoglu, S. Hariri, and M.-Y. Wu. Performance-Effective and Low-Complexity Task Scheduling for Heterogeneous Computing. *IEEE Transactions on Parallel and Distributed Systems*, 13(3), pp. 260-274, 2002.

[24] N. Woo and H.Y. Yeom. K-Depth Look-Ahead Task Scheduling in Network of Heterogeneous Processors. *Lecture Notes in Computer Science*, Vol. 2344, pp. 736-745, 2002.

PROTOTYPE IMPLEMENTATION OF A DEMAND DRIVEN NETWORK MONITORING ARCHITECTURE*

Augusto Ciuffoletti, Yari Marchetti
INFN/CNAF
Via B. Pichat 6a
Bologna - Italy
augusto@di.unipi.it yari.marchetti@cnaf.infn.it

Antonis Papadogiannakis, Michalis Polychronakis
FORTH
Heraklion (Crete) - Greece
[papadog,mikepo]@ics.forth.gr

Abstract   The capability of dynamically monitoring the performance of the communication infrastructure is one of the emerging requirements for a Grid. We claim that such a capability is in fact orthogonal to the more popular collection of data for scheduling and diagnosis, which needs large storage and indexing capabilities, but may disregard real-time performance issues. We discuss such claim analysing the gLite NPM architecture, and we describe a novel network monitoring infrastructure specifically designed for *demand driven* monitoring, named *gd2*, that can be potentially integrated in the gLite framework. We describe an implementation of *gd2* architecture on a virtual testbed.

Keywords: Network Monitoring, gLite, Network Measurement, XML Schema Description, User Mode Linux.

---

*This research work is carried out under the FP6 Network of Excellence CoreGRID funded by the European Commission (Contract IST-2002-004265).

1.   Introduction

End-to-end network monitoring substantially contributes to the usability of Grid resources, but it introduces distinctive problems.

One is that its complexity potentially scales up with the square of the size of the system. To ensure its scalability, end-to-end network monitoring must be selective in its targets: only a significantly small fraction of end-to-end paths can be monitored at each time. As a consequence, whatever the criteria to select which path is to be monitored, we need some sort of distributed infrastructure in order to activate and deactivate network monitoring selectively.

Another problem comes from the accessibility of the resource: we often observe that the monitoring tool requires some sort of cooperation from the resource itself: for instance, even the trivial ICMP ping requires that packets are freely propagated, which is not always true. As a general rule, an end-to-end network element must be treated as an opaque box, showing a performance which is traffic specific. One way to overcome this problem is to use passive measurement techniques, instead of active, thus analysing existing traffic.

Summarizing, we establish two cornerstones for an end-to-end network monitoring architecture capable of managing the scalability challenge offered by a Grid environment: i) *demand driven*, in the sense that its activity is not set by default, or with static configurations, but controlled by external agents, and ii) *passive monitoring oriented*, in the sense that only existing traffic is analysed in order to obtain the requested measurements.

The next section goes into the details of a novel architecture which is based on the above foundations: it is the result of a joint activity of INFN-CNAF (Italy) and FORTH (Greece), in the frame of the European CoreGRID project.

2.   The components of a demand driven network monitoring architecture

Our architecture, named *gd2*, partitions Grid end-points into *Domains* (see figure 1). A Network Monitoring Agent (Agent, in the rest of this paper) takes the responsibility of managing a number of Network Monitoring Sensors (Sensors, in the rest of the paper), and of agents enabled to submit network monitoring requests, the Network Monitoring Clients (Clients, in the rest of the paper) that compose the Domain. There are good reasons to introduce a partitioning, roughly the same that motivate its introduction in many aspects of networking: *reducing complexity* – one Agent concentrates the interface to the entities inside a domain; *security containment* – security issues can be managed using local credentials inside a domain; *limiting global state access* – only Agents have access to the global state, thus simplifying its management and ensuring security.

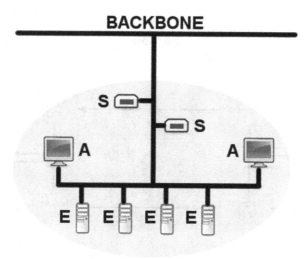

Figure 1. Deployment of *gd2* components in a Domain: E units represent generic monitoring endpoints, A labelled units represent Network Monitoring Agents, S units represent Network Monitoring Sensors

2.1 The Network Monitoring Agent

The services offered by an Agent can be divided into two quite separate sets: one towards the other Agents (back end), and another towards local sensors and clients (front end), this partitioning can be seen in figure 2. We examine these two faces, and next detail the internal structure of the agent.

The *back end* part is in charge of maintaining the membership of the Agents in the system. Such membership is the repository of two relevant data: 1) the credentials of the Agents, needed to enforce security in communications among the agents, and 2) the components of each domain.

As for the first point, we envision a public/private key scheme as adequate for our purpose: we consider that security primarily avoids the intrusion of malicious entities disguised as Agents. Whenever the results of the monitoring activity are considered confidential, Clients and Sensors will be in charge of encrypting sensitive data according to agreed methods. In order to control access to the membership, we assume the existence of an external entity in charge of key creation and assignment. This Authority, upon admission of a new agent, releases a certificate, which entrusts the use of the public key as authorized by the Certification Authority. Each Agent has access to a repository containing the certified public keys, and each communication within the

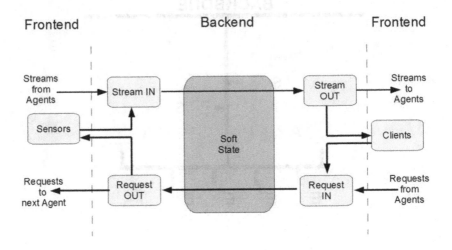

Figure 2.   Internal architecture of a Network Monitoring Agent. The Back End interfaces are located in the innermost stripe

membership is accompanied by the signature of the sender (not encrypted, in principle), which can be checked using the public key.

An agent offers a back end service for requests delivery: it routes requests coming from other Agents and from the front end toward their destination. For this purpose an agent analyses the content of the request to determine its next hop, and then it delivers the request: such routing is made possible through Agents' membership informations access. Every request passing through an Agent leaves a track in the Agent's Soft State: informations stored in the Soft State are later used for routing streams back to Clients.

An Agent offers another back end service for the transport of Network Monitoring data to the Client that requested it: such transport service consists of a stream from the Sensor to the Client, and is routed transparently through the reverse of the path used to deliver the request. The content of the stream may be encrypted, in case the network monitoring results are considered as confidential, but the client(s) must own the key to decrypt the data: here we assume that such keys are negotiated when the network monitoring task is accepted for execution.

The *front end* of the Agent is in charge of interacting with Clients and Sensors inside the Domain: the Agent accepts requests for Network Monitoring from the Clients, and drives the Sensors in order to perform the requested network monitoring activity.

The network monitoring activity is organized into *Network Monitoring Sessions* (or Sessions, in the rest of this paper). A session describes the endpoints of the Network Monitoring activity, as well as the kind of activity required. The request must determine, either implicitly or explicitly, the features of the stream that will be produced to return observations to the Client. In [5] we give an XML Schema Definition for such data structure, the Session Description.

The Clients submit their requests to the Agent as Session Descriptions. The Agent is in charge of checking whether the request comes from an authorized client: this functionality is achieved by a trust supported internally to the domain, independent from that used within the membership of the agents. This allows the possibility of merging domains with distinct security policies and support.

An agent, upon receiving a request for a domain it controls, analyses its content to assess its ability to configure a Sensor able to perform the the required task: to this purpose, the Agent must have access to a directory, internal to the domain, containing the descriptions of the sensors.

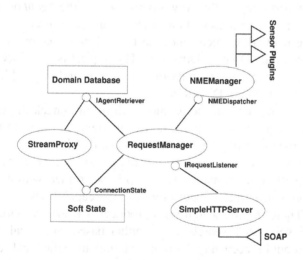

Figure 3. Modular view of a Network Monitoring Agent

The abstract functionalities described above have been implemented as a multi-threaded daemon (see figure 3). The *StreamProxy* thread is in charge of passing through the streams of data from sensors. It is composed of four threads that implement a pipe composed of four tasks: to receive the packet, to verify its signature, to generate the new signature, and to send the packet to the next hop. These threads utilize the AgentRetriever API provided by the database in order to have access to the Domain Directory, and the APIs used to access the shared Soft State through the interface *ConnectionState*. It implements the "Stream IN, Stream OUT" boxes in Figure 2.

The *RequestManager* is another thread in charge of routing network monitoring requests, and implements the "Request IN, Request OUT" boxes in Figure 2. As in the case of the *StreamProxy*, the ConnectionState and the AgentRetriever interfaces grant access to the Soft State and to the Domain Directory.

Requests are acquired by a *SimpleHTTPServer* thread that offers a SOAP interface to the Clients, and they are delivered to the *RequestManager* through its *IRequestInterface* interface.

The *RequestManager* controls the Sensors through a set of plugins, each of them specifically designed in order to drive a specific kind of sensor.

2.2   The Domain Database

In order to understand the role of the Domain Database, we illustrate the decisions that the Agents take on the basis of its content.

The first decision step on this way is performed by the *Agent* once it receives a request from a *Client*: it consists in determining the Source and Destination domain of the network element under test. Such information is obtained by way of a query to the Domain Directory. The request is then forwarded to an Agent in such domains: the identity of such agents and their address is again obtained from the Domain Directory.

Each agent on the way of the Request will in turn check the signature associated to the request, and replace it with its own. A query to the Domain Directory returns the public key needed to check the signature.

Each agent in turn will check the availability of the network monitoring functionality within the domain. This step is performed without further access to the Domain Directory, but browsing the capabilities available within the domain. Therefore the search for a producer is restricted within a limited number of sensors: such search can be either based on a local directory, or simply carried out broadcasting the request template to the local sensors.

The above discussion explains why the Domain Directory is to be considered a critical component in the structure: it is a potential single point of failure, and a performance bottleneck. A centralized implementation is therefore incompatible with the scalability of our architecture. However, the information stored in the Domain Directory is seldom updated, and this opens the way to strongly distributed solutions.

There are several options, that depend on the scale of the Grid of concern. One is to apply to a LDAP or DNS based implementation. Such well known tools are ready solutions for the maintenance of a distributed, that allow data replication in order to improve performance and fault tolerance. Such solution is probably adequate to most current scenarios.

Going beyond such scale, we indicate the implementation of a fully delocalized solutions: in essence, all Agents cache a part of the database, and updates are propagated according with a peer to peer protocol. Such approach may significantly improve scalability, while reducing the footprint for the maintenance of the Domain Directory. A theoretical investigation about the topic are reported in [3], while experimental results are in [4].

2.3 A passive Sensor and its plugin

Passive monitoring sensors are usually located at selected vantage points in the network that offer a broad view of the traffic of a domain, such as the access link that connects a LAN with another, or an Autonomous System to the Internet.

To support passive network measurements using the *gd2* architecture, we have developed a plugin within the Network Monitoring Agent which controls the passive monitoring sensors. The passive monitoring plugin first receives the configuration parameters for the passive network measurements from the client's request: available measurements are round-trip time [7], delay and jitter, packet loss rate [8], available bandwidth, and per-application bandwidth usage [1], based on the the Distributed Monitoring Application Programming Interface (DiMAPI) [13] developed at FORTH. These parameters are derived from the measurement specific part of the session description document, while the **MAPIOptions** element provides the relevant parameters for the passive monitoring tools.

When the starting time of a measurement comes, the passive monitoring plugin invokes the execution of a DiMAPI program that coordinates the remote monitoring sensors for the task. Dynamic configuration of the sensor includes the specification of packet filters, the definition of the processing operations that should be performed for each network packet, and the kind of results that should be produced, using the suitable DiMAPI functions [13]. The measurement results from each sensor are periodically sent to the DiMAPI program for aggregation and then returned to the plugin in the NMA. Finally, the plugin parses the results and sends them to the consumer through an encrypted connection.

Figure 4 presents an example of a passive measurement session for the packet loss ratio between two different domains: we emphasize that such a measurement requires sophisticated techniques in order to be performed according with a passive approach to network monitoring. Initially a client submits a request to the local NMA (**1**), and the request is forwarded to a corresponding NMA (**2**) that should perform the measurement. Then, the passive

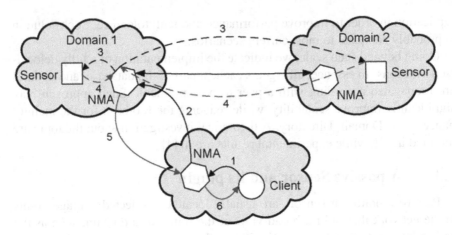

Figure 4.   Invoking a passive measurement for packet loss ratio in *gd2*: a plugin inside NMA initiates a DiMAPI program which gathers results from two remote sensors

monitoring plugin parses the request and initiates the execution of a DiMAPI program that computes the packet loss ratio between the two domains using data from two corresponding monitoring sensors. The program first configures the two sensors (**3**) and then the results are streamed from the sensors to the DiMAPI program (**4**), which computes the packet loss ratio and reports it to the passive monitoring plugin. Finally, the results are streamed to the local NMA (**5**) and to the client (**6**).

We have currently implemented the passive monitoring plugin to support appmon [1], a DiMAPI based tool that reports the accurate bandwidth usage for individual protocols and applications, and packet loss [8] measurement tools.

3.   Related works

The NPM architecture [9] is one of the most promising proposals for network monitoring, and is presently embedded in the gLite infrastructure, designed and implemented in the framework of the European Project EGEE. NPM is designed to provide two types of information: measurement data, in the form of data records conforming to OGF standards, and metadata, indicating what kind of data are available for a given network element. Such information is delivered to clients, whose role is to diagnose network performance problems.

NPM strongly focuses on the accessibility of historical data: this makes a relevant difference compared to our perspective. In fact, since we mainly address data collected on demand, we necessarily exclude, for performance reasons, a web service oriented architecture for the retrieval of measurements.

Instead we introduce a long lived communication entity, a stream. For the same reason we need not to address a large database of collected data: data are delivered to interested users, without being stored anywhere (unless a Client wants to do so). In our architecture the discovery activity focuses on a far less complex task: determining where to fire the measurement session.

We conclude our discussion remarking that a direct comparison is in fact inappropriate: the two frameworks, NPM and *gd2* address two distinct problems, and each of them is a poor solution when applied to the problem for which it has not been explicitly designed. A *gd2* Agent is designed to diagnose network problems once they have been detected, but has no detection tools: here we present a framework that helps detecting a network problem, and possibly overcome its presence without diagnosing its source. The NPM has an extremely heavy footprint when used to receive real time updates of the performance of a network element, which is needed to detect problems; our framework has no way to explore the past of an observation, tracking up to its cause.

Since their application domains are different, one may guess that they may live side-to-side in the same infrastructure. We believe that this is possible, at least in perspective.

The approach presented in this paper is also complementary with the **IPFIX** project [11]: the purpose of the IETF initiative is to design a protocol for flow metering data exchange between IPFIX Devices (corresponding to sensors in out framework) and IPFIX Collectors (Clients in our framework). Such a protocol roughly corresponds to the payload of the Sensor to Client stream, and can be used whenever network utilization has the characteristics of a flow. We plan to converge to an IPFIX compliant architecture, and an IPFIX interface for MAPI is under work.

A monitoring infrastructure which inspired our work is **CoMo** [6], a passive monitoring infrastructure invented by Intel. A branch of this project covers the placement of passive sensors [2], a relevant issue that is not considered in our paper. The CoMo research team explores many relevant aspects of network monitoring, but fails to give an exhaustive description of the conversation between the Sensor and the Client, which is the main purpose of our work.

4. Prototype layout and operation

The purpose of our prototype was to assess the feasibility of the whole *gd2* architecture, focussing on the communication infrastructure: therefore we tried to concentrate our efforts in order to produce a real scale support for a community of Agents, leaving behind other aspects.

We implemented a fully functional request delivery infrastructure, as well as the streaming in charge of returning the data to the requester. We took

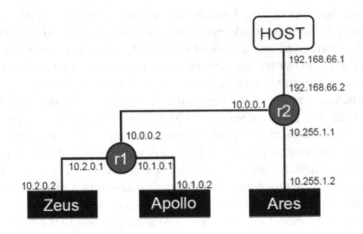

Figure 5. Development testbed

into account the security issues mentioned above, using signed communications among the Agents, taking care of the organization of the content of the database.

One of the aspects that are considered to a limited extent is the implementation of the database: we have implemented a solution based on an LDAP directory, whose scalability is similar to other solutions based on this technology.

In order to debug and demonstrate the functionality of the prototype, we have implemented a virtual testbed using NETKIT [12], based on the User Mode Linux technology, which allows to virtualize several distinct hosts, as well as an interconnection network, on a single computer. The major advantage of such an approach is that the experiments can be easily replicated on distant sites, thus allowing a collaborative development of the software without need of sharing hardware facilities, and always run under extremely controlled and uniform conditions. Demonstrations can be produced using any available Linux machine, and without installing experimental software on the real computer[1].

In our testbed we synthesize a network composed of three Agents and two routers (see figure 5): each of the Agents lives in a distinct domain. One of the Agents was equipped with a Client interface able to generate Network Monitoring Requests.

---

[1]The package with the virtual testbed (designed for Ubuntu Linux) is available at http://network-monitoring-rp.di.unipi.it/, with instruction for its installation

A real testbed is under development through a collaboration between INFN and FORTH institutes and we are working on the construction of a version whose allows to perform scalability and reliability tests on a real environment. With this real testbed we count to perform some rigorous evaluations on costs introduced by this architecture: we voluntary left them in the background to concentrate on a more clear architecture development.

5. Conclusions

Our investigation leads to a clear view of the problems related to *on demand* network monitoring, and to the change of attitude needed with respect to a *diagnosis-oriented* network monitoring. A demand driven architecture is not data-centric, in the sense that storage and indexing of measurements are not relevant, but more capability-centric, in the sense that operational network monitoring capabilities must be indexed, and protected against misuse. Therefore we need an architecture that is able to give a structure to the membership of the components that have monitoring capabilities, so to provide a capability based addressing of the monitoring resources.

Using such a capability-centric model it is nonetheless possible to collect data to be used for diagnosis purposes. the tools provided by *gd2* allow to collect and to keep an historical trace of measurements but also to request real time, non-periodic updates on the status of the network elements. This latter point discloses new horizons to network monitoring, by just not confining it to a problems detection role, but allowing to be used for a new set of activities, like, for example, best performance data source location in a replica management scenario.

We have identified a cornerstone concept in a topology-bound partitioning: such structure must be sufficiently stable, in order to allow a distributed management of the directory that describes the partitioning. In order to effectively abstract from the internal structure of a domain, we introduce components that manage the monitoring capabilities within a domain.

Data transfer must focus on long lived, low bandwidth data transfers: a *less than best effort* paradigm seems appropriate for their definition. This seems to match with a stream oriented protocol, that uses routing information obtained during the delivery of the network monitoring request.

In such scenario, passive monitoring is not only an option motivated by a low footprint. Passive end-to-end monitoring capabilities can be concentrated in a few locations within a domain, thus simplifying the indexing of available capabilities instead of scattered on each possible endpoint, which comes as a crucial advantage also in the deployment of the network monitoring infrastructure.

References

[1] Demetres Antoniades, Michalis Polychronakis, Spiros Antonatos, Evangelos P. Markatos, Sven Ubik, and Arne fflslebfi. Appmon: An application for accurate per application network traffic characterization. In *IST Broadband Europe 2006 Conference*, 2006.

[2] Gion Reto Cantieni, Gianluca Iannaccone, Christophe Barakat, Chadi Diot, and Patrick Thiran. Reformulating the monitor placement problem: Optimal network-wide sampling. Technical report, Intel Research, 2005.

[3] A. Ciuffoletti. The wandering token: Congestion avoidance of a shared resource. In *Austrian-Hungarian Workshop on Distributed and Parallel Systems*, page 10, Innsbruck (Austria), September 2006.

[4] Augusto Ciuffoletti. Secure token passing at application level. In *1st International Workshop on Security Trust and Privacy in Grid Systems*, page 6, Nice, September 2007. submitted to FGCS through GRID-STP.

[5] Augusto Ciuffoletti, Papadogiannakis Antonis, and Michalis Polychronakis. Network monitoring session description. Technical Report TR-0087, CoreGRID Project, July 2007.

[6] Gianluca Iannaccone, Christophe Diot, Derek McAuley, Andrew Moore, Ian Pratt, and Luigi Rizzo. The CoMo white paper. Technical Report IRC-TR-04-17, Intel Research, 2004.

[7] Hao Jiang and Constantinos Dovrolis. Passive estimation of tcp round-trip times. *SIGCOMM Comput. Commun. Rev.*, 32(3):75–88, 2002.

[8] Antonis Papadogiannakis, Alexandros Kapravelos, Michalis Polychronakis, Evangelos P. Markatos, and Augusto Ciuffoletti. Passive end-to-end packet loss estimation for grid traffic monitoring. In *Proceedings of the CoreGRID Integration Workshop*, 2006.

[9] Alistair Phipps. Network performance monitoring architecture. Technical Report EGEE-JRA4-TEC-606702-NPM NMWG Model Design, JRA4 Design Team, September 2005.

[10] Alistair Phipps. NPM services functional specification. Technical Report EGEE-JRA4-TEC-593401-NPM Services Func Spec-1.2, JRA4 Design Team, October 2005.

[11] J. Quittek, T. Zseby, B. Claise, and S. Zander. Requirements for IP Flow Information Export (IPFIX). RFC 3917 (Informational), October 2004.

[12] Massimo Rimondini. Emulation of computer networks with Netkit. Technical Report RT-DIA-113-2007, Roma Tre University, January 2007.

[13] Panos Trimintzios, Michalis Polychronakis, Antonis Papadogiannakis, Michalis Foukarakis, Evangelos P. Markatos, and Arne fflslebfi. DiMAPI: An application programming interface for distributed network monitoring. In *Proceedings of the 10th IEEE/IFIP Network Operations and Management Symposium (NOMS)*, April 2006.

A SCALABLE ARCHITECTURE FOR DISCOVERY AND COMPOSITION IN P2P SERVICE NETWORKS

Agostino Forestiero, Carlo Mastroianni
CNR-ICAR, Rende (CS), Italy
{forestiero,mastroianni}@icar.cnr.it

Harris Papadakis, Paraskevi Fragopoulou*
Institute of Computer Science, Foundation for Research and Technology-Hellas
P.O. Box 1385, 71 110 Heraklion-Crete, Greece
{fragopou,adanar}@ics.forth.gr

Alberto Troisi, Eugenio Zimeo
Department of Engineering, University of Sannio, Benevento, Italy
{altroisi,zimeo}@unisannio.it

Abstract   The desirable global scalability of Grid systems has steered the research towards the employment of the peer-to-peer (P2P) paradigm for the development of new resource discovery systems. As Grid systems mature, the requirements for such a mechanism have grown from simply locating the desired service to compose more than one service to achieve a goal. In Semantic Grid, resource discovery systems should also be able to automatically construct any desired service if it is not already present in the system, by using other, already existing services. In this paper, we present a novel system for the automatic discovery and composition of services, based on the P2P paradigm, having in mind (but not limited to) a Grid environment for the application. The paper improves composition and discovery by exploiting a novel network partitioning scheme for the decoupling of services that belong to different domains and an ant-inspired algorithm that places co-used services in neighbouring peers.

Keywords: Peer to peer, Service composition, Partitions, Ant-algorithm

---

*With the Department of Applied Informatics and Multimedia, Technological Educational Institute of Crete, Greece.

1.   Introduction

Future applications and services in Pervasive and Grid environments will need to support more and more distributed and collaborative processes. So, systems should have the ability to cope with highly dynamic environments in which resources change continuously and in unpredictable ways, and might even be not existent when designing the system, thus calling for runtime discovery and composition.

While expectations on the quality of these systems are increasing dramatically, current methods, techniques, and technologies are not sufficient to deal with adaptive software in such dynamic environments.

Service-oriented architecture (SOA) represents a promising model for these environments. Services, in fact, are becoming important building blocks of many distributed applications where a loose connection among components represents a key aspect to better implement functional distribution (i.e. contexts in which distribution is fundamental for implementing applications) and scalability (i.e. the ability to easily extend functional properties of a system). SOA can be usefully exploited in Grid computing to dynamically acquire available computational, communication or storage resources characterized by desired QoS offerings, to compose high-level functions for solving complex problems or to enable virtual organizations.

Despite its application in many domains, the supervised approach of SOA-based technology for service discovery, composition, and execution can be a strong limitation since it represents a bottleneck from a performance point of view and imposes a centralized knowledge to discover services useful to address a specific goal.

The paper presents an approach based on P2P to overcome currently adopted connection and coordination models, which enables fully distributed and co-operative techniques for discovery, composition and enactment of services, optimized through semantic overlays. In particular, the paper shows a technique that reduces the time for automatic service composition with respect to the centralized approach. The technique is mapped on P2P networks by exploiting two mechanisms for improving performance and scalability: (1) network partitioning to reduce message flooding and (2) an ant-inspired algorithm that allows for an efficient reorganization of service descriptors. This way, a service discovery procedure can discover the basic components of a composite service in a shorter time and with lower network traffic.

These two techniques, respectively proposed by FORTH [6] and CNR-ICAR [3] are integrated with a previous work implemented at the University of Sannio on P2P service composition [7] to improve its performance and scalability.

The rest of the paper is organized as follows. Section 2 analyzes the state of the art in service discovery and composition by discussing related work.

Section 3 presents a distributed planning technique to compose services in a workflow by exploiting a P2P model and discusses some possible mapping on P2P networks. Section 4 proposes a first improvement at network level by transforming an unstructured P2P network in a semi-structured one based on partitions that capture domains of knowledge in the service network. Section 5 shows an ant-inspired algorithm to aggregate descriptors of services related to the solution of the same problem or the most used services for solving a specific problem. Finally, Section 6 concludes the paper and highlights future work among the CoreGrid partners.

2.   Related Work

Service discovery is typically performed through centralized middleware components, such as registries, discovery engines and brokers. They will become a serious bottleneck when the number of services and organizations using services will grow, since service discovery requires using sophisticated matchmaking algorithms to identify semantic similarities between consumers template and providers target descriptions.

Distributed registries and registry federations have been proposed as a first approach to avoid bottlenecks in a service network [8–9]. METEOR-S [10] and PYRAMID-S [11], on the other hand, propose a scalable P2P infrastructure to federate UDDI registries used to publish and discover services; it uses an ontology-based approach to organize registries according to a semantic classification based on the kind of domains they serve. Even though these solutions well address scalability and fault-tolerance through federation of registries, they use a structured topology of registries built on the basis of a domain-specific ontology, so enforcing significant constraints on publication policies.

In [12], the authors propose a distributed federation of registries coordinated by a publish/subscribe infrastructure that is able to dispatch to the interested clients service availability as soon as a service is published in the network, by adopting a bus-oriented infrastructure to decouple registries. The proposed architecture is flexible but scalability is constrained by the number of organizations connected to the bus. Anyway, the infrastructure is mainly adopted to discover and not to compose existing services to solve a more complex problem than the ones directly solved with atomic published services.

Here, we propose a P2P model to exploit cooperative approaches for service discovery, composition and enactment. This goes beyond existing P2P technologies such as Gnutella and JXTA, which implement a primitive form of service composition through the dynamic construction of paths through the network to address queries.

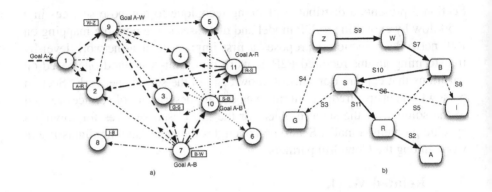

Figure 1. Cooperative composition of services to satisfy a goal. a) Space of peers and services. b) Space of states

3. Self-organizing P2P Service Network

A service network should be able to self-organize in a dynamic and adaptive way, in order to follow environmental changes and to structure the knowledge for continually optimizing service discovery and composition. In such a system of services, nodes should be able to communicate to find each other through discovery mechanisms that ensure high efficiency and scalability, with the aim of reducing response times. To this end, each node should be able to interpret an incoming goal and to give a partial or total contribution to the solution, even individuating other nodes in the network able to contribute with a piece of knowledge.

Figure 1 a) shows an example of cooperative composition in the space of services. Each node represents a peer hosting one or more services. Each sevice published on a peer exposes one operation identified through the label $Pr \rightarrow Po$, which means that Pr is the precondition and Po is the postcondition of an operation. Node 1 injects in the network a goal $(A \rightarrow Z)$ with the aim of discovering and composing the services whose execution changes the state of the system from A to Z.

Figure 1 b) shows the composition in the space of states. Each node represents a state whereas the transition between two states identifies a service that changes the system from a state to another one. The composition is the shortest path between the postcondition Z and the precondition A of the desired abstract services.

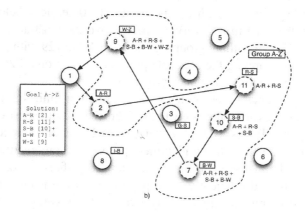

Figure 2.   Group identification after a composition

3.1   Discovery and composition

Each node in the network contributes to discover the peers that can originate useful compositions. According to the P2P model, peers become a crucial part of the architecture, since with this model the network lacks of structural components for discovery and composition.

Each peer is responsible of receiving requests from other nodes (goals), and fulfilling them (i) by relying on service operations or lower level features available on each peer or (ii) by forwarding the request to other known peers (see Fig. 1 a). In many cases a peer can be able to fulfill a request by composing some of its operations with operations made available by other peers (see peers 1, 9, 7, 11). In such a case, a peer is also responsible of composing these operations, to fulfill either partially or totally the request received.

When a goal is resolved, the submitter peer receives either the composition of services or simply the identifier of the first service/peer to contact in order to start a distributed execution.

3.2   Network topology and overlays

When a composition is identified (see Fig. 2), the network implicitly aggregates the participating peers to form a new group that will simplify successive discovery and composition operations. This process is executed continually in the network, giving rise to several virtual layers of peers able to solve different problems at different abstraction layers. Therefore we can imagine having two distinct dimensions for the specialization of services: (1) a first dimension that organizes services according to the domain in which they are used, and (2) a second dimension that organizes services in groups to simplify new and more complex compositions.

Simulation experiments with compositions of 10 services belonging to a space ranging from 10 to 640 services/peers have demonstrated a speed-up ranging from 3.5 to 19 without grouping and from 4.7 to 129 with groups. This demonstrates that mapping the concepts presented above on a P2P network is a crucial concern to achieve high performance.

However, techniques based on network information limit the traffic in the network since queries are routed only to the peers that host the desired resource. In Distributed Hash Tables (DHT) for example, each peer or resource is mapped to a unique identifier in a known identifier space. The combination of unique identifiers and a known space from which these identifiers are drawn, allows routing to be achieved efficiently. The payoff for this efficiency however, is that such architectures require a highly structured network and do not well support ad hoc configurations. The strong constraints imposed to the publication of service advertisements severely limit the possibilities for cooperation among peer nodes. The lack of a single point of failure in P2P unstructured networks ensures a better fault tolerance of the overall system whereas the availability of a potentially non-limited storage capacity for indexing increases significantly network scalability. Unfortunately, unstructured networks typically adopt flooding to broadcast discovery messages to all the reachable peers connected to the network.

4.   Network partitioning

One way to reduce the cost of flooding is to partition the overlay network into a small number of distinct subnetworks and to restrict the search for individual request to one network partition. The *Partitions* scheme, proposed in this section, enriches unstructured P2P systems with appropriate data location information in order to enable more scalable resource discovery, while not affecting at all the self-healing properties and the inherent robustness of these systems.

More specifically, Partitions employ a universal uniform hash function to map each keyword to an integer, from a small set of integers. Each integer defines a different category. Thus, keywords are categorized instead of services/content.

The keyword categories are exploited in a 2-tier architecture, where nodes operate as Ultrapeers and/or Leaves. The partitioning of the network is performed as follows (see Fig. 3):

- Each Ultrapeer is randomly and uniformly assigned responsibility for a single keyword category. Ultrapeers responsible for the same category form a random subnetwork. As a consequence, the network overlay is partitioned into a small number of distinct subnetworks, equal to the number of available categories.

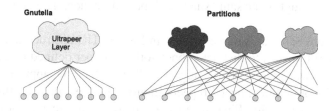

Figure 3.   Illustration of the Gnutella network and the Partitions design.

- Leaves randomly connect to one Ultrapeer per subnetwork. Furthermore, each Leaf sends to each Ultrapeer it is connected to all its keywords, in the form of a bloom filter, that belong to that same category. Thus, an innovative index splitting technique is used. Instead of each Leaf sending its entire index (keywords) to each Ultrapeer it is connected to, each Leaf splits its index based on the defined categories and constructs a different bloom filter for each keyword category. Each bloom filter is then sent to the appropriate Ultrapeer. An illustration of this technique can be found in Fig. 4.

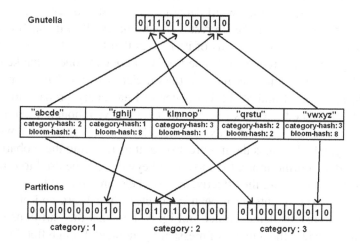

Figure 4.   The Partitions and Gnutella bloom filters.

We should emphasize that in this design Ultrapeers are de-coupled from their content, meaning that peers operating as Ultrapeers will have to also operate as Leaves at the same time in order to share their own content, which spans several categories. Furthermore, even though in this design each Leaf connects to more than one Ultrapeers, the volume of information it collectively transmits to all of them is roughly the same since each part of its index is send to a single Ultrapeer.

The Partitions scheme is demonstrated in Fig. 3. The unstructured overlay network is partitioned into distinct subnetworks, one per defined category. A search for a keyword of a certain category will only flood the appropriate subnetwork and avoid contacting Ultrapeers in any other network partition. The benefit of this is two-fold. First, it reduces the size of the search for each individual request. Secondly, it allows each Ultrapeer to use all its Ultrapeer connections to connect to other Ultrapeers in the same network partition, increasing the efficiency of 1-hop replication at the Ultrapeer level. One-hop replication dictates that each Ultrapeer contains an index of the contents of its neighbouring Ultrapeers (including the contents of their Leaves).

There are, however, two obvious drawbacks to this design. The first one is due to the fact that each Leaf connects to more than one Ultrapeers, one per content category. Even though each Leaf sends the same amount of index data to the Ultrapeers collectively upon connection as before, it requires more keepalive messages to ensure that its Ultrapeer connections are still active. Keepalive messages however are very small compared to the average Gnutella protocol message. In addition, query traffic is used to indicate liveliness most of the time, thus avoiding the need for keepalive messages.

The second drawback arises from the fact that each subnetwork contains information for a specific keyword category. Requests however may contain more than one keywords and each result should match all of them. Since each Ultrapeer is aware of all keywords of its Leaves that belong to a specific category, it may forward a request to some Leaf that contains one of the keywords but not all of them. This fact reduces the efficiency of the 1-hop replication at the Ultrapeer level and at the Ultrapeer to Leaf query propagation. This drawback is balanced in two ways. The first is that even though the filtering is performed using one keyword only, Leaves' bloom filters contain keywords of one category, which makes them more sparse, thus reducing the probability of a false positive. Furthermore, the most rare keyword can be used to direct the search, further increasing the effectiveness of the search method.

Simulation experiments have been conducted for 10, 30, and 60 network partitions. The results demonstrated in Fig. 5 show that the Partitions scheme reduces significantly the number of messages generated through flooding while simultaneously reducing the network load observed by each Ultrapeer.

5.   Ant-inspired reorganization of descriptors

Inside each partition, the construction of a composite service (workflow) needs the identification of the basic services that will compose the workflow, and the discovery of such services on the network. This is generally reduced

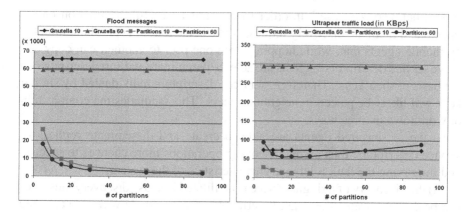

Figure 5.   (a) Number of messages generated in one flood.(b) Query traffic observed by each Ultrapeer.

to the problem of finding *service descriptors*, through which it is possible to access the corresponding services.

In general, the construction of a workflow implies the generation of a discovery request for each of the required basic services, which can result in long discovery times and high network loads. The technique described in Section 4 allows for reducing flooding generated by discovery operations (by creating different domains). To further enhance performances, it would be useful to place descriptors of services that are often used together (i.e., in the same composite services) in restricted regions of the system, so that a single discovery operation will have high chances to find all or most of the required services in a short time (groups). Accordingly, we propose an ant-inspired technique to reorganize and sort the service descriptors in order to facilitate the composition of workflows.

Descriptors are indexed through bit strings, or *keys*, that are generated by a hash function. The hash function is assumed to be locality preserving [2, 5], which assures that similar descriptor keys are associated to similar services. In this context, two services are defined as *similar* if they are often used together to compose a workflow. This type of similarity must be based on a statistical analysis of co-occurrences of services in the workflows characterized by similar semantics.

Our algorithm is inspired by the behavior of some species of ants [1], that sort items or corpses within their environment. The algorithm described in this paper has been specifically designed to *sort* service descriptors, i.e., to place descriptors of services that are often co-used in composite services in neighbor peers, in order to facilitate and speed up their discovery. This work is inspired by the work of Lumer and Faieta [4], who devised a method to spatially sort data items through the operations of robots. In our case, descriptors are not only sorted, but also *replicated*, in order to disseminate useful information on the system and facilitate discovery requests. The behaviour of ants is here imitated by mobile agents that, while hopping from one peer to another, can copy and move service descriptors. Agents are able to disseminate and sort descriptors on the basis of their keys. Therefore, services descriptors individuated by similar keys will likely be placed in neighbour peers. This facilitates the composition of workflows in three ways:

(i) the ant-inspired agents are able to create and disseminate replicas of service descriptors, thus giving discovery operations more chances to succeed and improving the fault tolerance characteristics of the system;

(ii) the discovery of a single service is facilitated because discovery messages can be driven towards the target descriptor in a very simple way. At each step the discovery message is sent to the neighbor peer whose descriptors are the most similar to the target descriptor. Due to the sorting of descriptors in most cases this method allows queries to reach peers that store a significant number of useful descriptors;

(iii) once a target descriptor has been reached, it is possible to locate other services, needed in the same workflow, in the same network region. Indeed, since services that are often co-used have similar keys, they have likely been placed into very close peers by mobile agents.

The ant-inspired algorithm is briefly described in the following, but more details can be found on [3]. Periodically each agent performs a small number of hops among peers. When an agent arrives at a new peer, if it is carrying some descriptors it must decide whether or not to *drop* these descriptors whereas, if it is currently unloaded, it must decide whether or not to *pick* one or more descriptors from the local host. When performing a pick operation, an agent must also decide if the descriptor should be replicated or not. In the first case, the descriptor is left on the current peer and the agent will carry a replica; in the other case, the descriptor is taken from the peer and carried by the agent. This way, agents are able to replicate, move and reorganize the descriptors.

In both cases, agent decisions are based on a similarity function, f, reported in formula (1), which is based on the basic ant algorithm introduced in [4]. This function measures the average similarity of a given descriptor $\bar{d}$ with all the descriptors d located in the local region R. In formula (1), N_d is the overall number of descriptors maintained in the region R, while $H(d, \bar{d})$ is the Hamming distance between d and $\bar{d}$. The parameter α is set to $B/2$, which is half the value of the maximum Hamming distance between vectors having B bits. The value of f assumes values ranging between -1 and 1, but negative values are truncated to 0.

$$f(\bar{d}, R) = \frac{1}{N_d} \cdot \sum_{d \in R} (1 - \frac{H(d, \bar{d})}{\alpha}) \qquad (1)$$

The probability of picking a descriptor stored in a peer must be inversely proportional to the similarity function f, thus obtaining the effect of averting a descriptor from co-located dissimilar descriptors. Conversely, the probability of dropping a descriptor carried by an agent must be directly proportional to the similarity function f, thus facilitating the accumulation of similar descriptors in the same local region.

The pick and drop probability functions, *Ppick* and *Pdrop*, are defined in formulas (2)a and (2)b. In this functions, the parameters k_p and k_d, whose values are comprised between 0 and 1, can be tuned to modulate the degree of similarity among descriptors.

$$(a) \; Ppick = \left(\frac{k_p}{k_p + f} \right)^2 \quad (b) \; Pdrop = \left(\frac{f}{k_d + f} \right)^2 \quad (2)$$

After evaluating the pick or drop probability function (which function depends whether the agent is carrying descriptors or not), the agent computes a random number comprised between 0 and 1 and, if this number is lower than the value of the corresponding function, it executes the pick or drop operation for the descriptor under examination. The inverse and direct proportionality with respect to the similarity function f assures that, as soon as the possible initial equilibrium is broken (i.e., descriptors having different keys begin to be accumulated in different Grid regions), the reorganization of descriptors is more and more facilitated.

6.   Conclusions

The paper proposes an innovative approach to the distributed and cooperative composition of Grid (and not only) services based on: (1) AI planning techniques, (2) service grouping and (3) overlays in large P2P networks. To this end, we integrated a system for distributed service composition with (1) an intelligent, ant-inspired search mechanism able to self-organize the location of the services to facilitate discovery and (2) a partitioning technique that reduces flooding. The end system is a composite mechanism that can scale to a large number of services and peers. Future work will consolidate the mechanism in a P2P infrastructure with the aim of comparing the results with those obtained by simulations. Furthermore, new techniques will be exploited for identifying service similarities for composition and their impacts on network partitioning.

Acknowledgments

This research work is carried out under the FP6 CoreGRID Network of Excellence which is funded by the European Commission (Contract IST-2002-004265).

References

[1] Eric Bonabeau, Marco Dorigo, and Guy Theraulaz. *Swarm intelligence: from natural to artificial systems*. Oxford University Press, New York, NY, USA, 1999.

[2] Min Cai, Martin Frank, Jinbo Chen, and Pedro Szekely. Maan: A multi-attribute addressable network for grid information services. In *GRID '03: Proceedings of the Fourth International Workshop on Grid Computing*, page 184, Washington, DC, USA, 2003. IEEE Computer Society.

[3] Agostino Forestiero, Carlo Mastroianni, and Giandomenico Spezzano. Antares: an ant-inspired p2p information system for a self-structured grid. In *BIONETICS 2007 - 2nd International Conference on Bio-Inspired Models of Network, Information, and Computing Systems*, Budapest, Hungary, December 2007.

[4] Erik D. Lumer and Baldo Faieta. Diversity and adaptation in populations of clustering ants. In *Proc. of SAB94, 3rd international conference on Simulation of adaptive behavior: from animals to animats 3*, pages 501–508, Cambridge, MA, USA, 1994. MIT Press.

[5] D. Oppenheimer, J. Albrecht, D. Patterson, and A. Vahdat. Design and implementation tradeoffs for wide-area resource discovery. In *Proc. of the 14th IEEE International Symposium on High Performance Distributed Computing HPDC 2005*, Research Triangle Park, NC, USA, July 2005.

[6] Harris Papadakis, Paraskevi Fragopoulou, Marios Dikaiakos, Alexandros Labrinidis and Evangelos Markatos. *Divide Et Impera: Partitioning Unstructured Peer-to-Peer Systems to Improve Resource Location*. CoreGRID Springer Volume, 2007.

[7] Alberto Troisi, Eugenio Zimeo Self-Organizing Service Network in a P2P environment. *Technical Report*, Research Centre on Software Technology - University of Sannio, Italy, 2007.

[8] ebXML. ebXML: electronic business using extensible markup language. http://www.ebxml.org

[9] UDDI 3.0 Universal description, discovery and integration version 3. http://www.uddi.org

[10] Kunal Verma, Kaarthik Sivashanmugam, Amit Sheth, Abhijit Patil, Swapna Oundhakar, John Miller. *METEORĐS WSDI: A Scalable P2P Infrastructure of Registries for Semantic Publication and Discovery of Web Services*. Information Technology Management, (6)1:17-39, 2005.

[11] T.Pilioura, G. Kapos, and A. Tsalgatidou. PYRAMID-S: a scalable infrastructure for semantic web services publication and discovery. In *Proc. of the 14th International Workshop on Research Issues on Data Engineering*, 28-29 March 2004.

[12] Luciano Baresi, Matteo Miraz. A Distributed Approach for the Federation of Heterogeneous Registries. In *Proc. of ICSOC 2006*, Chicago, USA, 2006.

OCM2PRV:PERFORMANCE VISUALIZATION OF GRID APPLICATIONS BASED ON OCM-G AND PARAVER

Wlodzimierz Funika and Maciej Zientarski
Institute of Computer Science AGH, Mickiewicza 30, 30-059 Kraków, Poland
funika@uci.agh.edu.pl
maciej.zientarski@gmail.com

Rosa M. Badia and Jesús Labarta
Univ. Politècnica de Catalunya, C/ Jordi Girona, 1-3, E-08034 Barcelona, Spain
rosab@ac.upc.edu
jesus@cepba.upc.es

Marian Bubak
Inst. Computer Science, AGH, al. Mickiewicza 30, 30-059 Kraków, Poland
Academic Computer Centre – CYFRONET, Nawojki 11, 30-950 Kraków, Poland
bubak@agh.edu.pl

Abstract   In grid computing where data processing takes place on many machines it is essential to have possibility to see a whole execution workflow. It enables the user to visually assess the computing-to-communication time ratio, frequency of executed probes or library functions, delay and volume of communication, or simply to observe how all nodes are actually working. In this paper we introduce the Ocm2Prv tool that makes it possible to visually analyze the execution of parallel applications developed with MPI library. The tool couples the functionality of two flexible environments - the OCM-G grid-enabled monitoring system and performance visualization tool Paraver. Implications coming from other Grid models, especially, GCM are also addressed.

Keywords: grid, monitoring, performance analysis, visualization, OCM-G, Paraver

1.   Introduction

Visualization as a graphic representation of abstract data relayed in text and numbers makes it easy to observe certain behaviors [1]. In the context of information systems, a visualizer is a computer program that presents data according to a particular pattern. Tracing parallel applications in most cases requires to instrument a program before it is executed (at compilation time). Such an instrumentation modifies the program so that it provides a kind of feedback of its execution. This can be information on functions it executes, time of these executions, parameters; it can also be information on communication, regarding its volume and participants.

There are many analysis tools that can visualize the performance of message-passing applications. Our focus is on creating a tool that is targeted strictly at visual analysis of grid applications which pose special requirements for performance visualization. In our research, its source of monitoring data is meant to be the OCM-G grid-enabled monitoring system [2]   which collects information about execution workflow, while for visualization purposes the Paraver visualization tool [3]   is chosen.

The purpose of the OCM-G coming from the CrossGrid project [4]   is to provide on-line information about a running grid application to application-development tools, specifically, performance analysis tools like G-PM [5], which is a tool designed for measurement and visualization purposes oriented towards interactive applications. OCM-G enables the user to choose which application performance aspect should be monitored by specifying standard or user-defined metrics. It does not visualize the gathered information itself, so external performance-oriented applications are needed for this purpose. One such an application is the performance measurement tool G-PM which focuses on taking precise measurements based on monitoring data supplied to it by OCM-G.

Paraver is a flexible performance visualization and analysis tool that can be used to visualize any data provided in its special file format. Paraver was developed to respond to the need to have a qualitative global perception of the application behavior by visual inspection and to be able to focus on the detailed quantitative analysis of performance problems. Paraver provides a large amount of information useful to improve the decisions on whether and where to invest the programming effort to optimize an application. Expressive power, flexibility and the capability of efficiently handling large traces are key features addressed in the design of Paraver. For user convenience, Paraver provides a configuration files where the user sets preferences such as colors and labels to make its output easy to understand.

The toolkit developed within the research under discussion, called Ocm2Prv, is aimed to support visual analysis of applications monitored by OCM-G. Unlike G-PM, Ocm2Prv is focused more on performance visualization than on the visualization of measurement results. The tool gathers data from OCM-G and produces Paraver-compliant trace files which contain performance information specified by the user. The visualization in Paraver comprises the whole picture of an analyzed application execution.

We are focusing on the performance visualization of applications using MPI, which is high-performance well-accepted platform, but programming on the Grid is not limited to the use of MPI, it goes much further, and its evolution towrads flexible, interoperable models and their implementations poses real challenges for performance evaluation tools.

This paper provides a brief review of exiting performance visualization tools that produce timelined displays of applications developed using MPI. This can be found in Section 2 followed by Section 3 in which we focus on the main requirements for our system. The next section describes the design of Ocm2Prv that comes up from the requirements to, finally, in Section 5 present implementation work. A sample case is presented in Section 6. A discussion on going beyond MPI in Section 7 is followed by concluding remarks and future plans.

2. Related work

Performance analysis of massively parallel systems is a very wide topic and as many different parallel computing libraries exist as many different tools for them have been developed to enable those analysis. One of such systems is Vampir (Visual Analysis od MPI Resources) [6]. It is an on-line performance analysis tool that visualizes four different types of information that the user may want to obtain. It is compatible with both C and Fortran77 compilers and provides tools that modify programs by injecting *probes*[1] of each MPI routine. Vampir has the capability to draw both dynamic and static representations of communication of application. It also provides statistics of executions and timeline views of nodes activities and global system views of nodes activity. Vampir supports an animation mode that can help to locate performance bottlenecks, and it provides flexible filter operations to reduce the amount of information displayed. It is a compact and efficient system that has ability to display many kinds of different information that enables performance analysis.

Another on-line MPI visualizer - G-PM [5] requires the analyzed program to be compiled using an OCM-G compiler wrapper so that it is instrumented to produce tracking information at run-time. G-PM enables the user to dynamically choose the scope of measurements based on data to be extracted from OCM-G to produce different types of diagrams including dynamic timelined

---

[1] some additional code designed specially to make possible inspection of the application process while it is executed

diagrams. The user is enabled to make use of standard metrics as well as of the PMSL language [7] to specify user-defined metrics.

The MPITrace[2] application is an instrumentation package that relies on dynamic interception mechanism. Like Vampir it does not require any changes or source code additions and works on an executed program code. Being provided with Paraver, MPITrace is completely integrated with it and both these tools working together offer a large analysis potential, both qualitative and quantitative. It produces a complete description of the application that can involve user defined probes (to use these probes, source code and compilers are required).

The other application that can produce time-line output and is worth mentioning is Jumpshot [8]. This Java-written application does postmortem performance analysis of information stored in SLOG[3] files. It is easy to use when we require to analyze a program quickly. It does not require any changes to source code but if we want to generate an SLOG file we have to compile an MPI application with a special option.

3.   Requirements

Each tool mentioned in Section 2 has its advantages and disadvantages. For example, Jumpshot is easy to use, it does not require changes to source code and is portable, but SLOG files generated by MPE contain absolutely all information that came from monitored application. If we imagine that such an application runs for a long time on huge number of nodes executing many MPI functions, so in this case a trace file can grow into enormous sizes and cause serious problems. That is why both Jumpshot and MPITrace programs may be used for big applications with care. G-PM is mainly a measurement-oriented tool, while Vampir does not support user-defined metrics which are very important for analyzing grid applications, especially, these with stress on interactiveness.

The toolkit under research is intended to couple the advantages of performance tools presented above. It should enable changing the scope of performance monitoring to avoid big trace files, it should allow the user to watch the monitored application at any time after it has finished and, finally, we would like to provide the user with a possibility to specify own metrics oriented towards qualitative and quantitative performance analysis based on visualization.

4.   Design

In order to develop a tool with the features stated in Section 3, we decided to use two already existing and mature tools: OCM-G and Paraver. OCM-G

---

[2] for more information about MPITrace please refer to Paraver web site: http://www.cepba.upc.edu/paraver/
[3] special file format for Jumpshot. These files are generated using the MPE package for MPI and a special converter

works as an on-line monitoring system that provides execution data on-the-fly. It gathers data which can be accessed via its OMIS-based API [9]. Paraver is an off-line visualization tool, i.e. it requires data for the whole computation, provided at once so it can visualize already completed executions only. A system that couples these two performance tools should use the OMIS API and supply to Paraver input files at its output.

The developed system should fulfill the following requirements:

1 connect to the OCM-G system

2 inform it that it wants to receive information from a set of nodes

3 inform it on what kind of information should be provided

4 collect this information and store it

5 transform the information obtained from OCM-G into a Paraver input file

The first two points can easily be achieved through the OCM-G API, while for point 4 there should be a kind of intermediate file and the last point can be realized in form of an application that translates this intermediate file into a Paraver trace file. The selection of information mentioned in point 3 will be enabled by a configuration file. This analysis implies the following implementation plan: The system should consist of two modules: one responsible for gathering data and the second one for translating it into a proper format. The data selected for visualization will be provided in a special configuration file. The file will be edited by the user to specify what information he/she is interested in. The designed system structure is shown in Fig.1.

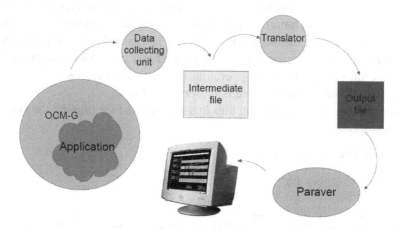

Figure 1.   Designed system structure

5.   Implementation work

Ocm2Prv prepares input files for Paraver, based on the data grabbed from
OCM-G system. To achieve that an application built of two cooperating modules was developed. Those modules are:

- Data Grabber

- Intermediate File Translator

Data Grabber is responsible for connecting to OCM-G Service Manager, reg-
istering probes[4] and starting the monitored application. It is developed using
OCM-G libraries. Data Grabber prints a list of probes execution to Intermediate File which is an input for Intermediate File Translator. The module is
a C language console-like application. Its execution flow can be described as
follows:

1 User-specified list of functions he wants to monitor is read at application
   startup

2 Information about all processes included in monitored application is gathered from Service Manager

3 All selected[5] MPI functions are registered to be monitored (to get information about its execution start end end times)

4 User-defined probes are registered

Intermediate File Translator is an application developed for the conversion
of data provided in Intermediate File to Paraver input file. It is also responsible
for sorting provided events by the time of occurrence and its type as specified
in Paraver Traces Generation documentation. It produces a correctly formatted
Paraver input file. Intermediate File Translator is a Java-developed application
which translates Intermediate File using a parser and stack based engine which
associates information about co-operating application processes.

The overall system architecture is presented in Fig.2.

There are several configuration files that are required for running the system.
They are:

- Ocm2Prv configuration file

- OCM-G probes file

---

[4]any function that comes from MPI standard library or a user defined function whose execution times and
parameters can be gathered by the OCM-G system. User defined probes must be specified in separate files
for both the monitored application compilation and Ocm2Prv execution
[5]A probe measuring the result of MPI_Comm_Rank() is always registered because it is required to form the
output file properly.

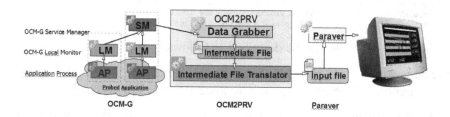

Figure 2.   Developed system architecture

- Paraver configuration file

Ocm2Prv configuration file contains a list of MPI functions which should be monitored and presented on time-line as process states as well as a list of user defined probes which will be interpreted as events. An example configuration file is shown below:

```
MPI_Finalize
MPI_Init
probe_sleep 10
```

In the example MPI_Finalize() and MPI_Init() are functions whose executions will be marked on output time-line as time spans. It is possible to show the execution times of the functions and threads which execute them. probe_sleep() is a user defined function. It will be shown on a time-line as an event (marked as a colored flag) of type 10^6 and a value equal to the second argument of the probe_sleep() function execution (both value and type can be read after clicking a proper flag). OCM-G probes file contains user defined probes declarations (functions without bodies). An example:

```
void probe_send(int vt,int dest) {}
void probe_recv(int vt,int src) {}
void probe_sleep(int vt,int time) {}
```

The first argument of the probes is obligatory and should be incremented by one each time any of the probes is executed. It is required for proper probes executions watched by the OCM-G system[7].

When executing Ocm2Prv, an Intermediate File is produced (it can be printed on a screen on-the-fly). The file contains lines similar to those shown below:

```
p_1836_n_a0000c8 : 4,["end@MPI_Init",1189065074.68863201,0,1]:
```

---

[6]The type of an event can be any number. It is used to distinguish different events only.

[7]For more details on defining probes, please refer to OCM-G's documentation which can be found at http://grid.cyfronet.pl/ocmg/files/userguide.pdf

```
p_1836_n_a0000cb : 4,["start@MPI_Comm_rank",1189065074.68888855,91,1]:
p_1836_n_a0000e4 : 4,["probe@probe_whoami",1189065074.68933868,0,0]:
p_1836_n_a0000fs : 4,["evnt@probe_sleep",1189065074.6894846,-1073918620,1]:
```

Generally each line can be described as follows:

```
<process_ID> : 4,["<end|start|probe|comm|evnt>@<probe_name>",
    <execution_time>,<probe_argument>,<probe_type>]:
```

end and start represent any MPI function (as specified in a configuration file) execution start and end times. In such a case, probe_argument is not taken into consideration and may be any value. probe is used with probe_whoami only. It is an artificial probe that should not be specified in configuration file. It is used to relate process_ID to MPI process number (returned by MPI_Comm_Rank()). It is done by relating process_ID to probe_argument. evnt represents a user-defined probe execution. comm represents communication between two threads. probe_argument is a second participant in such communication. comm is generated by probe_send() and probe_recv() only.

6.   Sample case

For illustrating the operation of the developed integrated tool we will consider a fragment of monitoring session on a ping-pong-like application. Three workers (threads 2,3, and 4) send some data to master (thread 1) which after receiving data from all workers sends it back to them.

```
if (rank==0)
{
    for(i=1;i<size;i++)
    {
        MPI_Recv(&msg,1,MPI_INT,MPI_ANY_SOURCE,tag,
            MPI_COMM_WORLD,&status);
        source_id = status.MPI_SOURCE;
        probe_recv(pc++,source_id);
    }
    for(i=1;i<size;i++)
    {
        MPI_Send(&msg,1,MPI_INT,i,tag,MPI_COMM_WORLD);
        probe_send(pc++,i);
    }
}
else
{
    probe_send(pc++,0);
    MPI_Send(&msg,1,MPI_INT,0,tag,MPI_COMM_WORLD);
    sleept=rand()%5;
```

```
    probe_sleep(pc++,sleept);
    sleep(sleept);
    MPI_Recv(&msg,1,MPI_INT,0,tag,MPI_COMM_WORLD,&status);
    source_id = status.MPI_SOURCE;
    probe_recv(pc++,source_id);
}
```

To compile the program we have to use the `mpicc` compiler wrapper provided
with OCM-G:

```
cg-ocmg-cc -probes probes.c mpicc <source_file.c>
 -o <binary_file_name>
```

`probes.c` is a file containing probes definitions for OCM-G.
The next step is to start OCM-G monitor:

```
cg-ocmg-monitor
```

This returns a special identifier used to run both the monitored application and
Ocm2Prv tool. Now it is time to start our application:

```
mpirun -np 4 <binary_file_name> --ocmg-mainsm <mainsm>
 --ocmg-appname <application_name>
```

and Ocm2Prv:

```
./ocm2prv --ocmg-mainsm <mainsm> <application_name>
 <configuration file> <intermediate_file_name> [-v]
```

−v (verbose) option makes Ocm2Prv to print intermediate file contents to the
screen. After a while the program completes its execution (or if it does not we
can stop it by typing *quit* and pressing *Enter*) and we can view its trace file
named `ocm2prv.out` by opening it in Paraver. This is what we should see on
the screen:

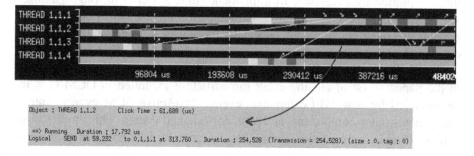

Figure 3.   Example output

Colorful stripes on time lines (Fig.3 upper window) represent threads states. The yellow ones represent executing the `MPI_Comm_Size()` function, pink ones are for `MPI_Comm_Rank()` and green ones show `MPI_Send()` function execution times. In the above example, other MPI functions were not specified in OCM2Prv configuration file so they are not presented in Paraver. The small green flags represent probes executions (`probe_*()` functions in the source code). Details on probes and their parameters can be seen after clicking on the flags as well as communication events (Fig.3 lower window). Yellow lines with yellow arrows show communication between two processes.

7.   Performance visualization beyond MPI

From the user's point of view, programming on the Grid is mainly seen as using MPI and its derivatives: it is a popular, well known platform which features high performance and acceptability. On the other side it lacks important properties like flexibility and interoperability, featured by other platforms like ProActive/GCM [8] [10]. One of the promising approaches to support Grid oriented programming is coupling the message passing paradigm and GCM [11]. Here important is to get a synergy of these two paradigms and not to loose the high performance of message passing.

From the performance monitoring's perspective, ProActive/GCM as well as its support for MPI-like programming pose some interesting issues from a number of viewpoints. First of all, the user will definitely be interested in similar performance data on their applications as when programming with pure MPI, e.g. data on communication operations. It would be certain that monitoring function calls or the execution of code fragments is also of interest; we need to consider extensions to MPI, e.g. new communicators and related primitives. The second point which is much more challenging is drilling down the performance world when coming from MPI to ProActive. This would need the performance assessment at the level of the wrapping code interfacing the native MPI code. Going down we need to address the performance of protocols, e.g. these exploited by ProActive to implement "inter-system" message passing. An interesting issue is to explore communication mechanisms between components in a hierarchical model, especially those used to improve performance, e.g. the shortcut mechanism.

The above issues imply enhancements to the performance tools discussed in the paper. First of all, the event infrastructure exploited in OCM-G is to be extended by new MPI-extensions events, ProActive/GCM events: intra-component-, inter-component- and protocol-oriented events. This implies also extensions to instrumentation techniques, fortunately, Java provides quite con-

---

[8]ProActive web page `http://proactive.inria.fr/`

venient mechanisms. We experimented with them when working on a Java applications-oriented sibling of OCM-G, J-OCM [12]. Another issue is to extend or not the current OCM-G's monitoring infrastructure, this needs special exploration. It is quite probable that a decentralized architecture can be more suitable in case of ProActive. From the performance visualization viewpoint, in addition to the current time-lined and profiling displays provided by Paraver there will be some other displays needed, most probably these oriented towards animation views to illustrate the states of the objects involved. The dynamics of Grid applications, especially when using ProActive will also necessitate to overcome the constraint of Paraver to off-line visualization towards semi- or fully-online visualization. And last but not least: using the PMSL language for programming user-defined metrics, which is supported by OCM-G, would make exploring the application's performance meaningful in terms of the application's semantics, which implies the necessity to introduce a mechanism for mapping user-defined metrics onto Paraver's display definitions.

8.   Conclusions

Our goal was to develop a tool that could become an alternative to the existing performance visualization tools via coupling the functionality of a flexible, low-intrusive monitoring system, OCM-G, and a powerful performance visualization tool, Paraver. The integrated toolkit produces trace files for MPI applications enabling their further visual analysis. Ocm2Prv focuses on the presentation of MPI function timings and types, but can also visualize communication between processes and execution of user defined functions (probes). It enables filtering information presented on time-line thus reducing the size of trace files. In the simplest scenario, no changes to application source code are required to use Ocm2Prv and Paraver environment.

Our further research will concentrate on adapting the PMSL language to map user-defined metrics onto OCM-G operation for visualization purposes and, reversely, onto Paraver diagrams. We will continue our on-going research on extending the capabilities of OCM-G and Paraver towards ProActive/GCM.

Acknowledgments

We are grateful to dr. Judit Gimenez (Universita Politècnica de Catalunya) for valuable help. This research is partly funded by the EU IST FP6-0004265 CoreGRID project. The comments of our reviewers were of great help, we thank them very much.

References

[1] M. Gerndt, et. al. Performance Tools for the Grid: State of the Art and Future, volume 30 of Research Report Series, LRR-TUM, Shaker Verlag, 2004.

[2] Balis, B., Bubak, M., Funika, W., Wismüller, R., Radecki, M., Szepieniec, T., Arodz, T., Kurdziel, M. Grid Environment for On-line Application Monitoring and Performance Analysis. In: Scientific Programming, vol. 12, no. 4, 2004, pp. 239-251.

[3] Vincent Pillet, Jesús Labarta, Toni Cortes, Sergi Girona. PARAVER: A Tool to Visualize and Analyze Parallel Code. In: Proceedings of WoTUG-18: Transputer and occam Developments, vol. 44, IOS Press(1995), p. 17-31

[4] EU IST CrossGrid project page http://www.eu-crossgrid.org/

[5] G-PM web page: http://gpm.icsr.agh.edu.pl/

[6] W. E. Nagel and A. Arnold and M. Weber and H. C. Hoppe and K. Solchenbach. VAMPIR: Visualization and Analysis of MPI Resources. In: Supercomputer (1996), vol.12, p. 69-80

[7] R. Wismüller, M. Bubak, W. Funika, and B. Balis. A Performance Analysis Tool for Interactive Applications on the Grid. In: Intl. Journal of High Performance Computing Applications, 18(3):305-316, Fall 2004.

[8] O. Zaki, E. Lusk, W. Gropp, D. Swider. Toward Scalable Performance Visualization with Jumpshot. In: The International Journal of High Performance Computing Applications, vol. 13, pp. 277–288

[9] T. Ludwig, R. Wismueller, V. Sunderam and A. Bode. OMIS – On-line Monitoring Interface Specification (Version 2.0). Shaker Verlag, Aachen, vol.9, LRR-TUM Research Report Series, (1997)

[10] Baude F., Baduel L., Caromel D., Contes A., Huet F., Morel M. and Quilici R. Programming, Composing, Deploying for the Grid. In: Jose C. Cunha and Omer F. Rana (Eds), GRID COMPUTING: Software Environments and Tool, Springer Verlag, January 2006.

[11] F. Baude, D. Caromel, N. Maillard, E. Mathias. Hierarchical MPI-like Programming using GCM Components as Implementation Support. Selected and presented at the CoreGRID workshop: Grid Systems, Tools and Environments, Gridswork II conference, Dec. 2006., pp. 5-14

[12] W. Funika, M. Bubak, M. Smetek, R. Wismueller. An OMIS-based approach to Monitoring Distributed Java Applications. In: Yuen Chung Kwong (ed.) Annual Review of Scalable Computing, vol. 6, World Scientific Publishing Co. and Singapore University Press, 2004, pp. 1-29

ANALYSING ORCHESTRATIONS WITH RISK PROFILES AND ANGEL-DAEMON GAMES *

Joaquim Gabarró, Alina García, Maria Serna
Universitat Politècnica de Catalunya, ALBCOM Research Group
Edifici Ω, Campus Nord Jordi Girona, 1-3, Barcelona 08034, Spain
{gabarro, agarcia, mjserna}@lsi.upc.edu

Peter Kilpatrick, Alan Stewart
School of Computer Science, The Queen's University of Belfast
Belfast BT7 1NN, Northern Ireland
{p.kilpatrick, a.stewart}@qub.ac.uk

Abstract   In this paper game theory is used to analyse the effect of a number of service failures during the execution of a grid orchestration. A service failure may be catastrophic in that it causes an entire orchestration to fail. Alternatively, a grid manager may utilise alternative services in the case of failure, allowing an orchestration to recover. A risk profile provides a means of modelling situations in a way that is neither overly optimistic nor overly pessimistic. Risk profiles are analysed using angel and daemon games. A risk profile can be assigned a valuation through an analysis of the structure of its associated Nash equilibria. Some structural properties of valuation functions, that show their validity as a measure for risk, are given. Two main cases are considered, the assessment of Orc expressions and the arrangement of a meeting using reputations.

Keywords: Fault tolerance, orchestrations, resource management, zero-sum games, two-person strategic games.

---

* J. Gabarró, P. Kilpatrick and A. Stewart are partially supported by the FP6 Network of Excellence CoreGRID funded by the European Commission (Contract IST-2002-004265). J. Gabarró, A. García and M. Serna are partially supported by FET pro-active Integrated Project 15964 (AEOLUS) and by Spanish projects TIN2005-09198-C02-02 (ASCE) and MEC-TIN2005-25859-E.

1. Introduction

In this paper a means of assessing the outcome of executing a grid orchestration in an untrusted environment is proposed. A grid orchestration is modelled by an Orc expression [8] which interacts with services on a grid network. A service provided by a site may be unreliable because of site overuse, site failure or network congestion. In this paper game theory is used to analyse the effects of a bounded number of service (site) failures during an orchestration evaluation. Two examples are used to motivate the use of game theory for orchestration assessment:

EXAMPLE 1 **Multiple job***:*
Consider a physicist who wishes to execute a program on a large number of data sets. The jobs will be executed in parallel on a computational grid. In order to draw conclusions the physicist requires that only a certain percentage of jobs return results. Suppose that the set of parallel jobs are executed on sites $S_1, .., S_n$ and that each site has an associated reliability rating. What is the probability that the physicist will receive sufficient experimental results? In this paper the problem of estimating the number of values published by an Orc expression evaluation is presented as a model of this problem. □

EXAMPLE 2 **Minimum Computing requirements:**
Consider a user who wishes to execute a distributed program with a very high computational workload on a grid. The user wishes to find a set of sites that will participate (simultaneously) in the execution of the job. The orchestration contains a management program which first interrogates a number of sites, $S_1, \ldots, S_n$, to determine which are prepared to engage in the computation. The job is scheduled among the sites that indicate that they are available to participate.

Suppose that site S_i has associated (i) a reputation, R_i, of being available to carry out a job and (ii) an amount of work, W_i, that can be computed in a time unit. If the user has a minimum requirement for the amount of work that can be carried out in a time unit, should the job proceed or not? There are a number of variants of this scenario: for example, (i) a user requires a minimum number of services to be available concurrently in order to implement dynamically a fork and join operation or (ii) a user has a maximum cost bound. In this paper a meeting scheduling problem is presented as an exemplar of problems of this type. □

Two model problems which represent *multiple job* and *minimum computing requirements* are presented and analysed by means of risk profiles and games. The set of sites participating in the evaluation of an orchestration is partitioned into sets $\mathcal{A}$ and $\mathcal{D}$ called *angels* and *daemons*, respectively. Each of the sets $\mathcal{A}$ and $\mathcal{D}$ is associated with a number of site failures, denoted by f_A and f_D, respectively. In an *angel-daemon game* the f_A sites in $\mathcal{A}$ which fail are chosen so that the damage to the application is minimized. In contrast, the f_D sites in $\mathcal{D}$ which fail are chosen so as to maximise damage to the application. When angels and daemons act simultaneously a competitive situation arises that can be represented as a game. We consider two different cases: games which are zero-sum games (*multiple job*) and games which are not (*minimum computing requirements*).

The study of systems under failure with games is not new [3, 9]; however, assessment of orchestrations where control is *exercised by a single user* is different from the analysis of distributed systems under failure[1].

In §2 an introduction to the orchestration language Orc [8] is given. A means of determining the number of outputs published by an expression evaluation is given in §3. The number of outputs published by an expression evaluation provides *one* means of assigning a valuation to a game. A formal definition of risk profile is given in §4. Some properties of risk profiles are given in §5. In §6 an assessment of a meeting scheduling problem using risk profiles is presented.

2. Orc

An orchestration is a user-defined program that utilises services on a grid. In Orc [8] services are modelled by sites which have some predefined semantics. Typical examples of services are: an eigensolver, a search engine or a database. A *site* accepts an argument and *publishes* a result value[2]. For example, a call to a search engine, $find(s)$, may publish the set of sites which *currently* offer service s. A site is *silent* if it does not publish a result. Site calls may induce *side effects*. A site call can publish *at most one response*. Although a site call may have a well-defined result it may be the case that a call to the site, in an untrusted environment, fails (silence). Orc contains a number of inbuilt sites: 0 is always silent while $1(x)$ always publishes x. $if(b)$ publishes a signal if b is true and remains silent otherwise. An orchestration which composes a number of service calls into a complex computation can be represented by an Orc expression. An orchestrator may utilise any service that is available on the grid. The simplest kind of Orc expression is a service (site) call. Two Orc expressions P and Q can be combined using the following operators:

- **Sequence** $P > x > Q(x)$: For each output, x, published by P an instance $Q(x)$ is executed. If P publishes the stream of values, $v_1, v_2, \ldots v_n$, then $P > x > Q(x)$ publishes some interleaving of the set $\{Q(v_1), Q(v_2), \ldots, Q(v_n)\}$. When the value of x is not needed we note $P \gg Q$.

- **Symmetric Parallelism** $P \mid Q$: Orchestration $P \mid Q$ publishes *some* interleaving of the values published by P and Q.

- **Asymmetric parallelism** P **where** $x :\in Q$: In this case P and Q are evaluated in parallel. P may become blocked by a dependency on x. The

---

[1] The analysis of risk is well studied in microeconomics (see [7], chapter 6). The study of grid and web applications under user's risk perception is new at the best of our knowledge. In particular the notion of risk profile introduced here seems to be new.

[2] The words "publishes","returns" and "outputs" are used interchangeably. The terms "site" and "service" are also used interchangeably.

first result published by Q is bound to x, the remainder of Q's evaluation is terminated and evaluation of the blocked residue of P is resumed.

EXAMPLE 3 *Consider the expression $s > x > (P|Q)$ where s is a site. However, if s fails to publish then this will result in a catastrophic failure in the evaluation of $s > x > (P|Q)$. If site t has the same functionality as s then the orchestration $(P|Q)$ where $x \in (t|s)$ will have the same functionality as $s > x > (P|Q)$ while being more robust.*

A service s implementing a total function is called *non-blocking* as $s(v_1, \ldots, v_n)$ must publish a result for all well-defined arguments $v_1, \ldots, v_n$; otherwise s is called *potentially blocking*. For example, site 1 is non-blocking while site if is potentially blocking. Given $E(z)$, depending on an input variable z, we denote by $E(\perp)$ the behavior of this expression when the value of z is undefined. This is equivalent to replace by 0 all subexpressions having a dependency on z. We keep $E(z)$ to represent the evaluation when z is defined.

3. The number of values published by an orchestration

Consider the example **Multiple job** executing in an environment where some sites are broken. The evaluation may still have value to the orchestrator provided that a certain minimum number of results are published. Given a complex orchestration E it is *unrealistic to assume that there will be no site failures* during execution. We use $\alpha(E)$ be the set of sites that are referenced in orchestration E and $\alpha_+(E) = \alpha(E) \setminus \{0\}$. Let $\mathcal{F} \subseteq \alpha_+(E)$ denote a set of sites that fail during an evaluation of E. The behaviour of the evaluation of E in this environment is given by replacing all occurrences of s, $s \in \mathcal{F}$, by 0. Let $\varphi_{\mathcal{F}}(E)$ denote this expression. The following assumptions are made in [4].

Reliability assumption. Sites are unreliable and can fail. When a site fails it remains silent; otherwise it publishes a result.

Value assumption. The evaluation of an orchestration has value even if some sites fail. For a particular failure set $\mathcal{F}$ the usefulness of the evaluation of $\varphi_{\mathcal{F}}(E)$ is measured by $v(\varphi_{\mathcal{F}}(E))$, the *value* or *benefit* of the orchestration $\varphi_{\mathcal{F}}(E)$. A valuation function v should be such that:

1　the range of v should be non-negative $\mathbb{R}$

2　the value of v must be 0 when all sites fail

3　$v(\varphi_{\mathcal{F}}(E)) \geq v(\varphi_{\mathcal{F}'}(E))$ when $\mathcal{F} \subseteq \mathcal{F}' \subseteq \alpha(E)$

4　$v(E)$ and $v_{\mathcal{F}}(E)$ have a low computational complexity.

We are interested in value functions v such that $v(E)$ and $v_{\mathcal{F}}(E)$ is easy to compute. A rough measure $v(E)$ is the number of outputs published by E denoted as out(E).

LEMMA 4 *The number of outputs,* out, *published by an expression meets the requirements needed for a value function. Moreover, given a non-blocking well formed expression E and $\mathcal{F} \subseteq \alpha_+(E)$, the values* out$(E)$ *and* out$(\varphi_{\mathcal{F}}(F))$ *can be computed in polynomial time with respect to the length of the expression E.*

Proof. The proof of the validity is straightforward. The computation bounds follow from standard techniques, taking into account the following considerations. The number of outputs of a single site call verifies $\mathsf{out}(0) = 0$, $\mathsf{out}(1) = 1$ and $\mathsf{out}(s(v_1, \ldots, v_k))$ is 1 if all the parameters are defined, 0 otherwise. For two non-blocking well formed expression E_1, E_2 we have $\mathsf{out}(E_1 | E_2) = \mathsf{out}(E_1) + \mathsf{out}(E_2)$, $\mathsf{out}(E_1 > z > E_2(z)) = \mathsf{out}(E_1) * \mathsf{out}(E_2(z))$ and $\mathsf{out}(E_1(z) \text{ where } z :\in E_2)$ is equal to $\mathsf{out}(E_1(z))$ if $\mathsf{out}(E_2) > 0$ otherwise is equal to $\mathsf{out}(E_1(\bot))$. □

4.   Risk profiles, angel-daemon games and assessments

Given an expression E we assume a partition of $\alpha_+(E)$ into two sets $\mathcal{A}$ and $\mathcal{D}$. Some ways of defining site partitions are given in [4]. An analysis is conducted where sites in $\mathcal{A}$ perform *as well as possible* while sites in $\mathcal{D}$ *maximise damage to the application*[3]. This results in an intermediate analysis lying between the best and worst cases. Let $f_\mathcal{A} \leq \#\mathcal{A}$ angelic sites and $f_\mathcal{D} \leq \#\mathcal{D}$ of daemonic sites fail during evaluation of E. The risk profile $(\mathcal{A}, f_\mathcal{A}, \mathcal{D}, f_\mathcal{D})$ gives a perception of risk from an assessor's point of view.

DEFINITION 5 *Given and Orc expression E, the tuple $\mathcal{R} = \langle E, \mathcal{A}, \mathcal{D}, f_\mathcal{A}, f_\mathcal{D} \rangle$ is a* risk profile *for E where $\mathcal{A} \cup \mathcal{D} = \alpha_+(E)$, $\mathcal{A} \cap \mathcal{D} = \emptyset$, $f_\mathcal{A} \leq \#\mathcal{A}$ and $f_\mathcal{D} \leq \#\mathcal{D}$.*

Given a risk profile $\mathcal{R} = \langle E, \mathcal{A}, \mathcal{D}, f_\mathcal{A}, f_\mathcal{D} \rangle$ a strategic situation occurs when E suffers the effects of two players, $\mathcal{A}$ and $\mathcal{D}$, with opposing behaviours. Consider the following zero sum game:

DEFINITION 6 ([4]) *The zero-sum* angel-daemon game *associated to risk profile $\mathcal{R}$ is the game $\Gamma(\mathcal{R}) = \langle \{\mathcal{A}, \mathcal{D}\}, A_\mathcal{A}, A_\mathcal{D}, u_\mathcal{A}, u_\mathcal{D} \rangle$ with two players, $\mathcal{A}$ the angel and $\mathcal{D}$ the daemon. The players have the following sets of actions, $A_\mathcal{A} = \{a \subseteq \mathcal{A} \mid \#a = f_\mathcal{A}\}$ and $A_\mathcal{D} = \{d \subseteq \mathcal{A} \mid \#d = f_\mathcal{D}\}$. As for an strategy profile $s = (a, d)$ the set of sites to fail associated with s is thus $a \cup d$, the utilities are $u_\mathcal{A}(s) = \mathsf{out}(\varphi_{a \cup d}(E))$ and $u_\mathcal{D}(s) = -u_\mathcal{A}(s)$.*

A *pure saddle point* is a strategy profile $s^* = (a^*, d^*)$ such that

$$u_\mathcal{A}(a^*, d^*) = \max_{a' \in A_\mathcal{A}} \min_{d' \in A_\mathcal{D}} u_\mathcal{A}(a', d') = \min_{a' \in A_\mathcal{A}} \max_{d' \in A_\mathcal{D}} u_\mathcal{A}(a', d')$$

---

[3] An important question is how this happen in practice. Given an orchestration E, a human or mechanical "user", has a belief about the behaviour of sites in $\alpha_+(E)$. This belief can be based on past experiences, common knowledge or any other information source. This should allow the user to partition the sites roughly into "good" and "bad". If there is no experience, the user can assume that all sites all are good (optimistic view) or all are bad (pessimistic view). Once the partition is found, the user has to consider failures. He can assume only that "all bad sites will fail for sure" or, alternatively, that "some good and some bad sites will fail". Assuming the latter case, the user has to address the following question "which good sites will fail" and similarly for daemons. Assuming that "good sites" fail damaging as little as possible seems a reasonable hypothesis. This approach is formalized with *risk profiles* and *angel-daemon games*.

$$SEQ\_of\_PAR \triangleq (P \mid Q) \gg (R \mid S) \,, \ PAR\_of\_SEQ \triangleq (P \gg Q) \mid (R \gg S)$$
$$\mathcal{R}_1 = \langle SEQ\_of\_PAR, \{P,Q\}, \{R,S\}, 1, 1\rangle, \mathcal{R}_2 = \langle SEQ\_of\_PAR, \{P,R\}, \{Q,S\}, 1, 1\rangle$$
$$\mathcal{R}_3 = \langle PAR\_of\_SEQ, \{P,Q\}, \{R,S\}, 1, 1\rangle, \mathcal{R}_4 = \langle PAR\_of\_SEQ, \{P,R\}, \{Q,S\}, 1, 1\rangle$$

	$\mathcal{D}$			$\mathcal{D}$			$\mathcal{D}$			$\mathcal{D}$	
	R	S		Q	S		R	S		Q	S
P	1	1	P	0	1	P	0	0	P	1	0
Q	1	1	R	1	0	Q	0	0	R	0	1

$\mathcal{A}$ appears to the left of each table ($\mathcal{A}\ P,Q$ / $\mathcal{A}\ P,R$ / $\mathcal{A}\ P,Q$ / $\mathcal{A}\ P,R$).

$$\nu(\mathcal{R}_1) = 1 \qquad \nu(\mathcal{R}_2) = 1/2 \qquad \nu(\mathcal{R}_3) = 0 \qquad \nu(\mathcal{R}_4) = 1/2$$

Figure 1. Angel-daemon games for SEQ_of_PAR and PAR_of_SEQ in different environments. The utility $u_\mathcal{A}$ is given by the number of outputs of the Orc expression. Games $\Gamma(\mathcal{R}_1)$ and $\Gamma(\mathcal{R}_3)$ have pure saddle points. Games $\Gamma(\mathcal{R}_2)$ and $\Gamma(\mathcal{R}_4)$ have mixed saddle points.

A pure saddle point does not necessarily exist (see the second game in Figure 1). A mixed strategy for $\mathcal{A}$ is a probability distribution $\alpha : A_\mathcal{A} \to [0,1]$ and similarly for $\mathcal{D}$. Let $\Delta_\mathcal{A}$ and $\Delta_\mathcal{D}$ be the set of mixed strategies for $\mathcal{A}$ and $\mathcal{D}$. A mixed strategy profile is a tuple (α, β) and the expected utility for $\mathcal{A}$ is $u_\mathcal{A}(\alpha, \beta) = \sum_{(a,d)\in A_\mathcal{A}\times A_\mathcal{D}} \alpha(a)\beta(d)u_\mathcal{A}(a,b)$. It is well known [6] that there always exists a mixed saddle point (α^*, β^*) satisfying

$$u_\mathcal{A}(\alpha^*, \beta^*) = \max_{\alpha'\in\Delta_\mathcal{A}} \min_{\beta'\in\Delta_\mathcal{D}} u_\mathcal{A}(\alpha', \beta') = \min_{\beta'\in\Delta_\mathcal{D}} \max_{\alpha,\in\Delta_\mathcal{A}} u_\mathcal{A}(\alpha', \beta')$$

Moreover, all the existing saddle points give the same utility; therefore such a value is called the *value* of the game $\Gamma(\mathcal{R})$.

DEFINITION 7 *Given a risk profile* $\mathcal{R} = \langle E, \mathcal{A}, \mathcal{D}, f_A, f_D\rangle$, *the assessment under* $\mathcal{R}$, *denoted by* $\nu(\mathcal{R})$, *is the value of the zero-sum game* $\Gamma(\mathcal{R})$.

EXAMPLE 8 *Consider two classical parallel workflow patterns (see [1]), SEQ_of_PAR and PAR_of_SEQ. PAR represents parallel execution (e.g. a farm) while SEQ is sequential composition. In Figure 1 the workflows SEQ_of_PAR and PAR_of_SEQ are analysed using angel-daemon games using utility function out. A "sequential composition of parallel processes" (SEQ_of_PAR) is denoted by* $\triangleq (P \mid Q) \gg (R \mid S)$ *while a "parallel composition of sequential expressions" (PAR_of_SEQ) is denoted by* $\triangleq (P \gg Q) \mid (R \gg S)$.

In Example 8 there are simple cases without pure saddle points. Pure saddle points arise in the following example:

EXAMPLE 9 *A farm (a kind of multiple job) is an embarrassingly parallel computation defined as* $FARM_n \triangleq (S_1 \mid \cdots \mid S_n)$. *For any* $\mathcal{R} = \langle FARM_n, \mathcal{A}, \mathcal{D}, f_A, f_D\rangle$ *it is easy to prove* $\nu(\mathcal{R}) = n - f_A - f_D$. *An angel failure has the same effect as a daemon failure (because of the simple structure of* $FARM_n$*). A sequential composition of farms [2] can be analysed* using angel-daemon games. The sequential composition of $k > 0$ farms is defined for $k = 1$ as $SEQ\_of\_FARM_{n,1} \triangleq FARM_n$ and for $k > 1$ as $SEQ\_of\_FARM_{n,k} \triangleq FARM_n \gg SEQ\_of\_FARM_{n,k-1}$. For the profile $\mathcal{R}_{SEQ} = \langle SEQ\_of\_FARM_{n,k}, \mathcal{A}, \mathcal{D}, f_{\mathcal{A}}, f_{\mathcal{D}} \rangle$ we have $\nu(\mathcal{R}_{SEQ}) = (n - f_{\mathcal{A}} - f_{\mathcal{D}})^k$. □

Under restricted circumstances, pure equilibria exist:

LEMMA 10 *Let E and F be two expressions, then we have*

$$\nu(\langle E \mid F, \alpha_+(E), \alpha_+(F), f_{\mathcal{A}}, f_{\mathcal{D}} \rangle)$$
$$= \max_{a \in A_{\mathcal{A}}} \mathsf{out}(\varphi_a(E)) + \min_{d \in A_{\mathcal{D}}} \mathsf{out}(\varphi_d(F))$$
$$\nu\langle E \gg F, \alpha_+(E), \alpha_+(F), f_{\mathcal{A}}, f_{\mathcal{D}} \rangle)$$
$$= \max_{a \in A_{\mathcal{A}}} \mathsf{out}(\varphi_a(E)) * \min_{d \in A_{\mathcal{D}}} \mathsf{out}(\varphi_d(F))$$
$$\nu(\langle E, \mathcal{A}, \mathcal{D}, f_{\mathcal{A}}, 0 \rangle) = \max_{a \in A_{\mathcal{A}}} \mathsf{out}(\varphi_a(E))$$
$$\nu(\langle E, \mathcal{A}, \mathcal{D}, 0, f_{\mathcal{D}} \rangle) = \min_{d \in A_{\mathcal{D}}} \mathsf{out}(\varphi_a(E))$$

Therefore, in all the four cases the associated game has a pure saddle point.

Proof sketch. Given the orchestration $E \mid F$ it is easy to see that $u_{\mathcal{A}}(a, d) = \mathsf{out}(\varphi_a(E)) + \mathsf{out}(\varphi_d(F))$. Observe that for $E \gg F$ we have that $u_{\mathcal{A}}(a, d) = \mathsf{out}(\varphi_a(E)) * \mathsf{out}(\varphi_d(F))$. In the case that $f_{\mathcal{D}} = 0$ we have that $u_{\mathcal{A}}(a, \emptyset) = \mathsf{out}(\varphi_a(E))$ and when $f_{\mathcal{A}} = 0$ we have that $u_{\mathcal{D}}(\emptyset, d) = \mathsf{out}(\varphi_a(E))$. Therefore, in all the four cases, the extreme values are achievable by pure strategies and the corresponding games have a pure saddle point. □

5. Properties of risk profiles and assessments

We study basic properties of risk profiles in relation to the assessment of orchestrations. The first establishes a basic monotonicity property. Assume that $\mathcal{A}$ and $\mathcal{D}$ remain unchanged.

LEMMA 11 *Given a risk profile $\mathcal{R} = \langle E, \mathcal{A}, \mathcal{D}, f_{\mathcal{A}}, f_{\mathcal{D}} \rangle$, consider the risk profiles $\mathcal{R}' = \langle E, \mathcal{A}, \mathcal{D}, f'_{\mathcal{A}}, f_{\mathcal{D}} \rangle$ and $\mathcal{R}'' = \langle E, \mathcal{A}, \mathcal{D}, f_{\mathcal{A}}, f'_{\mathcal{D}} \rangle$. Then, when $f'_{\mathcal{A}} \le f_{\mathcal{A}}$ we have that $\nu(\mathcal{R}) \le \nu(\mathcal{R}')$ and when $f'_{\mathcal{D}} \ge f_{\mathcal{D}}$, $\nu(\mathcal{R}) \ge \nu(\mathcal{R}'')$.*

Proof sketch. Consider the profile $\mathcal{R}'$, note $f'_{\mathcal{A}} = p'$, $f_{\mathcal{A}} = p$ and $\delta = p - p'$. Given a set $a \subseteq \mathcal{A}$ with $|a| = p$ and a set $a' \subseteq a$ with $|a'| = p'$, for any $d \subseteq \mathcal{D}$ we have that $\mathsf{out}(\varphi_{a \cup d}(E)) \ge \mathsf{out}(\varphi_{a' \cup d}(E))$, therefore $u_{\mathcal{A}}(a, d) \le u_{\mathcal{A}'}(a', d)$. The previous inequality can be extended to *dual pairs* of mixed strategies α and α' in which for any a there is $a' \subset a$ for which $\alpha(a) = \alpha'(a')$. Finally, to prove that $\nu(\mathcal{R}) \le \nu(\mathcal{R}')$ consider, for a dual pair α and α', the strategies β^* and $\hat{\beta}$ such that $u_{\mathcal{A}}(\alpha, \beta^*) = \min_\beta u_{\mathcal{A}}(\alpha, \beta)$ and $u_{\mathcal{A}}(\alpha', \hat{\beta}) = \min_\beta u_{\mathcal{A}'}(\alpha', \beta)$, then we can show that $u_A(\alpha, \beta^*) \leq u_{A'}(\alpha', \hat{\beta})$. Now considering the strategies α^* and $\hat{\alpha}$ with $u_A(\alpha^*, \beta^*) = \max_\alpha u_A(\alpha, \beta^*)$ and $u_{A'}(\hat{\alpha}, \hat{\beta}) = \max_\alpha u_{A'}(\alpha, \beta^*)$, then we can show that $\nu(\mathcal{R}) = u_A(\alpha^*, \beta^*)$ and that $\nu(\mathcal{R}') = u_{A'}(\hat{\alpha}, \hat{\beta})$, therefore $\nu(\mathcal{R}) \leq \nu(\mathcal{R}')$. □

One particular case is when the angel or the daemon is not allowed to act. For a given $\mathcal{R} = \langle E, A, D, p, q \rangle$, we consider $\mathsf{AngCut}(\mathcal{R}) = \langle E, A, D, p, 0 \rangle$ and $\mathsf{DaeCut}(\mathcal{R}) = \langle E, A, D, 0, q \rangle$. The previous result shows that the values verify $\nu(\mathsf{DaeCut}(\mathcal{R})) \leq \nu(\mathcal{R}) \leq \nu(\mathsf{AngCut}(\mathcal{R}))$.

It can be difficult to find more sophisticated properties as we see in the following example which shows that intuition is not necessarily a good guide.

EXAMPLE 12 *Given a risk profile we could try to trade-off properties such as, "increasing the failures of A and decreasing the failures of D so as to give a less risky situation". Unfortunately, this is false. Given $E = ((P \mid Q) \gg T) \mid R)$, profile $\mathcal{R} = \langle E, \{T, R\}, \{P, Q\}, 1, 1 \rangle$ gives us $\nu(\Gamma(\mathcal{R})) = 1$, trading a daemonic failure for an angelic one makes the situation worse because now the profile is $\mathcal{R}' = \langle E, \{T, R\}, \{P, Q\}, 2, 0 \rangle$ and $\nu(\mathcal{R}') = 0$.*

There are more extreme risk profiles.

THEOREM 13 *Given a risk profile $\mathcal{R} = \langle E, A, D, p, q \rangle$, consider the profiles*

$$\mathsf{Ang}(\mathcal{R}) = \langle E, \alpha_+(E), \emptyset, p + q, 0 \rangle, \mathsf{Dae}(\mathcal{R}) = \langle E, \emptyset, \alpha_+(E), 0, p + q \rangle$$

then we have $\nu(\mathsf{Dae}(\mathcal{R})) \leq \nu(\mathcal{R})) \leq \nu(\mathsf{Ang}(\mathcal{R}))$.

Proof sketch. Let $a^* \subseteq \alpha_+(E)$ be a set giving the maximal value for $\mathsf{out}(\varphi_d(E))$ and let $d_* \subseteq \alpha_+(E)$ be a set giving the minimal value for $\mathsf{out}(\varphi_d(E))$. Taking into account the definirion of the two games we have that $(a^*, \emptyset)$ is a saddle point of $\mathsf{Ang}(\mathcal{R})$ and that $(\emptyset, d^*)$ is a saddle point of $\mathsf{Dae}(\mathcal{R})$. Furthermore, for any $(a, d) \in A_A \times A_D$ it holds that $\mathsf{out}(\varphi_{d^*}(E)) \leq u_A(a, d) \leq \mathsf{out}(\varphi_{a^*}(E))$. Therefore, $\nu(\mathsf{Dae}(\mathcal{R})) \leq \nu(\mathcal{R}) \leq \nu(\mathsf{Ang}(\mathcal{R}))$. □

The $\mathsf{Ang}(\mathcal{R})$ profile adopts the viewpoint "the world is as good as possible even when failures cannot be avoided". In contrast, the $\mathsf{Dae}(\mathcal{R})$ profile is a conceptualization of "the world is as bad as possible and failures always happen to maximize dammage". Given a risk profile $\mathcal{R}$, the profiles $\mathsf{Ang}(\mathcal{R})$ and $\mathsf{Dae}(\mathcal{R})$ act as a basic bounds.

6.   Arranging a Meeting using Reputation

The following is an example of internet computing where sites are interpreted as interfaces between the members of a community. Consider a university rector who wishes to consult his staff before making a decision. He sends an email to professors in his university to arrange a meeting. Some professors answer; others do not. Assume that professors have a reputation metric. For example,

PROFESSOR	REPUTATION
Rector	0.3
Ex-Rector	0.3
Head of Dept.	0.2
Professor	0.1
Instructor	0.1
TOTAL	1.0

$r(a,d)$	E	H	P	$r_A(a)$
R	0.13...	0.16...	0.2	0.1
I	0.2	0.23...	0.26...	0.3
$r_D(d)$	0.15	0.2	0.25	

Figure 2. The first table gives the reputation and the second reflects the reputation values associated to the strategies in the game associated to the risk profile $< \mathcal{P}, \{R, I\}, \{E, H, P\}, 1, 1 >$.

reputation could be based on position. After a time ΔT the rector has to decide if the meeting will take place or not. The decision will be based on the *average reputation of the professors replying*. The following Orc expression *Meeting* is based on *MeetingMonitor* (see section 7.3 in [8]). It is assumed that a call to a professor's site p, with a message m, is denoted by $p(m)$. The call $p(m)$ either returns the reputation of the professor or is silent (this is represented as $p(m) > r$).

The expression $AskFor(L, m, t, \Delta T)$ gives the number and the total reputation of the answers received. In the expression $L = (h, t)$ is the list of professors, m is the message, t the suggested meeting time, and ΔT the maximum waiting time for responses. $AskFor$ publishes a pair $(count, total\_reputation)$. The average reputation is $r = reputation/count$. As the reputation r_i of any professor i satisfies $0 < r - i < 1$, it holds that $0 < r < 1$. Following [5, 11] we define a lower $0 \leq \omega \leq 1$ threshold in order to classify the relevance of data. The meeting will take place when the reputation is good enough: $\omega \leq r$; otherwise the meeting is cancelled. The final expression is *ProceedOrCancel*, where $L_{\mathcal{P}}$ is the email list of all the professors in the university.

$$AskFor([], m, t, \Delta T) \triangleq let(0, 0)$$
$$AskFor(H : T, m, t, \Delta T) \triangleq let(count, total\_reputation)$$
$$\textbf{where}$$
$$count :\in add(u.count, v.count)$$
$$total\_reputation :\in add(u.reputation, v.reputation)$$
$$u :\in \{h(m) > r > let(1, r) \mid Rtimer(\Delta T) \gg let(0, 0)\}$$
$$v :\in AskFor(T, m, t, \Delta T)$$
$$ProceedOrCancel(c, total\_r, \omega) \triangleq$$
$$average(c, total\_r) > r >$$
$$(if(\omega \leq r) \gg let(\text{``do''})) \mid if(\omega > r) \gg let(\text{``cancel''}))$$
$$Meeting(\mathcal{P}, \omega, t, \Delta T) \triangleq$$
$$AskFor(L_{\mathcal{P}}, m, t, \Delta T) > (c, r) > ProceedOrCancel(c, r, \omega)$$

Let us consider how to assess the meeting. To do this consider a strongly divided university with a set of professors $\mathcal{P}$ such that $\mathcal{P} = \mathcal{A} \cup \mathcal{D}$. As before the easy way to analyse this situation is introducing a risk profile.

DEFINITION 14 *For the meeting problem a risk profile contains information about the reputation and the threshold,* $\mathcal{R} = \langle \mathcal{P}, (r_i)_{i \in N}, \omega, \mathcal{A}, \mathcal{D}, f_{\mathcal{A}}, f_{\mathcal{D}} \rangle$.

This profile contains elements in common with that given in Definition 5 just replacing $\alpha_+(E)$ by $\mathcal{P}$. Let $a = \{a_1, \ldots, a_p\}$ be the failing sites (do not respond) for $\mathcal{A}$ and $d = \{d_1, \ldots, d_q\}$ the failing sites for $\mathcal{D}$ and, as before, the strategy profile is $s = (a, d)$. The set of sites answering the email (successful sites) are $S_a = \mathcal{A} \backslash a$ and $S_d = \mathcal{D} \backslash d$. Given a strategy profile (a, d), the average reputations of $\mathcal{A}$ and $\mathcal{D}$ and the average reputation of the strategy profile are defined as follows

$$r_{\mathcal{A}}(a) = \frac{\sum_{s \in S_a} r_s}{\# S_a}, r_{\mathcal{D}}(d) = \frac{\sum_{s \in S_d} r_s}{\# S_d}, r(a, d) = \frac{\sum_{s \in S_a \cup S_d} r_s}{\#(S_a \cup S_d)}$$

The angel $\mathcal{A}$ is happy when the meeting takes place and unhappy otherwise. The daemon $\mathcal{D}$ behaves in the opposite direction.

$$u_{\mathcal{A}}(a, d) = \begin{cases} +r_{\mathcal{A}}(a) & \text{if } \omega \leq r(a, d) \\ -r_{\mathcal{A}}(a) & \text{otherwise} \end{cases} \qquad u_{\mathcal{D}}(a, d) = \begin{cases} -r_{\mathcal{D}}(d) & \text{if } \omega \leq r(a, d) \\ +r_{\mathcal{D}}(d) & \text{otherwise} \end{cases}$$

Based on these utilities the Angel-Daemon game is adapted to this situation and we obtain the strategic game $\Gamma(\mathcal{R}) = \langle \mathcal{A}, \mathcal{D}, u_{\mathcal{A}}, u_{\mathcal{D}} \rangle$ called the Meeting game. Note that the Meeting game is not a zero-sum game.

EXAMPLE 15 *We have a university with* $N = 5$ *professors* $\mathcal{P} = \{R, E, H, P, I\}$ *partitioned as* $\mathcal{A} = \{R, I\}$, $\mathcal{D} = \{E, H, P\}$ *and* $f_{\mathcal{A}} = f_{\mathcal{D}} = 1$. *The Figure 3 give us several examples of the meeting game for diferent values of w. Observe that for* $w = 0.1, 0.18,$ *and* 0.3 *the meeting game has a pure Nash equilibrium, but that when* $w = 0.25$ *the game does not have a Nash equilibrium.*

		$\mathcal{D}$		
		E	H	P
$\mathcal{A}$	R	$0.1, -0.15$	$0.1, -0.2$	$0.1, -0.25$
	I	$0.3, -0.15$	$0.3, -0.2$	$0.3, -0.25$

$w = 0.1$

		$\mathcal{D}$		
		E	H	P
$\mathcal{A}$	R	$-0.1, 0.15$	$-0.1, 0.2$	$0.1, -0.25$
	I	$0.3, -0.15$	$0.3, -0.2$	$0.3, -0.25$

$w = 0.18$

		$\mathcal{D}$		
		E	H	P
$\mathcal{A}$	R	$-0.1, 0.15$	$-0.1, 0.2$	$-0.1, 0.25$
	I	$-0.3, 0.15$	$-0.3, 0.2$	$0.3, -0.25$

$w = 0.25$

		$\mathcal{D}$		
		E	H	P
$\mathcal{A}$	R	$-0.1, 0.15$	$-0.1, 0.2$	$-0.1, 0.25$
	I	$-0.3, 0.15$	$-0.3, 0.2$	$-0.3, 0.25$

$w = 0.3$

Figure 3. Some examples of the meeting game for the case in Example 15 for $w \in \{0.1, 0.18, 0.25, 0.3\}$.

THEOREM 16 *Given* $\mathcal{R} = \langle \mathcal{N}, (r_i)_{i \in N}, \omega, \mathcal{A}, \mathcal{D}, f_{\mathcal{A}}, f_{\mathcal{D}} \rangle$. *Let* $A = A_{\mathcal{A}} \times A_{\mathcal{D}}$
and define $\delta = \min_{(a,d) \in A} r(a,d)$, $\mu = \max_{(a,d) \in A} r(a,d)$, $\delta_{\mathcal{A}} = \min_{a \in A_{\mathcal{A}}} r_{\mathcal{A}}(a)$
and finally $\mu_{\mathcal{A}} = \max_{a \in A_{\mathcal{A}}} r_{\mathcal{A}}(a)$

- $\Gamma(\mathcal{R})$ *has a Nash equilibrium iff either (1)* $\exists a \in A_{\mathcal{A}}$ *with* $r_{\mathcal{A}}(a) = \mu_{\mathcal{A}}$
  such that $\forall d \in A_{\mathcal{D}}$ $r(a,d) \geq \omega$, *or (2)* $\exists d \in A_{\mathcal{D}}$ *with* $r_{\mathcal{D}}(d) = \mu_{\mathcal{D}}$ *such*
  that $\forall a \in A_{\mathcal{A}}$ $r(a,d) < \omega$.

- *If* $\omega \leq \delta$ *or* $\omega > \mu$, *the game* $\Gamma_{\mathcal{P}}(\mathcal{R})$ *has a Nash equilibrium.*

Furthermore, in any Nash equilibrium (a,d) *of the game (if one exists), either*
the meeting holds and $u_{\mathcal{A}}(a,d) = \mu_{\mathcal{A}}$ *and* $u_{\mathcal{D}}(a,d) = -\delta_{\mathcal{D}}$ *or the meeting is*
cancelled and $u_{\mathcal{A}}(a,d) = -\delta_{\mathcal{A}}$ *and* $u_{\mathcal{D}}(a,d) = \mu_{\mathcal{D}}$.

Proof Sketch. Observe that function r has some monotonicity properties. In
the case that $r(a,d) \geq \omega$, for any $a' \in A_{\mathcal{A}}$ with $r_{\mathcal{A}}(a') \geq r_{\mathcal{A}}(a)$, we have that
$r(a',d) \geq \omega$. Let (a,d) be a Nash equilibrium in which the meeting holds, that
is $r(a,d) \geq \omega$. This means that $r_{\mathcal{A}}(a_1) \geq 0$ and $r_{\mathcal{D}}(d_1) \leq 0$. Therefore, taking
into account the monotonicity, we have that $r_{\mathcal{A}}(a_1) = \mu_{\mathcal{A}}$ and $r_{\mathcal{D}}(d_1) = \delta_{\mathcal{D}}$,
otherwise a_1 will not be a best response to d_1 and viceversa. But in such a case
condition (1) holds. In the case that condition (1) holds, we have that a is the
best response to any action of the daemon d'. Furthermore, the best response
to a happens in the daemon strategy with minimum $r_{\mathcal{D}}$ value. Therefore the
game has a Nash equilibrium in which the meeting holds. Symmetrically if
$r(a,d) < \omega$, for any $d' \in A_{\mathcal{D}}$ with $r_{\mathcal{D}}(d') \leq r_{\mathcal{D}}(d)$, we have that $r(a,d') < \omega$.
Reversing the arguments we get the equivalence with the existence of a Nash
equilibrium in which the meeting does not hold and condition (2). Observe that
$\omega \leq \delta$ implies condition (1) and $\omega > \mu$ implies condition (2). □

7. Conclusions

We have addressed the question of the management of risk in orchestrations.
We captured an *ex-ante* vision of the risk in a risk profile and applied this
idea to two different types of orchestrations. Several open questions remain.
Perhaps it is possible to define a taxonomy or risk profiles for large families
of orchestrations. It also seems possible to define the behaviour in relation
to risk attitudes. The behaviour of an orchestration under failures can also be
studied using a probabilistic approach [13]. The relationship between the two
approaches merits investigation.

Acknowledgement. We thank the anonymous referees for their very helpful
comments and suggestions.

References

[1] Bougé, L.: Le mòdele de programmation à parallélisme de donés: une perspective sémantique. *Techniques et science informatiques*, Vol 12, 5, 541–562, 1993.

[2] Danelutto, M; Aldinucci, M. Algorithmic skeletons meeting grids. Parallel Computing Vol 32, Issues 7-8, September 2006, Pages 449-462.

[3] Eliaz, K: Fault Tolerant Implementation. *Review of Economic Studies*, 2002, vol. 69, issue 3, pages 589-610.

[4] Gabarro, J; García, A.; Clint, M; Stewart, A; Kilpatrick, P.: Bounded Site Failures: an Approach to Unreliable Grid Environments. CoreGRID Workshop. FORTH - Hellas , Heraklion - Crete, Greece. June 12-13, 2007.

[5] Marsh, S.: *Formalising Trust as a Computational Concept*. PhD. Thesis University of Stirling, 1994.

[6] von Neumann, J.; Morgenstern, O.: *Theory of Games and Economic Behavior*, Princeton, 1944.

[7] Mas-Colell, A.; Whinston, M; Green, J.: *Microeconomic Theory*. Oxford, 1995.

[8] Misra J.; Cook, W.: Computation Orchestration: A basis for wide-area computing. *Software & Systems Modeling*, 2006. DOI 10.1007/s10270-006-0012-1.

[9] Moscibroda, T., Schmid, S., Wattenhofer, R: When selfish meets evil: byzantine players in a virus inoculation game. PODC'06, 35 - 44, 2006.

[10] Osborne, M., Rubinstein, A.: *A Course on Game Theory*, MIT Press, 1994.

[11] Bin Yu, Munindar P. Singh. An Evidential Model of Distributed Reputation Management, Proceedings of First International Conference on Autonomous Agents and MAS, July 2002, 294–301.

[12] Silaghi, G.C., Arenas, A., Silva, L.: Reputation-based trust management systems and their applicability to grids. Technical Report TR-0064, Institute on Programming Models, CoreGRID-Network of Excellence, March 2007. http://www.coregrid.net/mambo/images/stories/TechnicalReports/tr-0064.pdf 21 May 2007.

[13] Stewart, A., Gabarro, J., Clint, M., Harmer, T., Kilpatrick, P., Perrott, R.: Assessing the reliability and cost of web and grid orchestrations. To appear in ARES 2008.

[14] Stewart, A., Gabarro, J., Clint, M., Harmer, T., Kilpatrick, P., Perrott, R.: Managing Grid Computations: An ORC-Based Approach. ISPA 2006, Sorrento, Italy, LNCS Vol. 4330, pp. 278–291, 2006.

TOWARDS COORDINATED DATA MANAGEMENT FOR HIGH-PERFORMANCE DISTRIBUTED MULTIMEDIA CONTENT ANALYSIS

Pierpaolo Giacomin and Alessandro Bassi
Hitachi Sophia Antipolis Laboratory
Immeuble Le Thélème, 1503 Route de Dolines
06560 Valbonne, France
giacomin@few.vu.nl
alessandro.bassi@hitachi-eu.com

Frank J. Seinstra and Thilo Kielmann
Vrije Universiteit, Computer Systems Group
Dept. Computer Science, De Boelelaan 1081a
1081 HV Amsterdam, The Netherlands
fjseins@cs.vu.nl
kielmann@cs.vu.nl

Abstract

In a few years, access to the content of multimedia data will be a problem of phenomenal proportions, as digital cameras may produce high data rates, and multimedia archives steadily run into petabytes of storage space. As a consequence, in the field of large-scale distributed Multimedia Content Analysis (MMCA) there is an urgent need for the coordinated handling of vast amounts of distributed and replicated data collections.

Any sustainable solution to the management problem of distributed (multimedia) data in Grids has to follow a layered approach, starting from a new generation of network controllers and, through a novel middleware, up to an interface to applications.

In this paper we report on our first steps of our bigger plan in this direction. Specifically, we introduce a new transport protocol layer (called HI-TP), which is capable of taking advantage of the storage capabilities of network devices, such as routers. The paper presents the protocol definition, and discusses initial performance results for basic transmission functionality. Results indicate that our protocol is capable of achieving higher throughput than traditional transport protocols, even in networks with significant latency.

Keywords: Multimedia, Grid, Network, Storage, Coupling

1.   Introduction

Multimedia data is rapidly gaining importance along with recent deployment of publicly accessible digital television archives, surveillance cameras in public locations, and automatic comparison of forensic video evidence. Consequently, for emerging problems in multimedia content analysis (MMCA), Grid architectures are rapidly becoming indispensable.

Any sustainable solution to the management problem of distributed (multimedia) data in Grids has to follow a layered approach, starting from a new generation of network controllers and, through a novel middleware, up to an interface to applications. To achieve the goals of scalability, security, versatility, location independence, and delivering a Quality-of-Experience driven performance over current network infrastructures, we are developing a solution where 'intelligence' in a globally scalable system is put in the middleware, where the lower level deals with local problems only, while all other properties are taken care of at the upper layers.

Today, network devices such as routers have transparent storage capabilities: when IP packets reach a router, they are stored in a queue, waiting to be processed. An *active network caching* scheme can take advantage of such storage, and buffer streams to be released only at a later stage. To achieve this, the network nodes should expose in some way the underlying storage, thus separating the basic forwarding functions from higher control capabilities. Furthermore, a middleware layer should provide interfaces to these advanced data management properties, to be available to Grid services and applications. Research and development in this direction, including the design and standardization of new protocols, is one of the core businesses of the Hitachi Sophia Antipolis lab.

To transparently make available the newly developed protocols to application developers, an integration effort is taking place with the advanced Grid programming tools developed by the Computer Systems group at Vrije Universiteit: (1) Ibis Grid communication system and environment [17] and (2) Java version of the Grid Application Toolkit (GAT) [1]. The group at the Vrije Universiteit also is engaged in a strong collaboration with MultimediaN, a Dutch national consortium integrating over 120 researchers from leading Dutch institutes in the field of multimedia technology [15]. In this collaboration, Ibis and Java-GAT are currently being integrated with a user transparent cluster programming framework for multimedia content analysis, called Parallel-Horus [10–12]. The work described in this paper complements these ongoing efforts, and will benefit from the availability of many existing state-of-the-art multimedia applications, and large-scale multimedia data sets.

In this paper we report on our first steps towards a solution for the coordinated management of vast amounts of multimedia data, for real-time and off-line content analysis.

This paper is organized as follows. Section 2 presents the rationale of active network caching, and signals the need for a new transport protocol. In Section 3 we present an overview of state-of-the-art transport protocols, and indicate problems and drawbacks with respect to our purposes. Section 4 presents a new transport protocol, which is capable of taking advantage of the storage capabilities of network devices, such as routers referred to as HI-TP. Section 5 describes the testbed applied in our measurements, and discusses our initial performance results for basic transmission functionality. In Section 6 we give a brief overview of the set of tools in which our newly developed transport protocol will be integrated. Concluding remarks are given in Section 7.

2. Logistical Networking: Active Network Caching

As stated in the introduction, network devices such as routers have transparent storage capabilities: when IP packets reach a router, they are stored in a queue, waiting to be processed. An active, intelligent *network caching* scheme can take advantage of such storage, and buffer streams to be released only at a later stage. To achieve this, the network nodes should expose in some way the underlying storage, thus separating the basic forwarding functions from higher control capabilities.

Our work in this direction is a natural follow-up to the Internet Backplane Protocol (IBP), which aims to exploit a unified view of communication that creates a strong synergy between storage and networking [7]. IBP allows data to be stored at one location while en route from sender to receiver, adding the ability to control data movement temporally as well as spatially. This generalized notion of data movement is called *logistical networking*, drawing an analogy with systems of warehouses and distribution channels. Logistical networking can improve application performance by allowing files to be staged near where they will be used, data to be collected near their source, or content to be replaced close to its users.

Our current work, as part of the Intelligent Network Caching Architecture (INCA [2]), extends these ideas. In particular, we believe that any envisaged solution to logistical networking must be comprehensive, and must follow a layered approach, starting from a new generation of network equipment controllers and, through a novel middleware, up to the interface to applications.

The INCA system aims at *exposing* and *expanding* the storage capabilities of network equipment, such as routers. In particular, our goal is to implement an active network caching scheme that can take advantage of network storage, to buffer streams that are to be released only at a later stage. As an example, the INCA architecture aims to support files which can be replicated and scattered over the network, or at least in a defined network domain. To achieve this, we need to rethink the current architecture of network nodes, allowing them to expose their underlying storage. In other words, the network equipment should move towards a modular, or distributed, architecture, separating the basic forwarding functions from higher control capabilities.

This paper focuses on the lowest layer of transmission protocols, in particular at the IP level. At this level we need new mechanisms and protocols to make data storage available *inside* the network boundaries. This particular storage should have very basic properties and very simple failure modes, in order to allow for maximum scalability of the framework. The middleware above, which is not the focus of this paper, would act as the transport layer in networking; it would provide all those properties that allow the framework to be useful to services and applications.

The following section gives a brief overview of state-of-the-art network transmission protocols, and indicates problems and drawbacks with respect to our purpose of efficient and reliable network caching. In the subsequent section we introduce our newly developed transport protocol, referred to as HI-TP (High-volume INCA Transport Protocol).

3.   State-of-the-Art Network Transmission Protocols

The Transmission Control Protocol (TCP) is one of the core protocols of the Internet protocol suite [9]. TCP provides reliable, in-order delivery of data streams, making it suitable for applications like file transfer and e-mail. Despite its importance, TCP has many drawbacks. The most significant problem for our purposes is that TCP does not perform well on broadband high latency networks. This is because the maximal bandwidth usable by TCP is an inverse function of the latency.

An alternative to TCP is the User Datagram Protocol (UDP), which is yet another core protocol of the Internet protocol suite [8]. Using UDP, networked computers can send short messages (known as datagrams) to one another. UDP does not guarantee reliability or ordering in the way that TCP does. Datagrams may arrive out of order, appear duplicated, or go missing without notice. Avoiding the overhead of checking whether every packet actually arrived makes UDP faster and more efficient, at least for applications that do not need guaranteed delivery. Despite this increased performance potential, the lack of reliability and congestion control makes UDP not suitable for our purposes.

The problems of TCP and UDP have been acknowledged in the field, and have led to many extended and adapted data transfer protocols. One important research effort in this direction is UDT (or UDP-based Data Transfer Protocol), developed at the National Center for Data Mining (NCDM) at the University of Illinois at Chicago [4]. UDT is designed to effectively utilize the rapidly emerging high-speed wide area optical networks. It is built on top of UDP with reliability control and congestion control. A significant result of UDT is that it was capable of reaching 711Mb/s (peak 844Mb/s) disk to disk data transfer between the United States and Russia. This result still represents the highest recorded information transfer between these countries.

Another reliable data delivery protocol, that proxy TCP connections over UDP, is Airhook [3]. Unlike TCP, Airhook gracefully handles intermittent, unreliable, or delayed networks. Other features include session recovery, congestion control, and delivery status notification. In particular, Airhook continuously transmits small status packets to keep both endpoints aware of connection status; lost data packets are transmitted immediately when their absence is reported.

Despite the impressive results obtained with UTP and Airhook, both protocols can not exploit network storage capabilities. As there is not a straightforward manner to integrate such capabilities (efficiently) within existing protocols, it is essential to define a new transport protocol for our purposes. Our proposed protocol will be introduced in the following section.

3.1 Related Approaches to Wide-Area File Transmission

Apart from low level transport protocols, there are several related efforts that must be mentioned here, and that must be compared in our evaluations. First, there is the distributed file system implementation created by Sun Microsystems, called NFS. Over the years, NFS has been the only satisfactory solution for a Network Attached Storage (NAS). Although NFS is much more than a file transfer system, it is relevant to compare NFS with our efforts, in particular due the recent trend to use NAS/SAN storage in Grid environments.

Second, the 'scp' application, part of the OpenSSH package, even if it is partially out of the scope of this paper, as it relies on SSL and TCP, is worthwhile to incorporate 'scp' in this paper's evaluation due to the fact that it is such a commonly used tool.

Finally, 'Sendfile()' is an operating system kernel primitive that aims to send a file in a 'zero copy' manner, using as little CPU time as possible. It is available in recent kernel editions of major operating systems. Sendfile() is particularly useful in our evaluations, as it allows us to send a file over TCP without any kind of overhead.

4. HI-TP: High-volume INCA Transport Protocol

In this section we introduce our new transport protocol, which we refer to as HI-TP, or High-volume INCA Transport Protocol. The aim of HI-TP is to transfer very large volumes of data in the most efficient way. The protocol is connectionless, such that it can deal with multiple peers easily and get easily proxied.

Table 1. HI-TP header

0	1-15	16	17-31
mo	offset	mr	rid
ml	length	checksum	
payload...			

Table 2. Simplified HI-TP header

0-15	16-31
offset	rid
lenght	checksum
mblock	Mblock
payload...	

A natural way to optimize data transport is to minimize overhead. To this end, HI-TP tries to identify the minimal amount of information needed to transfer a byte-sequence across the Internet successfully. In addition, HI-TP is made generic and extensible to allow it to deal with underlying heterogeneous network infrastructures and overlying applications. For these reasons, we have chosen the scheme in table 1 as the packet header of our prototype protocol implementation. A very important role is played by the most significant bits (msb) of the fields rid, checksum and offset. A more detailed explanation of the header fields is available in [2]. We believe that, using this strategy, we are able to keep the protocol extremely expandable. Each extension field is placed after the checksum in the same order as the basic fields. Each extension field of the same type is placed contiguously.

All HI-TP packets carry from a sender, identified by its IP address in the field Source Address of the IP protocol header, to a receiver, identified by his IP address in the field Destination Address of the IP protocol header, the amount of data specified by the length field of the HI-TP. When the packets arrive at the receiver side the data are stored in a buffer identified by the rid at the offset specified by the HI-TP header.

4.1   A Simplified Header

A simplified header, which is more targeted to current network infrastructures, could be considered as an alternative. For such a simplified header definition, we apply the following basic assumptions: (1) 64 KB is sufficiently large as a single packet size, (2) a peer will never have to handle more than 65536 incoming memory buffers at a time, and (3) a single dataset is limited to 256 TB. Under these assumptions our HI-TP header would look as in table 2. This simplified header definition incorporates two new field definitions: **m block**, minor block, and **M block**, major block. Not very different from offset they allows one to address blocks of 64 KB and 4 GB respectively.

With this simplified definition, the implementation performance is expected to increase significantly due to the fixed header size, and (thus) a reduced complexity of packet analysis. Still it is important to note that, even though a 256 TB addressing space is not perceived as a limit today, this may (and probably will) change in the future. Hereinafter we will refer to this simplified version as HI-TP.

5. Performance Evaluation

The following presents the results obtained with our new protocol using a basic sender-receiver scenario.

We have performed our measurements on a testbed system comprising of three standard desktop PCs running Debian GNU/Linux "etch". The first machine, i.e. the 'sender', is a DELL Dimension 4400 with a Pentium 4 1.7 Mhz processor and 512 MB of RAM. The second machine, i.e. the 'receiver', is a DELL Dimension 4500 with a Pentium 4 2.4 Mhz processor and 512 MB of RAM. The traffic between these two hosts, or 'peers', is entirely routed through the third machine, hereafter referred to as the 'gateway/router'. In the initial stages of our measurements the gateway/router machine was a DELL Dimension L667. Due to an unfortunate malfunction of this particular machine, it has been replaced by a DELL PowerEdge 600SC. Importantly, the replacement of the gateway/router machine had no measurable effect on performance. We have performed measurements using several Fast Ethernet network cards, without noticing significant differences in the performance behavior of our testbed.

The gateway/router machine is of essential importance in our testbed system, as it is used to introduce controlled packet loss, latency, and packet reordering in a transparent way. These variations in network and transmission behavior have been incorporated using the 'netem' network emulation suite, which consist of a kernel component, and an user space extension to iproute2. Hence, all applied software components are either open source, or developed by ourselves.

5.1 Theoretical Scenarios vs. Real-world Scenarios

As it is quite difficult, if not impossible, to realistically compare protocols acting on different layers, it is important to realize that — for our purposes — it is sufficient to simply transfer a static buffer and to see under which protocol the highest throughput is obtained. For this reason, we generated our own static buffer, consisting of the first 100 Mbytes of the Linux kernel 2.6.18 tar archive. This buffer has been transmitted under varying circumstances to analyze the behavior of our system in comparison with other protocols.

In our evaluation we have followed two alternative approaches. In the first approach we have studied the behavior of our protocol under variations in emulated network latency (ranging from no additional emulated latency up to 110 ms of emulated latency), and variations in packet loss (in the range of 0-2%).

In the second approach we have tried to create a real-world scenario with all sorts of 'network perturbations' occurring concurrently: i.e., variable latency and packet loss. We have decided to ignore issues such as packet duplication and packet corruption. Even though these issues are essential for testing a protocol, if no bugs are present in the protocol implementation, packet duplication has no significant effect on performance. Similarly, packet corruption has the same effect as packet loss, and thus can be ignored safely.

5.2   Measurements

In our first measurement (see Figure 1), we compare HI-TP, TCP and UDP under variations in emulated latency, but without any emulated packet loss or emulated packet reordering. Essentially, we should also add a small value representing real network latency.

In Figure 1 we can immediately see that TCP throughput is significantly and negatively influenced by increased latency, which is a well-known property of TCP. UDP, in contrast, performs much better under increased latency. If latency becomes significantly large, however, UDP also suffers from a significant decrease in throughput. In the graph it is clear that throughput obtained with our newly defined HI-TP protocol hardly suffers from variations in latency at all.

In our second measurement (see Figure 2) we compare the throughput performance of HI-TP, UDT, NFS, TCP Sendfile, and TCP Sendfile on top of Airhook using a link without latency (or less than 1 ms, as stated above), and no packet reordering, under variations in packet loss ranging from 0% to 2%. As can be seen in Figure 2, in this emulated scenario HI-TP again performs better than all other protocols. However, we can also observe that HI-TP is affected by packet loss in the same relative amount as all other protocols, with the exception of TCP Sendfile on top of Airhook. At this time of writing the exact reasons for this behavior of Airhook are unknown. This will be investigated further in the near future.

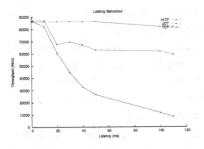 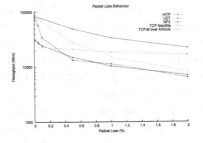

Figure 1.   Theory: Throughput under latency varying from 0ms to 115ms

Figure 2.   Theory: Throughput under packet loss varying from 0% to 2%

In our third evaluation we reconstruct a real world scenario, as can be expected on a link between Amsterdam and Paris. On such a link, the latency for http traffic is around 29 ms, with a variation of +/- 1 ms. As a consequence, packet reordering is a realistic and common phenomenon. Hence, for real-world scenarios we must evaluate how the different protocols react to packet reordering as well. Figure 3 shows that UDT seems to perform better under at least a certain amount of packet loss (i.e., around 0.5%). This is because an increased packet loss results in an increased number of acknowledge messages, and hence and increased sensitivity to packet reordering. Figure 3 also clearly shows that HI-TP is not at all influenced by packet reordering. Essentially, this is because the HI-TP buffer in the receiver is addressed directly from the packet.

In our final measurements (see Figure 4) we compare the absolute time for a file transfer as obtained in user space for UDT, scp, and HI-TP. In this measurement 25% of the packets (with a correlation of 50%) will be sent immediately, while all others will be delayed by 10 ms. Also, the scp measurements have been performed without any latency or packet reordering introduced, just to use the optimal scp case as a reference, for a real user-perspective comparison. In Figure 4 we can again observe that HI-TP performs best, and that it is not at all affected by packet reordering. More importantly, end-users are not at all bothered by any such troubles on the underlying network.

Based on all our measurements we conclude that HI-TP is only marginally influenced by increased network latency, and not at all affected by packet reordering. HI-TP is still vulnerable to packet loss, but this is a condition which is rather unusual in high-speed optical Grid network links.

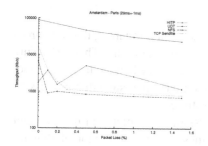

Figure 3. Real world: a file transferred from Amsterdam to Paris

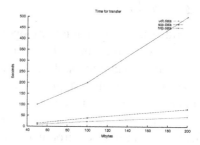

Figure 4. Time for transferring a file: scp in a LAN environment against HI-TP and UDT under packet reordering conditions

6. Future work

The HI-TP protocol initially is intended to be applied in a set of tools that allows straightforward development of high-performance distributed multimedia applications, which are to be executed on a very large scale. To this end, the Vrije Universiteit is developing a set of advanced Grid programming tools, each of which will be described briefly in the following. This section concludes with a brief description of a set of target applications.

6.1   Java-GAT

Today, Grid programmers generally implement their applications against a Grid middleware API that abstracts away part of the complexities of the underlying hardware. This is a daunting task, because Grid APIs change frequently, are generally low-level, unstable, and incomplete [6]. The Java Grid Application Toolkit (JavaGAT [16]), developed at the Vrije Universiteit, solves the above problems in an integrated manner. JavaGAT offers high-level primitives for access to the Grid, independent of the Grid middleware that implements this functionality. JavaGAT integrates multiple middleware systems into a single coherent system. It dynamically forwards calls on the JavaGAT API to one or more middlewares that implement the requested functionality. If a Grid operation fails, it will automatically dispatch the API call to an alternative Grid middleware. Using JavaGAT, Grid applications can, among other functionality, transparently access remote data and spawn off jobs within Grid installations. JavaGAT further provides support for monitoring, steering, resource brokering, and storing of application-specific data. The importance of JavaGAT is illustrated by the fact that, based on these efforts, the Open Grid Forum is now standardizing the next generation Grid programming toolkit: the Simple API for Grid Applications (SAGA).

JavaGAT is freely available at: https://gforge.cs.vu.nl/projects/javagat/.

6.2   Ibis

Grid systems, by nature, are open world and faulty, meaning that resources can be added and removed at will, and crash at any moment. Thus, to ensure robust Grid execution, application programmers must be handed the basic functionality to allow their applications to be made malleable, such that processors can be added and removed at application run-time.

Ibis [17], developed at the Vrije Universiteit, is a platform-independent Grid programming environment that combines flexible treatment of dynamically available resources with highly efficient object-based communication. Given his results it follows that Ibis provides a stable, efficient, and platform-independent communication layer that supports the open, dynamic, and faulty nature of real-world Grid systems.

Ibis is freely available at: http://www.cs.vu.nl/ibis/.

6.3   Parallel-Horus

Whereas JavaGAT and Ibis provide the basic functionality to allow supercomputing applications to execute efficiently and transparently in a Grid system, it is still up to the programmer to identify the available parallelism in a problem at hand. For the application programmer — generally a domain-expert with limited or no expertise in the field of supercomputing — this is often an insurmountable problem. Clearly, there is a need for programming models that either alleviate the burden somewhat or, preferably, shield the user from all intrinsic complexities of parallelization.

Parallel-Horus [11, 10, 12] is a cluster programming library that allows its users to implement parallel multimedia applications as fully sequential programs, using a carefully designed set of building block operations. These algorithmic patterns of parallel execution cover the bulk of all commonly applied multimedia functionality, while hiding all complexities of parallelization behind a familiar sequential API (identical to that of an existing sequential multimedia computing library: Horus [5]). Notably, Parallel-Horus was applied in recent international benchmark evaluations for content-based video retrieval, and played a crucial role in achieving top-ranking results [13–14]. A proof-of-concept implementation of Parallel-Horus is freely available at http://www.science.uva.nl/~fjseins/ParHorusCode/.

6.4 Integration of Tools

The Parallel-Horus programming model is being extended for use in Grid systems [10]. To this end, an innovative runtime system (RTS) is being developed, based on the notion of a SuperServer — i.e., a lightweight server implementation that allows for uploading of data as well as program codes (i.e., transferring Java byte codes by way of dynamic class loading over the network). With JavaGAT's transparent job submission functionality, the RTS starts a pool of SuperServers on behalf of a coordinating (client) application, hidden from the user. The pool of SuperServers is then applied by the RTS on behalf of the client application on a need-be basis, by uploading objects (data) and related program codes. Importantly, in this way — and in contrast to the common use of (web) services in Grid computing — it is the application programmer who implements the actual program code executed by a SuperServer. In case the uploaded code represents a (sequential) sequence of Parallel-Horus calls, the SuperServer, when running on a cluster, executes these calls transparently in data parallel fashion. By transparently outsourcing the running of Parallel-Horus code to multiple SuperServers in a fully asynchronous manner, we arrive at a 'wall-socket' computing solution: *transparent task parallel execution of data parallel services.*

6.5 Target Applications

The research group at the Vrije Universiteit closely collaborates with the University of Amsterdam on urgent MMCA problems, classified in two groups: real-time analysis and off-line categorization. Realistic examples from both groups include (1) the comparison of objects and individuals in video streams obtained from surveillance cameras, as researched in close cooperation with the Dutch Forensic Institute (NFI), (2) iris-scan based identification and automatic fingerprint checks (e.g. to be performed at international airports), also with the NFI, (3) the international NIST TRECVID evaluation [14], i.e. the yearly bench-mark evaluation for approaches to finding semantic concepts in archives of TV news broadcasts from (a.o.) ABC and CNN, (4) interactive access to Petabytes of current and historic TV broadcasts, as researched in close collaboration with the Dutch Institute for Sound and Vision (Beeld&Geluid). These examples represent urgent MMCA problems that will serve as targets in our future research.

7.   Conclusions

In this paper we have presented and validated a new transport protocol (HI-TP) conceived for active network caching, initially intended for coordinated data management in large scale distributed multimedia computing applications. To this end we have presented the rationale of logistical networking and active network caching, and indicated the need for a new data transmission protocol. In our overview of state-of-the-art transport protocols we have indicated problems and drawbacks with respect to our purposes, mostly from an end-user application and integration perspective. We have presented the new protocol, referred to as HI-TP, or High-volume INCA Transport Protocol, focusing on its ability of addressing, potentially, unlimited buffers in a simple manner. We have performed an initial set of measurements using our new protocol on a simple testbed environment, and compared our results with those obtained with other protocols. Our main conclusions are that HI-TP performs better than existing protocols, under many realistic variations in transmission and network behavior. Most importantly, HI-TP is only marginally influenced by increased network latency, and not at all affected by packet reordering. HI-TP is still vulnerable to packet loss, but this is a condition which is rather unusual in high-speed optical Grid network links. Finally, we have given a brief overview of the set of tools in which our newly developed transport protocol will be integrated in the near future.

Acknowledgments

This research is carried out under the FP6 *CoreGRID* Network of Excellence funded by the European Commission (Contract IST-2002-004265). This paper's first author is supported via CoreGRID's Industrial Fellowship Programme under grant no. CIFP-4/06.

References

[1] G. Allen, K. Davis, T. Goodale, A. Hutanu, H. Kaiser, T. Kielmann, A. Merzky, R. van Nieuwpoort, A. Reinefeld, F. Schintke, T. Schütt, E. Seidel, and B. Ullmer. The Grid Application Toolkit: Towards Generic and Easy Application Programming Interfaces for the Grid. *Proceedings of the IEEE*, 93(3):534–550, 2005.

[2] A. Bassi, S. Denazis, and P. Giacomin. Towards a Noah's Ark for the Upcoming Data Deluge. In *3rd VLDB Workshop on Data Management in Grids*, Sept. 2007.

[3] D. Egnor. Airhook: Reliable, Efficient Transmission Control for Networks that Suck.

[4] Y. Gu and R. Grossman. UDT: UDP-based Data Transfer for High-Speed Wide Area Networks. *Computer Networks*, 51(7):1777–1799, May 2007.

[5] D. Koelma et al. Horus C++ Reference, Version 1.1. Technical report, ISIS, Faculty of Science, University of Amsterdam, The Netherlands, Jan. 2002.

[6] R. Medeiros, W. Cirne, F. Brasileiro, and J. Sauvé. Faults in Grids: Why are they so bad and What can be done about it? In *Proceedings of the Fourth International Workshop on Grid Computing*, 2003.

[7] J. Plank, A. Bassi, M. Beck, T. Moore, M. Swany, and R. Wolski. Managing Data Storage in the Network. *IEEE Internet Computing*, 6(5):50–58, Sept. 2001.

[8] J. Postel. User Datagram Protocol, Aug. 1980. Internet standard RFC 768.

[9] J. Postel. Transmission Control Protocol, Sept. 1981. Internet standard RFC 793.

[10] F. Seinstra, J. Geusebroek, D. Koelma, C. Snoek, M. Worring, and A. Smeulders. High-Performance Distributed Video Content Analysis with Parallel-Horus. *IEEE Multimedia*, 15(4):64–75, Oct. 2007.

[11] F. Seinstra, D. Koelma, and A. Bagdanov. Finite State Machine-Based Optimization of Data Parallel Regular Domain Problems Applied in Low-Level Image Processing. *IEEE Transactions on Parallel and Distributed Systems*, 15(10):865–877, Oct. 2004.

[12] F. Seinstra, C. Snoek, D. Koelma, J. Geusebroek, and M. Worring. User Transparent Parallel Processing of the 2004 NIST TRECVID Data Set. In *Proceedings of the International Parallel & Distributed Processing Symposium (IPDPS 2005)*, Denver, Colorado, USA, Apr. 2005.

[13] C. Snoek, M. Worring, J. Geusebroek, D. Koelma, F. Seinstra, and A. Smeulders. The MediaMill TRECVID 2005 Semantic Video Search Engine. In *Proceedings of the 3rd TRECVID Workshop*, Gathersburg, USA, Nov. 2005.

[14] C. Snoek, M. Worring, J. Geusebroek, D. Koelma, F. Seinstra, and A. Smeulders. The Semantic Pathfinder: Using an Authoring Metaphor for Generic Multimedia Indexing. *IEEE Transactions on Pattern Analysis and Machine Intelligence*, 28(10):1678–1689, 2006.

[15] Stichting MultimediaN. *MultimediaN, Project proposal Bsik*, Feb. 2003. http://www.multimedian.nl/.

[16] R. van Nieuwpoort, T. Kielmann, and H. Bal. User-friendly and Reliable Grid Computing Based on Imperfect Middleware. In *Proceedings of SC'07*, Nov. 2007.

[17] R. van Nieuwpoort, J. Maassen, G. Wrzesinska, R. Hofman, C. Jacobs, T. Kielmann, and H. Bal. Ibis: a Flexible and Efficient Java-based Grid Programming Environment. *Concurrency and Computation: Practice and Experience*, 17(7–8):1079–1107, 2005.

TOWARDS A STANDARDS-BASED GRID SCHEDULING ARCHITECTURE

Christian Grimme, Joachim Lepping, Alexander Papaspyrou, Philipp Wieder, and Ramin Yahyapour
Dortmund University of Technology, IRF & ITMC
44221 Dortmund, Germany
{christian.grimme, joachim.lepping, alexander.papaspyrou, philipp.wieder, ramin.yahyapour}@udo.edu

Ariel Oleksiak
Poznan Supercomputing and Networking Center
Noskowskiego 10 61-704, Poznan, Poland
ariel@man.poznan.pl

Oliver Wäldrich and Wolfgang Ziegler
Fraunhofer SCAI, Department of Bioinformatics,
53754 Sankt Augustin, Germany
{oliver.waeldrich, wolfgang.ziegler}@scai.fraunhofer.de

Abstract   The definition of a generic Grid scheduling architecture is the concern of both the Open Grid Forum's Grid Scheduling Architecture Research Group and a CoreGRID research group of the same name. Such an architecture should provide a blueprint for Grid system and middleware designers and assist them in linking their scheduling requirements to diverse existing solutions and standards. Based on work executed within the Open Grid Forum related to scheduling use cases and requirements, which tackles the problem from a more theoretical point of view, we approach in this paper the problem practically by evaluating the teikoku Grid Scheduling Framework in the light of standards-compliance. The results of this evaluation and the existing Grid Scheduling Architecture proposal are set into context, existing gaps are described and potential solutions to bridge them are introduced. In doing so, we concentrate on the interoperability of schedulers and the necessity of a Scheduling Description Language to achieve it.

Keywords: Grid Scheduling Architecture, Grid Standards, Interoperability, Open Grid Forum, Scheduling Description Language

1.   Motivation

The overall goal of our work is the provision of a generic Grid scheduling architecture. This work is primarily conducted by the *Grid Scheduling Architecture Research Group* (GSA-RG[1]) of the Open Grid Forum (OGF) and a research group of the same name placed within CoreGRID's Institute on Scheduling and Resource Management[2]. The primary objectives defining the architecture are the following three:

Standards-compliance. The Grid scheduling architecture should, wherever possible, be based on languages, protocols, and specifications which are standards-compliant.

Interoperability. Implementations following the Grid scheduling architecture blueprint should be interoperable.

Universality. A realisation of the Grid scheduling architecture should be possible without following a specific design paradigm or using a certain technology.

We approach the problem space from two viewpoints, a generic (and more theoretical) one defining generic use cases and requirements, and from a practical one evaluating a standards-based Grid scheduler (cf. Section 2). As the former has already been described in a number of publications, we concentrate here on the latter by outlining the features, design, and architecture of the *teikoku Grid Scheduling Framework* (TGSF; cf. Section 3). Based on this framework and the research as well as production requirements set, we outline the gaps in the current standards landscape, reflect upon interoperability of Grid schedulers, and sketch the efforts necessary towards a standards-compliant, interoperable, and universal Grid scheduling architecture definition (cf. Section 4). In a concluding section we describe the efforts already under way and the steps to be taken in the near future.

Please note that we use the term "standards" in a broad sense throughout this paper. We do not merely refer to fully specified, tested, and certified standards, but also to specifications which are under development and are likely to become standards some time in the future.

2.   Problem Space

The scheduling and allocation of tasks, jobs, or workflows on a set of heterogeneous resources in a dynamically changing environment is a

---

[1]https://forge.gridforum.org/sf/projects/gsa-rg
[2]http://www.coregrid.net/mambo/content/blogcategory/16/295

complex problem. There are still no common Grid scheduling strategies available which solve this problem and implementations of scheduling systems still require specific architectures customised for the target computing platform and the application scenarios. Moreover, the complexity of applications, variety of user requirements, and system heterogeneity do not permit the efficient manual performance of any scheduling procedure.

Although no common and generic Grid scheduler yet exists, several common aspects can be found examining existing Grid scheduling uses cases [12] and Grid schedulers [11]. This leads to the assumption that a generic architecture may be conceivable not only to simplify the implementation of different schedulers but also to provide an infrastructure that enables interoperability between those different systems.

Furthermore, a number of standards that are useful in a Grid scheduling context are already specified and are also implemented in a number of Grid middlewares and services. Such standards are – ideally – being developed by consortia comprising representatives from academia and industry. Regarding Grids, the respective consortium is the Open Grid Forum[3]. It has produced a number of scheduling-related standards, which we briefly introduce here:

The *OGSA High Performance Computing Profile* (OGSA-HPCP) narrows two other specifications in order to provide a common submission interface for HPC jobs to HPC resources. It comprises a subset of the *Job Submission Description Language* [2] (JSDL), an XML dialect for the description of job requirements and specifications, and the *OGSA Basic Execution Service* [9] (OGSA-BES), a Web Service definition for supplying arbitrary activities to generalized resources.

The *Web Services Agreements* specification [1] (WS-Agreement) defines a language and a protocol to represent services through Service Level Agreement (SLA) templates, create agreements based on offers and and monitor agreement compliance during service execution.

The OGSA Resource Usage Service (OGSA-RUS)[4] and the OGSA Usage Records (OGSA-UR)[5] provide means to store resource usage and accounting information respectively.

The *Distributed Resource Management Application API* [3] (DRMAA) specification provides high-level functional interfaces for the submission and control of jobs to Distributed Resource Management (DRM) sys-

---

[3]http://www.ogf.org
[4]http://forge.ogf.org/sf/projects/rus-wg/
[5]http://forge.ogf.org/sf/projects/ur-wg/

tems. It is integrated in a number of academic and commercial Grid systems.

The *OGSA Resource Selection Services* (OGSA-RSS)[6] defines protocols and interfaces for the Candidate Set Generator (CSG) and the Execution Planning System (EPS). The CSG generate a set of (computational) resources that could potentially execute a job, while the EPS actually makes the decision.

Since we have already gained good understanding of common requirements regarding a Grid Scheduling Architecture, we decided within CoreGRID to tackle the problem also from a practical perspective in order to adjust our theoretical findings. Our candidate Grid scheduler, which is described in detail in the following section, has been designed and implemented with standards-compliance in mind. It is evaluated in the light of our architectural objectives (see Section 1) and the findings are related to the general Grid scheduling requirements.

3.   A Standards-based Grid Scheduler

Although Grid scheduling has become an important topic in various businesses and many commercial Enterprise Grid solutions[7] are available at the market, the development of advanced scheduling strategies and algorithms is mainly a matter of scientific research. However, the transferability of the gained results into production environments is problematic at best, since model assumptions are usually not in line with the conditions in enterprise scenarios.

The teikoku Grid Scheduling Framework tries to bridge the gap between research and production systems, the requirements of which differ significantly: *Research Requirements* include the availability of an extensible toolbox that supports the development and analysis of different models, algorithms, and strategies [8], [7]. Also, there is a strong need for high-performance simulation capabilities and efficient evaluation tools. *Production Requirements*, however, comprise support for easy deployment and configuration, and scalability in large Grid communities [6]. Furthermore, in order to enable interoperation with other existing systems, compliance with open standards is needed.

Following, we depict the features and design of TGSF as a basis for reviewing requirements and best practices of real-world scheduling solutions. In this context, we highlight coverage and desiderata of current

---

[6]https://forge.gridforum.org/sf/projects/ogsa-rss-wg
[7]Such as LSF (http://www.platform.com).

standards and protocols regarding various requirements and features in such implementations.

3.1   Features & Design

As depicted in Figure 1, the architecture of TGSF is divided into four layers, namely the Foundation Layer, the Commons Layer, the Site Layer, and the Grid Layer. Note that, although the usage of Foundation and Commons are mandatory and highly recommended, respectively, the different layers are loosely coupled and the inclusion of Site and Grid into a system instance is mutually optional.

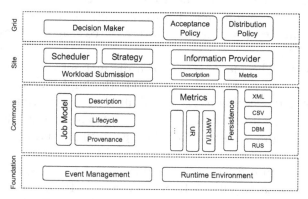

Figure 1.   Architectural view of the Teikoku Scheduling Framework

Here the different layers with their features and integration points into common standards are described.

Foundation Layer. The basis for TGSF is an event-driven *kernel* responsible for time management and event dispatching. This kernel component uses an internal clock to isolate higher layers from the real-time clock and provide a common abstraction for time instants and periods. Furthermore, it provides an extensible type system which allows the handling of domain-tailored events.

The behaviour of TGSF, however, does not depend on the kernel itself: in fact, it is determined by the *Runtime Environment*, which – depending on the implementation – allows the realisation of real-time as well as simulation or debugging systems.

Commons Layer. To provide general abstractions for management-related concepts, a *Job Model*, *Metrics*, and *Persistence* services are supplied in this layer.

The job model uses a holistic view on units of work within a Grid environment: it consists of a description of static job characteristics and resource requirements, a life-cycle which represents current and historic states of the job, and a provenance that denotes the track or route a job has taken from its original submission until final assignment and execution. In this context, JSDL can be used to at least tackle the specification of static properties and resource constraints for a job.

The metrics services provide a unified interface to the measurement data during runtime: values regarding different aspects can be stored and retrieved, e.g. for supporting advanced decision strategies. Such metrics may include traditional performance objectives such as response time and utilisation as well as accounting information such as OGSA-UR.

The persistence services offer a common access to different storage mechanisms for recording and replaying metrics values, e.g. files and relational databases as well as standard resource usage services as defined by OGSA-RUS.

Site Layer. The management of a distinct set of resources is conducted by the Site Layer, which abstracts the implementation of scheduler functionality, see Figure 2. In addition to appropriate data structures for keeping information on the current schedule, it allows the application of assignment strategies during runtime, and offers a Service Provider Interface (SPI) towards traditional local resource management systems. These interfaces might conform to the wide-spread DRMAA standard, but also to OGSA-BES, OGSA-HPCP, or more traditional protocols such as Globus WS-GRAM [5] or the POSIX batch management family of commands [10].

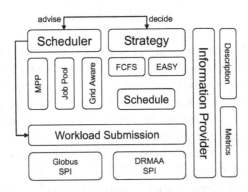

Figure 2.   ᴛGSF's Site Layer

Although the strategies calculate the assignment of work to resources, their results have advisory character: they propose their solutions to the scheduler which in turn decides on the actions to take. This allows the scheduler to consult multiple strategies at a time and select the most appropriate solution.

The information provider bundles static as well as dynamic site information such as number of resources, current utilisation etc. and exposes this data to the other Site Layer components and – at least partly – to the global environment.

Grid Layer. In order to enable an interaction component for the distribution of workload to other participating sites within a Grid environment, the Grid Layer provides facilities for the policy-based exchange of jobs.

Depending on the Grid environment's scheduler topology, the *Decision Maker* component has different responsibilities. In centralised or hierarchical environments, it's main task is the acceptance of jobs and their assignment to underlying resources or subordinate brokers. In decentralised scenarios, the redistribution to other decision makers is conducted additionally; the decision on the modalities is based on a set of policies regarding acceptance and distribution of jobs. A basic standard to be used in this context is the WS-Agreement specification.

4. Bridging the Gap – The Grid Scheduling Architecture

The previous section gave some architectural details of the TGSF and pointed out several interfaces between services and layers where standardised protocols can be used to ensure a flexible and customisable application of the framework.

Although there are already a couple of possible solutions for workload submission, job description, metrics and persistence, for several important interfaces in the grid scheduling context either no or not adequate standards exist, yet. One goal of this section is to highlight these gaps and to define requirements for possible solutions (cf. Sub-section 4.1).

Furthermore, this section outlines the efforts necessary to bridge the gaps (cf. Sub-section 4.2) and links them with existing standards to provide a Grid scheduling framework to test the interoperability of Grid schedulers (cf. Sub-section 4.3). This interoperability test together with the theoretical work described in this paper provide the foundations to define the Grid scheduling architecture. A side-effect of our work is that we evaluate the relations of the different OGF specifications and groups in the scheduling domain, point out where things are missing, and help to sketch a broad picture.

4.1 Existing Gaps

4.1.1 Job Model. The description of a job is mainly covered by JSDL: many aspects such as resource requirements, execution parameters, and input/output data definitions are defined therein and its extension mechanism allows proprietary enhancements. However, JSDL does not support the description of user-specified and scheduling-related constraints such as requested start times, due dates and deadlines, or runtime estimations.

The tracking of a job's life-cycle is also currently not properly standardised. Although OGSA-BES defines a very basic state model, it does not relate to intermediate states during the process of scheduling a job. Furthermore, no common interface to access the entire life-cycle of a job exists; one can only retrieve its current state.

The same holds for storing and retrieving provenance data of a job. Especially in distributed architectures this information is essential not only to the user, but also highly beneficial for supporting the decision process of scheduling strategies.

4.1.2   Algorithm & Policy Model.   Since the design of advanced scheduling strategies is a complicated task which is mostly conducted in research, an easy integration of developed results into available Grid scheduling products would be highly desirable.

To this end, a standardised interface for pluggable decision strategies is needed to enable the simple deployment of newly created algorithms into production systems. Besides that, such an approach would support an integrated development life-cycle for such algorithms, since both test/simulation environments as well as real-world systems would behave in a similar way. A possible first step towards such an interface could be the aforementioned advisory characterisation of strategies, where the scheduler requests possible solutions to reach an adequate decision.

The same problem applies for acceptance and distribution policies on the Grid interaction level.

4.2   Bridging the Gaps

From the architectural point of view, which is the focus of our work and hence this paper, solutions to overcome the issues related to the Job Model are those of interest since they prevent us from realising a Grid scheduling architecture with the characteristics given in the first section. The Algorithm & Policy Model related shortcomings outlined above need solutions, too, but those are currently not in the focus of our work as they are related to scheduler-internal architecture which we treat as a black box in the light of a general Grid scheduling architecture.

JSDL's extension mechanism has a negative and a positive effect. Negative is the fact that it can (and is) used to extend JSDL to realise proprietary enhancements which run counter to the idea of interoperability. Advantageous, however, is the extension mechanism to specify all the missing scheduling-related constraints.

To restrict the usage of JSDL to a limited number of attributes we decided to define a *JSDL Profile*, like it is e.g done by the OGSA-HPC group, to achieve an "a priori" agreement between interoperable schedulers. This profile defines in detail the supported JSDL attributes and how they are to be interpreted. Regarding the scheduling-related attributes which are not included in JSDL, we introduce the *Scheduling Description Language* (SDL). The goal is to provide a basic set of scheduling attributes that must be handled by Grid schedulers. Candidate attribute categories are time constraints, job dependencies, job priorities, scheduling objectives/preferences, data-dependent scheduling information, and queue-based scheduling information. These attributes may be referenced in SLAs negotiated between Grid schedulers, used for scheduling decisions, or exploited to execute a job by a local resource management system.

Regarding the life-cycle of a job, there is the OGSA-BES extension mechanism to its state model which allows the definition of domain-specific sub-states. But as far as the access to the life-cycle of a job and and its provenance data is concerned, only initial effort has been taken by the JSDL group.

4.3   Scheduler Interoperability

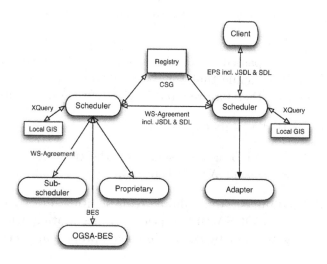

Figure 3.   Interoperability of Grid Schedulers using OGF standards

The interoperability test of Grid schedulers is another major step towards a Grid scheduling architecture. The purpose of this test is to show that Grid schedulers that are compliant to the standards-based Grid scheduling architecture we propose, are able to delegate scheduling requests to other schedulers. For this purpose, we investigated, in addition to TGSF, two other schedulers, namely the VIOLA MetaScheduling Service (MSS) [4] and the Grid Resource Management System (GRMS)[8]. With the help of the systems' developers, who will adapt their systems once the Grid scheduling architecture is fully specified, we gathered the requirements of the three schedulers regarding the minimal set of JSDL parameters and the SDL. In combination with the Grid scheduling uses cases and requirements, the findings from the evaluation of the schedulers are the foundation for the integration of the JSDL Profile and the SDL with existing standards towards a Grid scheduling architecture.

The interoperability scenario we consider captures a common case: a scheduler is unable to fulfil a scheduling request. In existing Grid environments this often implies that the requesting user or service is informed that the request cannot be fulfilled. In case of interoperable schedulers, however, the scheduler, which is unable to fulfil a scheduling request, delegates it to another scheduler. In the context of OGF standards and based on the afore mentioned investigations and documents, we define the following interactions to reach agreement on the delegation of a scheduling decision are required (see Figure 3):

- Scheduler A, which realises an OGSA-RSS Execution Planning Service (EPS), cannot fulfil a scheduler request. The JSDL Profile-compliant job together with the SDL attributes is part of this request.

- The request is passed to Scheduler B, using WS-Agreement (please note that we assume that this request crosses administrative domains and we therefore rely on Service Level Agreements).

- Scheduler B checks its capabilities.

- Scheduler A and B agree/disagree on the conditions to fulfil the request (again using WS-Agreement).

- Scheduler B fulfils the scheduling request either directly by passing the job to an OGSA-BES service, by negotiating with another (local) scheduler, or by contacting some proprietary service.

[8]http://www.gridge.org/content/view/18/99

Calls to a registry, which has OGSA-RSS' Candidate Set Generator capabilities, to check schedulers' capabilities and queries to local Grid Information Services (GIS) are also part of the information flow of the interoperability test.

Please note that one could define ways different from the one outlined above to delegate scheduling requests, e.g. without negotiating an Service Level Agreement at all, but within the OGF landscape and with the requirements derived from the different scheduling systems, the proposed set of interactions guarantees reliable scheduling services.

Once the participating schedulers have implemented the interoperability interfaces and protocols and the test has been conducted, the GSA-RG will be able to finally define a Grid scheduling architecture in an standards-compliant landscape.

5. Status Quo & Outlook

The JSDL Profile and the SDL, which have been introduced in the previous section as potential instruments to fill the most important gaps en route to defining a standards-compliant, interoperable, and generic Grid scheduling architecture, exist as draft specifications. The GSA-RG is currently working on the finalisation of these documents together with other groups at the Open Grid Forum. This work is executed under the umbrella of an scheduler interoperability test where CoreGRID partners plan to implement the interoperability architecture sketched in Figure 3. In this test currently participate the Viola MetaScheduling Service[9] and the Grid Resource Management System[10], but other CoreGRID partners have already expressed their interest. The evaluation of this test together with the findings from the theoretical evaluations will finally result in the definition of a standards-compliant, interoperable, and generic Grid scheduling architecture.

Acknowledgments

This paper includes work carried out jointly within the CoreGRID Network of Excellence funded by the European Commission's IST programme under grant #004265.

References

[1] A. Andrieux, K. Czajkowski, A. Dan, K. Keahey, H. Ludwig, T. Nakata, J. Pruyne, J. Rofrano, S. Tuecke, and M. Xu. WS-Agreement - Web Services

---

[9]http://www.viola-testbed.de
[10]http://www.gridge.org

Agreement Specification. Grid Forum Document, GFD.107, Open Grid Forum, May, 2007.

[2] A. Anjomshoaa, F. Brisard, M. Drescher, D. Fellows, A. Ly, S. McGough, D. Pulsipher, and A. Savva. Job Submission Description Language (JSDL) Specification, Version 1.0. Grid Forum Document, GFD.56, Open Grid Forum, November, 2005.

[3] R. Brobst, W. Chan, F. Ferstl, J. Gardiner, A. Haas, B. Nitzberg, H. Rajic, D. Templeton, J. Tollefsrud, and P. Träger. Distributed Resource Management Application API Specification 1.0. Recommendation GFD.22, Open Grid Forum, Lemont (IL), USA, April 2004.

[4] Th. Eickermann, W. Frings, O. Wäldrich, Ph. Wieder, and W. Ziegler. Co-allocation of mpi jobs with the viola grid metascheduling framework. In *Proceedings of the German e-Science Conference 2007*, Baden-Baden, May 2007. Max Planck eDoc Server, Max Planck Digital Library.

[5] I. Foster and C. Kesselman. Globus: A Toolkit-Based Grid Architecture. In *The Grid: Blueprint for a Future Computing Infrastructure*, pages 259–278. Morgan Kaufman, San Mateo (CA), 1st edition, 1998.

[6] Ch. Grimme, T. Langhammer, A. Papaspyrou, and F. Schintke. Negotiation-based Choreography of Data-intensive Applications in the C3Grid Project. In *Proceedings of the German e-Science Conference (GES)*, Baden-Baden, Germany, May 2007. Max-Planck Society (online).

[7] Ch. Grimme, J. Lepping, and A. Papaspyrou. Identifying Job Migration Characteristics in Decentralized Grid Scheduling Scenarios. In *Proceedings of the 19th International Conference on Parallel and Distributed Computing and Systems (PDCS)*, Cambridge (MA), USA, November 2007. IASTED, ACTA Press. To appear.

[8] Ch. Grimme, J. Lepping, and A. Papaspyrou. Prospects of Collaboration between Compute Providers by Means of Job Interchange. In E. Frachtenberg and U. Schwiegelshohn, editors, *Proceedings of the 13th Workshop on Job Scheduling Strategies for Parallel Processing (JSSPP)*, Lecture Notes on Computer Science (LNCS), Seattle (WA), USA, June 2007. Springer. To appear.

[9] A. Grimshaw, S. Newhouse, et al. OGSA Basic Execution Service Version 1.0. online [http://forge.gridforum.org/projects/ogsa-bes-wg], December 2006.

[10] IEEE Computer Society Portable Applications Standards Committee. Portable Operating System Interface (POSIX). Shell and utilities. In *Standard for Information Technology*, volume 6 of *The Open Group Base Specifications*. IEEE Press, 2004.

[11] N. Tonellotto, Ph. Wieder, and R. Yahyapour. A Proposal for a Generic Grid Scheduling Architecture. In S. Gorlatch and M. Danelutto, editors, *Proceedings of the Integrated Research in Grid Computing Workshop 2005*, CoreGRID Series, pages 227–239. Springer, 2007.

[12] R. Yahyapour and Ph. Wieder. Grid scheduling use cases. Grid Forum Document, GFD.64, Global Grid Forum, March, 2006.

DYNAMIC SERVICE-BASED INTEGRATION OF MOBILE CLUSTERS IN GRIDS *

Stavros Isaiadis and Vladimir Getov
Harrow School of Computer Science
University of Westminster, London, UK
S.Isaiadis@wmin.ac.uk, V.S.Getov@wmin.ac.uk

Ian Kelley and Ian Taylor
School of Computer Science
Cardiff University, Cardiff, UK
I.R.Kelley@cs.cardiff.ac.uk, Ian.J.Taylor@cs.cardiff.ac.uk

Abstract   The emergence of pervasive and mobile computing has drawn research attention
to integrated mobile Grid systems. These new hybrid Grids consist of a typical SOA backbone extended to include mobile and small scale devices such as
personal digital assistants, smart-phones, multimedia devices, and intelligent sensors. In a fully integrated model, mobile devices are able to act both as consumers
and providers to open up a completely new range of very interesting possibilities
in exploiting their mobile nature, unique functionality, and context awareness.
However, in resource-limited environments, traditional SOA frameworks cannot
easily be deployed since they assume a plethora of available device resources,
and have a number of complex dependencies, thus rendering them unsuitable for
resource-constrained devices. Therefore, a smaller and simpler server-side container with reduced requirements and dependencies is needed. The contribution
of this paper is two-fold: first, we have designed a J2ME-compliant socket-
based server-side container, and second, we have demonstrated how an aggregator framework enables such mobile services to be accessed using standard-based
Web services in a high-level manner.

Keywords: Hybrid Grid, Service aggregation, Pervasive systems, Mobile services.

---

*This research work has been carried out partly under the FP6 Network of Excellence CoreGRID funded by
the European Commission (Contract IST-2002-004265).

1.   Introduction

The emergence of pervasive and mobile computing has drawn research attention to integrated mobile Grid systems. Such systems consist of a typical SOA (Service-Oriented Architecture) backbone extended to include mobile and small scale devices (Personal Digital Assistants, smart-phones, sensors and more). There are three hybrid system classes: first, mobile interfaces to grid resources, where mobile devices are merely interfaces to functionality available in the Grid system, and do not contribute any services. Second, exploitation of raw resources (CPU, memory, storage) in small-scale devices, where focus is on distributing applications for parallel execution usually requiring the partitioning of the application into small independent tasks. However, we believe that the core competence of such devices is their flexibility, pervasiveness, and location awareness and not their (limited) raw resources. Third, exploitation of services in mobile and small-scale devices, where the focus is in supporting mobile services in a SOA system, while also enabling small-scale devices to contribute services.

The last model is the one that provides the most complete integration where mobile and micro-devices can be both consumers and providers of services. Such integration could open up a completely new range of very interesting possibilities in exploiting the mobile nature of these devices. SOA systems could extend to reach geographical areas where before it was not possible allowing, for example, an organization to better control its field operations personnel. The functional benefits are also significant as mobile devices increasingly offer unique functionality not found in traditional Grid nodes, such as location aware equipment, multimedia cameras, intelligent wireless sensors, Global Positioning Systems and more.

However, a hybrid Grid system presents a number of interesting challenges. In a limited environment, pure SOA frameworks cannot easily be deployed. For example, typical Web Service (WS) and Grid Service (GS) containers (such as Axis/Tomcat or the Globus Toolkit) assume a plethora of available device resources, and have a number of complex dependencies. These requirements render them unsuitable for resource-constrained devices, where a smaller and simpler container with reduced requirements and dependencies is needed. But even with the development of such container, it is unreasonable to assume that all limited devices will adopt the same approach. In dedicated and relatively static environments certain guidelines can be enforced and adopted so that all members comply with the same policies. But in a dynamic environment that aims at agile and opportunistic computing, flexibility and mobility, imposing such restrictions is undesired.

The contribution of this paper is two-fold: first, we present the design of a fully J2ME compliant (Java 2 Micro Edition) socket-based server-side container that enables the user to export Java classes available in the device (Section 3). Second, we demonstrate how an aggregator framework enables such mobile services to be accessed using standard-based Web services in a high-level manner (Section 4). An aggregator service acts as a proxy to a group of heterogeneous and mobile underlying server-side components (supporting RMI, WS, GS, plain sockets and more). Further, aggregators provide an abstraction layer that hides the dynamicity and heterogeneity of the grouped services, in order to ease programming and provide a simpler view to high-level clients. The paper is completed with an evaluation of the LSC framework that verifies its superiority in terms of performance and resource utilization (Section 5).

2. Related Work

Mobile OGSI.NET [3] is an implementation of an OGSI (Open Grid Services Infrastructure [4]) based Grid services container for mobile devices based on Microsoft's PocketPC. Mobile OGSI.NET, despite being one of the earliest efforts, has been abandoned due to its restrictive implied programming model and nature, and has become obsolete due to the emergence of new standards in the form of the Web Services Resource Framework (WSRF) [5].

A generic component-based platform has been presented in [6–7] and has been part of research work conducted under CoreGRID [8]. Its design goals are the generality, reconfigurability, dynamic adaptation to system conditions and expandability of the platform. While this approach does not focus on small-scale devices, it offers a generic approach and an attractive model that could be adapted to suit the atypical environment of mobile hybrid Grid systems. At the time of writing, the platform remains at a design level.

WSPeer is a generic SOA-oriented toolkit based on the core Web services technology of SOAP that enables applications to perform the core SOA operations in an environment agnostic manner [9]. It has three bindings to different underlying middleware systems: the conventional HTTP and UDDI binding to the most-frequently used SOA stack; bindings to Peer-to-Peer middleware, such as JXTA and P2PS [10]; and a binding for constrained devices called WSKPeer. It also supports many WS-* specifications, including WS-Security, WS-Addressing, WS-Transfer and WS-RF. WSKPeer [11] ('K' for kilobytes) exposes a WSPeer restraint-device binding but focuses on the message abstraction, reducing all activity to asynchronous XML message exchanges. WSPeer is implemented using kXML and J2ME and can support service description parsing, including complex types, and sophisticated message exchanges that support notions of state and events, in particular WS-RF, despite the limited availability of processing power. WSKPeer provides an interesting approach to service orientation but it is at an early alpha stage of development and therefore premature for integration in the work presented here.

KSOAP [13] and kXML [12] have been successfully used in experimental settings to support mobile servers, SOAP engines, and XML parsing, installed on limited Java-based devices. One such implementation is the MicroServices framework [1] developed at the Monash University in Australia. This framework comprises of a stripped down mobile HTTP server, supported by a number of components to handle either HTTP or SOAP requests, thus allowing the deployment of Web services in resource-limited devices. The system allows only restricted Web services in terms of functionality, method complexity, and supported data types, while scalability is also reduced, with the number of simultaneous connected clients kept to low numbers to preserve resources.

Raccoon [2] is an effort to port Apache's popular httpd daemon into the Symbian-powered S60 Nokia phones. Raccoon encompasses a connectivity solution able to provide a mobile phone with a unique global URL accessible through HTTP from anywhere once online, thus enabling the concept of mobile Web sites (or "mobsites"). A significant benefit from having a mobile Web server is the enabling foundation for developing and deploying Web services on the smart phone. This would greatly widen the applicability, and allow for more familiar, service-oriented communication with the mobile devices.

3. Lightweight Server-side Container (LSC)

The inherent limitations of mobile devices enforce certain restrictions regarding the nature of the hosted server-side components. First, while typically a service can handle complex operations, the nature and role of mobile devices in an agile, pervasive, and context-aware environment suggest otherwise. Such services should perform very well defined, simple, and short operations, optimized for resource-constrained devices. Further, the nature of the services must not be transient (like in the WS paradigm) as there is limited scalability and even a small number of client requests can quickly deplete available resources. Instead, permanent and stateful services must be employed, first to simplify service lifecycle management and reduce the cost of service initialization, second, to support state and context aware operations.

Several technical requirements were identified for the LSC design. First, the CPU, memory, and storage footprint of the LSC must be as low as possible. Further, in an effort to preserve battery energy for end-user operations, when the level of battery is low the LSC is automatically shut down and does not accept any new requests. Second, the prototype must be fully J2ME compliant to ensure a high degree of interoperability and compatibility with a wide range of mobile devices. Third, it must be autonomous with no software or technological dependencies to enable easy deployment and wide adoption. Finally, it should offer a user-friendly GUI to enable the easy exportation of server-side components.

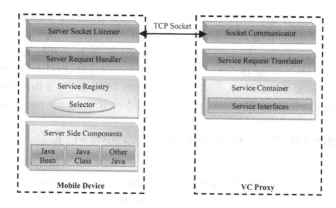

Figure 1.   Architectural Overview of MPA/LSC and VC Proxy

The LSC is part of the Mobile Platform Agent (MPA), a small software component that accompanies the Virtual Clusters (VC) platform (more details in the next section), and is responsible for several non-functional properties such as monitoring, discovery, activation and more. The MPA encapsulates the LSC to provide the necessary GUI and high-level function management.

The LSC consists of three distinct components: the Server Socket Listener (SSL), the Server Request Handler (SRH), and the Service Registry (SR) (Fig. 1). The SSL is responsible for initializing, maintaining, and terminating the server socket in the mobile device, listening and receiving client requests on that socket, and forwarding them to the SRH. The SRH validates the TCP requests (against the required protocol format) and interacts with the SR in order to activate the relevant Java service and invoke the requested method. The LSC message protocol has the following format:

```
LSC_INV|<service URL>|<method name>|<serialized arguments>
```

for instance:

```
LSC_INV|lsc://192.168.1.3:5678/vclustercdc.ImageService|
processImage|1984592123<arg byte array>
```

All the service method arguments, as well as the return value if any, are serialized into plain byte arrays before TCP transmission. The SRH is then responsible for the de-serialization of the arguments before supplying them to the relevant Java service. Finally, the SR is a permanent storage facility that stores information relating to the local shared Java services, namely the Implementation and the Interface classes. This information is supplied by the service provider through the GUI, a screenshot of which is shown in Fig. 4.

At the other end (the VC proxy), a number of components perform the opposite operations than the LSC. The Service Request Translator (SRT) is responsible for transforming high-level method invocations into low-level LSC protocol requests, ready to be transmitted through the TCP socket. The SRT also serializes all method arguments into plain byte arrays, before forwarding them to the Socket Communicator (SC), which is responsible for the actual transmission. It has to be noted that developers would never directly make use of the LSC protocol but instead will only access LSC devices through the VC Proxy which knows how to "talk" in LSC (see Section 4.1 for more details).

4.   Aggregator Services and LSC Framework

Aggregator services are at the core of the VC platform. The VC architecture focuses on providing the means to overcome the resource limitations, dynamicity, and mobility that humble the mobile domain. The main conceptual idea is to hide the big cardinality of the mobile domain by exposing all mobile devices as a single virtual entity, thus enabling a smooth integration and reduce the administrative and performance overhead. In order to present a group of devices as a single entity, a representative proxy node is required. Hence, the VC approach is a proxy-based, partially centralized design, where the grid system is merely extended to include a single extra node: the proxy, which acts as the gateway for the underlying group of mobile devices [14–15].

The main entity in the realization of a VC is the aggregator service (or simply 'Aggregator'). The Aggregator resides at the proxy node, and is responsible for a group of mobile devices that provide a similar resource or service (where similarity is determined by the implemented interfaces). Aggregators expose single, consistent, and permanent interface points to functionality available in the fabric service layer. Each Aggregator is generated and deployed on the fly, the first time that a particular type of service is made available for sharing in a VC -there is one Aggregator for each different type of service or resource. Fig. 2 depicts the VC architecture, which focuses primarily on providing the functionality of the proxy layer, which consists of the Aggregators, the core platform services that support various non-functional aspects, and a collective layer that enables coordinated and concurrent access to fabric services. Aside of these components, an API is also provided, to enable the development of sophisticated VC-aware hybrid grid applications. Each main service group is associated with, and is responsible for, one or more of the main challenge areas: monitoring for controlling dynamicity, discovery for managing mobility, collective layer for efficient management of large numbers of dynamic nodes, and there is also a number of supporting service groups, including indexing, invocation and more.

4.1   Overview of Communication Models

The LSC on its own presents a number of interesting challenges. Despite its efficiency (see Section 5) and functionality, it is not an interoperable ap-

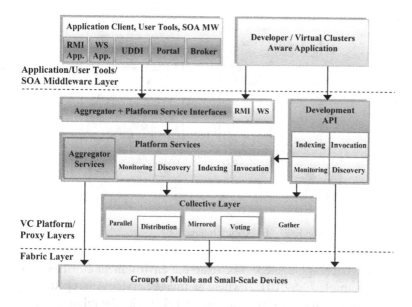

Figure 2. High Level Overview Depicting the Most Important Components

proach as it is based on a customized communication protocol format over TCP sockets. The low-level socket based communication model employed must be encapsulated to provide a more abstract development environment. The VC platform is used in this case, to decouple the high-level clients from the socket-dependant LSC services on mobile devices and enable high-level interactions. Communication at a conceptual level still flows between the client and the LSC-exposed services, but underneath, the VC proxy is the intermediary that translates the network-agnostic client requests into low-level LSC/TCP socket streams. Communication between the client and the VC proxy (in essence the relevant Aggregator that represents the specific type of service) is unmodified WS based HTTP/SOAP. The Aggregator then translates the request, and contacts the LSC through a TCP socket using the LSC communication protocol. The same socket is used to return the results once the execution on the mobile device finishes.

4.2 Interaction Patterns

Assuming that the mobile device is within the range of a VC, a complete exemplary scenario is presented here, from the local registration of the shared LSC services in the MPA, to the handling of the client request and the return of the results (Fig. 3). The example functionality includes a Java class that returns a Java image stored locally in the device, after scaling it to the specified size. A further assumption to simplify this scenario is that this specific type of Image

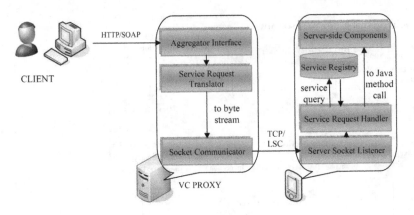

Figure 3. Invocation Interactions

service has already been aggregated. The example environment consists of a VC proxy (in our example 79.69.101.2) where an Image Service Aggregator has already been deployed in the Axis/Tomcat framework, under the relative URL: /axis/services/aggregators/ImageAggregator, to make up the full Aggregator endpoint address of:

`http://79.69.101.2:8080/axis/services/aggregators/ImageAggregator`.

A mobile device such as Sony Ericsson P990i (79.69.99.35), implementing the Image Service, registers and contributes to the VC.

1. **Registration of Local Services**. The service provider specifies which Java components to share. For each Java component, the server-side framework (WS, RMI, or LSC), the implementation and interface classes, and an optional human readable description must be specified (Fig. 4). Obviously, a relevant container must be already running, for instance, the MicroServices framework or Raccoon for WS, an RMI registry for RMI, or the LSC/TCP for plain Java-based services. All service information is first validated and then stored locally either as an XML file in the local file system, or using the Persistence J2ME API for very limited devices. In this example, the Image Gather Java application is registered as an LSC server-side component.During the local registration process, the current possibly dynamic IP address of the device is not important (the device can even be offline), while the LSC port defaults at 12345. The endpoint invocation address of the Image service thus becomes:

`lsc://79.69.99.35:12345/vclustercdc.ImageApp.ImageServer`

2. **Initialization of the MPA**. When one or more services have been registered locally, the mobile user can initialize the MPA. MPA initialization involves discovering and binding to a nearby VC proxy, and automatic activation of the locally registered Java services. If this is the first time this MPA registers with

Figure 4.   The MPA GUI

a VC proxy, a new globally unique ID is generated and assigned to it for future activations, in the form of: 9f941ea6-4579-30b2-96c4-f3a6812e60ce. Since the Image service is hosted on the LSC, the latter is also initialized along with the MPA. Initialization of the LSC is a two-step process: first, the Service Registry is loaded from the permanent storage, and second, the Server Socket Listener creates a local server socket on the designated port (12345), and starts listening for service requests.

3. **Automatic Activation of Local Services**. Immediately after binding to a VC proxy, the MPA activates and thus contributes the Image service (and any other registered services). As already assumed, an Aggregator for the Image service is already deployed in the VC proxy; otherwise, a new Aggregator is generated to represent the Image interface. The Image service is bound to the relevant Aggregator and is now ready to use.

4. **Aggregator Method Invocation**. A potential client connects to the representative Aggregator and invokes the getImage method having no knowledge of the Virtual Cluster and the underlying aggregated services. The communication is facilitated with SOAP over HTTP in typical WS fashion. Programmatically an Aggregator method invocation facilitating the Axis Dynamic Service Invocation API could look like:

```
...
Call call = (new Service()).createCall();
call.setEndpointAddress(
"http://79.69.101.2:80/axis/services/aggregators/ImageAggregator");
Image img = (Image)call.invoke("getImage", new Object[] {640, 480});
...
```

Alternatively, the client could use a portal framework, a web interface, or some other grid submission software.

5. **Aggregator Processing**. The Aggregator acquires the mobile service's address and binding details from the VC platform component, and forwards the method invocation to the Socket Request Translator (SRL). The SRL serializes the method arguments into a plain byte array, and translates the request into the LSC protocol format, before forwarding it to the Socket Communicator. The method invocation translated in the LSC protocol format would look like:

```
LSC_INV|lsc://79.69.99.35:12345/vclustercdc.ImageApp.ImageServer
|getImage|3982746...<byte array of the parameters>
```

The Socket Communicator opens a client socket connection (in a random available port, for instance 7008) to the LSC server socket (which listens on 79.69.99.35:12345) on the mobile device, and streams the translated request to it.

6. **LSC processing**. The Server Socket Listener receives the TCP socket stream in LSC format, and forwards it to the Service Request Handler (SRH). The SRH validates the stream against the LSC protocol format, and, if valid, extracts the service name from the supplied URL, in this case: vclustercdc.ImageApp.ImageServer, and the method name. The SRH then consults the Service Registry to acquire the registered information for the specified Java service, in order to dynamically recreate the method arguments from the byte array. When the arguments have been recreated, a new instance of the service class is created, and the requested method is invoked. The result of the method invocation is then serialized back to a byte array, and forwarded to the client end of the socket, in this case 79.69.101.2:7008.

7. **Aggregator Returns**. When the TCP stream with the result reaches the Aggregator, the Socket Communicator closes the client socket connection (port 7008), and forwards the result to the SRT. The latter de-serializes the byte array into the respective Java type, and returns. The client acquires the result from the Aggregator in typical WS fashion.

8. **MPA and LSC can be shut down if further sharing is not desired**. The mobile end user can easily shut down the MPA if no further contribution to the VC is required. During shut down, the MPA de-activates the Image service by informing the Active Index component of the VC proxy. Finally, the LSC shuts down the server socket and frees up any allocated resources.

5.   Evaluation

The evaluation of the LSC consists of two parts: performance or stress testing, and resource requirements testing. For the performance testing, three different devices where used as described in Table 1.

Table 1. Experimental Environment Nodes Specification

Type	Base Model	Memory	OS	Server-side framework
Laptop A	2.2GHz Intel-based	1GB	Win XP	Tomcat/Axis, RMI, LSC
Laptop B	1.6GHz AMD-based	512MB	Win XP	Tomcat/Axis, RMI, LSC
PDA	Sony P990i	128MB	Win Mobile	Microservices, RMI-OP, LSC

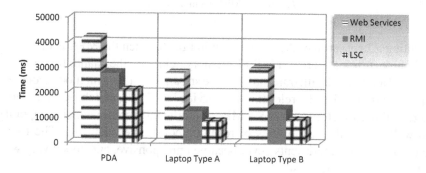

Figure 5. Comparison of WS, RMI, and LSC Single Invocation Performance

For each device, we tested the overall performance for invoking a simple image transformation service method (image size 2048KB, scale factor 3:1) facilitating all three available technologies – WS, RMI, and LSC/TCP. All requests originated from a desktop client where the VC Proxy was installed. Fig. 5 demonstrates the well-documented difference between WS and RMI performance, but most importantly, the significantly better performance of the LSC. This does not come as a surprise as generally sockets represent the fastest possible communication method among the three, while the interoperability and low-level programming restrictions are diminished with the use of the VC Aggregator scheme. Clients or developers will never have to make direct use of the LSC protocol. Instead it is meant to be accessed through the standards-based Aggregators in the VC Proxy.

Regarding the storage requirements, a total disk space of approximately 76 KB is required, including 42 KB for the vcluster-mobile.jar component, 31 KB for the LSC.jar component, 2 KB for the service-registry.xml component, and 1 KB for the startup scripts. This, however, does not include the RMI-Optional Package, which is required for some non-functional aspects of the VC platform, thus an additional 144KB is required to install the full package. The current version of the VC platform implementation is publicly available.

Evaluating the memory requirements entails testing the MPA under two different states: running/passive and running/active. In the first mode, the MPA and LSC have been bound to a VC proxy, but there are no pending requests. In the active state, the LSC has received an invocation request and is currently

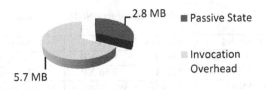

Figure 6.   MPA Memory Usage

executing a Java service. As can be seen in Fig. 6, when the MPA is in passive mode it occupies a mere 2.8 MB of memory. On the other hand, the memory overhead associated with translating a byte stream into a Java method invocation request, and invoking the relevant Java service is 5.7 MB, and the total memory usage in this case climbs up to 8.5 MB, a significant increase, albeit temporary and well within the capabilities of resource-constrained devices. The P990i we used in these experiments never became unresponsive, and coped very well with all invocation requests.

6.   Conclusions and Future Directions

The LSC is a lightweight performance-based container that is very easily able to run on any number of pervasive and resource limited mobile devices due to its small memory and storage requirements. To achieve this widespread functionality, certain value-added features that are present in the core MPA have been purposely left out of the LSC, such as the monitoring, dynamic service discover, and activation features. Future research in this project is moving towards the direction of enabling lightweight Peer-to-Peer mechanisms that would facilitate the dynamic loading of extra modules into the LSC depending on the capabilities of a given device. In this scenario, each client in the VC is guaranteed to have a base functionality of those provided by any LSC, however, if they are capable of performing more resource intensive operations, such as sending and receiving notifications of neighborhood monitoring information, or acting as a VC proxy, they would then be promoted on a need-based basis to act as higher-level network participants.

The MPA complements the VC platform and consists of two distinct parts: the core MPA that supports fundamental non-functional properties of the VC platform, such as monitoring, dynamic service discovery and activation, and the LSC that provides a lightweight and performance-oriented alternative to standard containers (such as WS or RMI) suitable for resource constrained devices. The properties, interface, usability, and evaluation of the LSC were presented in detail in this paper.

The LSC framework manages to marry the high performance of low-level TCP sockets with the interoperability of the standards-based Web Services paradigm through the high-level interfaces of Aggregators. Furthermore, usability is ensured with a fully J2ME-compliant graphical interface to assist the mobile service provider in selecting and exporting his services.

The resource requirements evaluation verified the suitability of the LSC framework for even very limited devices, while the performance evaluation puts it ahead of typical service hosting environments at approximately half the cost of RMI interactions. In the context of the VC platform it presents a performance-oriented container, albeit still interoperable through the Aggregator framework.

References

[1] Schall, D., Aiello, M. and Dustdar, S., *Web Services on Embedded Devices,* International Journal of Web Information Systems (IJWIS), 2007.

[2] J. Wikman, F. Dosa, *Providing HTTP Access to Web Servers Running on Mobile Phones,* Nokia Technical Report NRC-TR-2006-005, May 24, 2006

[3] Chu, D. and Humphrey, M., *Mobile OGSI: Grid Computing on Mobile Devices,* 5th International Workshop on Grid Computing (GRID), 2004.

[4] Tuecke, S., Czajkowski, K., Foster, I., Frey, J., Graham, S., Kesselman, C., Maguire, T., Sandholm, T., Snelling, D., Vanderbilt, P., *Open Grid Services Infrastructure (OGSI) Specification,* [Online] http://www.ggf.org/documents/GFD.15.pdf, 27 Jun, 2003.

[5] Czajkowski, K., Ferguson, D., Foster, I., Frey, J., Graham, S., Sedukhin, I., Snelling, D., Tuecke, S., Vambenepe, W., *The Web Services Resource Framework,* [Online] http://www.ibm.com/developerworks/library/ws-resource/ws-wsrf.pdf, 3 May, 2004.

[6] Thiyagalingam, J., Isaiadis, S. and Getov, V., *Towards Building a Generic Grid Services Platform: A Component-Oriented Approach,* in V. Getov and T. Kielmann [ed.], *Component Models and Systems for Grid Applications,* Springer, 2004.

[7] Thiyagalingam, J., Parlavantzas, N., Isaiadis, S., Henrio, L., Caromel, D., Getov, V., *Proposal for a Lightweight, Generic Grid Platform Architecture,* IEEE HPC-GECO/Compframe Workshop, HPDC-15, 2006.

[8] CoreGRID. [Online] http://www.coregrid.net.

[9] A. Harrison and I. Taylor, The Web Services Resource Framework In A Peer-To-Peer Context, Journal of Grid Computing, vol. 4(4): 425–445, December 2006.

[10] I. Wang, P2PS (Peer-to-Peer Simplified), in Proceedings of 13th Annual Mardi Gras Conference - Frontiers of Grid Applications and Technologies. Louisiana State University, pp. 54–59, February 2005.

[11] A. Harrison and I. Taylor, Service-oriented Middleware for Hybrid Environments, in Advanced Data Processing in Ubiquitous Computing (ADPUC 2006), 2006.

[12] kXML Project. [Online] http://www.kxml.org.

[13] kSOAP Project. [Online] http://www.ksoap.org.

[14] Isaiadis, S. and Getov, V., *Integrating Mobile Devices into the Grid: Design Considerations and Evaluation,* Proc. of the 11th Int. Euro-Par Conference on Parallel Processing. pp. 1080-1088, 2005.

[15] Isaiadis, S. and Getov, V., *Dependability in Hybrid Grid Systems: a Virtual Clusters Approach,* IEEE JVA International Symposium on Modern Computing, 2006.

COMPARISON OF MULTI-CRITERIA SCHEDULING TECHNIQUES

Dalibor Klusáček and Hana Rudová
Faculty of Informatics, Masaryk University
Botanická 68a, Brno, Czech Republic
{xklusac, hanka}@fi.muni.cz

Ranieri Baraglia[1] and Marco Pasquali[1,2] and Gabriele Capannini[1]
[1] *ISTI - Institute of the Italian National Research Council,*
Via Moruzzi 1, Pisa, Italy
{ranieri.baraglia, marco.pasquali, gabriele.capannini}@isti.cnr.it

[2] *IMT Lucca, Lucca institute for advanced studies,*
Lucca, Italy
marco.pasquali@imtlucca.it

Abstract
    This paper proposes a novel *schedule-based* approach for scheduling a continuous stream of batch jobs on the machines of a computational Grid. Our new solutions represented by dispatching rule Earliest Gap—Earliest Deadline First (EG-EDF) and Tabu search are based on the idea of filling gaps in the existing schedule. EG-EDF rule is able to build the schedule for all jobs incrementally by applying technique which fills earliest existing gaps in the schedule with newly arriving jobs. If no gap for a coming job is available EG-EDF rule uses Earliest Deadline First (EDF) strategy for including new job into the existing schedule. Such schedule is then optimized using the Tabu search algorithm moving jobs into earliest gaps again. Scheduling choices are taken to meet the Quality of Service (QoS) requested by the submitted jobs, and to optimize the usage of hardware resources. We compared the proposed solution with some of the most common queue-based scheduling algorithms like FCFS, EASY backfilling, and Flexible backfilling. Experiments shows that EG-EDF rule is able to compute good assignments, often with shorter algorithm runtime w.r.t. the other queue-based algorithms. Further Tabu search optimization results in higher QoS and machine usage while keeping the algorithm runtime reasonable.

Keywords: Grid, Scheduling, Dispatching Rule, Local Search, Backfilling

1.   Introduction

The building of a Grid infrastructure requires the development and deployment of middleware, services, and tools. At middleware level the scheduler is central to efficiently and effectively schedule jobs on available resources. It should both maximize the overall resource utilisation and guarantee nontrivial QoS for the user's applications. The scheduling problem has shown to be *NP-complete* in its general as well as in some restricted forms. Moreover, to meet the QoS requirements of applications flexible scheduling mechanisms are required. A typical QoS requirement is the time at which user wants to receive results, i.e., the job turnaround time.

In the past, a lot of research effort has been devoted to solve both static and dynamic job scheduling problems. Many of the proposed algorithms, such as backfilling, are queued-based techniques. Current production systems like PBS [7], Condor [21], LSF [23] or meta-scheduling systems such as Grid Service Broker [22], GridWay [11] and Moab [6] are mostly queue-based solutions. On the other hand, solutions using *schedule-based* [10, 19] approaches are poorly investigated, in particular to solve dynamic job scheduling problems [4]. In dynamic environments, such as Grids, resource may change, jobs are not known in advance and they appear while others are running. Schedule-based approach allows precise mapping of jobs onto machines in time. This allows us to use advanced scheduling algorithms [16, 8] such as local search methods [8] to optimize the schedule. Due to their computational cost, these approaches were mostly applied to static problems, assuming that all the jobs and resources are known in advance which allows to create schedule for all jobs at once [2–3]. CCS [10] as well as GORBA [19] are both advanced resource management systems that use schedule instead of a queue(s) to schedule workflows (GORBA), or sequential and parallel jobs while supporting the advanced reservations (CCS). GORBA uses simple policies for schedule creation and an evolutionary algorithm for its optimisation while CCS uses FCFS, Shortest/Longest Job First when assigning jobs into the schedule and a backfill-like policy that fills gaps in the constructed schedule. Both CCS and GORBA re-compute the schedule from scratch when a dynamic change such as job arrival or machine failure appears. It helps to keep the schedule up to date, however for large number of jobs this approach may be quite time consuming as was discussed in case of GORBA [17]. Works [1] and [18] propose local search based methods to solve Grid scheduling problems. The schedule is kept valid in time without total re-computation, however no experimental evaluation was presented in [1], and [18] does include resource changes but no dynamic job arrivals.

In this paper we propose novel schedule-based solutions to schedule *dynamically arriving* batch jobs on the machines of a computational Grid. In comparison with other approaches [10, 19], we are using *dispatching rule* and *local search* in an *incremental* fashion [13]. It means that current computed schedule can be used as the starting point for building a new schedule after each job arrival. This leads to a reasonable computational cost since the schedule is not rebuilt from scratch. We propose a multi-criteria approach which is based on providing nontrivial QoS to the end users, while satisfying the system administrators requirements as well. User requirements are expressed by the objective function focusing on maximising the number of jobs that meet their deadline, while system administrators needs are expressed by a machine usage criterion [5]. Moreover we developed an efficient method which detects and fills existing gaps in the schedule with suitable jobs. It allows us to increase both the QoS and machine usage by limiting fragmentation of the processor time.

The feasibility of the solutions we propose has been evaluated by comparing with a FCFS, an EASY backfilling, and a Flexible backfilling algorithms. The evaluation was conducted by simulations with the Alea simulator [12] using different streams of synthetically generated jobs.

2. Problem Description

In our study we consider a continuous stream of sequential or parallel batch jobs, which arrive to the system and are placed into a single job queue (FCFS, Easy and Flexible backfilling) or into the schedule (EG-EDF, Tabu search). Each job J is characterized by a submission time $Submit_J$, which represents the time when the job arrives, a deadline $Deadline_J$, the number Req_J of CPUs requested for its execution, an estimation of its duration $Estimated_J$, and a benchmark score BM_m, which represents the CPU speed of a machine m used for the time estimation. Precise J execution time for a specific machine $\bar{m}$ is calculated as $(Estimated_J \cdot BM_m)/BM_{\bar{m}}$. All the jobs are considered non-preemptible.

The target architecture is a computational Grid made up of multiprocessor machines. Each machine m is characterized by a number R_m of CPUs, and all CPUs within one machine have the same speed BM_m. Different machines may have different speeds and number of CPUs. Machines use the Space Sharing processor allocation policy which allows parallel execution of k jobs on machine m if $R_m \geq \sum_{J=1}^{k} Req_J$.

Various objective functions can be considered such as makespan or average flow time. Our scheduler aims to maximize both the resource utilisation and the number of jobs with the respected deadlines [5]. A higher resource utilisation fulfills resource owner expectations, while a higher number of non delayed jobs guarantees a higher QoS provided to the users.

3.   Applied Approaches

In this section we describe two different approaches we propose to solve the considered job scheduling problem. First principles of queue-based Flexible backfilling are explained. Next we focus on the schedule-based solutions. They are represented by a dispatching rule, which is used to create an initial schedule and Tabu search algorithm, which optimizes the initial solution according to the objective function.

3.1   Flexible Backfilling

Flexible backfilling [20] is a variant of the EASY backfilling algorithm which is an extension of the original backfilling algorithm [14]. In the Flexible backfilling, a priority value $P(J)$ is computed for each job J by exploiting a set of heuristics. Each heuristics follows a different strategy to satisfy both users and system administrator requirements.

After selection of the set of machines suitable to perform a job, the priority value assigned to such job is the sum of the values computed by each heuristics. In our study, to select the set of machines we considered only the number of available processors on a machine. Priority values are re-computed at scheduling events, which are job submission and completion. We defined the following heuristics: *Aging, Deadline*, and *Wait Minimization*.

Aging aims to avoid job starvation. For this reason higher scores are assigned to those jobs which have been present in the queue for a longer time. The value of the priority assigned to the job J is increased as follows: $P(J)+ = agefactor \cdot age(J)$, where $age(J)$ equals to $wallclock - Submit_J$ and $agefactor$ is a multiplicative factor set by the administrator according to the adopted system management policies. The value of the system wall-clock is represented by $wallclock$ parameter equal to the time when the heuristic is computed.

Deadline aims to maximize the number of jobs that terminate their execution within their deadline. It requires an estimation of the job execution time in order to evaluate its completion time with respect to the current wall-clock time. The heuristic assigns a minimal value (Min) to any job whose deadline is far from its estimated termination time.

When the distance between the completion time and the deadline is smaller than a threshold value (Max), the score assigned to the job is increased in inverse proportion with respect to such distance. The threshold value may be tuned according to the importance assigned to this heuristics. Without loss of generality, in our work, when a job goes over its deadline before it is scheduled, its updating priority value is set to Min. Each job is scheduled on the first most powerful available machine. Since jobs with a closer deadline receive higher priority, this strategy should improve the number of jobs executed within their deadline. Let $Estimated_J$ to be the estimated execution time of job J, we define:

$$Nxtime_J = Estimated_J \cdot \frac{BM_{\bar{m}}}{BM_m}$$
$$Extime_J = Now + Nxtime_J$$
$$t_J = Deadline_J - k \cdot Nxtime_J$$

where BM_m is the most powerful cluster machine m (optimistic prediction), and $BM_{\bar{m}}$ is the power of the machine $\bar{m}$ utilised to estimate the execution time of J. $Nxtime_J$ denotes the job's estimated execution time and $Extime_J$ denotes the estimated termination time of the job with respect to the current wall-clock (Now). t_J is the time from which the job must be evaluated to meet its deadline (i.e., the job priority is updated to consider its deadline too). k is a constant value fixed by the installation, which permits us to overestimate $Nxtime_J$.

The value $P(J)$ is increased by the Deadline heuristics according to the following formula:

$$P(J)+ = \begin{cases} Min & \text{if } Extime_J \leq t_J \\ a(Extime_J - t_J) + Min & \text{if } t_J < Extime_J \leq Deadline_J \\ Min & \text{if } Extime_J > Deadline_J \end{cases}$$

where a is the angular coefficient of the straight line passing through the points (t_J, Min) and $(Deadline_J, Max)$.

Finally, *Wait Minimization* favors jobs with the shortest estimated execution time. The rationale is that shorter jobs are executed as soon as possible in order to release the resources they have reserved and to improve the average waiting time of the jobs in the scheduling queue. Let *boostvalue* be the factor set by administrator according to system management policies and $minext = min(Estimated_J)$. The value of $P(J)$ is increased by the heuristics as follows:

$$P(J)+ = \frac{boostvalue \cdot minext_J}{Estimated_J}$$

In this paper the parameters used in Flexible backfilling were hand tuned to following values: $agefactor = 0.01$, $k = 2.0$, $max = 20.0$, $min = 0.1$ and $boostvalue = 2.0$. At each scheduling event the value of $P(J)$ for all queued jobs is reset to zero and then these heuristics are applied for each job to compute new $P(J)$ values so that $P(J) = Aging + Deadline + Wait\ Minimization$. Then the queue is sorted according to new $P(J)$ values and the backfilling procedure starts.

3.2   Earliest Gap—Earliest Deadline First Rule

In this section the proposed schedule-based approach *Earliest Gap—Earliest Deadline First (EG-EDF)* dispatching rule is described. It places a new submitted job into the *existing schedule* to built the schedule incrementally. It permits us to compute a new job scheduling plan saving running time for scheduling since the new plan is not re-computed from scratch. To do this, it is necessary to choose a good place in the schedule for the job being scheduled, otherwise resource utilisation may drop quickly due to the *gaps* appearing in the schedule. A gap is considered to be a period of idle CPU time. A new gap appears in the schedule every time the number of currently available CPUs by the machine is lower than the number of CPUs requested by a job. In such situation job has to be placed in the schedule to a time when a sufficient number of CPUs is available. Gaps can also appear when there are more CPUs than required by the jobs. They generally lead to processor fragmentation which results in a bad system utilisation.

In order to reduce the processor fragmentation, we developed a method that is able to optimize the schedule by placing the jobs into existing gaps. It is a key part of EG-EDF rule which works in the following way. Suppose a new job J arrives to the system. Using the existing schedule the *Earliest Gap (EG)* suitable for J is identified for each machine. Let S denotes the number of found EGs ($S \leq \#\ of\ Machines$). We consider three different cases: $S \geq 2$, $S = 1$, and $S = 0$. $S \geq 2$ means there is more than one EG for the job assignment. A *weight* is computed for each assignment of J to EG according to Equation 1, and the EG with the highest weight is chosen. The weight function is defined as:

$$
\begin{aligned}
weight &= weight_{makespan} + weight_{deadline} \qquad (1)\\
weight_{makespan} &= \frac{makespan_{old} - makespan_{new}}{makespan_{old}}\\
weight_{deadline} &= \frac{nondelayed_{new} - nondelayed_{old}}{nondelayed_{old}}
\end{aligned}
$$

Here the $makespan_{old}$ is the expected makespan[1] of the current schedule, $makespan_{new}$ is the makespan of the new schedule. $nondelayed_{old}$ and $nondelayed_{new}$ are the number of jobs executed within their deadline before and after the job assignment, respectively.

$S = 1$ simply means there is just one EG for the job J and this is used for the job assignment. $S = 0$ means there are no suitable gaps. In such case the job is placed into each machine's schedule according to the Earliest Deadline First (EDF) strategy. Each of these assignments is evaluated separately and the one with the highest weight is accepted.

3.3 Tabu Search

Although EG-EDF rule is trying to increase the machine usage and also to meet the job deadlines by finding suitable gaps, it only manipulate with the newly arrived job. The previously scheduled jobs are not considered by EG-EDF rule when building a new schedule. In such case many gaps in the schedule may remain. To reduce their effect, we propose a Tabu search [9] optimization algorithm which increases both machine usage and the number of jobs executed respecting their deadline. It only works with jobs prepared for running—jobs already running are not affected since the job preemption is not supported.

Tabu search selects the last job from the schedule of a certain machine, which has the highest number of delayed jobs. Such job must not be in the *tabu list* to prevent cycling. The tabu list contains jobs that were selected in previous iterations. It has limited size and the oldest item is always removed when the list becomes full. Selected job is put into the tabu list and then the method for finding the *Earliest Gap (EG)* for this job in a specific machine's schedule is executed. If suitable EG is found the job is moved to it and the weight value is computed according the Equation 1. If *weight* > 0 the move is accepted since it improves the quality of current schedule, $makespan_{old}$ and $nondelayed_{old}$ values are updated, and a new iteration is started. Otherwise, the move is not accepted, the job is not moved, and next machine's schedule is used to find an EG for this job. If none of the remaining machines has a suitable gap in its schedule, a new iteration is started by selecting a different job, since the previous choice is now banned by the tabu list. It can happen that the machine with the highest number of delayed jobs contains only jobs present in the tabu list. Then the machine with the second highest number of delayed jobs is selected. The process continues until there are no delayed non-tabu jobs or the upper bound of iterations is reached.

---

[1]Makespan is the completion time of the last job in the schedule.

4.   Experimental Evaluation

In order to verify the feasibility of the EG-EDF and Tabu search solutions, some experiments have been conducted. The evaluation was performed by comparing our solutions with FCFS, EASY backfilling (Easy BF), and Flexible backfilling (Flex. BF). Concerning the Flex. BF, job priorities are updated at each job submission or ending event and the reservation for the first queued job is maintained through events. We used our Alea Simulator [12], which is an extended version of the GridSim toolkit. The evaluation was conducted by simulations using five different streams of jobs synthetically generated according to a negative exponential distribution with different inter-arrival times between jobs [5, 20]. According to the job inter-arrival times a different workload is generated through a simulation. Smaller this time is, greater the system workload is. Inter-arrival times were chosen in a way that the available computational power is able to avoid the job queue increasing when it is fixed equal to 5. Moreover, each job and machine parameter was randomly generated according to a uniform distribution[2].

The experimental tests were conducted by using a Grid made up of 150 machines with different CPU number and speed, and 3000 jobs. Job scheduling plans were carried out by exploiting the Space Sharing processor allocation policy, and both parallel and sequential jobs were simulated—up to now parallel jobs are always executed on only one machine with a sufficient number of CPUs. In order to obtain stable values, each simulation was repeated 20 times with different job attributes values. The experiments were conducted on an Intel Pentium 4 2.6 GHz machine with 512 MB RAM.

To evaluate the quality of schedules computed by EG-EDF rule and Tabu search, we exploited different criteria: the percentage of jobs executed do not respecting their deadline, the percentage of system usage, the average job slowdown, and the average algorithm runtime.

The system usage was computed at each simulation time by using the following expression:

$$System\ usage = \frac{\#\ of\ active\ CPUs}{min(\#\ of\ available\ CPUs, \#\ of\ CPUs\ requested\ by\ jobs)}$$

It permits us to not consider situations when there are not enough jobs in the system to use all the available machines. It happens at the beginning and at the end of the simulation.

---

[2]Following ranges were used: Job execution time [500–3000], jobs with deadlines 70%, number of CPUs required by job [1–8], number of CPU per machine [1–16], machine speed [200–600]

4.1   Discussion

In Figure 1 (left) the percentage of jobs executed not respecting their deadline is shown. As expected, when the job inter-arrival time increases, the number of late jobs decreases. Moreover, it can be seen that both EG-EDF rule and Tabu search produced much better solutions than Flexible backfilling, Easy backfilling, and FCFS. Tabu search outperforms all the other algorithms. In particular, it obtains nearly the same results of EG-EDF rule when the system contention is low (job inter-arrival time equal to 5). In Figure 1 (right), the percentage of system usage is shown. Schedule-based algorithms are, in general, able to better exploit the system computational resources. However, when there is not contention in the system the solutions we propose obtained worse results than the other ones. When the available computational power is able to avoid the job queue increasing, the Tabu search and EG-EDF solutions do not improve, or improve very little, the previous schedule. In this situation, the schedule-based approach is less effective concerning the resource utilisation. In such situation the schedule is almost empty so a newly arrived job is often immediately executed on an available machine, therefore the Tabu search has a very limited space for optimization moves.

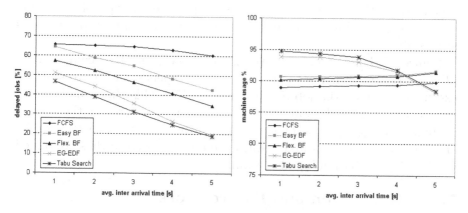

Figure 1. Average percentage of delayed jobs (left) and system usage (right).

Figure 2 (left) shows the average scheduling times spent by the scheduler for conducting the tests on the simulated computational environment. It is computed by measuring the scheduling time at each scheduling event. The runtime of FCFS is very low w.r.t. to Easy and Flexible backfilling for which it grows quickly as a function of the job queue length. Although the Flexible backfilling has to re-compute job priorities at each scheduling event, and then has to sort the queue accordingly, it

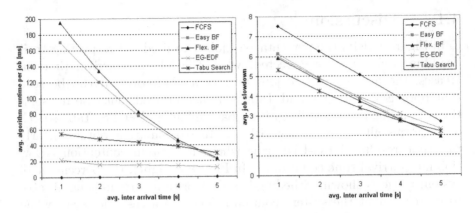

Figure 2.   Average algorithm runtime (left) and the average job slowdown (right).

causes minimal growth of its run time compared to the Easy backfilling. This is due to the application of an efficient sort algorithm.

Local search based algorithms are often considered to be very time consuming. Our implementation, which exploits an incremental approach based on the previously computed schedule, is able to guarantee a shorter and stable execution time w.r.t. the other algorithms. In particular, EG-EDF rule is fast and it always generates acceptable schedule, so we can stop Tabu search optimization at any time if prompt decisions are required.

Figure 2 (right) shows the average job slowdown. It is computed as $(Tw + Te)/Te$, with Tw the time that a job spends waiting to start its execution, and Te the job execution time [15]. This shows us how the system load delays the job execution. As expected, greater the system contention is, greater the job slowdown is. In this case the better results are obtained by Tabu search, which are enough close to those obtained by the Flexible backfilling algorithm.

5.   Conclusion and Future Work

Both Flexible backfilling and schedule-based algorithms demonstrated significant improvement when decreasing the number of late jobs while keeping the machine usage high. This would not be possible without the application of effective gap-filling method in case of the schedule-based algorithms. Tabu search algorithm proved to be more successful in decreasing the number of delayed jobs over Flexible backfilling—on the other hand precise job execution time was known in this case so the advantage of schedule-based solution took effect. The incremental approach used in the schedule-based solutions allowed to keep the algorithm runtime stable and low. From this point of view both Easy and Flexible backfilling are more time consuming since their runtime is growing with the size of the queue more quickly.

In the future we would like to include job execution time estimations to study their effect on the performance of schedule-based methods. Usually this is not a crucial issue for the queue-based algorithms because they are designed to deal with dynamic changes. However, the schedule-based approach relies on the precision of execution time prediction much more. We expect that some changes will have to be done when the estimates will not meet the real job execution time. It is probable that in such situation local change or limited rescheduling will be necessary. Also, we would like to introduce failure tolerance and investigate job preemption and job migration effects. Next we plan to compare these solutions with other scheduling techniques such as Convergent Scheduling [5].

Acknowledgments

This work was supported by the Ministry of Education, Youth and Sports of the Czech Republic under the research intent No. 0021622419, by the Grant Agency of the Czech Republic with grant No. 201/07/0205, and by the EU CoreGRID NoE (FP6-004265) which we highly appreciate.

References

[1] A. Abraham, R. Buyya, and B. Nath. Nature's heuristics for scheduling jobs on computational Grids. In *The 8th IEEE International Conference on Advanced Computing and Communications (ADCOM 2000)*, pages 45–52, 2000.

[2] V. A. Armentano and D. S. Yamashita. Tabu search for scheduling on identical parallel machines to minimize mean tardiness. *Journal of Intelligent Manufacturing*, 11:453–460, 2000.

[3] R. Baraglia, R. Ferrini, and P. Ritrovato. A static mapping heuristics to map parallel applications to heterogeneous computing systems: Research articles. *Concurrency and Computation: Practice and Experience*, 17(13):1579–1605, 2005.

[4] J. Bidot. *A General Framework Integrating Techniques for Scheduling under Uncertainty*. PhD thesis, Institut National Polytechnique de Toulouse, 2005.

[5] G. Capannini, R. Baraglia, D. Puppin, L. Ricci, and M. Pasquali. A job scheduling framework for large computing farms. In *ACM/IEEE International Conference for High Performance Computing, Networking, Storage and Analysis (SC'07)*, 2007.

[6] Cluster Resources. *Moab Workload Manager Administrator's Guide*, 2008.

[7] J. P. Jones. *PBS Professional 7, Administrator Guide*. Altair, April 2005.

[8] F. W. Glover and G. A. Kochenberger, editors. *Handbook of Metaheuristics.* Kluwer, 2003.

[9] F. W. Glover and M. Laguna. *Tabu Search.* Kluwer Academic Publishers, 1998.

[10] M. Hovestadt, O. Kao, A. Keller, and A. Streit. Scheduling in HPC Resource Management Systems: Queuing vs. Planning. In *Job Scheduling Strategies for Parallel Processing,* volume 2862 of *LNCS,* pages 1–20. Springer, 2003.

[11] E. Huedo, R. Montero, and I. Llorente. The GridWay framework for adaptive scheduling and execution on Grids. *Scalable Computing: Practice and Experience,* 6(3):1–8, 2005.

[12] D. Klusáček, L. Matyska, and H. Rudová. Alea – Grid Scheduling Simulation Environment. In *Workshop on scheduling for parallel computing at the 7th International Conference on Parallel Processing and Applied Mathematics (PPAM 2007),* LNCS. Springer, 2008. To appear.

[13] D. Klusáček, L. Matyska, H. Rudová, R. Baraglia, and G. Capannini. Local Search for Grid Scheduling. In *Doctoral Consortium at the International Conference on Automated Planning and Scheduling (ICAPS'07),* USA, 2007.

[14] D. A. Lifka. The ANL/IBM SP Scheduling System. In *Job Scheduling Strategies for Parallel Processing,* volume 949 of *LNCS,* pages 295–303. Springer, 1995.

[15] A. W. Mu'alem and D. G. Feitelson. Utilization, predictability, workloads, and user runtime estimates in scheduling the IBM SP2 with backfilling. *IEEE Transactions on Parallel and Distributed Systems,* 12(6):529–543, 2001.

[16] M. Pinedo. *Planning and Scheduling in Manufacturing and Services.* Springer, 2005.

[17] K. Stucky, W. Jakob, A. Quinte, and W. Süß. Solving scheduling problems in Grid resource management using an evolutionary algorithm. In R. Meersman and Z. Tari, editors, *OTM Conferences (2),* volume 4276 of *LNCS,* pages 1252–1262. Springer, 2006.

[18] R. Subrata, A. Y. Zomaya, and B. Landfeldt. Artificial life techniques for load balancing in computational Grids. *Journal of Computer and System Sciences,* 73(8):1176–1190, 2007.

[19] W. Süß, W. Jakob, A. Quinte, and K. Stucky. GORBA: A global optimising resource broker embedded in a Grid resource management system. In S. Zheng, editor, *International Conference on Parallel and Distributed Computing Systems, PDCS 2005,* pages 19–24. IASTED/ACTA Press, 2005.

[20] A. D. Techiouba, G. Capannini, R. Baraglia, D. Puppin, and M. Pasquali. Backfilling strategies for scheduling streams of jobs on computational farms. In *CoreGRID Workshop on Grid Programming Model, Grid and P2P Systems Architecture, Grid Systems, Tools and Environments.* Springer, 2008. To appear.

[21] D. Thain, T. Tannenbaum, and M. Livny. Distributed computing in practice: the Condor experience. *Concurrency - Practice and Experience,* 17(2-4):323–356, 2005.

[22] S. Venugopal, R. Buyya, and L. Winton. A Grid Service Broker for scheduling distributed data-oriented applications on global Grids. In *MGC '04: Proceedings of the 2nd workshop on Middleware for grid computing,* pages 75–80. ACM Press, 2004.

[23] M. Q. Xu. Effective metacomputing using LSF multicluster. In *CCGRID '01: Proceedings of the 1st International Symposium on Cluster Computing and the Grid,* pages 100–105. IEEE Computer Society, 2001.

COMPARISON OF CENTRALIZED AND DECENTRALIZED SCHEDULING ALGORITHMS USING GSSIM SIMULATION ENVIRONMENT

Marcin Krystek, Krzysztof Kurowski, Ariel Oleksiak
Poznan Supercomputing and Networking Center
Noskowskiego 10
61-704 Poznan, Poland
mkrystek,krzysztof.kurowski,ariel@man.poznan.pl

Krzysztof Rzadca
LIG, Grenoble University
51, avenue Jean Kuntzmann
38330 Montbonnot Saint Martin, France
and Polish-Japanese Institute of Information Technology
Koszykowa 86
02-008 Warsaw, Poland
rzadca@imag.fr

Abstract   Various models and architectures for scheduling in grids may be found both in the literature and in practical applications. They differ in the number of scheduling components, their autonomy, general strategies, and the level of decentralization. The major aim of our research is to study impact of these differences on the overall performance of a Grid. To this end, in the paper we compare performance of two specific Grid models: one centralized and one distributed. We use GSSIM simulator to perform accurate empirical tests of algorithms. This paper is a starting point of an experimental study of centralized and decentralized approaches to Grid scheduling within the scope of the CoreGrid Resource Management and Scheduling Institute.

Keywords: Decentralized scheduling, scheduling architecture, scheduling algorithms, grid, GSSIM simulator

1.   Introduction

Decentralization is a key feature of any architectural part of the grid, a system that is crossing organizational boundaries [7]. Nevertheless, standard approaches to scheduling, both theoretical and practical, concern mainly centralized algorithms. In large-scale grids, the centralized approach is clearly unfeasible. Firstly, centralized scheduling requires accurate, centralized information about the state of the whole system. Secondly, sites forming the grid maintain some level of autonomy, yet classic algorithms implicitly assume a complete control over individual resources.

We model the grid as an agreement to share resources between independent organizations. An organization is an entity that groups a computational resource (a cluster) and a group of users that submit jobs. Each organization, by granting access to its resource, in return expects that its jobs will be treated fairly in the system.

In the paper, we compare two classes of scheduling algorithms, centralized and decentralized. In centralized scheduling, one grid scheduler maintains a complete control over the clusters. All the jobs are submitted through the grid scheduler. In contrast, in decentralized scheduling, organizations maintain (limited) control over their schedules. Jobs are submitted locally, but they can be migrated to another cluster, if the local cluster is overloaded. The possibilities of migration are, however, limited, so that migrated jobs do not overload the host system.

The aim of this paper is to compare performance centralized and decentralized scheduling algorithms. Using GSSIM simulation environment, we perfom realistic simulation of example scheduling algorithms that use both approaches, and compute various performance measures of jobs.

In literature, decentralization has two distinct meanings in grid systems, composed of resources under different administrative domains [7]: the decentralization of the algorithm or the decentralization of the optimization goals. A *decentralized algorithm* does not need complete, accurate information about the system. An algorithm with *decentralized goals* optimizes many performance measures of different stakeholders of the system. Classic scheduling algorithm are centralized algorithms that optimize a centralized goal, such as the average completion time of jobs or the makespan. Such scheduling problems have been thoroughly studied, both theoretically [2] and empirically [6]. Decentralized algorithms optimizing decentralized goals include mainly economic approaches [3]. Decentralized algorithms optimizing system-level goal include e.g. [11], that proposes a load-balancing algorithm for divisible task model. Finally, in optimization of decentralized goals with a centralized algorithm, multi-objective algorithms are usually used [13, 10].

The paper is organized as follows. The architecture of the scheduling system and algorithms for centralized and decentralized implementations are proposed in Section 2. Section 3 contains a description of GSSIM, the simulation environment. Section 4 presents results of experiments.

2. Scheduling Algorithms

In this section we present the model of the grid and scheduling algorithms. In the first case, we assume that there is a single grid scheduler while local schedulers are not autonomous, i.e. they must accept decisions of a grid scheduler. In the second approach, there is no central grid scheduler and local schedulers are autonomous. However, they must obey certain rules agreed between organizations. In both cases, jobs come from users from considered organizations, i.e. there are no external jobs. The next sections contains used notation and details of algorithms.

2.1 Notation and the Model of the Grid

By $\mathcal{O} = \{O_1, \ldots, O_N\}$ we denote the set of independent organizations forming the grid. Each organization O_k owns a cluster M_k. By $\mathcal{M}$ we denote the set of all clusters. Each cluster M_k has m_k identical processors. Cluster have different processing rates. The inverse of M_k processing speed is denoted by s_k.

The set of all the jobs *produced* by O_k is denoted by $\mathcal{I}_k$, with elements $\{J_{k,i}\}$. By $\mathcal{J}_k$ we denote the set of jobs *executed* on O_k's cluster M_k. If $J_{k,i} \in \mathcal{J}_k$, the job is executed *locally*, otherwise it is *migrated*. Job $J_{k,i}$ must be executed in parallel on $q_{k,i}$ processors of exactly one cluster M_l during $p_{k,i} \cdot s_l$ time units. It is not possible to divide a job between two, or more, clusters. The system works on-line. $J_{k,i}$ is not known until its *release date* $r_{k,i}$. Each job has a due date $d_{k,i}$.

In a schedule, by $C_{k,i}$ we denote the completion (finish) time of job $J_{k,i}$. Flow time of job $J_{k,i}$ is defined as the total time the job stays in the system, i.e. $f_{k,i} = C_{k,i} - r_{k,i}$. Tardiness $l_{k,i}$ of job $J_{k,i}$ is defined as the difference between job's completion time and its due date $l_{k,i} = C_{k,i} - d_{k,i}$, if $J_{k,i}$ is completed after its due date ($C_{k,i} > d_{k,i}$), or 0 otherwise.

Organization O_k, in order to measure the performance of its jobs $\mathcal{J}_k$, computes aggregated measures. In this work, we will consider *sum*-type aggregations, such as the sum of flow times $\Sigma_i f_{k,i}$, or the sum of tardiness $\Sigma_i l_{k,i}$, or the number of late jobs U_k.

The performance of the system is defined as a similar aggregation over all the jobs. For instance, system's sum of completion times is defined as $\Sigma_{k,i} C_{k,i}$.

2.2   Centralized Scheduling Algorithm

This algorithm assumes that all the jobs in the system are scheduled by a centralized Grid scheduler, that produces schedules for all clusters $\mathcal{M}$. Each organization must accept decisions of the Grid scheduler, which means that Grid scheduler is the single decision maker and enforcement point within the system.

The algorithm works in batches. This approach is motivated by a possibility of schedule optimization within a batch. In the worst case, on-line FCFS policy may result in linearly increased makespan (compared to the optimal). Moreover, FCFS prevents Grid scheduler from taking full advantage of available information. We applied the following approach for creating batches. We introduced two parameters batch size s and batch length l. Batch size is a number of jobs that form a batch. Batch length is an amount of time between start time of the last and first job in the batch. The current batch is scheduled if a threshold related to any of these two parameters is achieved or exceeded, i.e. if $s \geq S$ or $l \geq L$. The size limit threshold prevents batches from being to large while the length limit decrease delays of jobs waiting in the next batch. Use of batches has also a practical justification. It causes that local schedules grow more slowly which helps to react in case of failures or imprecise job execution times. Some experimental studies on impact of batch sizes on the performance can be found in [10].

The algorithm consist of two independent policies. The first policy defines the order of jobs in a batch while the second determines the way job is assigned to a given cluster M_k. As the first policy the earliest due date (EDD) has been used. This policy ensures that jobs within a batch are sorted by increasing deadline. Every job J_i must be at position k such as that $d_{j(k-1)} \leq d_i \leq d_{j(k+1)}$, where $j(k)$ denotes a number of a job at position k in a queue.

Jobs J_i from the queue are assigned to one of clusters $\mathcal{M}$ using a greedy list-scheduling algorithm based on [8, 5]. To this end, the Grid scheduler queries each organization O_k about a list of free slots $\psi_{ki} \in \Psi_k, \psi_{ki} = (t', t'', m_{ki}), i = 1..|\Psi|$. Parameters t' and t'' denote start and time of a slot, respectively. m_{ki} is a number of processors available within the slot i at organization O_k. Slots are time periods within which a number of available processors is constant. The Grid scheduler sorts collected slots by increasing start time. The schedule is constructed by assigning jobs in the Grid scheduler's queue to processors in given slots in a greedy manner. For each slot ψ_{kI} (starting from the earliest one) the scheduler chooses from its queue the first job J_j requiring no more than m_{ki} processors in all subsequent slots $i \geq I$ such as $t''_{ki} \geq t'_{kI} + p_j$, which simply means that jobs' resource requirements must be met for the whole duration of a job. If such a job was found the scheduler schedules it to be started at t'_{kI}, and removes it from the queue. If there is no such a job, the scheduler applies the same procedure to the next free slot with a number of available processors larger than the current one.

2.3 Distributed Scheduling Algorithm

The proposed algorithm consists of two parts. Most of the local jobs are scheduled on the local machine with a list-scheduling algorithm working in batches (Section 2.3.1). Moreover, the scheduler attempts to migrate jobs which would miss their due dates when executed locally. Section 2.3.2 shows an algorithm for handling such migration requests from the receiver's point of view. Although migration improves the performance of the originator, migrated jobs can possibly delay local jobs, and, consequently, worsen the local criterion. We solve this dilemma by introducing limits on the maximum total size of jobs an organization must accept (as a result of the grid agreement), and, at the same time, is able to migrate. These limits are proportional to the length of the current batch multiplied by a *cooperation coefficient* c_k, controlled by each organization O_k.

2.3.1 Scheduling local jobs. Let us assume that the scheduling algorithm was run at time t_0 and returned a schedule which ends at t_1. For each job $J_{k,i}$ released between t_0 and the current makespan t_{max}, the algorithm tries to schedule $J_{k,i}$ so that no scheduled job is delayed and t_{max} is not increased (conservative backfilling). If it is not possible, $J_{k,i}$ is deferred to the next batch, scheduled at t_{max}. However, if it caused $J_{k,i}$ to miss its due date (i.e. $t_{max} + p_{k,i}s_k > d_{k,i}$), the scheduler tries to migrate the job to other clusters, by sending migration requests (Section 2.3.2). If cluster M_l can accept $J_{k,i}$ before its due date, the job is removed from the local queue and migrated. If there is more than one cluster ready to accept $J_{k,i}$, the earliest start time is chosen.

At t_{max}, a list scheduling algorithm schedules all the deferred jobs. Jobs are sorted by increasing due dates (EDD). Then, jobs are scheduled with a greedy list-scheduling algorithm [8, 5]. The schedule is constructed by assigning jobs to processors in a greedy manner. Let us assume that at time t, m' processors are free in the schedule under construction. The scheduler chooses from the list the first job $J_{k,i}$ requiring no more than m' processors, schedules it to be started at t, and removes it from the list. If there is no such job, the scheduler advances to the earliest time t' when one of the scheduled jobs finishes. At t', the scheduler checks if there is any unscheduled job $J_{k,i}$ that missed its due date (i.e. $t + p_{k,i}s_k < d_{k,i}$, but $t' + p_{k,i} > d_{k,i}$). For each such job $J_{k,i}$, scheduler tries to migrate it, using the same algorithm as described in the previous paragraph. The rest of the delayed jobs are scheduled locally.

After all the jobs are scheduled, O_l broadcasts the resulting makespan.

2.3.2   Handling migration requests.   Acceptance of a migration request depends on the total surface of migrated jobs already accepted by the host in the current batch, on the total surface of jobs already migrated by the owner and on the impact of the request on the local schedule. Moreover, each organization can control these parameters by means of *cooperation coefficient* c_k ($c_k \geq 0$).

Assuming that the current batch on M_k started at t_0 and will finish at t_1, until the current batch ends, O_k is obliged to accept foreign jobs of total surface of at most $L_k = c_k \cdot (t_1 - t_0) \cdot m_k$. Moreover, O_k can reject a foreign job, if the makespan of the current batch increases by more than $c_k \cdot (t_1 - t_0)$. In order to motivate O_k to declare $c_k > 0$, any other organization O_l can reject O_k's migration requests, if the total surface of jobs exported by O_k in the current batch exceeds L_k.

O_k is obliged to answer to foreign migration requests on-line. Let us assume that, at time t' ($t_0 < t' < t_{\max}$), O_k receives a migration request for job $J_{l,i}$. O_k can reject $J_{l,i}$ straight away in two cases. Firstly, when the total surface of the jobs migrated by the sender O_l exceeds its current limit L_l. Secondly, when O_k has already accepted enough foreign jobs of surface of at least L_k.

Otherwise, O_k's local scheduler finds the earliest strip of free processors of height of at least $q_{l,i}$ and of width of at least $p_{l,i}s_k$ (an incoming, foreign job never delays a scheduled job). If such a strip exists only at the end of the schedule, O_k can reject $J_{l,i}$, if the makespan is increased by more than $c_k \cdot (t_1 - t_0)$. Otherwise, a positive response is returned to the sender O_l. If O_l finally decides to migrate $J_{l,i}$, this decision is broadcasted so that all other organizations can update the surface of O_l's migrated jobs.

2.3.3   Setting the Cooperation Coefficient.   Each organization O_k periodically broadcasts its cooperation coefficient c_k, that specifies the organization's desire to balance its load with other organizations. In general, larger values of c_k mean that more migration requests must be locally accepted, but also more local jobs can be migrated. Consequently, c_k value should depend on the local load and on the observed load (by means of migration requests) of other clusters. An algorithm for setting c_k is beyond the scope of this paper.

In order to make the system more stable, the delay T between two broadcasts of c_k value for an organization must be strongly greater than the average batch size.

3.   GSSIM Simulation Environment

To perform experimental studies of models and algorithms presented above we used the Grid Scheduling SIMulator (GSSIM) [9]. GSSIM has been designed as a simulation framework which enables easy-to-use experimental studies of various scheduling algorithms. It provides flexible and easy way to describe, generate and share input data to experiments. GSSIM's architecture

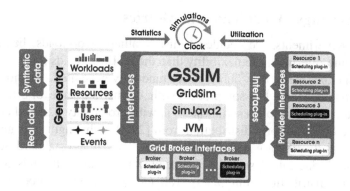

Figure 1. GSSIM architecture

and a generic model enables building multilevel environments and using various scheduling strategies with diverse granularity and scope. In particular, researchers are able to build architectures consisting of two tiers in order to insert scheduling algorithms both to local schedulers and grid schedulers. To enable sharing of the workloads, algorithms and results, we have also proposed a GSSIM portal [1], where researchers may download various synthetic workloads, resource descriptions, scheduling plugins, and results.

The GSSIM framework is based on GridSim [4] and SimJava2 packages. However, it provides a layer added on top of the GridSim adding capabilities to enable easy and flexible modeling of Grid scheduling components. GSSIM also provides an advanced generator module using real and synthetic workloads. The overall architecture of GSSIM is presented in Figure 1.

In the centralized case, the main scheduling algorithm is included in a single Grid scheduler plugin (Figure 1, grid broker interfaces). This plugin include implementation of the algorithm presented in Section 2.2. The input of this plugin consists of information about a queue of jobs in a current batch and available resources. Local schedulers (resource providers in the right part of Figure 1) can be queried about a list of time slots. The output of the Grid scheduling plugin is a schedule for all clusters for the batch of jobs.

The implementation of the decentralized version of scheduling algorithm is included exclusively within the local scheduling plugins. Plugins receive as an input a queue of jobs, description of resources and the requests from other local schedulers. Each plugin produces a schedule for its resource.

4. Experiments

This section contains a description of experiment defined using GSSIM. The following subsections contain information about applied workload, how scheduling components were modeled, and results

4.1   Settings: Workload and Metrics

In our experiments, we decided to use synthetic workloads, being more universal and offering more flexibility than the real workloads ([12, 9]).

In each experiment, $n = 500$ jobs are randomly generated. The job arrival ratio is modeled by the Poisson process with λ either the same, or different for each organization. A job is serial ($q_i = 1$) with probability 0.25, otherwise q_i is generated by a uniform distribution from [2,64]. Job length p_i is generated using normal distribution with a mean value $\mu = 20$ and standard deviation $\sigma = 20$. Job's due date d_i set to be d_i' time units its release date. d_i' is generated by a uniform distribution from $[p_i * s_S, 180]$ ($p_i * s_S$ is the job's processing time at the slowest resource).

We used $N = 3$ organizations in the experiment. Each organization owns a single homogeneous cluster. Clusters have 32, 64, and 128. For the sake of simplicity we assumed that their relative processing speed identical.

In order to measure the performance of the system experienced by the users, we used metrics such as the mean job flow time $\bar{F} = (\Sigma_{k,i} f_{k,i})/n$, and the mean job tardiness $\bar{L} = (\Sigma_{k,i} l_{k,i})/n$. The tightness of a schedule for a cluster is expressed by resource utilization $\bar{R}$, defined as $\frac{\Sigma_k \Sigma_{i \in J_k} p_{k,i} q_{k,i}}{\Sigma_k m_k (t_k^{end} - t_k^{start})}$, where $t_k^{end} = \max_i C_{k,i}$, and $t_k^{start} = \min_i r_{k,i}$. Results may be often distorted by first and last jobs that are executed when load of clusters is relatively low. In order to avoid this inconvenience we did not consider within our results first and last 10% of jobs.

In order to check how equitable are obtained results for all organizations we used the corresponding performance metrics for every single organization O_k. Then we tested how disperse are these values by calculating the standard deviation and comparing extreme values. We also compared the performance metric of each organization to the performance achieved by *local* scheduling algorithm, scheduling jobs on clusters where they are produced (i.e. it is the same as *decentralized*, but with no migration). If there is no cooperation, *local* scheduling is the performance each organization can achieve.

4.2   Results

We performed two series of tests, comparing centralized, decentralized and local algorithm. Firstly, we measured system-level performance in order to check how the decentralization of the algorithm infuences the whole system. In this series of tests, we assumed that all the organizations have similar job streams. Secondly, we compared the fairness proposed by algorithms when organizations' loads differ. Jobs incoming from overloaded clusters cannot lower too much the performance achieved by underloaded organizations.

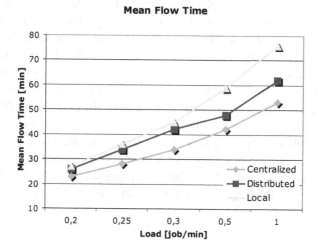

Figure 2.   Mean Flow Time for three strategies: centralized, distributed, and local

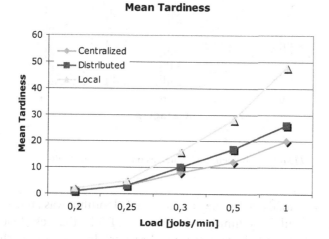

Figure 3.   Mean Tardiness for three strategies: centralized, distributed, and local

Generally, the decentralized algorithm schedules slightly worse than the centralized algorithm. However, migration considerably improved the results comparing to the local algorithm. This observation is valid especially for tardiness as this criterion is used by a distributed algorithm to decide about job migration.Typical results of experiments comparing system-level performance are presented in Figure 2 and 3 for mean flow time and tardiness, respectively. In Figure 2 it is easy to notice that mean flow time of the distributed algorithm is comparable to local strategy for low load. These poor results are caused by low number of migrations since majority of jobs can be executed without exceeding their due dates. This situation changes for higher loads when number of migrations is increased and the distributed algorithm outperforms the local one. We achieved similar results for different performance metrics and different sets of parameters.

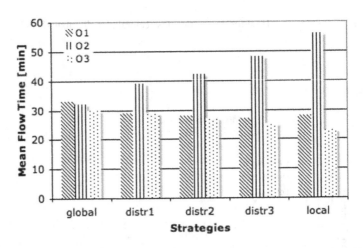

Figure 4.   Influence of strategies on fairness of results

When clusters' loads differ, the decentralized algorithm was able to increase the fairness of results, by limiting the number of jobs that less-loaded clusters must accept. Figure 4 presents typical results. In this case, performance measures depend strongly on the collaboration factor c_k of less-loaded clusters. Strategies 'distr1', 'distr2', and 'distr3' denotes distributed approach with cooperation factors for organizations $O1$, $O2$, and $O3$ equal to (0.25, 0.25, 0.25), (0.2, 0.2, 0.3), and (0.1, 0.1, 0.5), respectively. When their c_k is too low the system as a whole starts to be inefficient, although the performance of the less-loaded clusters is not affected. As it is illustrated in Figure 4 the total performance can be improved for certain values of c_k, while mean flow time of less-loaded clusters does not differ dramatically from the local ("selfish") approach. Consequently, we consider that there must be some minimal value of c_k that results from a grid aggreement. As in real systems the job stream changes, this minimal c_k can be also interpreted as an "insurance" to balance the load.

5. Conclusion and future work

In this paper we proposed an experiment to compare centralized and decentralized approaches to scheduling in grid systems. We have chosen two extreme architectures. In centralized scheduling, the grid scheduler had total control over resources. In decentralized scheduling, local schedulers maintained almost complete control over their resources, as each scheduler sets a limit on the maximum migrated workload that it would have to accept. We have proposed to compare these approaches using GSSIM, a realistic simulation environment for grid scheduling. The main conclusion from experiments is that the decentralized approach, although slightly worse for the system-level performance, provides schedules that are much more fair, especially for less-loaded grid participants.

This work is a start of a longer term collaboration in which we plan to study decentralized scheduling algorithms in context of organizationally-distributed grids. We plan to extend the algorithms to support features or constraints present in current grid scheduling software, such as reservations, preemption or limitation to FCFS scheduling. We also plan to validate experimentally by realistic simulation our previous theoretical work on this subject.

References

[1] The gssim portal. http://www.gssim.org, 2007.

[2] J. Blazewicz. *Scheduling in Computer and Manufacturing Systems*. Springer, 1996.

[3] R. Buyya, D. Abramson, and S. Venugopal. The grid economy. In *Special Issue on Grid Computing*, volume 93, pages 698–714. IEEE Press, 2005.

[4] GridSim Buyya R., Murshed M. A toolkit for the modeling and simulation of distributed resource management and scheduling for grid computing. *Concurrency and Computation: Practice and Experience*, 14(13-15):1175–1220, 2002.

[5] L. Eyraud-Dubois, G. Mounie, and D. Trystram. Analysis of scheduling algorithms with reservations. In *Proceedings of IPDPS*. IEEE Computer Society, 2007.

[6] D. G. Feitelson, L. Rudolph, and U. Schwiegelshohn. Parallel job scheduling âĹ" a status report. In *Proceedings of JSSPP 2004*, volume 3277 of *LNCS*, pages 1–16. Springer, 2005.

[7] I. Foster. What is the grid. http://www-fp.mcs.anl.gov/~foster/Articles/WhatIsTheGrid.pdf, 2002.

[8] R.L. Graham. Bounds on multiprocessor timing anomalies. *SIAM J. Appl. Math*, 17(2), 1969.

[9] K. Kurowski, J. Nabrzyski, A. Oleksiak, and J. Weglarz. Grid scheduling simulations with gssim. In *Proceedings of ICPADS'07*. IEEE Computer Society, 2007.

[10] K. Kurowski, J. Nabrzyski, A. Oleksiak, and J. Weglarz. Multicriteria approach to two-level hierarchy scheduling in grids. In J. Nabrzyski, J. M. Schopf, and J. Weglarz, editors, *Grid resource management: state of the art and future trends*, pages 271–293. Kluwer, Norwell, MA, USA, 2007.

[11] J. Liu, X. Jin, and Y. Wang. Agent-based load balancing on homogeneous minigrids: Macroscopic modeling and characterization. *IEEE TPDS*, 16(7):586–598, 2005.

[12] U. Lublin and D. Feitelson. The workload on parallel supercomputers: Modeling the characteristics of rigid jobs. *Journal of Parallel and Distributed Computing*, 11(63):1105Ð1122, 2003.

[13] F. Pascual, K. Rzadca, and D. Trystram. Cooperation in multi-organization scheduling. In *Proceedings of the Euro-Par 2007*, volume 4641 of *LNCS*. Springer, 2007.

A DATA-CENTRIC SECURITY ANALYSIS OF ICGRID

Jesus Luna*, Michail Flouris[†], Manolis Marazakis and Angelos Bilas[‡]
Institute of Computer Science (ICS).
Foundation for Research and Technology - Hellas (FORTH)
PO Box 1385. GR-71110. Heraklion, Greece.

jluna@ics.forth.gr
flouris@ics.forth.gr
maraz@ics.forth.gr
bilas@ics.forth.gr

Marios D. Dikaiakos and Harald Gjermundrod
Department of Computer Science. University of Cyprus. PO Box 1678. Nicosia, Cyprus
mdd@cs.ucy.ac.cy
harald@cs.ucy.ac.cy

Theodoros Kyprianou
Intensive Care Unit, Nicosia General Hospital
Nicosia, Cyprus
drtheo@cytanet.com.cy

Abstract   The Data Grid is becoming a new paradigm for eHealth systems due to its enormous storage potential using decentralized resources managed by different organizations. The storage capabilities in these novel "Health Grids" are quite suitable for the requirements of systems like ICGrid, which captures, stores and manages data and metadata from Intensive Care Units. However, this paradigm depends on a widely distributed storage sites, therefore requiring new security mechanisms, able to avoid potential leaks to cope with modification and destruction of stored data under the presence of external or internal attacks. Particular emphasis must be put on the patient's personal data, the protection of which is

---

*This work was carried out for the CoreGRID IST project n°004265, funded by the European Commission. The author is also with the Dept. of Computer Science, University of Cyprus, PO Box 1678, Nicosia, Cyprus

[†] Also with the Dept. of Computer Science, University of Toronto, Toronto, Ontario M5S 3G4, Canada.

[‡] Also with the Dept. of Computer Science, University of Crete, P.O. Box 2208, Heraklion, GR 71409, Greece.

required by legislations in many countries of the European Union and the world in general. Taking into consideration underlying data protection legislations and technological data privacy mechanisms, in this paper we identify the security issues related with ICGrid's data and metadata after applying an analysis framework extended from our previous research on the Data Grid's storage services. Then, we present a privacy protocol that demonstrates the use of two basic approaches (encryption and fragmentation) to protect patients' private data stored using the ICGrid system.

Keywords: Data Grid, eHealth, Intensive Care Grid, privacy, security analysis.

1.   Introduction

Modern eHealth systems require advanced computing and storage capabilities, leading to the adoption of technologies like the Grid and giving birth to novel *Health Grid* systems. In particular, Intensive Care Medicine uses this paradigm when facing a high flow of data coming from Intensive Care Unit's (ICU) inpatients. These data needs to be stored, so for example data-mining techniques could be used afterwards to find helpful correlations for the practitioners facing similar problems. Unfortunately, moving an ICU patient's data from the *traditionally isolated* hospital's computing facilities to Data Grids via public networks (i.e. the Internet) makes it imperative to establish an integral and standardized security solution to avoid common attacks on the data and metadata being managed.

As mandated by current Data Protection Legislations [1], a patient's personal data must be kept private because *data privacy means eHealth trust*, therefore comprehensive privacy mechanism are being developed for the Health Grid, harmonizing legal and technological approaches. To provide solutions it is necessary to consider privacy from a *layered* point of view: legal issues are the common base above which state-of-the-art security technologies are deployed. In our previous research related with the security analysis of Grid Storage Systems [2] we concluded that current technological mechanisms are not providing comprehensive privacy solutions and worst of all, several security gaps at the storage level are still open.

There is a clear need not only to identify the vulnerabilities associated with Health Grids, but also for designing new mechanisms able to provide confidentiality, availability, and integrity to the Data Grid in general. Towards this end, the first part of the research presented in this paper shows the result of applying a security analysis framework (extended at the Foundation for Research and Technology - Hellas) over an *Intensive Care Grid* scenario (the ICGrid system developed by the University of Cyprus [3]); this has proven that the greatest threat to patient's privacy comes in fact from the Data Grid's Storage Elements, which are untrusted and may easily leak personal data. In an effort to cover these privacy gaps, the second part of this paper contributes with a *low-level* protocol for providing privacy to current Intensive Care Grid systems from a data-centric point of view, but taking into account the legal framework and keeping compliance with *high-level* mechanisms. The contributed protocol proposes the use of two basic mechanisms to enhance a patient's data assurance: cryptography and fragmentation.

The rest of this paper is organized as follows: Section 2 reviews the basic terminology related with Intensive Care Medicine and the ICGrid system. The basic underlying technological and legal security approaches for Health Grids are presented in Section 3. Section 4 briefly presents and then applies the security analysis framework to ICGrid's data and metadata. Section 5 uses the analysis' results to introduce a privacy protocol proposed for ICGrid, able to use encryption and fragmentation to protect a patient's personal data at rest. Finally, Section 6 presents our conclusions and future work.

2. The ICGrid system

In this Section we introduce the required background and the respective terminology for Intensive Care Medicine, which is the basis of the ICGrid system analyzed in this paper.

2.1 Intensive Care Medicine

An Intensive Care Unit (ICU) is the only environment in clinical medicine where all patients are monitored closely and in detail for extended periods of time, using different types of *Medical Monitoring Devices (MMD)*. An MMD may be defined as a collection of sensors that acquire the patients' physiological parameters and transform them into comprehensible numbers, figures, waveforms, images or sounds. Taking clinical decisions for the ICU patients based on monitoring can be a very demanding and complex task requiring thorough analysis of the clinical data provided: *even the most skilled physicians are often overwhelmed by huge volumes of data, a case that may lead to errors, or may cause some form of life threatening situation* [4]. Providing systems that actively learn from previously stored data and suggest diagnosis and prognosis is a problem that, to our knowledge, has been overlooked in previous Intensive Care Medicine research.

Traditionally, medical research is guided by either the concept of patients' similarities (clinical syndromes, groups of patients) or dissimilarities (genetic predisposition and case studies). Clinical practice also involves the application of commonly (globally) accepted diagnostic/therapeutic rules (*evidence-based medicine* [5]) as well as *case-tailored approaches* which can vary from country to country, from hospital to hospital, or even from physician to physician within the same hospital. These different approaches in treating similar incidents produce knowledge which, most of the times, remains a personal/local expertise, not documented in detail and not tested against other similar data. Global sharing of this cumulative national/international experience would be an important contribution to clinical medicine in the sense that one would be able to examine and follow up implementation of and adherence to guidelines as well as to get the benefit of sharing outstanding experience from physicians.

2.2   ICGrid: data and metadata architecture

Although a number of dedicated and commercially available information systems have been proposed for use in ICUs [6], which support real-time data acquisition, data validation and storage, analysis of data, reporting and charting of the findings, none of these systems was appropriate in our application context. Another important issue with ICU is the need for data storage: an estimate of the amount of data that would be generated daily is given in the following scenario. Suppose that each sensor is acquiring data for storage and processing at a rate of 50 bytes per second (it is stored as text) and that there are 100 hospitals with 10 beds each, where each bed has 100 sensors. Assuming that each bed is used for 2 hours per day, the data collected amounts to 33.5275 GB per day. But this number only represents the data from the sensors. Additional information includes metadata, images, etc.

Because Grids represented a promising venue for addressing the challenges described above, the Intensive Care Grid (ICGrid) system [3] has been prototyped over the EGEE infrastructure (Enabling Grids for E-sciencE [7]). ICGrid is based on a hybrid architecture that combines a heterogeneous set of monitors that sense the inpatients and three Grid-enabled software tools that support the storage, processing and information sharing tasks. The diagram of Figure 1 depicts the acquisition and annotation of parameters of an inpatient at an ICU Site (bottom left) and the transfer of data replicas to two ICGrid Storage Sites. The transfer comprises the actual sensor data, denoted as *Data*, and the information which is provided by physicians during the annotation phase, denoted as *Metadata*. We utilize the notion of a *Clinically Interesting Episode (CIE)* to refer to the captured sensor data along with the metadata that is added by the physician to annotate all the events of interest. Data and Metadata are transferred to Storage Elements and Metadata servers (currently a gLite Metadata Catalogue -AMGA- service [8]) respectively, so afterwards they can be accessed by all the authorized and authenticated parties that will be entities of an ICGrid Virtual Organization. About security, the sharing and collaborative processing of medical data collected by different ICUs raises important privacy, anonymity, information integrity challenges that cannot be addressed by existing commercial ICU information systems. The rest of this paper overviews current security solutions, along with our proposal for a comprehensive low-level privacy approach.

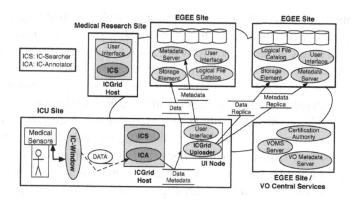

Figure 1. ICGrid System Architecture. White rectangles represent different sites of the infrastructure (each site represents resources of one administrative domain/institution), shaded rectangles represent computer nodes, and shaded ovals depict required Grid services and tools of the ICGrid framework.

3. Health Grid Privacy: legal and technological aspects

As mentioned in Section 1, comprehensive privacy solutions for Health Grids need the synergy of two different factors, legislation and technology.

3.1 Legal aspects

A major concern in eHealth is the confidentiality of the personal data that are stored and managed electronically. The core component of many eHealth systems is the Electronic Health Record (EHR), which is basically the patient's health record in digital format. Nowadays EHR protection is the focus of privacy legislations around the globe. In the European Union, several Directives of the European Parliament and the European Council regulate the processing and management of the EHR. The common foundation of all these initiatives is the EU Directive on Data Protection [1], which provides the general framework for the protection of privacy with respect to the processing of personal data in its widest sense. The Directive concerns more than the protection of the privacy of the natural persons, since it defines *personal data* as all data related to an individual's private, public, or professional life. However, the European Working Party on Data Protection, which was established under article 29 of the Directive [1] and comprises all national data protection authorities of EU Member States, has recently acknowledged that some special rules may need to be adopted for key eHealth applications.

A fundamental term referenced in current eHealth legislations is the concept of *consent*, which is defined as any unambiguous, freely given, specific and informed indication of the patient's wishes, with which she agrees to the processing of her personal data. In other words, *a patient's consent enables the legal processing of her EHR*. However, what happens if, for instance, after an accident the patient is unable to give her consent for accessing her personal data at the Intensive Care Unit? Most of the legal issues and ambiguities related to eHealth regulations are being carefully studied. In the particular case of the European Union, the European Health Management Association (EHMA) along with the Commission established the "Legally eHealth" [9] project to study these issues. This document defines the basic recommendations regarding the protection of patients' data, which can be used towards implementing a comprehensive and harmonized technological solution as the one proposed in Section 5.

3.2   Technological approach

Enforcing privacy of patient's data in Health Grids have spawned the development of a broad range of mechanisms. Two of these are particularly important for our research because of their wide use: the Electronic Health Card and the Grid Security Infrastructure.

The Electronic Health Card [10] is a new health card that stores basic patient data such as name, age, insurance details, and electronic prescriptions, including also physical features to identify the owner, i.e. a photograph and human-readable information. Basically this is a smartcard that stores information in a microchip supporting authentication, authorization and even digital signature creation, and will soon replace EU's existing health insurance cards. Data protection issues are critical in the design of Electronic Health Cards, since they store sensitive personal data that must be as secure and confidential as possible, while operating smoothly in practice. A comprehensive security concept assures the protection of the sensitive data, so with few exceptions, the health card can only be used in conjunction with an *Electronic Health Professional Card*, which carries a "qualified" electronic signature (one that meets strict statutory criteria for electronic signatures). Electronic Health Cards being deployed in EU Member States represent a big step towards a citizen-centered health system.

Along with the Electronic Health Card, Health Grids security is strengthened thanks to the Grid Security Infrastructure (GSI) [11] . This is a set of protocols, libraries, and tools that allow users and applications to securely access Grid resources via well defined authentication and authorization mechanisms relying on X.509 entity certificates, and XML-based protocols that retrieve security assertions from third-party services (i.e. the *Virtual Organization Membership Service* VOMS [12] used in EGEE).

Despite their security features, Electronic Health Cards and GSI do not provide adequate confidentiality guarantees for the data at rest, as our security analysis shows in the next Section.

4. Use Case: security analysis of ICGrid

From the point of view of a typical Health Grid system, its subsystems may be attacked in several ways. Nevertheless, for the purposes of our research on data privacy, the framework proposed in [13] and extended in [2] will be used to pinpoint the main concerns linked with the security of its data and metadata. In a nutshell, the use of this framework consists of determining the basic components related with the system's security (players, attacks, security primitives, granularity of protection, and user inconvenience), so that afterwards they can be summarized to clearly represent its security requirements. As a proof of concept, the security analysis in this Section will be performed in the content of the *Intensive Care Grid* system (ICGrid) (introduced in Section 2), considering also the underlying security mechanisms presented in Section 3.

4.1 Identifying the Elements for the Security Analysis

As mentioned at the beginning of this Section, the first step in our analysis is to identify the elements that play a security-related role in ICGrid:

1 *Players:* four data readers/writers are involved *(i)* the ICU and Medical Research sites that produce and consume the data; *(ii)* the EGEE Central Services that perform VO authentication and authorization as mentioned in Section 3.2; *(iii)* the EGEE *storage facilities* for data and metadata; and finally *(iv)* the "wire" or WAN links (public and private) conveying information between the other players.

2 *Attacks:* the generic attacks that may be executed over ICGrid are related with *(i)* Adversaries on the wire; *(ii)* Revoked users using valid credentials on the Central Services during a period of time -while the revocation data is propagated through the Grid-; and *(iii)* Adversaries with *full control* of the EGEE storage facilities. Each one of these attacks may result in data being leaked, changed or even destroyed.

3 *User inconvenience:* It is critical for IGGrid operation to have minimum latencies when reading and retrieving the stored data and metadata from the EGEE Site. Since smartcards -like the Electronic Health Card explained in Section 3.2- are beginning to be introduced into National Health Systems, it is feasible to consider that involved entities (i.e. patients and physicians) will require them for performing operations into our Health Grid scenario.

4 *Security Primitives:* Two security operations take place within the ICGrid: *(i) Authentication and Authorization* via GSI-like mechanisms and, *(ii) Consent* just as explained in Section 3.1.

5 *Trust Assumptions:* We assume that *(i)* the security tokens used for authentication and consent (i.e. Electronic Health Cards) are personal, intransferable and tamper-resistant; *(ii)* EGEE Sites and/or ICU premises have full control over the data and metadata stored on them; *(iii)* data are encrypted on the public link thanks to secure functionalities (i.e. via SSL); and *(iv)* the EGEE Central Services are *trusted* because they are managed in a secure manner, therefore providing high assurance to its operations.

4.2   Security Analysis Results

Based on the elements identified in the previous Section, Table 1 summarizes the vulnerabilities identified in the ICGrid system. Results are categorized by possible attacks (main columns) and types of damage – the Leak (L), Change (C), Destroy (D) sub-columns. Cells marked with a "Y" mean that the system (row) is vulnerable to the type of damage caused by this particular attack. Cells marked with a "N" mean that the attacks are not feasible, or cannot cause a critical damage.

Table 1.   Summary of security issues related with ICGrid

	Adversary on the wire			Revoked user w/Central Service			Adversary w/Storage Site		
Damage	L	C	D	L	C	D	L	C	D
ICGrid	N	N	Y	Y	Y	Y	Y	Y	Y

From Table 1 we conclude that current Health Grid Authentication and Authorization systems like the ones presented in Section 3.2 are unable to enforce access control close to the Storage Elements and the data itself. In other words, an attacker that bypasses these security mechanisms (by using a local account with administrative privileges or by physical access to the disks) will have full control over the stored data. Unfortunately, merely using cryptography at the Storage Elements is not a viable solution, and moreover imposes a significant performance penalty. In the following Section, we introduce a protocol designed to address these particular privacy concerns.

5. Protecting the patient's personal data at-rest

Up to now we have seen that the most vulnerable and critical part of Health Grid systems are the patient's personal data while at-rest on the storage elements. State of the art distributed storage systems mostly rely on fragmentation[1] ([15] and [16]), encryption ([17]) or even a mix of both ([18], [19] and [20]) for enhancing stored data assurance. Our proposal is a low-level privacy protocol that protects data and metadata from attacks targeting compromised Storage Elements, while *implementing data confidentiality and consent-like mechanisms* (in compliance with current Legislations), by using encryption and fragmentation at the ICGrid Uploader (which uses functionalities of the EGEE Storage Resource Manager -SRM- [21]).

Using the entities from ICGrid architecture (Figure 1), in Figure 2 we show the messages exchanged with the proposed protocol when data and metadata are being stored. Under this scenario the following steps will take place when an IC-Annotator (ICA) is writing a patient's private data file *(D)*:

1 The ICA computes the hash *H(D)* and *signs* this with his private key (using his Electronic Health Professional Card 3.2), that is $E_{KPrivProd}(H(D))$. This enforces non-repudiation, integrity and also provides the basis for an "electronic" consent-like mechanism.

2 Upon reception of $(E_{KPrivProd}(H(D)), D)$, the ICGrid Uploader:

   (a) Generates a nonce *N* and concatenates it to the received hash for generating the symmetric encryption key *H(D)+N*.

   (b) Uses the new key to symmetrically encrypt the data *D*, thus obtaining $E_{H(D)+N}(D)$. This provides patient's data confidentiality, therefore enforcing his right to privacy.

   (c) *Fragments* $E_{H(D)+N}(D)$ into *n-parts* and disperses these to the *Storage Elements at the EGEE Sites*.

   (d) Sends via a secure channel (using GSI) the encryption key *H(D)+N* to a VO Metadata Server hosted at the trusted EGEE Central Services. This service can be seen as a Secure Key Store possibly implemented in cryptographic hardware.

---

[1]In a fragmentation scheme [14], a file *f* is split into *n* fragments, all of these are signed and distributed to *n* remote servers, one fragment per server. The user then can reconstruct *f* by accessing *m* fragments ($m \leq n$) arbitrarily chosen.

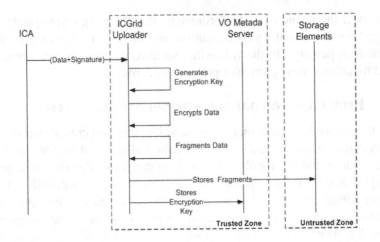

Figure 2.   Privacy Protocol proposed to protect patient's data within ICGrid

Correspondingly, when an IC-Researcher (ICS) tries to retrieve a data with this protocol, the inverse sequence takes place, first of all using the ICGrid Up-loader to defragment the encrypted file and then by securely retrieving the cor-respondent encryption key from the Central Service's Key Store. Encryption at the ICGrid Uploader is a promising solution if security issues related with the Key Store (high availability and protection of the symmetric key) and overall performance can be achieved. However, new research lines also have begun to analyze the performance gains that could be achieved if the *untrusted* Storage Elements participate in the whole encryption scheme or, if the whole fragmen-tation and encryption processes are performed by the *trusted* Key Store.

6.   Conclusions

The computing and storage potential of the Grid are projected to play an important role for implementing Health Grid systems, able to store and man-age Intensive Care Units' data. However, the deployment of production-level Health Grids, such as the ICGrid system presented in this paper, should provide assurances of the patient's data, in particular when referring to personal infor-mation, which is currently the subject of increasing concerns in most countries in the European Union. Unfortunately, when personal data is being transferred from the Hospital to the Grid new vulnerabilities may appear: on the wire, at-rest, with the metadata servers, etc. As a first step on proposing a secu-rity mechanism for Health Grids, in this paper we have performed a security analysis of ICGrid's data and metadata by applying a framework previously ex-tended and used in Grid storage services. The results of the analysis show the need to protect the system from *untrusted Data sites*, which have full control over the stored information, thus allowing its leak, destruction of change due to successful external or even internal attacks. It is also worth highlighting that our analysis takes into consideration the use of commonly deployed security mechanisms. After the security analysis, our research focused on proposing a privacy protocol able to protect the patient's personal data at the Storage Elements with a combination of encryption and fragmentation. The contributed protocol not only provides data confidentiality, but also integrity, high availability and a consent-like mechanism fully compliant with the legal and technological aspects discussed in this paper.

Our next steps include focusing on performance tests that will provide more information about the optimal design of the privacy protocol presented in this paper: encryption/fragmentation at ICGrid Uploader or, fragmentation at ICGrid Uploader with encryption at Storage Elements. A second promising solution refers to using the proposed Central Service's Key Store for encryption and fragmentation; this will greatly improve data assurance (encryption key are never transferred through the network), however communication overhead may become an issue. As future work we plan to base the design of the proposed Key Store into the Hydra system [20], because it resembles our needs in its application field (EGEE's Health Grid) and uses similar security mechanisms.

Acknowledgments

We thankfully acknowledge the support of the European FP6-IST program through the UNISIX project, the CoreGRID Network of Excellence and EGEE-II (contract number INFSO-RI-031688).

References

[1] European Parliament. Directive 95/46/EC of the European Parliament and of the Council of 24 October 1995 on the protection of individuals with regard to the processing of personal data and on the free movement of such data. Official Journal of the European Communities of 23 November 1995 No L. 281 p. 31., October 1995.

[2] Jesus Luna et al. An analysis of security services in grid storage systems. In *CoreGRID Workshop on Grid Middleware 2007*, June 2007.

[3] K. Gjermundrod, M. Dikaiakos, D. Zeinalipour-Yazti, G. Panayi, and Th. Kyprianou. Icgrid: Enabling intensive care medical research on the EGEE grid. In *From Genes to Personalized HealthCare: Grid Solutons for the Life Sciences. Proceedings of HealthGrid 2007*, pages 248–257. IOS Press, 2007.

[4] B. Hayes-Roth et al. Guardian: A prototype intelligent agent for intensive care monitoring. *Artificial Intelligence in Medicine*, 4:165–185, 1992.

[5] DL Sackett et al. *Evidence-Based Medicine: How to Practice and Teach EBM*. Churchill Livingstone, 2nd edition, 2000.

[6] B.M. Dawant et al. Knowledge-based systems for intelligent patient monitoring and management in critical care environments. In Joseph D. Bronzino, editor, *Biomedical Engineering Handbook*. CRC Press Ltd, 2000.

[7] Enabling Grids for E-SciencE project. http://www.eu-egee.org/.

[8] N. Santos and B. Koblitz. Distributed Metadata with the AMGA Metadata Catalog. In *Workshop on Next-Generation Distributed Data Management HPDC-15*, June 2006.

[9] European Health Management Association. Legally eHealth - Deliverable 2. http://www.ehma.org/_fileupload/Downloads/Legally_eHealth-Del_02-Data_Protection-v08(revised_after_submission).pdf, January 2006. Processing Medical data: data protection, confidentiallity and security.

[10] Federal Ministry of Health. The Electronic Health Card. http://www.die-gesundheitskarte.de/download/dokumente/broschuere elektronische gesundheitskarte engl. pdf, Octuber 2006. Public Relations Section. Berlin, Germany.

[11] Von Welch. Globus toolkit version 4 grid security infrastructure: A standards perspective. http://www.globus.org/toolkit/docs/4.0/security/GT4-GSI-Overview.pdf, 2005. The Globus Security Team.

[12] R. Alfieri, R. Cecchini, V. Ciaschini, L. dellAgnello and A. Frohner, A. Gianoli, K. Lorentey, and F. Spataro. VOMS, an Authorization System for Virtual Organizations. In *First European Across Grids Conference*, February 2003.

[13] Erik Riedel, Mahesh Kallahalla, and Ram Swaminathan. A framework for evaluating storage system security. In Darrell D. E. Long, editor, *FAST*, pages 15–30. USENIX, 2002.

[14] Michael O. Rabin. Efficient dispersal of information for security, load balancing, and fault tolerance. *J. ACM*, 36(2):335–348, 1989.

[15] Mark W. Storer, Kevin M. Greenan, Ethan L. Miller, and Kaladhar Voruganti. Secure, archival storage with potshards. In *FAST'07: Proceedings of the 5th conference on USENIX Conference on File and Storage Technologies*, pages 11–11, Berkeley, CA, USA, 2007. USENIX Association.

[16] Cleversafe. http://www.cleversafe.com, 2007.

[17] Atul Adya, William J. Bolosky, Miguel Castro, Gerald Cermak, Ronnie Chaiken, John R. Douceur, Jon Howell, Jacob R. Lorch, Marvin Theimer, and Roger Wattenhofer. Farsite: Federated, available, and reliable storage for an incompletely trusted environment. In *OSDI*, 2002.

[18] Adam L. Beberg and Vijay S. Pande. Storage@home: Petascale distributed storage. In *IPDPS*, pages 1–6. IEEE, 2007.

[19] John Kubiatowicz, David Bindel, Yan Chen, Steven E. Czerwinski, Patrick R. Eaton, Dennis Geels, Ramakrishna Gummadi, Sean C. Rhea, Hakim Weatherspoon, Westley Weimer, Chris Wells, and Ben Y. Zhao. Oceanstore: An architecture for global-scale persistent storage. In *ASPLOS*, pages 190–201, 2000.

[20] Encrypted Storage and Hydra. https://twiki.cern.ch/twiki/bin/view/EGEE/DMEDS, September 2007.

[21] Graeme A. Stewart, David Cameron, Greig A Cowan, and Gavin McCance. Storage and Data Management in EGEE. In *5th Australasian Symposium on Grid Computing and e-Research (AusGrid 2007)*, January 2007.

A FRAMEWORK FOR RESOURCE AVAILABILITY CHARACTERIZATION AND ONLINE PREDICTION IN THE GRIDS*

Farrukh Nadeem, Radu Prodan, Thomas Fahringer
Institute of Computer Science, University of Innsbruck, Austria.
{farrukh,radu,tf}@dps.uibk.ac.at

Alexandru Iosup
Faculty of Electrical Engineering, Mathematics, and Computer Science
Delft University of Technology, The Netherlands.
A.Iosup@tudelft.nl

Abstract   Production grids integrate today thousands of resources into e-Science platforms. However, the current practice of running yearly tens of millions of single-resource, long-running grid jobs with few fault tolerance capabilities is hampered by the highly dynamic grid resource availability. In additional to resource failures, grids introduce a new vector of resource availability dynamics: the resource sharing policy established by the resource owners. As a result, the availability-aware grid resource management is a challenging problem for today's researchers. To address this problem, we present in this work GriS-Prophet, an integrated system for resource availability monitoring, analysis, and prediction. Using GriS-Prophet's analysis tools on a long-term availability trace from the Austrian Grid, we characterize the grid resource availability for three resource availability policies. Notably, we show that the three policies lead to very different capabilities for running the typical grid workloads efficiently. We introduce a new resource availability predictor based on Bayesian inference. Last but not least, using GriS-Prophet's prediction tools we achieve an accuracy of more than 90% and 75% in our instance and duration availability predictions respectively.

Keywords: Resource Availability characterization, Availability Aware Resource Selection, Resource Availability Prediction

---

*This work is partially supported by the European Union through IST-2002-004265 CoreGRID and IST-034601 edutain@grid projects. Part of this work was also carried out in the context of the Virtual Laboratory for e-Science project (www.vl-e.nl), which is supported by a BSIK grant from the Dutch Ministry of Education, Culture and Science (OC&W). Part of this work is also supported by Higher Education Commission (HEC) of Pakistan.

1.   Introduction

Today's grids, e.g., CERN's LCG [6], the TeraGrid [18], the Austrian Grid [17], integrate into a single e-Science platform (tens of) thousands of resources provided by various owners. On these platforms, the typical grid workload comprises yearly millions of single-resource, long-running jobs, with few or even no fault tolerance capabilities [8, 6]. However, the highly dynamic resource availability of the current grids [9, 4] increases for the typical workload the difficulty of resource capacity planning and of scheduling. In traditional computing centers, a human administrator can respond to unavailability events usually after they have occurred; often, on-line tools are employed to predict errors before they occur [5, 19, 12]. In grids, human administration of the system would be required for each participating resource owner, leading to unmanageable costs of ownership. To build predictive tools, more knowledge is needed about the characteristics of the grid resource availability, and about the accuracy and the overhead of on-line predictors. To this end, in this work we present **Grid reSource Prophet (GriS-Prophet)**, a system for resource availability characterization and prediction.

Similarly to other computing resources, grid resources may become unavailable due to failures in hardware, the operating system, or the middleware. In addition, the grid resource owners may set different resource availability policies, from resources that are dedicated to grid use [9] to desktop grids [4] and to resources that are available on-demand from computing centers. Currently, there is no tool to characterize the resource availability in a grid system in which the different resource availability policies coexist. To address this situation, we design GriS-Prophet to characterize the grid resource availability per resource availability policy.

The large number of resources present in grids increases the difficulty of accurate on-line resource availability predictions. While several approaches exist in the context of clusters [19, 12], it is unclear if they can be applied directly in a grid context. Similar work in grids has recently begun [7], but more research is needed before such approaches can be widely deployed. To this end, we propose and implement in GriS-Prophet two methods from pattern recognition and classification: *Bayesian Inference* [3] and the *Nearest Neighbor Predictor*.

In this *work in progress*, our contribution is threefold:

1 We introduce the design of the GriS-Prophet, a system for resource availability characterization and prediction (Section 3);

2 Using GriS-Prophet on a long-term availability trace from the Austrian Grid, we characterize the grid resource availability for three resource availability policies (Section 4);

3 We evaluate the use of two methods from pattern recognition and classification, and in particular of one based on Bayesian Inference, for grid resource *instance* and *duration* availability predictions (Section 5).

We design and build different predictors that take advantage of different availability properties, and compare their effectiveness. We further investigate our predictions by taking trace data of different past durations. Our results show that more specific information is critical for better predictions. On average, we are able to get more than 95% accuracy in our instance availability predictions and more than 75% accuracy in duration predictions.

2. Related Work

Much research has been devoted to analyzing or modeling the resource availability in multi-computers and supercomputers [16, 15], clusters of computers [1, 15], pools of desktop computers [11, 14], cluster-based grids [9], desktop grids [4], and even peer-to-peer systems [2]. However, none of these efforts presents data for a system integrating supercomputers, clusters of computers, and pools of desktop computers at the same time. Futhermore, much of the related work uses few traces or traces from early systems, and needs further research to confirm their findings. Iyer et al. [16] model the failures and the resource availability for the Tandem multi-computer. Arguably the largest study of a large computing environment to date, the work of Schroeder and Gibson [15] characterizes 22 clusters and supercomputers from the LANL environment using data spanning 9 years. Closest to our work, Kondo et al. [4] and Iosup et al. [9] analyze long-term traces from an enterprise desktop grids and from cluster-based, respectively. The former uses two-minutes sampling coupled with the execution of probe applications to collect availability information from the system. The latter introduces cross-cluster resource availability properties.

For resource availability prediction in computing systems, the many research efforts have to date employed a wide variety of data mining techniques: time-series analysis [12, 11, 13], rule-based classification [19, 12], Bayesian statistics [12], signal processing [10], and hybrid models [7]. However, different methods have been found to give better predictions for various data sets; in particular, the Nearest Neighbor predictor (see Section refsec:predictions:nn) gives surprisingly accurate availability state estimates [12, 10, 13, 7]. Sahoo et al. [12] compare time-series analysis, rule-based classification, and Bayesian networks to make accurate on-line predictions about system reliability parameters and availability events. Mickens and Noble [10] and Ren et al. [13] predict the resource availability over the next period of time, under the assumption of the independence of failures across computing nodes.

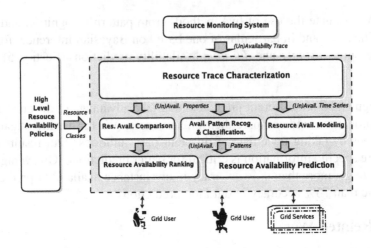

Figure 1.   The GriS-Prophet Architecture.

For resource availability prediction in computing systems, the many research efforts have to date employed a wide variety of data mining techniques: time-series analysis [12, 11, 13], rule-based classification [12], Bayesian statistics [12], signal processing [10], and hybrid models [7]. However, different methods have been found to give better predictions for various data sets; in particular, the Nearest Neighbor predictor (see Section refsec:predictions:nn) gives surprisingly accurate availability state estimates [12, 10, 13, 7]. Sahoo et al. [12] compare time-series analysis, rule-based classification, and Bayesian networks to make accurate on-line predictions about system reliability parameters and availability events. Mickens and Noble [10] and Ren et al. [13] predict the resource availability over the next period of time, under the assumption of the independence of failures across computing nodes.

3.   The GriS-Prophet Architecture

In this section we present GriS-Prophet, an integrated system for resource availability monitoring, characterization, and prediction. With GriS-Prophet, we address two main goals: building a framework for resource availability characterization in grids, and building a framework for resource availability predictions in grids. For both goals, we focus on the concept of resource availability policy, through which the resource owner can specify a dynamic participation of the resource in the grid. Our framework can analyze the characteristics for each resource availability policy, or for a class of related resource availability policies. We also provide a generic prediction framework that takes into account availability policies.

Figure 1 depicts the GriS-Prophet architecture. The GriS-Prophet aggregates resource availability characteristics for each of the resource classes defined through the High Level Resource Availability Policies. The main input for the system is the monitoring data concerning resource availability that is provided by the Resource Monitoring System. The Resource Trace Characterization module analyzes these data based on the resource class, and extracts the resource availability properties over time. The Resource Availability Modeling module tries to model the main input data by fitting them against well-known distributions, e.g., fitting the inter-arrival time between consecutive failures using the Weibull distribution [15, 9]. The Availability Pattern Recognition and Classification module is a general toolbox of data mining tools that uses expert knowledge about grid systems to provide fast and accurate predictions for grid resource availability. Finally, the Resource Availability Comparison and Ranking modules rank resources in the same class based on their suitability to run jobs of different durations and fault-tolerance capabilities.

4. Resource Availability Characterization

In this section we characterize the availability of the Austrian Grid resources. First, we present the Austrian Grid and the general characteristics of a long-term availability trace taken from this environment. Then, we extract from this trace the detailed characteristics for each of the resource availability policies used in the Austrian Grid: the dedicated resources, the temporary resources, and the on-demand resources. Finally, we propose a resource availability classification, and a novel reliability metric specific to grids, the resource stability.

4.1 The Austrian Grid Resource Availability Trace

The Austrian Grid is a nation-wide, multi-institutional, -administrative and -VO Grid platform, consisting of 28 grid sites geographically distributed in Austria. Eeach grid site comprises multiple computational nodes; in total, there are over 1500 processors in the Austrian Grid.

There are three availability policies in the Austrian Grids: the *dedicated resources*, which are meant to be always available to the grid users for production and experimental work, the *temporary resources*, which are resources belonging to university laboratories that join the grid when powered and left idle by their users, and the *on-demand resources*, which are made available to the grid only on user demand and only for large scale jobs or experiments. We define a resource class for each availability policy; for each resource class the class name is identical to that of its associated availability policy. We argue that these classes are most likely to be found in other grids; in particular, the dedicated resources and the temporary resources correspond to traditional cluster-based grids [9] and to desktop grids [4], respectively.

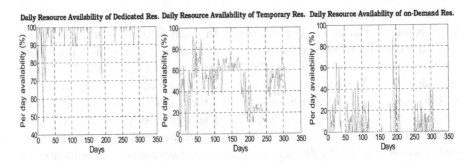

Figure 2. The daily resource availability for the three resource classes in the Austrian Grid: (left) dedicated resources; (middle) temporary resources; (right) on-demand resources.

We accessed, organized, and analyzed a long-term Austrian Grid resource availability trace, from mid-June 2006 to mid-April 2007, for a total of 274 days. The trace records availability information at intervals of 5 minutes; altogether this trace comprises of more than 23 million events occurring in the whole Austrian Grid. Each trace event represents the availability status of a grid resource (i.e., available or unavailable) with the time stamp at which the status of the resource is recorded. A resource is considered available if it is accessible remotely, otherwise unavailable.

4.2   Time Patterns in Resource Availability

We first investigate the evolution of resource availability over time. Figure 2 shows the evolution over time of the daily resource availability for each resource class from the Austrian Grid. On average, the resource availability in Austrian Grid is 33%, with a minimum (maximum) of 4% (71%) per day. The dedicated resources have the highest availability of 92% with a minimum (maximum) of 48% (100%) per day. The temporary resources collectively show a relatively lower average daily availability of 47% with a minimum (maximum) of 0% (92%) per day. The on-demand resources are the least available: on average 9% daily, with a minimum (maximum) of 0% (88%) per day.

We further analyze the patterns that occur in the resource availability time series. We report the average availability of the three resource classes in the Austrian Grid as a function of *hour of the day* (daily patterns) and *day of the week* (weekly patterns). We have also investigates individual resources, as opposed to resource classes, and found more patterns, sometimes even inverse from the resource class patterns; the individual resource patterns are used by the Resource Availability Comparison and Ranking module (see Section 3).

Figure 3 shows the daily resource availability patterns for the three resource classes in the Austrian Grid. The resource availability peaks for all classes

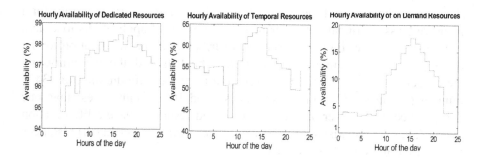

Figure 3. Daily resource availability patterns for the three resource classes in the Austrian Grid: (left) dedicated resources; (middle) temporary resources; (right) on-demand resources.

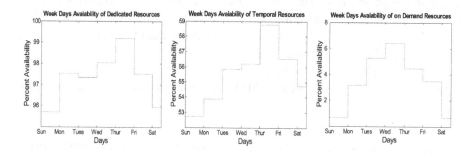

Figure 4. Weekly resource availability patterns for the three resource classes in the Austrian Grid: (left) dedicated resources; (middle) temporary resources; (right) on-demand resources.

during 10AM to 8PM. The dedicated resources show an additional peak between 2AM and 3AM, while the temporary resources show a high level of availability during the night hours. The resource availability is minimal between 4AM and 8AM, the time when most of the resources are turned off or automatically restart. Figure 4 depicts the weekly resource availability patterns for the three resource classes in the Austrian Grid. The peak is observed for all resources from the middle to the end of the work days (i.e., Wednesday for on-demand resources, Thursday for the other resource classes). This corresponds to the typical grid users behavior patterns, where most of the work (job submission) is done in the last half of the week.

4.3   Resource Availability Duration

We now look at the duration of resource availability. We define the *life time* of a resource as the time period between two consecutive failures, and the *life duration* as the length of the life time. The distribution of life durations for a resource class is critical for understanding the types of applications that class can reliably service. Figure 5 shows the distribution of the life duration for the three resource classes in the Austrian Grid. The dedicated, the temporary, and the on-demand resources have on average a maximum life duration of 93495 minutes (65 days), 5275 minutes (4 days), and 1000 minutes (less than one day), respectively. Over 50% of the dedicated resources have a life duration over a day; by comparison, over 50% of the temporary (on-demand) resources have a life duration below 6 hours.

4.4   Resource Availability Classification

Based on the results obtained for the time patterns in resource availabilitys, we propose four classes of resource availability: high, medium upper, medium lower, and low. The four resource availability classes correspond respectively to the daily availability percentage ranges $(75\%, 100\%]$, $(50\%, 75\%]$, $(25\%, 50\%]$, and $[0\%, 25\%]$, and to the availability duration ranges (in hours) $(72, \infty)$, $(36, 72]$, $(24, 36]$, and $[0, 24]$.

By mapping the resources from each resource class are mapped to the resource availability classes, we are able to better understand how each resource

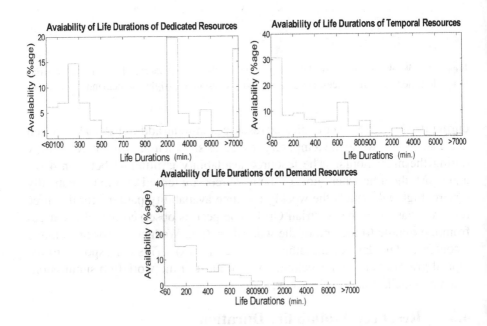

Figure 5.   Lifetime distributions in three resource classes

class can reliably service jobs of various durations. Table 1 describes the resource availability classes, and maps to them the three resource classes in the Austrian Grid. Considering the daily availability, none of the dedicated resources fall in the *low* category; in contrast, all on-demand resources fall in this category. Most of the temporary resources (90%) have low availability. Roughly 78% of dedicated resources are highly available during the day and only 14% of their total are suitable for jobs longer than 72 hours. Most of temporary and all of the on-demand resources are suitable for jobs smaller than 24 hours of duration.

Table 1. Resource classification based on their average availability duration within the resource classes in Austrian Grid.

			Percentage of resources		
		Res. classes	Ded. Res.	Temp. Res.	on-Dem. Res.
High		daily avail.(75%, 100%].	78.57	0	0
		avg. dur. $(72, \infty)$hrs.	14.28	10	0
Med. Upper		daily avail.(50%,75%].	14.28	10	0
		avg. dur. $(36, 72]$hrs.	35.71	0	0
Med. Lower		daily avail.(25%,50%].	7.14	0	0
		avg. dur. $(24, 36]$hrs.	50	0	0
Low		daily avail.[0%, 25%].	0	90	100
		avg. dur. $[0, 24]$hrs.	0	90	100

4.5 Resource Stability

We introduce in this section the *resource stability*, a new reliability metric that defines the ability of a resource (or group of resources) to run multiple jobs of a given duration. The motivation for this new metric is that while grid workloads are dominated both numerically and in terms of resource consumption by groups of single-resource jobs, the core grid resource management middleware (e.g., Globus GRAM) deals with each individual job in turn, incurring high overhead (and, in turn, higher job wait time than expected for the remaining jobs). Selecting one resource with high availability and running on it several jobs of the same runtime characteristics is critical for achieving low overhead.

We define a job duration as the job's uninterrupted run time, i.e., the run time of the job if the job cannot use checkpointing, and the time between checkpoints otherwise. Then, we define the stability of a grid resource r for a job duration ΔJ as:

$$S_r(\Delta J) = \sum_{i=1,n} \lfloor \frac{\Delta t_i}{\Delta J} \rfloor \times P(\Delta t_i)$$

where n is the number of life time periods for the resource r, the set of Δt_i are the unique life durations for the resource r, and $P(\Delta t_i)$ denotes the probability of life duration Δt_i for the resource r. The integral term $\lfloor \frac{\Delta t_i}{J} \rfloor$ counts the number of jobs of duration Δt_k that can be run on resource r consecutively; for $\Delta t_i < \Delta J$ the count is 0.

Figure 6 depicts the resource stability for the three resource classes in the Austrian Grid. The dedicated resources have the highest stability: on average more than 8 times that of the the class with the lowest stability, the on-demand resources. For job durations of 1 hour, the average dedicated resource can run over 40 consecutive jobs; by comparison, the average temporary (on-demand) resources can run 10(5) consecutive jobs.

5.   Resource Availability Prediction

In this section, we present and evaluate parts of our resource prediction framework.

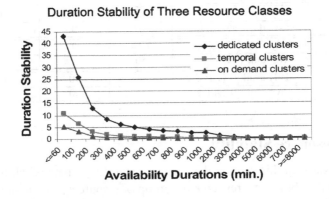

Figure 6.   Resource stability for the three resource classes in the Austrian Grid.

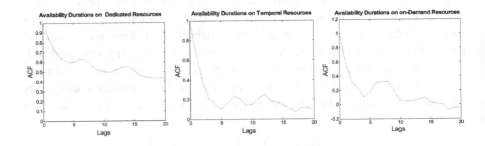

Figure 7.   The auto-correlation function for the three resource classes in the Austrian Grid: (left) dedicated resources; (middle) temporary resources; (right) on-demand resources.

5.1   The Predictors

The autocorrelation functions of availability for the three resource classes are shown in Figure 7. The wave like shapes of the curves indicate similar patterns over time, and high value of autocorrelation for smaller lags (1-3) indicate that the most recent values will yeild better predictions. To exploit the availability features and patterns over time, we employ two methods from *Pattern Recognition and Classification*, the *Bayesian Inference* [3] and *Nearest Neighbor* predictor to serve resource *instance* or *point* availability and *duration* availability predictions. Instance availability predictions describes resource availability at the next monitoring instance, and the duration availability prediction describes resource availability for the immediate next duration of a certain time span.

The bayesian inference (BI) enables estimating the possibility of an event from its *likelihood* and *prior probability* as its probability conditional to its characteristics. We first model resource availability with as either available or unavailable. Then, we predict the resource availability using BI as follows. Let σ_a and σ_u represent the two classes to which our resource state may belong. The *prior probabilities* $P(\sigma_a), P(\sigma_u)$ are known from the characterization phase, and can be calculated as . These can be calculated as $P(\sigma_i) = N_i/N$ for $i = a, u$, where N is the total number of events and N_i the number of number of events for event that leads to state σ_i. We will use as specific BI features the availability features found in Section 4: $x=[day\_of\_week, hour\_of\_day, hour\_of\_day \ \& \ day\_of\_week]$. Then, $p(x|\sigma_i)$ for $i = a, u$ represents the class-conditional probability density functions (PDFs), describing the distributions of a feature vector x for each BI feature. The class-conditional PDFs are also calculated from the trace data during the characterization phase. Then according to BI:

$$P(\sigma_i|x) = \frac{p(x|\sigma_i)P(\sigma_i)}{p(x)} \qquad (1)$$

where $p(x)$ is the PDF of x and for our resource availability model $p(x) = \sum_{i=a,u} p(x|\sigma_i)P(\sigma_i)$. We consider one feature from the feature vector x at a time, which can have any value from its feature space, e.g., $\{0, 1, 2, ..., 23\}$ for the feature "hour_of_day". In our case feature vector only takes discrete values, thus the density functions $p(x|\sigma_i)$ are equivalent to the probabilities $P(x|\sigma_i)$.

The Nearest Neighbor (NN) predictor is a well known pattern classification technique, which selects the the nearest neighbor as a prediction for the current location. To predict resource availability, the last monitored status is used as the nearest neighbor [12, 10, 13, 7]. This method typically suits to the machines with high MTBF(Mean Time Between Failure) and MTR(Mean Time to Reboot).

5.2   Resource Ranking

We now focus on the problem of resource ranking based on the predicted life time duration. Let $\{\gamma_1, ..., \gamma_m\}$ be a set of m resources that can execute a job. The *loss* function $\eta(\gamma_i|\sigma_j)$ describes the loss incurred for selecting resource γ_i when resource state is σ_j, computed as:

$$\eta(\gamma_i|\sigma_j) = Tl_{\gamma_i} + T_{\gamma_k} - Tg(\gamma_i, \gamma_k)$$

where Tl_{γ_i} represents the time lost on resource γ_i in case the resource fails after selection, T_{γ_k} represents total time (including overheads) taken to execute job on next potential resource γ_k, and $Tg(\gamma_i, \gamma_k)$ represents expected time gain in selecting γ_i over γ_k.

Suppose that we select one property from the feature space x and the resource γ_i. If the true state of the resource is σ_j but the predicted state is $\sigma_i \neq \sigma j$ then we will incur a loss of $\eta(\gamma_i|\sigma_j)$. Since $P(\sigma_j|x_i)$ is the probability that the true state of the resource is σ_j, the expected loss with selecting resource γ_i is:

$$R(\gamma_i|x) = \sum_{j=a,b} \eta(\gamma_i|\sigma_j)P(\sigma_j|x_i)$$

In decision-theory terminology, an expected loss is called a risk; thus, we call $R(\gamma_i|x_i)$ the *conditional risk* for selecting a resource property x_i from feature vector x. Our objective is to minimize the overall risk that is given by $\int R(\gamma(x_i)|x_i)p(x_i)dx$, where $\gamma(x_i)$ represents selection of resource γ when feature x_i is selected, d is our notation for *d-space* volume element and integral intends over the entire feature space. To minimize the overall risk, we compute the conditional risk for all the m resources and select resource γ_i for which $R(\gamma_i|x_i)$ is minimum.

5.3   Experimental Results

We now present initial results of our work on resource availability predictions. The work on resource selection risk analysis is in progress.

The first experiment evaluates the accuracy of the predictions for availability instances, that is, for predicting the resource availability state at arbitrary moments in time. We simulate the Austrian Grid environment based on the availability traces taken from the Austrian Grid (see Section 4.1). For each of the 274 days present in the Austrian Grid traces, and for every resource, we make predictions for 24 moments of time, one for each hour where the minuts and the seconds are selected at random. We define the *daily prediction accuracy* as the percentage of correct vs. incorrect predictions for one day, using the traces as ground truth. Figure 8 depicts the daily prediction accuracy using BI for three resource availability properties: *hour-of-the-day, day-of-the-week* and *hour-of-the-day:day-of-the-week*. The last predictor exhibits the best average accuracy: 97% for dedicated resources, and above 90% for temporal and on-demand resources. The *hour-of-the-day* predictor showed the second best accuracy for the three classes, with the *day-of-the-week* predictor proving to be the least accurate (59% average accuracy for temporary resources). In comparison, the NN predictor achieves a higher accuracy for availability instance predictions, of over 97% for all classes of resources, as shown by Figure 9. In addition, the NN predictor never reacher a prediction accuracy below 55%, while the BI predictor can lead to a prediction accuracy as low as 20%.

The second experiment evaluates the accuracy of the predictions for availability duration. We use the same setup as for the first experiment. For each of the 274 days present in the Austrian Grid traces, and for every resource, we evaluate the predictions for all the time durations between 10 minutes and

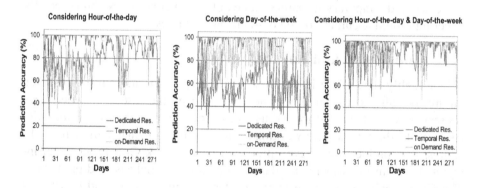

Figure 8. The daily prediction accuracy for availability instances using the BI predictor for three availability properties: (left) hour of the day; (middle) day of the week; (right) combined properties.

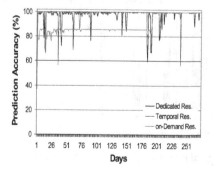

Figure 9. The daily prediction accuracy for availability instances using the NN predictor.

24 hours in increments of 5 min. The accuracy for each prediction duration was evaluated over 100 trials where the date and time of the prediction were selected randomly. For the BI predictor, the likelihood and priori probabilities were computed from the data in the time window before the prediction moment. Figure 10(a)(a) depicts the average accuracy of the availability duration predictions using the BI predictor, for windows of size 7 to 50 weeks. The prediction accuracy decreases as amount of historical data more distant from the prediction moment is included while calculating prior probabilities, this was also confirmed by investigating the auto-correlation function (ACF) of the availability durations in the Austrian Grid traces. The best accuracy using the BI predictor is achieved for windows of 7 weeks: 80%, 75%, and 69% accuracy for dedicated, temporary, and on-demand resources, respectively. Figure 10(a)(b) depicts the accuracy of availability duration predictions using the NN predictor. The NN predictor yields better or similar results to the BI predictor for dedicated and temporary resources, but exhibits lower accuracy and especially lower minimum accuracy for the on-demand resources.

6.   Conclusion and Future Work

The highly dynamic grid resource availability is due not only to resource failure, but also to the sharing policy enforced by the resource owners: resources may be dedicated to grid use, or become temporary part of the grid. As a result, the typical grid workloads are difficult to manage efficiently. To address this problem, we have introduced in this work GriS-Prophet, an integrated system for resource availability monitoring, analysis, and prediction. The GriS-Prophet receives resource availability information, and transforms it into useful predictions for the grid resource management systems. For this

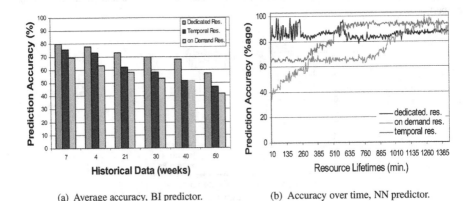

(a) Average accuracy, BI predictor.   (b) Accuracy over time, NN predictor.

Figure 10.   The accuracy of duration predictions using the BI and the NN predictors.

work in progress, we have first used the analysis tools on a long-term availability trace from the Austrian Grid, and characterized the grid resource availability for three resource availability policies. Notably, we have shown that the three policies lead to very different capabilities for running the typical grid workloads efficiently. We have also introduced a new resource availability metric, the resource stability, which characterizes the ability of a resource to execute groups of jobs of a given duration; we argued that selecting resources based on this metric will greatly increase the efficiency of the grid resource selection process. For the GriS-Prophet prediction component, we have introduced a new resource availability predictor based on Bayesian inference, and the notion of resource selection risk. Compared with a predictor used often in resource availability predictions, the Nearest Neighbor, we have shown that our new predictor can deliver better accuracy for specific cases.

For the future, we plan to extend the predictors with traditional data mining algorithms adapted to the grid resource availability data, and to follow our investigation of novel metrics for grid resource availability. Last but not least, we plan to research the optimization problem related to the notion of resource selection risk.

References

[1] A. Acharya, G. Edjlali, and J. H. Saltz. The utility of exploiting idle workstations for parallel computation. In *SIGMETRICS*, pages 225–236, 1997.

[2] R. Bhagwan, S. Savage, and G. M. Voelker. Understanding availability. In *IPTPS*, pages 256–267, 2003.

[3] W. M. Bolstad. *Introduction to Bayesian Statistics*. Aug. 2007.

[4] Derrick Kondo et al. Characterizing resource availability in enterprise desktop grids. *Future Generation Comp. Syst.*, 23(7):888–903, 2007.

[5] P. A. Dinda. A prediction-based real-time scheduling advisor. In *IPDPS*. IEEE Computer Society, 2002.

[6] EGEE Team, LCG. [Online] http://lcg.web.cern.ch/, 2007.

[7] S. Fu and C.-Z. Xu. Exploring event correlation for failure prediction in coalitions of clusters. In *SC*. ACM, 2007.

[8] A. Iosup, C. Dumitrescu, D. H. J. Epema, H. Li, and L. Wolters. How are real grids used? the analysis of four grid traces and its implications. In *GRID*, pages 262–269. IEEE, 2006.

[9] A. Iosup, M. Jan, O. Sonmez, and D. Epema. On the dynamic resources availability in grids. In *Grid 2007*, Austin, TX, USA, September 19-21.

[10] J. W. Mickens and B. D. Noble. Exploiting availability prediction in distributed systems. In *NSDI*. USENIX, 2006.

[11] R. Wolski et al. Automatic methods for predicting machine availability in desktop grid and peer-to-peer systems. In *CCGRID '04*.

[12] Ramendra et al. Critical event prediction for proactive management in large-scale computer clusters. In *KDD*, pages 426–435, 2003.

[13] X. Ren, S. Lee, R. Eigenmann, and S. Baghci. Resource availability prediction in fine-grained cycle sharing systems. In *HPDC*, 2006.

[14] B. Rood and M. J. Lewis. Multi-state grid resource availability characterization. In *Grid 2007*, Austin, TX, September 17-19,.

[15] B. Schroeder and G. A. Gibson. A large-scale study of failures in high-performance computing systems. In *DSN*, pages 249–258. IEEE Computer Society, 2006.

[16] D. Tang and R. K. Iyer. Dependability measurement and modeling of a multicomputer system. *IEEE Trans. Comput.*, 42(1):62–75, 1993.

[17] The Austrian Grid Consortium. [Online] http://www.austriangrid.at, 2007.

[18] The TeraGrid Project. [Online] http://www.teragrid.org/, 2007.

[19] R. Vilalta, C. Apté, J. L. Hellerstein, S. Ma, and S. M. Weiss. Predictive algorithms in the management of computer systems. *IBM Systems Journal*, 41(3):461–474, 2002.

A GRID ENVIRONMENT FOR REAL-TIME MULTIPLAYER ONLINE GAMES*

Radu Prodan, Vlad Nae, Thomas Fahringer
Institute of Computer Science, University of Innsbruck, Austria
CoreGRID Institutes on Grid Information, Resource and Workflow Monitoring Services; on Resource Management and Scheduling
{radu,vlad,tf}@dps.uibk.ac.at

Sergei Gorlatch, Frank Glinka, Alexander Ploß, Jens Müller-Iden
University of Münster, Germany
CoreGRID Institutes on Programming Model; on Grid Information, Resource and Workflow Monitoring Services; on Resource Management and Scheduling
{gorlatch,glinkaf,a.ploss,jmueller}@uni-muenster.de

Abstract   We present joint work between the University of Innsbruck and University of Münster on targeting online games as a novel class of Grid applications, whose user community (general public) is much broader than of contemporary scientific Grids. Online games are a new, large, generic class of applications not yet studied by the Grid community, with the following distinctive features in comparison to traditional parameter studies or scientific workflows: large number of concurrent users connecting to a single application instance, frequent real-time user interactions, negotiation and enforcement of precise Quality of Service (QoS) parameters, adaptivity to changing loads and levels of user interaction, and competition-oriented interaction between users, other actors, and services.

We develop a novel multi-layer, service-oriented architecture for executing online games in a distributed Grid infrastructure. Firstly, scheduling and runtime steering services assist the users in transparently connecting to game sessions while maintaining certain levels of QoS. Secondly, resource allocation, monitoring, and capacity planning services allow efficient resource management that removes the cost and scalability barriers in game hosting. Finally, a Real-Time Framework (RTF) provides the fundamental technology for scaling game sessions to an increased number and density of users through real-time protocols and a variety of parallelization and distribution techniques.

*This work is supported by the European Union through the projects: IST-004265 *CoreGRID* and IST-034601 *edutain@grid*.

1.   Motivation

Within the last ten years, *online gaming* has become a dominant component in the video game market. Every game genre has been impacted and even redefined by the multiplayer network feature, completely transforming the players' experience. This trend is developing further as all the hardware devices released on the market today have built-in network support and thus allow the game developer to rely on network availability. In contrast to existing interactive applications like those provided by Amazon and eBay exclusively oriented towards business transactions, online games have severe realtime and scalability requirements (like the minimum state update rate per second to all clients) which makes them rather unique and yet to be studied by the Grid community.

The online game market is nowadays dominated by three classes of online games: (1) *Massively Multiplayer Online Role Playing Games (MMORPGs)* (e.g. Anarchy Online, Silkroad Online, World of Warcraft) are slow-paced games with few thousands of players sharing one game session in a huge game world map; (2) *First Person Shooter (FPS)* (e.g. Counter Strike Source, Battlefield 2142) are fast-paced action games that only scale to a few players (maximum 64) due to the extremely frequent action processing and communication (up to 60 Hz) required for updating the state of each player in order to experience a realistic environment; (3) *Real-Time Strategy (RTS)* games (e.g. Command & Conquer, Starcraft) are comparatively fast-paced games that typically contain a high number of ongoing interactions in the game world. Users usually have direct control over a huge amount of in-game objects, e.g. military units, and can trigger actions on them that can cause interactions with a lot of other in-game objects and consume a lot of bandwidth and processing time. In this paper we present a novel multi-layer service-oriented architecture as a platform that eliminates the following three main barriers which currently hinder the scalability of online games.

Firstly, to improve the scalability of MMORPG game sessions, game developers and hosting companies currently divide the game world in zones (often representing different realms) which are hosted on different machines. The zones are typically predefined and managed manually by the Hosters. The transition of a client between two zones is in general not a seamless action and requires an important amount of waiting time. This solution has therefore the same limitations as a monotonic environment, since the number of players within one zone is still limited and cannot be extended. To address this limitation, we propose a *Real-Time Framework (RTF)* providing the fundamental technology for dynamic on-the-fly scaling of game sessions to the user demands through real-time protocols and a variety of novel parallelization and distribution techniques. RTF is not limited to MMORPG games, but addresses the more dynamic and harder to satisfy FPS and RTF games too.

Secondly, the only significant attempts in terms of hosting to apply Grid technologies to online games are the Butterfly.net [3] and BigWorld [1] environments. Both are commercial Grid systems for MMORPGs which optimise resource utilisation within a single data centre typically residing within the same local area network. However, because of this restriction, this solution is subject to the same limitations as with any data centre as there is no way to add substantially more resources if those assigned become insufficient. This limitation has also negative economic impacts by preventing any but the largest hosting centres from joining the market which will dramatically increase prices because those centres must be capable of handling peaks in demand, even if the resources are not needed for much of the time. We propose in this paper an architecture that uses the potential of the global Grid to provide on-demand access to a potentially unbounded amount of cheap compute resources connected to the Internet through three advanced middleware services: *resource allocation, monitoring,* and *capacity planning.*

Thirdly, current online game infrastructures are usually based on the best-effort Internet protocol with no QoS support, which is needed for a smooth and realistic experience. We provide *scheduling* and *runtime steering* services to assist the users in transparently connecting to game sessions while enforcing certain levels of QoS for the entire duration of the interaction through proactive load balancing and session steering decisions.

We present our architecture design in Section 2, followed by implementation and experimental results in Section 3. We conclude our paper with an outlook into the future collaboration work in Section 4.

2. Architecture

We designed a distributed service-oriented architecture depicted in Figure 1 to support transparent and scalable access of an increased number of users (compared to current state of the art) to existing online gaming applications. The architecture is based on the interaction of four main actors. (1) *End-user* is the game player that accesses the

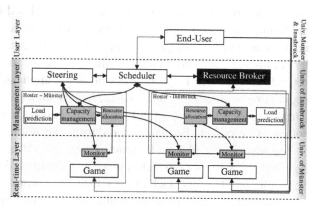

Figure 1. The overall Grid architecture.

online game sessions through graphical clients, typically purchased as a DVD; (2) *Scheduler* is an intermediary that negotiates on behalf of the end-user appropriate game sessions based on the user-centric QoS requirements (e.g. connection latency, game genre, friends, expertise); (3) *Hoster* is an organisation (e.g. Universities of Innsbruck and Münster in the current project) that provides some computational and network infrastructure for running game servers; (4) *Resource broker* provides a mechanism for application Schedulers and Hosters (and possibly other actors) to find each other in a large-scale Grid environment and negotiate QoS relationships.

2.1   User layer

The user layer consists of the end-user game application which should be simple and easy to install and manage. One important requirement is that the Grid middleware must not add additional complexity to existing game installation procedures based on a DVD purchase and several mouse clicks. Rather, we aim at simplifying today's process of initiating and connecting to online game sessions, such that the user no longer needs to memorise and edit IP server addresses or manually edit custom configuration files.

2.2   Scheduling layer

The scheduling layer developed by the University of Innsbruck is where the different interactions between the actors are supported. Apart from an off-the-shelf Resource Broker [4] that we integrated into the environment for resource discovery, we designed two novel services as part of this layer.

2.2.1   Scheduling service.   The Scheduler receives from the user specific QoS requirements which can be performance-related (e.g. maximum latency, minimum bandwidth, minimum throughput) or game-specific (e.g. game genre, minimum number of players, difficulty, tournament planning). Our Scheduler goes beyond the current state-of-the-art practice in scientific computing (i.e. centralised best-effort optimisation of single application-specific metrics), by negotiating with several distributed Hosters multiple and often contradictory (from each actor's perspective) QoS requirements (e.g. execution time versus computation cost) to be maintained during execution.

The mapping of players to game servers, as well as the allocation of Hoster resources to game servers, takes place as a distributed negotiation between the Scheduler and Hosters, each of them trying to optimise its own specific metrics expressing individual interests. While the Scheduler purely negotiates in terms of users-centric QoS parameters, the Hosters try to selfishly optimise metrics related to their own and often contradicting interests such as maximising resource utilisation or income. A centralised Scheduler, as typically approached in the scientific Grid community, is therefore not a feasible solution in such a distributed non-collaborative environment. Rather, we approach the problem using game theory [8], where a number of parties having different objectives and utility functions negotiate using cooperative or non-cooperative techniques, possible enhanced with auctioning or bargaining models. It is proven that such theories converge to a Nash equilibrium that represents a balance between risks and rewards for all participating parties. The result of the negotiation process is a performance contract that the Scheduler offers to the end-user and which does not necessarily match the original QoS request. The user has the option to accept the contract and connect to the proposed session, or reject it.

2.2.2   Runtime steering service.   There may occur factors during the execution of a game session which affect the performance, such that the negotiated contracts are difficult or impossible to be further maintained. Typical perturbing factors include external load on unreliable Grid resources, or overloaded servers due to an unexpected concentration of users in certain "hot spots". The steering service interacts at runtime with the monitoring service of each Hoster in the management layer for preserving the negotiated QoS parameters for the entire duration of the game session. Following an event-action paradigm, a violation of a QoS parameter triggers appropriate adaptive steering or rescheduling actions using the API provided at the real-time layer.

The QoS parameters of online games to be enforced may be of two kinds:

(1) *Client-related QoS parameters* include requirements between the local game client and the remote server such as latency and bandwidth constraints collected by special sensors embedded in the client application (hidden to the end-user) that monitor the traffic on the real-time connection links. Upon violation of these requirements, users will be transparently migrated to new game servers (of the same distributed session) that maintain the original QoS parameters negotiated by the Scheduler.

(2) *Game session-related QoS parameters* include application-specific requirements such as efficient use of Grid resources, maximum load, or proper load balancing. Typical game session-related steering actions are: starting a new game server (potentially at a different Hoster site) for distributing the user load of an overloaded session; load balancing by migrating users between game servers within one or across several Hosters; switching-off underutilised game servers (after migrating the users) for improved resource utilisation; or cloning game servers upon critical QoS values to hide user migration latencies.

All of these actions must be performed transparently from the user's point of view who should not notice any change or experience minimum delay in the execution environment. To meet this challenge, we consider defining performance contracts based on fuzzy logic [11] (rather than based on exact boolean variables) that allows one to linguistically state smooth transitions between areas of acceptance and violation. The user can express the contracts by defining a membership function with the following signature: $\mu : \mathbb{R} \rightarrow [0,1]$, where $\mathbb{R}$ denotes the set of real numbers (representing performance values such as current user load). A very simple membership function could be a step function with three linguistic values: fulfil (indicating proper execution), critical (indicating that the contract is in danger and needs steering), and violate (when the contact has already been broken). Fuzzy logic is a powerful technique that will provide flexibility in performing proactive steering actions before the actual contracts are violated, for example through anticipated migration or cloning when the load of the game sessions enters a critical stage.

2.3   Resource management layer

The resource management layer, mostly developed by the University of Innsbruck (apart from monitoring developed in Münster), focuses on the development of generic Grid management services within each Hoster, while dealing with the challenges raised by the main requirements of online games: scalability to thousands of online user connections, optimised allocation of resources, and monitoring and steering to maintain the QoS parameters in dynamic environments like the Grid. The traditional way of allocating resources in a Grid environment employs opportunistic matchmaking models based on runtime resource requests and offers [9], which are known to converge to local minima as we demonstrated in previous work on scientific workflows [4]. We improve on the state of the art by designing a management layer consisting of three services described in the following.

2.3.1   Resource allocation.   Typically, each Hoster in the management layer owns one Resource Allocation service responsible for allocating local resources to a large number of connecting clients. The Resource Allocation service receives from the Scheduler connection requests formulated in terms of QoS requirements such as minimum latency, maximum bandwidth or maximum load, and returns either a positive answer if it can accommodate the client, or a negative answer otherwise.

It is important to notice that, for online games, the resource allocation problem is significantly different than in scientific computing. Scientific applications are typically owned by single users and consist of a set of computationally intensive jobs to be mapped to individual processors. Online games, in contrast, are characterised by a large number of users that share the same application instance and interact within the same or across different game servers. The atomic resource allocation units for users are, therefore, no longer coarsegrain processors, but rather fine-grained threads and memory objects, which are obviously harder to address and more sensitive to external perturbations.

2.3.2 Monitoring. High-level monitoring services implemented by the University of Münster are aiming at observing the QoS parameters previously negotiated by the Hoster as performance contracts which must be preserved throughout the user's participation in the game session. Several monitoring parameters are summarized in particular profiles. To support a wide range of game types, we distinguish between two different types of profiles: basic profiles common to all games, and the custom profiles which allow the compilation of customised parameter sets adapted to the requirements of any particular game.

The basic profiles, already developed and implemented by the University of Münster, support monitoring of low-level QoS parameters, as well as of game-related metrics crucial for guaranteeing an adequate game play experience to the users. The *system profile* and *network profile* contain generic low-level system parameters which do not depend on the game inner state and represent an assessment of the game server resource use. The *entity model profile*, *client data profile*, and *game world profile* monitor information related to internal game mechanisms like entity positions, messages sent or received, or end-user activity information such as idle, spectator, or active.

2.3.3 Capacity Planning. The load of a game session depends heavily on internal events such as the number of entities that find themselves in each other's area of interest and interact altering each other's stare. Alongside internal events, there may also occur external events such as the user fluctuation over the day or week with peak hours in the early evening [5]. Hence, it becomes crucial for a Hoster to anticipate the future game load which brings the following benefits: (1) enhanced confidence in guaranteeing the fulfilment of global QoS parameters for the entire distributed game session (like smooth response time or proper load balancing) through ahead-planning of resource allocation; (2) anticipation of critical game stages by predicting potential contract violations and performing proactive steering actions before the contracts are actually broken; (3) opportunities for more aggressive resource allocation that accommodates a larger number of users.

Projecting future load in highly dynamic Grid environments of game players needs to take into account a multitude of metrics such as processor, memory, and network latencies and load. All these metrics can be deterministically expressed as a (game-specific) function of the human factor, which is the hardest and most unpredictable parameter. We therefore reduce the prediction problem to the task of estimating the entity distribution in the game world at several equidistant time intervals. Our solution goes towards neural networks due to a number of reasons which make them appropriate to being applied on online games: they adapt to a wide range of time series, they offer better results than other simple methods, and they are sufficiently fast compared to other more sophisticated statistical analysis.

We employ a neural network for load prediction that has a signal expander as input to ensure a non-linear expansion of the input space fed to the hidden neuron layers (see Figure 2). The input fed into the fuzzy layer consists of the positions of the players in the game world at several successive equidistant time intervals (Δt). As output signal, network provides a similar space representing a prediction of the players' layout in the next time interval ($t + \Delta t$). Because the input is expanded, the expected output will not be a precise estimation of each player's position,

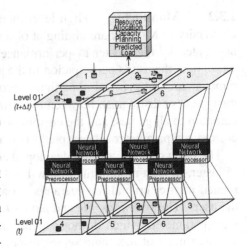

Figure 2.   Neural network capacity planning.

but a world of subarea estimations. Each zone of the map is analysed by dividing it into subareas and providing a local prediction. An interesting aspect is that the edges of the subareas are overlapped to hide latencies upon player transitions.

Two offline phases are required for utilising the neural network-based prediction. The *data set collection* phase is a long process in which the game is observed by gathering entity count samples for all subareas at equidistant time steps. The training phase uses most of the previously collected samples as training sets, and the remaining as test sets. The *training phase* runs for a number of eras, until a convergence criterion is fulfilled. A training era has three steps: (1) presenting all the training sets in sequence to the network; (2) adjusting the network's weights to better fit the expected output (the real entity count for the next time step); and (3) testing the network's prediction capability with the different test sets.

These two stages are performed only once per world and game type since they are the main game characteristics that determine the player behaviour. Once successfully trained, the network can be serialised and reused at a later time, when the same world and game type combination is played.

2.4   Real-time layer

As part of the real-time layer, the University of Münster is developing the Real-Time Framework (RTF) [6] that hides the Grid management infrastructure for the game servers. For the in-game communication, we designed a custom and highly optimised communication protocol independent from the XML-based protocols within the management infrastructure. To improve the

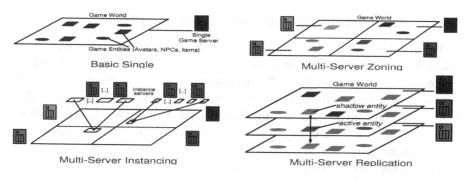

Figure 3.   Game distribution strategies.

game scalability to a high number and density of users, we distribute game sessions based on several distribution strategies illustrated in Figure 3.

The concept of *zoning* [2] is based on the distribution of the game world into several geographical zones, each zone being assigned to one game server. Players are able to move freely between zones with little overhead such that no interruptions in the game play are experienced. *Instancing* uses multiple, independently processed copies of highly frequented subareas of the geographical world, each copy being processed by one separate server. If a user moves into one such highly frequented subarea, he is assigned to one of the available copies. *Replication* is a novel technique developed in Münster [7] which assigns multiple servers to a single game world zone with a high load. The responsibility of computing the entities' states in that zone is divided equally among the assigned processors. Each processor has a local copy of the states of all entities in the game world zone which, after the assigned computations are done, is synchronised with the other servers.

The main novel features of the RTF are as follows: (1) Highly optimised and dynamic real-time communication links which adapt to changes in the dynamic Grid environment and allow the RTF, e.g. to redirect the communication to new servers underneath without a required reaction from the game developer; (2) Hidden background preparations like speculative connection establishments, which allow the runtime transfer and redistribution of parts of a game onto additional Grid resources without noticeable interruptions for the participating users; (3) An interface for the game developer that abstracts the game processing from the location of the participating resources. This is the technical basis that allows the management layer to dynamically reassign the game processing to the available resources; (4) Monitoring data gathering in the background about, e.g., the number of exchanged events, number of in-game objects on a server, and connection latencies. This data is used by the management layer for capacity planing and steering services.

3.   Implementation Issues and Experiments

We are developing the scheduling and resource management layers as a set of WSRF-based services deployed in the Austrian Grid environment that aggregates a large collection of heterogeneous parallel computers distributed across several major cities of Austria. We provide a *management portal* developed by the University of Innsbruck and depicted in Figure 4, which offers means of visualising the available machines in the Grid, the game sessions running at each Hoster site, and important monitoring metrics such as user load on each game server. The portal also offers key management features such as start-up and shut-down of sessions for games using RTF as well as stand-alone proprietary game server.

University of Münster implemented the RTF as a C++ library, since C++ is the dominating language in game development mainly due to performance reasons. The C++ library hides the underlying complexity of the distributed Grid from the game developers and allows them to realise their games without a major shift compared to contemporary client-single server development. Additionally, we realised a Java interface to the C++ library for exporting monitoring and management capabilities to the upper layers.

In order to generate load patterns suitable for testing and validating our prediction method, we developed a distributed FPS game simulator supporting the zoning and inter-zone migrations of the entities (see Figure 5). The simulator integrates the real-time layer implemented and generates dynamic load by simulating interaction hot-spots between large numbers of entities managed by one server. In order to simulate an as realistic environment as possible, the entities are driven by several Artificial Intelligence (AI) profiles which determine their behaviour during a game session: *aggressive* determines the entity to seek and interact with opponents; *team player* causes the entity to seek or form a group with its teammates; *scout* leads the entity into uncharted zones of the game-world (not guaranteeing any interaction); and *camper* simulates a well-known FPS game tactic to hide and wait for the enemy. To better emulate player behaviour in a realistic session, each entity is able to dynamically switch between all AI profiles during the simulation (e.g. from aggressive to camper once wounded) with a certain degree of randomness. We configured the entity speed and interactions to a highly dynamic value making the prediction in our belief harder than in existing fast-paced FPS games.

To validate our neural network prediction in the first instance, we generated using our game simulator eight different trace data sets with different characteristics by running 17 hours of simulations for each set and sampling the game state at every two minutes. The first four data traces simulate different scenarios of a highly dynamic FPS game, while the other four are characteristic to different MMORPG sessions. We use this trace data for training the neural

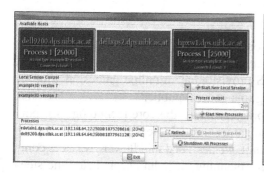

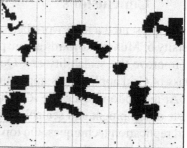

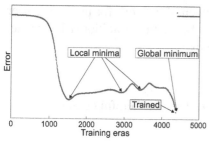

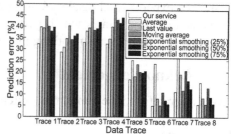

Figure 5. Game simulator snapshot

Figure 4. Management portal snapshot

Figure 6. Error trend during neural network training

Figure 7. Comparison of neural network prediction against other methods

network as presented in Section 2.3.3 until the process converges to a global minimum (see Figure 6). The majority of the traces are used as training sets and the rest as test sets.

To quantify the quality of our prediction, we compared the prediction error of the neural network against other fast prediction methods such as moving average, last value, average, exponential smoothing, which are known to be among the most effective in large and dynamic environments as the Grid [10]. Figure 7 illustrates that, apart from producing better results, our neural network prediction has the main quality of being adaptive to time series with different characteristics which related methods fail to achieve. The drawback of these conventional methods is that it is not universally clear during a game play which of them should be applied as the real-time prediction method for the next time step. Our prediction successfully manages to adapt to all these heterogeneous types of signals and always delivers good results, especially in the case of highly dynamic FPS action games (i.e. first four data traces).

4. Conclusions

We presented a joint work between the University of Innsbruck and the University of Münster towards a transparent, four-layer Grid environment designed to improve the scalability and QoS provisioning in online games, as a novel class of Grid applications appealing to a general public.

At the bottom layer, the RTF library provides the core technology for portable development and scalability of games through the combination of zoning and replication techniques. On top of it, we designed middleware services comprising resource allocation, capacity planning, scheduling, and runtime steering for automatic on-the-fly management, scaling, and provisioning of QoS parameters required for a smooth and efficient execution on the underlying Grid resources. We integrated the RTF library into a game simulator capable of delivering realistic user loads required for validating our methods, and we showed experimental results of using a neural network for predicting user behaviour in online games which performs better than traditional last value, averaging, or exponential smoothing methods.

5. Acknowledgement

We are grateful to the anonymous referees for their helpful comments.

References

[1] BigWorld. BigWorld Technology, http://www.bigworldtech.com.

[2] W. Cai, P. Xavier, S. J. Turner, and B.-S. Lee. A scalable architecture for supporting interactive games on the internet. In *16th workshop on parallel and distributed simulation*, pages 60–67, Washington, DC, USA, 2002. IEEE Computer Society.

[3] Emergent Game Technologies. Butterfly.net, http://www.emergentgametech.com.

[4] T. Fahringer, R. Prodan et al. ASKALON: a Grid application development and computing environment. In *6th Int. Workshop on Grid Computing*. IEEE Computer Society, 2005.

[5] W.-C. Feng, D. Brandt, and D. Saha. A long-term study of a popular MMORPG. In *NetGames'07*, ACM Press., 2007.

[6] F. Glinka, A. Ploss, J. Müller-Iden, and S. Gorlatch. RTF: A Real-Time Framework for Developing Scalable Multiplayer Online Games. In *NetGames'07*, ACM Press., 2007.

[7] J. Müller-Iden and S. Gorlatch. Rokkatan: Scaling an RTS game design to the massively multiplayer realm. *Computers in Entertainment*, 4(3):11, 2006.

[8] R. B. Myerson. *Game Theory: Analysis of Conflict*. Harvard University Press, 1997.

[9] R. Raman, M. Livny, and M. H. Solomon. Matchmaking: An extensible framework for distributed resource management. *Cluster Computing*, 2(2):129–138, 1999.

[10] R. Wolski. Experiences with predicting resource performance on-line in computational grid settings. *ACM SIGMETRICS Performance Evaluation Review*, 30(4):41–49, 2003.

[11] L. A. Zadeh. Fuzzy logic. 21(8), 1988.

IANOS: AN INTELLIGENT APPLICATION ORIENTED SCHEDULING FRAMEWORK FOR AN HPCN GRID

*Hassan Rasheed, Ralf Gruber and Vincent Keller
*EPFL, Lausanne, Switzerland, *CoreGRID Fellow*
Hassan.Rasheed, Ralf.Gruber, Vincent.Keller@epfl.ch

Wolfgang Ziegler and Oliver Waeldrich
Fraunhofer SCAI, Germany
Oliver.Waeldrich, Wolfgang.Ziegler@scai.fraunhofer.de

Philipp Wieder
University of Dortmund, Dortmund, Germany
philipp.wieder@udo.edu

Pierre Kuonen
EIF, Fribourg, Switzerland
Pierre.Kuonen@eif.ch

Abstract   We present the architecture and design of the IANOS scheduling framework. The goal of the new Grid scheduling system is to provide a general job submission framework allowing optimal positioning and scheduling of HPCN applications. The scheduling algorithms used to calculate best-suited resources are based on an objective cost function that exploits information on the parameterization of applications and resources. This standard-based, interoperable scheduling framework comprises four general web services and three modules. The middleware is complemented with one client and one admin console. The implementation is based on proposed Grid and Web services standards (WSRF, WS-Agreement, JSDL, and GLUE). It is agnostic to a specific Grid middleware. The beta version of IANOS has been tested and integrated with UNICORE. The validation of IANOS is in progress by running different types of HPCN applications on a large-scale Grid testbed.

Keywords: HPCN, Grid Scheduling, Meta Scheduling

1.   Introduction

In this paper we describe the integration of the Meta Scheduling Service (MSS) developed within the German VIOLA project [6], with the Swiss Intelligent Grid Scheduling (ISS) project [2], and the new monitoring system VAMOS [4]. The result is the new Grid scheduling framework IANOS (Intelligent ApplicatioN-Oriented Scheduling) aims at increasing the throughput of a Grid of High Performance Computing and Networking (HPCN) resources. The first testbed includes parallel machines in Germany and Switzerland.

With respect to existing Grid scheduling systems, the IANOS framework uses information about the behavior of HPCN applications on computational resources and communication networks. The goal is to place an application on a well suited resource in a Grid, reducing costs and turn-around time and improving throughput of the overall computing resources. In future, a Grid should include different types of resources. Some have high processor performances, others a high main memory bandwidth, others a low latency network, others a high inter-node communication bandwidth, or a good access to huge data storage systems. In the set of target applications there are those needing a fast processor, a high main memory bandwidth, a low network latency, a high inter-node communication bandwidth, or need a good data access. It is an art to recognize the right resource for each type of applications. For this purpose, applications and computational resources are characterized by a set of parameters [1]. These parameters can be fix or are determined after each execution by the new VAMOS [4] application-oriented monitoring system. They are then used to make a-priori estimations demanding prediction models for the CPU time, the waiting time, or on the overall execution costs.

The IANOS is a standard based, interoperable scheduling framework. It comprises four general web services and three modules: the *Meta Scheduler* (MSS) performs resource discovery, candidate resource selection and job management; the *Resource Broker* is responsible for the selection of suitable resources based on a Cost Function model; the *System Information* is a frontend to Data Warehouse module, analyzes the stored execution data of a given application to compute certain free parameters to be used by scheduling models; the *Monitoring Service* passes the submission information received from MSS to the Monitoring Module and sends monitored data received from the Monitoring Module to the System Information; the *Monitoring Module* monitors the application during execution and computes execution relevant quantities; the *Data Warehouse* module is part of SI and stores information on applications, Grid resources and execution related data; the *Grid Adapter* module provides generic interfaces and components to interact with different Grid middlewares. The framework is complemented with one *IANOS client* that submits the application to the MSS using WS-Agreement, and the *Web Admin* that provides a web interface to store application and resource relevent parameters and data into the Data Warehouse.

IANOS allocates computing and network resources in a coordinated fashion [3]. The IANOS MSS prepares a list of candidate resources and sends it to the Broker. The Broker collects all the data needed to evaluate the cost function model, prepares a list of potentially optimal schedules that is sent back to the MSS. If still available, the latter module submits the application to the machine with lowest costs. Otherwise, the second most cost efficient resource is chosen and so on. If all the five proposals are not available, the Broker is reactivated to recompute another set of proposals.

The implementation is based on state-of-the-art Grid and Web services technology as well as existing and emerging standards (WSRF, WS-Agreement, JSDL, and GLUE). The IANOS is a general scheduling framework that is agnostic to a Grid middleware, and therefore can easily be adapted to any Grid middleware. The beta version of IANOS has been tested and integrated with UNICORE 5 by implementing a Grid Adapter for it. The present version includes all the models and monitoring capabilities. The free parameters in the cost function model have been validated on GbE clusters with well-known applications. The next step is to build a Grid of different type of resources and a fine tuning of the free parameters using a set of relevant applications coming from the HPCN community.

The IANOS middleware helps not only in optimal scheduling of applications but also the collected data on Grid resources and the monitored data on past application executions can be used to detect overloaded resources and to pin-point inefficient applications that could be further optimized.

The IANOS middleware architecture is detailed in Section 2. The reference scheduling scenario is explained in Section 3. In Section 4, a short description of IANOS scheduling models is presented. The last Section provides summary and information on future work.

2. Architecture & Design

The IANOS architecture is presented in Figure 1. In the following subsections the different modules are presented.

2.1 Grid Adapter

The Grid Adapter mediates access to a Grid System through a generic set of modules as shown in Figure 2. It provides information on the Grid resources including CPU time availability and handles the submission of jobs on the selected resources. The SiteManager queries the Grid system for a list of available Grid Sites based on their type, for example, Globus site or UNICORE site. The InfoManager provides static information on the hardware and soft-

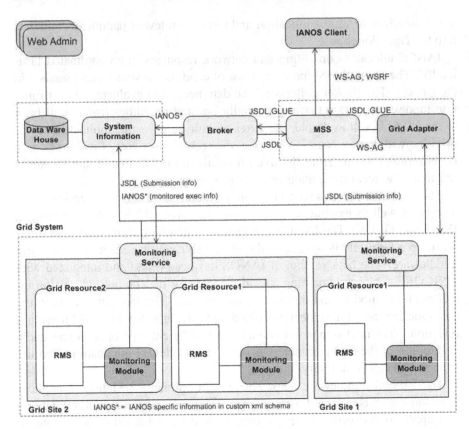

Figure 1.   IANOS Middleware Architecture:

ware configurations, on usage policies, and dynamic information on resource availability, i.e. on the current loads. All this information is modeled as an *extended GLUE schema* [8]. The TemplateManager contacts available Grid Sites for their installed applications. Each application is modeled as a *WSAG-Template*. The DataManager is responsible for the stag in/out of job files. The SubmissionManager is responsible for job submission and management. The ReservationManager handles the reservation of computational and network resources for a job submission. The resources are reserved for certain duration of start and end time. The JobManager and the DataManager receives *JSDL* [7] as input while the ReservationManager receives *WS-Agreement* as an input.

The Grid Adapter is the only IANOS module that is connected to a Grid system. Therefore, necessary interfaces are defined for each Grid adapter module for easy integration with different Grid middlewares. We do not need to implement a new Grid Adapter for each Grid middleware. Instead, a plugin mechanism is used in the design of Grid Adapter modules. At the moment, Grid adapter plugins for the UNICORE Grid middleware have been implemented.

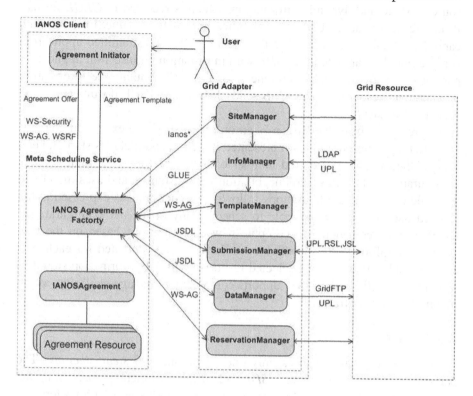

Figure 2.   Grid Adapter Modules & their Interaction with MSS and Grid Resource

2.2   Meta Scheduling Service (MSS)

The MSS is the only IANOS service that is accessible by the client. It performs client authentication and candidate resources selection. It uses the Grid Adapter to access the Grid system, and the access to the client is provided by an *AgreementFactory* interface. The client and the MSS communicate over the WS-Agreement protocol. The Client requests installed applications by issuing an *AgreementTemplate* request. The MSS first validates user requests and then queries the underlying Grid system for the list of installed applications based on user authorization filtering and application availability. The MSS sends these applications to the client in the form of *AgreementTemplates*. The client selects and submits the application to MSS by sending an *AgreementOffer*. This *AgreementOffer* includes a job description, application parameters, and user QoS preferences (maximum cost, maximum turnaround time).

Upon receiving an *AgreementOffer* from client, it first identifies potential candidate resources and then queries the Grid Adapter for each candidate resource's static and dynamic information, which is received in *GLUE* format. It also retrieves the CPU time availability information (TimeSlots) for each candidate resource by contacting their local RMS. The submitted application is represented by an extended *JSDL* with information on instrinsic application parameters, and user QoS preferences, and *GLUE* contains the information on candidate resources. The MSS sends JSDL and GLUE documents to the Resource Broker.

The response from the Broker is an ordered list of five execution configurations. Each configuration is represented by JSDL and includes start and end time of the execution, required number of nodes, and the cost value for this configuration. The MSS starts negotiation with resources and uses the GA to schedule one of the configurations following the preferences expressed in the ordered list. If it is not possible to schedule any of the five configurations, the Broker is recontacted to compute new configurations based on the new availability information. A *WS-Agreement Resource* is created for each successfully submitted job on a selected resource, with job information stored as resource properties. The MSS supports complete job management, such as job monitoring and control.

2.3   Broker

The Broker service exposes only one operation, *getSystemSelection*. The parameters of this operation are *JSDL* and *GLUE* documents; representing the candidate resources, the application parameters, and the user QoS preference. The Broker uses two modules to decide on the suitable resources for a given application. The *EtemModule* implements the Execution Time Evaluation model, and the *CfmModule* implements the Cost Function model. Applications can use the standard cost function implementation or a separate plugin tailored to a specific application can be implemented. This implementation framework allows separating implementations of different models and to extend or provide new implementations of the models.

Each candidate resource's availability information is in the form of TimeSlots, where every TimeSlot is represented by the start and the end time, and by the free number of nodes during this available time. To compute a cost function value for each TimeSlot of the candidate resources, the RB needs IANOS relevant resource parameters shown in Table 1, and data on the characteristics and requirements of the submitted application. The RB contacts the System Information for this data, and, based on the application requirements (nodes, memory, libraries etc), filters out unsuitable candidate resources. It then calculates the cost values for all suitable (execution time is less than available time)

TimeSlots of the candidate resources, prepares an ordered list of suitable configurations (including start-time and deadlines), and sends it to the MSS. Each configuration along with job requirements is represented by *JSDL*.

2.4   System Information

It exposes three operations: *getAppISSInfo*, *updateAppExecutionInfo* and *updateISSInfo*. The *getAppISSInfo* operation provides data on given resources and applications to the Broker. The *updateAppExecutionInfo* operation receives execution related data from the Monitoring service. The *updateISSInfo* operation receives IANOS relevant static resource information from Monitoring service.

The System Information is a frontend to the Data Warehouse module. An interface is designed to allow integration between System Information and Data Warehouse independent of the specific implementation of the Data Warehouse. The Data Warehouse is contacted by the System Information to query, add or update a stored data. It includes the ETEM Solver module that recomputes the execution time prediction parameters after each job execution. These parameters are then used by the Broker to predict the execution time for the next application submission.

2.5   Data Warehouse

The Data WareHouse is a repository of all information related to the applications, to the resources found, to the previous execution data, and to the monitoring after each execution. Specifically, the Data Warehouse contains the following information:

- Resources: Application independent hardware quantities, IANOS related characteristic parameters

- Applications: Application characteristics and requirements (software, libraries, memory, performance)

- Execution: Execution data for each executed run (Execution dependent hardware quantities, application intrinsic parameters, free parameters)

A Web Admin interface is designed to add or update information about resources and applications into the Data Warehouse.

2.6   Monitoring Service & Module

The Monitoring service receives submission information in JSDL from MSS and passes them to the Monitoring Module to monitor the "IANOS" application. Upon receiving the monitored execution data from the Monitoring Module, it sends the same data to the System Information.

The Monitoring Module [4] measures and collects IANOS relevant execution quantities (MFLOPS/s rate, memory needs, cache misses, communication and network relevant information, etc) during application execution. These quantities can be computed through a direct access to hardware counters using PAPI. It performs a mapping between hardware monitored data using the Ganglia service and application relevant data using the RMS (Local Scheduler, Torque/Maui). At the end of the execution, it prepares and sends monitored data to the Monitoring Service as shown on the right side of Table 1.

2.7   Integration with UNICORE Grid System

In a first phase of the IANOS project, we have integrated the IANOS framework with the UNICORE Grid System. The Grid Adapter with its generic functionality and the modules plugins specific for UNICORE has been implemented and tested. On the client side, a UNICORE Client plugin has been developed for this purpose. This client plugin provides a GUI interface to interact with the MSS.

3.   Scheduling Scenario

This section describes a reference scenario of job submission using IANOS framework.

1 User log in to the client

2 User requests applications from MSS by sending WS-Agreement Template request

2a MSS validates and authenticates the client request, contact Grid Adapter for all Grid Sites, and then queries these sites for the list of installed applications based on user authorization filtering

2b Prepare and return WS-Agreement Templates (representing the applications) to the client

3 User selects one application; specifies application intrinsic parameters and QoS preference (Cost, Time, Optimal), and submits the application as an AgreementOffer to MSS

3a MSS validates agreement offer, selects candidate resources based on the user access rights and the application availability, queries the Grid Adapter for each candidate resource's static and dynamic information including the resource's local RMS availability

4 MSS sends candidate resources and application along with intrinsic parameters and user QoS preferences to Broker

5 Broker requests data on candidate resources and given application from System Information

7 System Information requests the required information from Data Warehouse through Data Warehouse interface

8 Data Warehouse sends collected information to System Information on the candidate resources, on the application, and on the previous execution data of the same application

9 System Information sends requested data including the free parameters to Broker

10 Broker filters out unsuitable candidate resources based on the application requirements (nodes, memory, libraries etc). It then evaluates the cost function model and prepares a list of cost function values and tolerances for all candidate resources based on user QoS preference

11 Broker selects an ordered list of suitable configurations after applying the cost function and sends them to MSS

12 MSS uses Grid Adapter to schedule one of the configurations following the preferences expressed in the ordered list, and WS-Agreement Resource is created for each successfully submitted configuration

13 MSS sends submission information along with configuration to Monitoring Service, which in turn sends the same submission information to Monitoring Module

14 Monitoring Module monitors the execution of application, computes the execution relevant quantities and sends them to Monitoring Service

15 Monitoring Service sends the monitored data received from Monitoring Module to System Information

16 At the end of execution, results are being sent to the client

17 System Information computes ETEM model's free parameters from previous execution data and application intrinsic parameters

4. IANOS Scheduling Models

The Broker of the IANOS middleware uses two models: Cost Function model and the Execution Time Evaluation model. They are based on a parameterization of the applications and the resources [1]. The *Cost Function model* calculates the cost value for each candidate resource. Details can be found in [2]. The *Execution Time Evaluation model* forecasts the execution time of a given application on a given resource that needs to know the CPU node performance of the application.

4.1   Assumptions

- User provides some input parameters such as size of the problem, number of time iterations, etc

- Applications are well balanced in computation, communication, and storage needs

- The Grid resources are homogeneous

- All Grid resources share their IANOS relevant resource and cost parameters as shown in Table 1

4.2   Cost Function Model (CFM)

The job submission process is based on an estimation of the overall cost of the HPCN application. A Cost Function model has been developed that depends on

- CPU Costs K_e

- Licensing Costs K_ℓ

- Waiting Time Costs K_w

- Energy Costs K_{eco}

- Data Transfer Costs K_d

All these quantities depend on the application, on the per hour costs of a resource, on the number of processors used, and on data transfer costs over the networks. We express the money quantity as Electronic Cost Unit ([ECU]). The best schedule is obtained when the cost function [2]

$$z = \alpha(K_e + K_\ell) + \beta K_w + \gamma K_{eco} + \delta K_d \qquad (1)$$

is minimized. The four parameters α, β, γ, and δ can be used to weight user preferences. When a user wants to get the result as soon as possible, regardless of costs, he chooses $\alpha = \gamma = \delta = 0$ and $\beta > 0$. If he demands that execution costs are as small as possible, then $\beta = 0$. The user can prescribe two constraints: Maximum Cost and Maximum Turnaround Time. Then, the minimal cost solution satisfying the constraints is computed by the model.

4.3   Execution Time Evaluation Model (ETEM)

The execution time cost K_e is part of the cost function z. The execution time includes the CPU time and the communication time. Sometimes these timings have to be added, sometimes there is overlap. Their estimations are computed using historical execution data stored in the DataWarehouse. By means of the parameterization of the resources and the application, we estimate the execution time of an application on an unknown Grid resource based on the performance and on the execution time of the same application on a known resource. Then, we are able to predict the costs of this application on all the Grid resources. For this purpose, the application user has to deliver execution-relevant data such as the number of time steps, the matrix size, or other typical data that defines the job to be submitted. This model is quite complex and will be described somewhere else.

Table 1.   IANOS Cost Function relevent Quantities.

Cost Parameters	Resource Parameters	Execution Parameters
Machine Online Time	Number of nodes	Execution Time
Regression Factor	Processors Per Node	Average Efficiency
Factor (in [1/Year])	Cores Per Processor	Average Performance
Insurance Fee	Peak CPU Performance	Packets Sent
Investment Cost	CPU Performance Factor	Packets Received
Interest Cost	Peak Main Memory Bandwidth	Sent Packet Size
Personal Cost	Peak Network Bandwidth	Received Packet Size
The cost for a KWh	Machine Architecture	Memory used
Infrastructure Cos	Operating System	Swap used
Software licence Cost	Network Topology	
Management Overhead	Network NIC's Type	
Host Efficiency (over the year)		
Amortissement Time (in years)		
Hours (non-bissextile year)		
Node's Energy Consumption		

5.   Conclusion and Future Work

We have presented the design and implementation of IANOS scheduling framework for HPCN applications aiming at optimizing the usage of an HPCN Grid and improve the QoS. It is Grid middleware independent and is based on proposed Grid and Web services standards. The present version of IANOS has been integrated within UNICORE and includes all the functionalities needed to compute the Cost Function model and to submit the application to a well-suited resource. In a first validation step, a small Grid of GbE clusters and simple, well-known applications have been used.

Currently, we are validating IANOS framework on a large scale testbed by running different types of HPCN applications. This testbed includes diverse classes of resources from three institutes: EPFL, Fraunhofer SCAI, and University of Dortmund. This new testbed will enable us to fine-tune the free parameters in the Cost Function model. It is planned to have a well-tested version by the end of the CoreGRID project end of August 2008.

Acknowledgments

The ISS project is funded by the Swiss National Supercomputing Centre CSCS. MSS is funded by the German Federal Ministry of Education and Research through the VIOLA project. The IANOS integration work is carried out jointly within the CoreGRID Network of Excellence funded by the European Commission IST programme under grant #004265.

References

[1] Gruber, R., Volgers, P., De Vita, A., Stengel, M., Tran, T.-M. Parameterisation to tailor commodity clusters to applications, Future Generation Computer Systems,**19** (2003) 111-120.

[2] Gruber, R., Keller, V., Thiemard, M., Waeldrich, O., Wieder, P., Ziegler, W., and Manneback, P., Integration of Grid cost model into ISS/VIOLA meta-scheduler environment, Lecture Notes in Computer Science **4375** (Springer, 2007) 215-224.

[3] Waeldrich, O., Wieder, P., and Ziegler, W. A Meta-Scheduling Service for Co-allocating Arbitrary Types of Resources. Lecture Notes in Computer Science **3911** (Springer, 2006) 782-791.

[4] Keller,V. VAMOS web frontend to the Pleiades clusters.
http://pleiades.epfl.ch/~vkeller/VAMOS.

[5] UNICORE Open Source Download,
http://www.unicore.eu/download/unicore5

[6] VIOLA, Vertically Integrated Optical Testbed for Large Application in DFN.
http://www.viola-testbed.de

[7] A. Anjomshoaa, F. Brisard, M. Drescher, D. Fellows, A. Ly, A. S. McGough, D. Pulsipher, and A. Savva. Job Submission Description Language (JSDL) specification, version 1.0. Internet, 2007.
http://forge.ogf.org/sf/projects/jsdl-wg

[8] S. Andreozzi, S. Burke, L. Field, S. Fisher, B. K'onya, M. Mambelli, J. M. Schopf, M. Viljoen, and A. Wilson. Glue schema specification version 1.2. Internet, 2007.
http://glueschema.forge.cnaf.infn.it/Spec/V12

ON CONSISTENCY OF DATA IN STRUCTURED OVERLAY NETWORKS *

Tallat M. Shafaat[†], Monika Moser[‡], Ali Ghodsi[†], Thorsten Schütt[‡],
Seif Haridi[†], Alexander Reinefeld[‡]

Abstract   Data consistency can be violated in Distributed Hash Tables (DHTs) due to inconsistent lookups. In this paper, we identify the events leading to inconsistent lookups and inconsistent responsibilities for a key. We find the inaccuracy of failure detectors as the main reason for inconsistencies. By simulations with inaccurate failure detectors, we study the probability of reaching a system configuration which may lead to inconsistent data. We analyze majority-based algorithms for operations on replicated data. To ensure that concurrent operations do not violate consistency, they have to use non-disjoint sets of replicas. We analytically derive the probability of concurrent operations including disjoint replica sets. By combining the simulation and analytical results, we show that the probability for a violation of data consistency is negligibly low for majority-based algorithms in DHTs.

*This research work is carried out under the SELFMAN project funded by the European Commission and the Network of Excellence CoreGRID funded by the European Commission.

[†]Royal Institute of Technology (KTH), {*tallat,haridi*}(*at*)*kth.se*
[‡]Zuse Institute Berlin (ZIB), {*moser,schuett,ar*}(*at*)*zib.de*
[†] Swedish Institute of Computer Science (SICS), *ali*(*at*)*sics.se*

1.   Introduction

Peer-to-peer systems have gained tremendous popularity in recent years due to characteristics of scalability, fault-tolerance and self-management. Structured Overlay Networks (SONs) are a major class of these peer-to-peer system, examples of SONs include Chord [3], Chord# [6], Pastry [10] and DKS [7]. SONs provide lookup services for Internet-scale applications. Distributed Hash Tables (DHTs) use a SON's lookup service to provide a put/get interface for distributed systems with eventual consistency guarantees [11]. In contrast, many distributed systems require stronger consistency guarantees, relying on services such as consensus [12] and atomic commits [13]. These services employ quorum techniques at their core to guarantee consistency.

Quorum based algorithms are not well-suited for DHTs. Quorum based techniques provide consistency guarantees as long as quorums overlap *i.e.* are never disjoint. On the contrary, the number of replicas of an item are not constant in a DHT. Hence, due to the extra replicas in a DHT, two quorums might not intersect, leading to inconsistent results.

Like most distributed systems, DHTs replicate a data item on different nodes in the SON to avoid loosing data. In DHTs, the number of replicas may become greater than the replication degree for two reasons: *lookup inconsistencies* and *partitions*. Consider a DHT with replication degree three and an item replicated on nodes $N1, N2$ and $N3$. Due to lookup inconsistencies in the underlying SON[1], another node $N4$ might think that it is also responsible for the data item and will replicate the item. In such a case, a majority-based quorum technique [16] will result in inconsistent data as there are disjoint majority sets *e.g.* $\{N1, N2\}$ and $\{N3, N4\}$.

DHTs tolerate partitions in the underlying network by creating multiple independent DHTs. Due to consistent hashing [14], new nodes take responsibilities of inaccessible nodes and replicate data items. Thus, in the aforementioned case, if a partition occurs such that $N1, N2$ (partition P1) are separated from $N3$ (partition P2), owing to consistent hashing, replacement node $N3'$ will replicate the item in P1, and replacement nodes $N1'$ and $N2'$ will replicate the item in P2. This will result in the two partitions to have disjoint majority sets which will lead to data inconsistency.

It has been proved that it is impossible for a web service to provide the following three guarantees at the same time: consistency, availability and partition-tolerance [9]. These three properties have also been proved to be impossible to guarantee by a DHT working in an asynchronous network such as the Internet [7]. Thus, choosing to provide guarantees for two properties will violate

---

[1]Informally, a lookup inconsistency means multiple nodes believe to be responsible for the same identifier. The term will be discussed in detail later.

the guarantee for the third. Since lookups are always allowed in DHTs, this implies DHTs are always available, thus consistency cannot be guaranteed.

In this paper, we study the causes and frequency of occurrence of lookup inconsistency under different scenarios in a DHT. We focus solely on lookup inconsistency leaving scenarios where complete partitions can happen, resulting in creation of multiple separate DHTs. We discuss and evaluate techniques that can be used to decrease the effect of lookup inconsistencies. Based on our simulation results while considering lookup inconsistencies to be the only reason for creation of extra replicas, we give an analytical model that gives the probability under which a majority-based quorum technique works correctly. Using techniques to decrease the effect of lookup inconsistency, we show that the probability of a quorum technique to produce consistent results is very high.

2. Background

Basics of a Ring-based SON. A SON makes use of an *identifier space*, which for our purposes is a range of integers from 0 to $N - 1$, where N is the length of the identifier space and is a large, fixed and globally known integer. For ring-based SONs, this identifier space is perceived as a ring by arranging the integers in ascending order and wrapping around at $N - 1$.

Every node in the system has a unique identifier drawn from the identifier space. Each node p has a pointer, *succ*, to its *successor*, which is the node immediately succeeding p, going in clockwise direction on the ring starting at p. Similarly, each node q has a pointer, *pred*, to its *predecessor*, which is the node immediately preceding q, going in anti-clockwise direction on the ring starting at q. To enhance routing performance, SONs also maintain additional routing pointers.

Handling Joins and Failures. Apart from *succ* and *pred* pointers, each node p also maintains a *successor-list* consisting of p's c immediate successors, where c is typically set to $\log_2(n)$, n being the network size.

Chord [3] handles joins and failures using a protocol called *periodic stabilization*. Each node p periodically checks to see if its *succ* and *pred* are alive. If *succ* is found to be dead, it is replaced by the closest alive successor in the successor-list. If *pred* is found to be dead, p sets *pred* := *nil*.

Joins are also handled periodically. A joining node makes a lookup to find its successor s on the ring, and sets *succ* := s. Each node periodically asks for its successor's *pred* pointer, and updates its *succ* pointer if it gets a closer successor. Thereafter, the node notifies its current *succ* about its own existence, such that the successor can update its *pred* pointer if it finds that the notifying node is a closer predecessor than *pred*. Hence, any joining node is eventually properly incorporated into the ring.

Failure Detectors.   SONs provide a platform for Internet-scale systems, aimed at working on an asynchronous network. Informally, a network is asynchronous if there is no bound on message delay. Thus, no timing assumptions can be made in such a system. Due to the absence of timing restrictions in an asynchronous model, it is difficult to determine if a node has actually crashed or is very slow to respond. This gives rise to wrong suspicions of failure of nodes.

Failure detectors are modules used by a node to determine if its neighbors are alive or dead. Since we are working in an asynchronous model, a failure detector can only provide probabilistic results about the failure of a node. Thus, we have failure detectors working probabilistically.

Failure detectors are defined based on two properties: *Completeness* and *Accuracy* [5]. In a crash-stop model, completeness is the property that requires a failure detector to eventually detect as dead a node which has actually crashed. Accuracy relates to the mistake a failure detector can make to decide if a node has crashed or not. A perfect failure detector is accurate all the times, while the accuracy of an unreliable failure detector is defined by its probability of working correctly.

For our work, we use a failure detector similar to the baseline algorithm used by Zhuang et. al [4]. A node sends a ping to its neighbors at regular intervals. If it receives an acknowledgment within a timeout, the neighbor is considered alive. Not receiving an acknowledgment within the timeout implies the neighbor has crashed. The timeout is chosen to be much higher than the round-trip time between the two nodes.

3. Lookup and Responsibility Consistency

Data consistency is based on lookup consistency and responsibility consistency in the routing layer. We define these concepts and explain how a violation of these happens. The notion of a SON's configuration comprises the set of all nodes in the system and their pointers to neighboring nodes. A SON evolves by either changing a pointer, or adding/removing a node.

Lookup Consistency.   *A lookup on a key is consistent, if lookups made for this key in a configuration from different nodes, return exactly the same node.*

Lookup consistency can be violated if some node's successor pointer does not reflect the current ring structure. Figure 1a illustrates a scenario, where lookups for key k can return inconsistent results. This configuration may occur if node $N1$ falsely suspected $N2$ as failed, while at the same time $N2$ falsely suspected $N3$ as failed. A lookup for key k ending at $N2$ will return $N4$ as the responsible node for k, whereas a lookup ending in $N1$ would return $N3$.

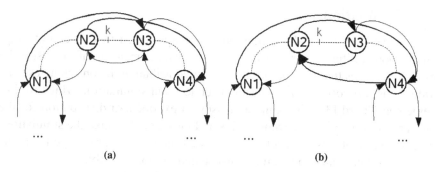

Fig. 1: (a) *Lookup inconsistency* caused by wrong successor pointers. (b) *Responsibility inconsistency* caused by wrong successors and backlinks resulting in overlapping responsibilities.

Responsibility. *A node n is said to be* locally responsible *for a certain key, if the key is in the range between its predecessor and itself, noted as* $(n.pred, n]$. *We call a node globally responsible for a key, if it is the only node in the system that is* locally responsible *for it.*

The responsibility of a node changes whenever its predecessor is changed. If a node has an incorrect predecessor pointer, it might have an overlapping range of keys with another node. However, to have concurrent operations on an item i with key k working on two different physical copies i' and i'', the concurrent lookups should be inconsistent, and there should be an overlap of responsibility for key k. Thus the following definition on responsibility consistency combines lookup consistency and global responsibility.

Responsibility Consistency. *The responsibility for a key is consistent if there is a globally responsible node for that key in the configuration.*

A situation where responsibility consistency for key k is violated is shown in Figure 1b. Here, lookup consistency for k cannot be guaranteed and both nodes, $N3$ and $N4$, are locally responsible for k. However, in Figure 1a, there is only one node $N3$ that is globally responsible despite lookup inconsistency. At node $N4$ the item is simply unavailable. The situation depicted in Figure 1b arises as the situation in Figure 1a with an additional wrong suspicion of node $N4$ about its predecessor $N3$.

As lookup consistency and responsibility consistency cannot be guaranteed in a SON it is impossible to ensure data consistency. However the violation of lookup consistency and responsibility consistency is a result of a combination of very infrequent events. In the following section we present simulation results that measure the probability of lookup inconsistencies and the probability of having an inconsistent responsibility, which turns out to be almost negligible.

4.   Evaluation

In this section, we evaluate how often lookup inconsistencies and overlapping responsibilities occur. For our experiments, the measure of interest is the fraction of nodes that are correct, i.e. do not contribute to inconsistencies. The evaluations were done in a stochastic discrete event simulator in which we implemented Chord [3]. The simulator uses an exponential distribution for the inter-arrival time between events (joins and failures). To make the simulations scale, the simulator is not packet-level. The time to send a message from one node to another is an exponentially distributed random variable.

For our simulations, the level of unreliability of a failure detector is defined by its probability of working correctly. For the graphs, the probability of a *false positive* [2] is the probability of inaccuracy of failure detectors. Thus, a failure detector with a probability of false-positives equal to zero is a perfect failure detector.

In our experiments, we implemented failure detectors in two styles, *independent* and *mutually-dependent* failure detectors. For independent failure detectors, two separate nodes falsely suspect the same node as dead independently. Thus, if a node n is a neighbor of both m and o, the probability of m detecting n as dead is independent of the probability of o detecting n as dead. For mutually-dependent failure detectors, if a node n is suspected dead, all nodes doing detection on n will detect n as dead with higher probability. This may be similar to a realistic scenario where due to n or the network link to n being slow, nodes do not receive ping replies from n thus detecting it as dead. In the afore-mentioned case, if n is suspected, both m and o will detect it dead with higher probability than the probability of false-positive. Henceforth, we use independent failure detectors unless specified.

For our simulations, we first evaluate lookup inconsistencies for different degrees of false-positives. Next, we evaluate overlapping responsibilities in a system with and without churn. Furthermore, we compare lookup inconsistency and overlapping responsibilities. Finally, we present the results with mutually dependent failure detectors.

Our simulation scenario has the following structure: Initially, we successively joined nodes into the system until we had a network with 1024 nodes. We then started to gather statistics by regularly taking snapshots (earlier defined as a configuration) of the system. In each snapshot, we counted the number of correct nodes i.e. do not contribute to lookup inconsistency and overlapping responsibilities. For the experiments with churn, we introduced node joins and failures between the snapshots. We varied the accuracy of the failure detectors from 95% to 100%, where 100% means a perfect failure de-

---

[2] detect an alive node as dead

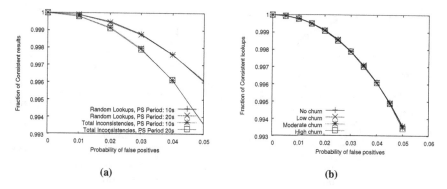

Fig. 2: (a) Evaluation of lookup inconsistency. (b) Evaluation of lookup inconsistency under churn with only node joins.

tector. This range seems reasonable, since failure detectors deployed on the Internet are usually accurate 98% of the time [4]. The results presented in the graphs are averages of 1800 snapshots and 30 different seeds.

Lookup Inconsistency. Figure 2a illustrates the increasing lookup inconsistency when the failure detector becomes inaccurate. The plot denoted 'Total Inconsistencies' shows the maximum over all possible lookup inconsistencies in a snapshot, whereas 'Random Lookups' shows the number of consistent lookups when – for each snapshot – lookups are made for 20 random keys, where each lookup is made from 10 randomly chosen nodes. If all lookups for the same key result in the same node, the lookup is counted as consistent. As can be seen, changing the periodic stabilization rate does not effect the lookup inconsistency in this case. This is due to the fact that there is no churn in the system.

Next, we evaluated lookup inconsistencies in the presence of churn. We varied the churn rate with respect to the periodic stabilization (PS) rate of Chord. For our experiments, we defined churn as node session times, to be in tens of minutes [15]. Short session times produce 'high churn' while long session times produce 'low churn'. Figure 2b shows the results for our experiments. The Y-axis gives a count of the number of lookup inconsistencies per snapshot. As expected, churn does not effect lookup inconsistencies much. Though, even with a perfect failure detector (probability of false positive=0), there will be a non-zero though extremely low number of lookup inconsistencies given churn (2.79×10^{-7} for a high churn system). The reason is that an inconsistency in such a scenario only happens if multiple nodes join between two old nodes m, n (where $m.succ = n$) before m updates its successor pointer by running PS.

This effect of churn is due to node joins on lookup inconsistency can be reduced to zero if we allow lookups to be generated only from nodes that are fully in the system. A node is said to be *fully in the system* after it is accessible from any node that is already in the system. Once a node is fully in the system,

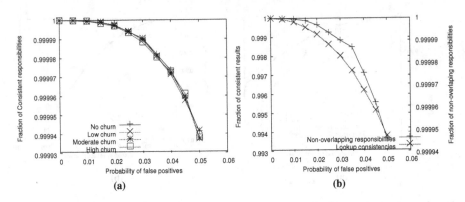

Fig. 3: (a) Evaluation of overlapping responsibilities under churn with only node joins. (b) Comparison of lookup inconsistency and overlapping responsibilities. Lookup inconsistency is plotted against Y-axis while overlapping responsibilities is plotted against Y2-axis.

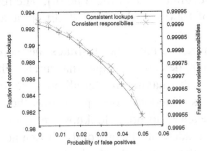

Fig. 4: Evaluation of lookup inconsistency and overlapping responsibilities with mutually dependent failure detectors. Lookup inconsistency is plotted against Y-axis while overlapping responsibilities is plotted against Y2-axis.

it is considered to be in the system until it crashes. We define the first node which creates the ring as fully in the system.

Responsibility Inconsistency.   Next, we evaluate the effect of unreliable failure detectors and churn on the responsibility consistency. The results of our simulations are presented in Figure 3a which shows that responsibility consistency is not effected by churn. Figure 3b shows that even with a lookup inconsistency, the chances of overlapping responsibilities are decreased roughly 100 times. This can be seen by the scale of the lookup inconsistency (Y-axis) and overlapping responsibility (Y2-axis).

Figure 4 shows results for a scenario without churn using mutually dependent failure detectors, where if a node n is suspected, the probability of nodes doing accurate detection on n drops to 0.7. In the scenario for the simulations, we suspect 32 random nodes. Compared to independent failure detectors, mutually dependent failure detectors produce higher lookup inconsistencies, but still low.

5. Data Consistency with Majority-Based Algorithms

To prevent loss of items stored in a SON, items are replicated on a set of nodes. The set of nodes that are responsible for the replicas, is determined by some replication scheme. Here we consider replication schemes that have a fixed replication factor r. An example for such a replication scheme is the DKS symmetric replication [2], where a globally known function determines the set of keys under which replicas for an item are stored. The set of replicas for an item is called *replica set*.

In dynamic environments, some replicas might be temporary unavailable. However operations on an item should be able to succeed if they can access a subset of the replica set. Majority based algorithms require that at least a majority of replicas are available and tolerate the unavailability of the rest. Thus they are well suited for a SON. We refer to a set with a majority of replicas as a *majority set*. As each write operation includes such a majority set, two concurrent write operations have at least one replica in common, such that a conflict can be detected. It is crucial that the number of replicas in the system is never increased, otherwise one cannot guarantee that concurrent operations work on *non-disjoint majority sets*. However responsibility inconsistencies temporarily lead to an increase in the number of replicas. In the following, we analyze the probability of two concurrent operations working on *disjoint majority sets* given i inconsistencies in the replica set, to which we refer as *inconsistent replicas*.

Probability for Disjoint Majority Sets.   In this section we model the probability that two operations work on disjoint majority sets in a given configuration. We assume that each responsibility inconsistency involves at most two nodes. More than two concurrent operations working on disjoint majority sets are not considered as the probability for it is considered as negligibly small.

The size of the smallest majority set is defined by $m = \lfloor \frac{r}{2} \rfloor + 1$. $T_{i,r}$, as shown in Equation (1), counts the number of all possible combinations for two majority sets, given $i > 0$ inconsistent replicas and the replication factor r. The formula takes into account the number of inconsistency j that are included in the majority sets. Each included inconsistency involves two possibilities to select a node that stores the replica.

$A_{i,r}$, in Equation (2), calculates the number of possible combinations for two disjoint majority sets, $m1$ and $m2$, given $i > 0$ inconsistent replicas in the replica set and a replication factor r. We compute $A_{i,r}$ by choosing set $m1$ and count all possible sets $m2$ that are disjoint to $m1$. Part a of $A_{i,r}$ counts all possibilities to choose $m1$, such that at least one inconsistency is included. Again, j denotes the number of included inconsistencies. The second majority set $m2$ shares k of the j inconsistencies (part b). For the remaining replicas of m2 we have to consider how many inconsistencies l it will include from those that are left (part c).

$$T_{i,r} = (\sum_{j=max(m-(r-i),0)}^{min(i,m)} \binom{r-i}{m-j}\binom{i}{j} * 2^j)^2 \tag{1}$$

$$A_{i,r} = \sum_{j=lb_j}^{ub_j} \sum_{k=lb_k}^{j} \sum_{l=lb_l}^{ub_l} \overbrace{\binom{r-i}{m-j}\binom{i}{j} * 2^j}^{a}$$
$$* \underbrace{\binom{j}{k}}_{b} * \underbrace{\binom{(r-m)-(i-j)}{m-k-l}\binom{i-j}{l} * 2^l}_{c} \tag{2}$$

where   (ub short for upper bound, lb short for lower bound)

$$lb_j = max(1, m-(r-i))$$
$$ub_j = min(i,m)$$
$$lb_k = max(1, m-(r-m))$$
$$lb_l = max(0, (m-k)-((r-m)-(i-j)))$$
$$ub_l = min(i-j, m-k)$$

$$pi_r = \sum_{i=1}^{r} (1-p)^{r-i} * p^i * \frac{A_{i,r}}{T_{i,r}} \tag{3}$$

pi_r calculates the overall probability in the system that two concurrent operations on one item operate on disjoint majority sets, where p is the probability of an inconsistency at a node as measured in our simulations.

Table 5 contains the probabilities for disjoint majority sets of two concurrent operations as calculated by $\frac{A_{i,r}}{T_{i,r}}$. As with an even replication factor the minimum number of replicas in common for two majority sets is two in contrast to one for an odd number of replicas, the probability for disjoint majorities is lower for an even number of replicas. In Figure 6 the results of the simulations are combined with Equation 3, where p denotes the simulated probability for an inconsistency. Depending on the failure detector accuracy it plots the probability to get non-disjoint majority sets. An even replication factor increases the probability of having non-disjoint majority sets, however less unavailable replicas can be tolerated.

6.   Related Work

DHTs have been the subject of much research in recent years, with substantial amount of work on resilience of overlays to churn. While these studies show that overlays tolerate failures, they also show how lookups are effected by churn.

Rhea *et. al.* [1] have explored lookup inconsistencies for a real implementation under churn. Their approach differs from ours as they define a lookup

r	i = 1	i = 2	i = 3	i = 4
1	0.5			
2	0	0.25		
3	0.16	0.31	0.42	
4	0	0.05	0.14	0.22
5	0.05	0.11	0.19	0.26

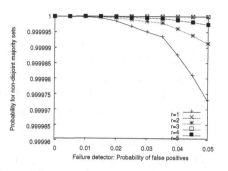

Fig. 5: Probability for disjoint majority sets depending on the replication factor *r* and the number of inconsistencies *i* in the replica set.

Fig. 6: Probability for non-disjoint majority sets in a SON, depending on the accuracy of the failure detector

to be consistent if a majority of nodes concurrently making a lookup for the same key get the same result. For our work, we require all results of making the lookup for the key to be the same. Furthermore, our work is extended to responsibility consistency. In their work, Rhea *et. al.* also study lookup inconsistency in an implementation of Pastry [10] called FreePastry [18], while we experiment with Chord.

Liben-Nowell *et. al.* [17] study the evolution of Chord under churn. Their study is based on a fail-stop model *i.e.* they assume perfect failure detection and reliable message delivery. Consequently, they ignore "false suspicions of failure", which is the main topic of our study as we observe that imperfect failure detectors are the main source of lookup inconsistencies.

Zhuang *et. al.* [4] studied various failure detection algorithms in Overlay Networks. They also use the same approach as Rhea *et. al.* [1] to define inconsistencies, which differs from our work.

7. Conclusion

This paper presents an evaluation of consistency in SONs. Data consistency cannot be achieved if responsibility consistency is violated. We describe why it is impossible to guarantee responsibility consistency in SONs. By simulating a Chord SON, we show that the probability of violating responsibility consistency is negligibly low.

We analytically derive the probability that majority-based operations are working on non-disjoint majority sets given an inconsistent responsibility for at least one replica. Operations that work on disjoint majority sets lead to inconsistent data. By combining the results from simulations and analysis, we show that the probability for getting inconsistent data when using majority based algorithms is significantly low. Furthermore, we conclude that since the accuracy of the failure detector greatly influences lookup and responsibility consistency, significant attention should be paid to the failure detection algorithm.

References

[1] S. Rhea, D. Geels, T. Roscoe and J. Kubiatowicz. Handling Churn in a DHT. In *Proceedings of USENIX Annual Technical Conference*, 2004 Berkeley

[2] A. Ghodsi, L. Onana Alima and S. Haridi. Symmetric Replication for Structured Peer-to-Peer Systems. *DBISP2P*, 2005, Trondheim, Norway

[3] I. Stoica, R. Morris, D. Liben-Nowell, D. R. Karger, M. F. Kaashoek, F. Dabek, H. Balakrishnan. Chord: A Scalable Peer-to-peer Lookup Protocol for Internet Applications. newblock *IEEE/ACM Transactions on Networking (TON)*, 11(1):17.32, 2003.

[4] S.Q. Zhuang, D. Geels, I. Stoica, R.H. Katz. On Failure Detection Algorithms in Overlay Networks. In *Proceedings of INFOCOM'05*, Miami, 2005

[5] T. D. Chandra and S. Toueg. Unreliable Failure Detectors for Reliable Distributed Systems. *Journal of the ACM*, 43:2, 1996

[6] T. Schütt, F. Schintke and A. Reinefeld. Structured Overlay without Consistent Hashing: Empirical Results. In *Proceedings of GP2PC'06*, 2006

[7] A. Ghodsi. Distributed *k*-ary System: Algorithms for Distributed Hash Tables. *PhD Dissertation*, KTH—Royal Institute of Technology Oct, 2006

[8] M. Moser, S. Haridi. Atomic Commitment in a Transactional DHT. In *Proceedings of the CoreGRID Symposium*, 2007

[9] S. Gilbert and N. Lynch. Brewer's conjecture and the feasibility of consistent, available, partition-tolerant web services. In *SIGACT News*, 2002

[10] A. Rowstron and P. Druschel. Pastry: Scalable, distributed object location and routing for large-scale peer-to-peer systems. In *Proceedings of MIDDLEWARE.01*, volume 2218 of Lecture Notes in Computer Science (LNCS), Germany, 2001

[11] F. Dabek. A Distributed Hash Table. *Doctoral Dissertation,* MIT — Massachusetts Institute of Technology, 2005

[12] L. Lamport. The part-time parliament. *ACM Trans. Comput. Syst.*, ACM Press, 1998, 16, 133-169

[13] N. Lynch, M. Merritt, W. Weihl, and A. Fekete. Atomic Transactions. Morgan Kaufmann Publishers, 1994

[14] D. Karger, E. Lehman, F. Leighton, M. Levine, D. Lewin, R. Panigrahy. Consistent hashing and random trees: Distributed caching protocols for relieving hot spots on the World Wide Web. In *Proceedings of the 29th ACM Symposium on Theory of Computing*, El Paso, 1997

[15] K. Gummadi, R. Dunn, S. Saroiu, S. Gribble, H. Levy, and J. Zahorjan. Measurement, Modeling, and Analysis of a Peer-to-Peer File-Sharing Workload. In *Proceedings of SOSP*, 2003.

[16] D. K. Gifford. Weighted voting for replicated data. In *Proceedings of SOSP '79*, New York, USA, 1979

[17] D. Liben-Nowell, H. Balakrishnan, D. Karger Analysis of the Evolution of Peer-to-Peer Systems In *Proceedings of PODC '02*, USA, 2002

[18] Freepastry. http://freepastry.rice.edu/

LOOPO-HOC: A GRID COMPONENT WITH EMBEDDED LOOP PARALLELIZATION

Johannes Tomasoni, Jan Dünnweber, and Sergei Gorlatch
University of Münster
CoreGRID Institute on Programming Model
{jtomasoni | duennweb | gorlatch}@uni-muenster.de

Michael Claßen, Philipp Claßen, and Christian Lengauer
University of Passau
CoreGRID Institute on Programming Model
{classenm | classen | lengauer}@fim.uni-passau.de

Abstract   This work integrates two distinct research areas of parallel and distributed computing, (1) automatic loop parallelization, and (2) component-based Grid programming. The latter includes technologies developed within CoreGRID for simplifying Grid programming: the Grid Component Model (GCM) and Higher-Order Components (HOCs). Components support developing applications on the Grid without taking all the technical details of the particular platform type into account (network communication, heterogeneity, etc.). The GCM enables a hierarchical composition of program pieces and HOCs enable the reuse of component code in the development of new applications by specifying application-specific operations in a program via code parameters. When a programmer is provided, e. g., with a compute farm HOC, only the independent worker tasks must be described. But, once an application exhibits data or control dependences, the trivial farm is no longer sufficient. Here, the power of loop parallelization tools, like LooPo, comes into play: by embedding LooPo into a HOC, we show that these two technologies in combination facilitate the automatic transformation of a sequential loop nest with complex dependences (supplied by the user as a HOC parameter) into an ordered task graph, which can be processed on the Grid in parallel. This technique can significantly simplify GCM-based systems which combine multiple HOCs and other components. We use an equation system solver based on the successive overrelaxation method (SOR) as our motivating application example and for performance experiments.

Keywords: Higher-Order Components (HOCs), Loop Parallelization, GCM, Grid Programming

1.   Introduction

We demonstrate the benefits of using software components together with loop parallelization techniques for Grid programming. In recent years, component technology [22] has reached wide-spread acceptance for the development of large-scale distributed software infrastructures. Almost no project that requires an interconnection of multiple resources, e. g., databases, compute clusters and Web clients, is started from scratch anymore. Developers rather rely on modern component frameworks, which provide them with reusable implementations of the functionality needed for their applications. This approach to code reuse goes much further than traditional libraries, since frameworks usually provide not only executable code but also the required configuration (i. e., setup descriptions, typically in the form of XML files) for deploying the components in the target context. This context may be, e. g., a middleware like Globus [19] for interconnecting multiple components and remote clients, across the boundaries of heterogeneous hardware and software.

In the CoreGRID community [24], the *Grid Component Model* GCM [16] has recently become the commonly agreed reference specification of software components for the Grid. The GCM combines efforts of multiple CoreGRID partners, e. g., the GCM predecessor *Fractal* [1] whose principle of hierarchical composition has been adopted, the ProActive library [3] for asynchronous communication among components, and Higher-Order Components (HOCs [17]) that accept as input not only data but also pieces of code supplied via an Internet connection.

For assisting programmers in building parallel applications of Grid components, this work combines HOCs with the automatic loop parallelization tool LooPo [7]. The idea is to apply the LooPo loop parallelization mechanism to HOC parameters, i. e., code pieces supplied to a HOC as parameters. These parameters often carry a loop nest to be executed by some worker hosts (i. e., any free processing nodes) in the Grid. A typical example is the Farm-HOC, implementing the popular master/worker pattern for running a set of independent tasks [17]. The original Farm-HOC is not able to deal with inter-task dependences: they would make it necessary either to design a new HOC which takes the dependences into account or to remain with a sequential, less efficient solution. Instead of requiring the developer to build one new HOC per possible dependence pattern, we suggest a more flexible component, called LooPo-HOC, which embeds the LooPo loop parallelizer [20].

Dependences in code parameters of the LooPo-HOC in the form of nested loops are automatically resolved: code parameters (the loop nests) are transformed into an ordered task graph. The processing pattern employed by the LooPo-HOC can be viewed as an adapted farm whose master schedules the tasks as specified by this graph.

In our previous work, we suggested to combine HOCs with LooPo [13] and discussed a farm implementation version for processing task graphs [18]. This paper presents the implemetation of the LooPo-HOC plus application examples and performance experiments.

HOCs use a Web service-based code transfer technology that extends the Globus middleware [19] by the *Code Service* and the *Remote Code Loader* (both are available open-source, within the scope of the Globus incubator project HOC-SA [15], see Fig. 1). The Code Service and Remote Code Loader can be viewed as an add-on to the Globus Resource Allocation Manager WS GRAM [10]. Their purpose is facilitating software components, which hold the code for solving recurring problems and expect the user to supply only application-specific code pieces via the network. The Code Service and the Remote Code Loader support the transfer of such code pieces across the network [12]. In contrast, programmers using only GRAM are supposed to transfer their programs on the whole rather than in pieces, which limits the potential of code reuse in component-based software architectures.

The structure of the paper is as follows. In Section 2, we introduce the LooPo-HOC: Section 2.1 introduces the `mwDependence` service which implements our adapted version of the master/worker processing pattern, for executing ordered task graphs (taking dependences into account). Section 2.2 explains the automatic parallelization mechanism of LooPo. Section 2.3 describes the challenges of integrating LooPo into a Grid-aware component and how we addressed them in the LooPo-HOC. Section 2.4 shows how the internal workload monitor of the LooPo-HOC works. Section 3 introduces an example application: the parallel SOR system solver. Performance measurements are presented in Section 4, and we draw the conclusions from our work in Section 5.

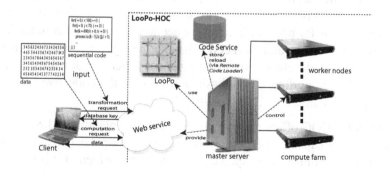

Figure 1. General setup of the LooPo-HOC in the HOC-SA

2.   Implementation of the LooPo-HOC

The LooPo-HOC is composed of LooPo itself for transforming code (Section 2.2), the Web service for clients to connect (Section 2.3), controller software for task queue management and workload monitoring (Section 2.4), and an internal farm implementation for running the actual application tasks. These parts are available to the client via a single Web service, as shown in Fig. 1.

2.1   The Internal Compute Farm of the LooPo-HOC

To explain how the compute farm in the LooPo-HOC works, let us briefly recall the functionality of the Farm-HOC [17] and explain the setup shown Fig. 1: clients upload (sequential) application code to a central Web service. This service is provided by the master server which stores the code at the Code Service where it is assigned a key and saved in a database (using OGSA-DAI [25]). Clients can send the master a request to reload the code and run it on multiple remote worker nodes for processing data in parallel. The master controls the distributed computations without requiring the user to be aware about the number of involved workers and the (Web service-based) communication between itself and the workers.

The compute farm in the LooPo-HOC differs from a common compute farm implementation for Grids [2] in two ways:

1 the LooPo-HOC embeds, besides a farm of workers, the LooPo tool and uses it for ordering tasks in the form of a task graph taking dependences among tasks into account. The farm executes the tasks according to this order, freeing the user from dealing with task dependences.

2 the communication does not rely on a single protocol, but to increase the efficiency, a Web service is used only as the remote interface for supplying input to the farm via an Internet connection. All internal communication (between master and workers) is handled using a light-weight protocol, specifically developed for this component which is a distributed, version of MPI, supporting all the basic and most of the collective operations, using only Java and TCP sockets [5].

The LooPo-HOC offers a universal farm implementation for Java code [2], i. e., this farm is capable of executing applications without dependences as well (and has shown almost linear speedup in various experiments) It is included in the open-source distribution of the HOC-SA [15] in the package mwDependence.

The worker nodes in Fig. 1 are fully decoupled from each other, i. e., they need no communication between each other, and are supposed to run in a distributed environment. In the following, we describe in more detail the transformation process, the scheduling and the workload monitoring, which make up the core of the LooPo-HOC and which are supposed to run locally, on the same server, ideally on a multiprocessor machine.

2.2 Transforming Loop Nests into Task Graphs

For the automatic parallelization of loop nests, LooPo uses a mathematical model, the so-called *polytope model* [20]. In this model, affine linear expressions are used to represent loop iterations, dependences and accesses to array elements. LooPo is an implementation of various methods and tools for analyzing a given loop program, bringing it into model representation and performing a dependence analysis and the actual parallelization using integer linear programming. The result of the code transformation done by LooPo is a task graph in which groups of independent tasks are arranged in a sequence.

For the automatic parallelization of loop nests using LooPo, there are a number of steps involved, as follows [18].

The first step is to analyze the input program and bring it into the polytope model representation. This is done by analyzing the (affine linear) expressions in loop bounds and array accesses. The resulting model consists of one so-called *index space* per statement. The index space contains the coordinates, i.e., the values of the loop variables, of all steps in which the statement is executed. LooPo keeps track of all array accesses and computes the resulting data dependences.

In the second step, we use mathematical optimization methods to compute two piecewise affine functions: the *schedule* maps each computation to a logical execution step, and the *placement* maps each computation to a virtual processor. The objective is to extract all available parallelism, independently of any machine parameters, e.g., the number of processors. The result of this step is the so-called *space-time mapping*.

In order to adjust the granularity of parallelism to a level that is optimal for task farming (our method for the distributed execution of the parallel tasks, as discussed in Section 2.1), the *tiling* technique is used in the third step to aggregate time steps and virtual processors into larger chunks, called *tiles*.

Each tile produced by LooPo represents a *task* for the LooPo-HOC and contains the corresponding set of computation operations for the time steps and virtual processors that were aggregated. Information about data dependences between tasks is stored in the form of a *task graph* that is used by the master for scheduling them, i.e., to choose an order of execution between dependent tasks. Thus, the master is responsible for arranging the execution order, whereas the target processor for the execution can be determined using an advanced scheduling system [11] to exploit task locality. In Grid environments which do not provide a scheduling system with tunable policies (e.g., KOALA [11]), users of the LooPo-HOC can also directly adapt the master, such that the complete scheduling is handled there. This way, programmers can, e. g., arrange chains of tasks that should be executed on the same worker. For data dependences between tasks that make the exchange of computed data elements necessary, the master provides a method to *join* a new (dependent) task with a finished task. This way, the dependent task is decoupled from its predecessor, gets the updated data and is scheduled for execution.

2.3   Integration of the LooPo-HOC with the Middleware

Beside the workers (executing the single tasks, as described in Section 2.1) and the master (running LooPo, as described in Section 2.2), the LooPo-HOC comprises a Web service for remote access and a resource configuration for maintaining the distributed application state (status data and intermediate results), as is typical in the Web Service Resource Framework (WSRF) [19].

While the service interface itself is stateless, the resources connected to it (as configured in a setup file) hold their state (in the form of transient variables, called *resource properties* in WSRF [19]) even past the scope/duration of a session. The LooPo-HOC makes use of this feature, e. g., for parallelizing a loop nest and preserving the resulting task graph as a data record in a resource, which can be referenced by a key and reused in multiple applications. Another

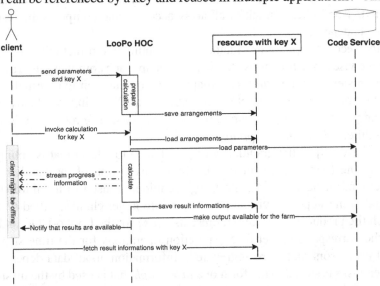

Figure 2.   Sequence Diagram for using the LooPo-HOC

feature, through which the LooPo-HOC benefits from the WSRF middleware, is its support for asynchronous operations. While LooPo transforms loop nests, the client can disconnect or even shut down. The LooPo-HOC can restore the task graph from a former session, when the client sends it the corresponding resource key. The LooPo-HOC uses two types of WSRF resources. For every code transformation request, one new resource instance (i. e., transient storage) for holding the resulting task graph is created dynamically. The other resource is static (i. e., instantiated only once and shared globally among all processes), called *monitor* and explained in Section 2.4.

The task graph resources are instantiated following the factory pattern, returning a unique remote reference (the resource key) to the client. As shown in Fig. 2, the client sends the resource key on every communication with the LooPo-HOC, which uses the key afterwards to retrieve the corresponding resource data (the task graph and intermediate results). Thus, a LooPo-HOC server is not a single point of failure, but rather a service provider that permits clients to switch between mirror hosts during a session.

2.4   Workload Monitoring in the LooPo-HOC

The transformation of loop nests into tasks graphs is a computation-intensive operation, which is quite unusual for Web services: typically, a Web service operation retrieves or joins some data remotely and terminates immediately. Due to the asynchronous operations of the LooPo-HOC, the clients produce processing load right *after* their requests are served, since this is, when the code transformations begin (concrete time costs follow in Section 4).

From the user's viewpoint, the asynchrony is advantageous, since local application activities are not blocked by the code transformations running remotely. However, when multiple users are connected to the same LooPo-HOC server, the workload must be restricted to a certain (server-specific) maximum of concurrrent requests. For this purpose, the LooPo-HOC workload monitor (Fig. 3) provides status information to the clients.

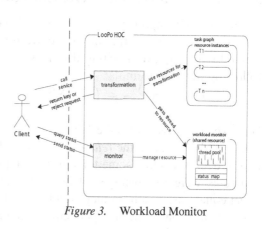

Figure 3.   Workload Monitor

The monitor consists of two parts, a fixed-size thread pool and a status map. For every transformation, the LooPo-HOC first checks if an idle thread is available. If the thread pool is fully loaded, then the LooPo-HOC creates a new transformation thread and adds it to the pool. The maximum threshold for the thread pool is set by the server administrator and is usually equal to the number of CPUs of the hosting server. Once the number of executing threads has reached this maximum, incoming requests are queued.

The status map (shown bottom right in Fig. 3) is a structured data store, used to keep track of the successive transformations. The client can read the map by issuing an XPath query [9] to the monitor at any time. This feature is useful when the client reconnects during a loop transformation. The map also allows one application to execute the tasks resulting from transforming the sequential loops submitted by another application: via the map, users can track the status of transformations (and run the resulting tasks), even if they connect to the LooPo-HOC for the first time (and, consequently, receive no automatic notification about status updates). This scenario arises, e. g., if the Web service for connecting to the LooPo-HOC is deployed to multiple servers, allowing clients to switch between hosts, when a connection fails or some host's request queue is full.

As future work, we are considering to use the workload monitor and the status map, for automatically balancing workload: instead of queuing requests that exceed some threshold, another server will take over the processing load. Implementing load balancing this way is probably also an interesting case study for on-demand deployment of HOCs and combining multiple code transfer technologies [12].

3.   Case Study: The SOR Equation System Solver

As an example application, we have implemented a solver for linear equation systems, $A\phi = b$, using the successive overrelaxation method (SOR). The SOR method works by extrapolating the Gauss-Seidel method [6], as shown in the following iteration formula:

$$\phi_i^{(k+1)} = (1 - \omega)\phi_i^{(k)} + \frac{\omega}{a_{ii}} \left(b_i - \sum_{j=1}^{i-1} a_{ij}\phi_j^{(k+1)} - \sum_{j=i+1}^{n} a_{ij}\phi_j^{(k)} \right)$$

Here, vector $\phi^{(k)}$ denotes the kth iterate, the a_{ij} are elements of the input matrix A, and ω is called the *relaxation factor* which is reduced in each iteration, until it declines below some tolerance. Roughly speaking, the SOR algorithm computes weighted averages of iterations, leading to a triangular system of linear equations, which is much simpler to solve than the original arbitrary system. There is one control dependence in the SOR solver, i.e., in each pair of successive iterations the follow-up statement depends on its predecessor.

```
1: @LooPo("begin loop", "constants: m,n; arrays: a{n+1}")
2: for (int k = 1;  k <= m;  k++)  {
3:     for (int i = 2;  i <= n - 1;  i++)  {
4:         // average computation
5:         a[i] = (a[i - 1] + a[i + 1]) / 2.0; ... } }
6: @LooPo("end loop")
```

Figure 4.   The sequential code parameter

To run this application in parallel on the Grid, the user supplies the LooPo-HOC with the application name (here, SOR) and a sequential description of the computations expressed in Java notation, as shown in Fig. 4. Any loop nest (with metadata, as the delimiting annotations in lines 1 and 6) can be used as input for the LooPo-HOC. The annotations have the purpose of delimiting the code that is automatically parallelized. The parallelization itself is applied to the Java source code using the steps from Section 2.2, resulting in a task graph. First, a model of the input program is derived (Fig. 5). For the space-time transformation, the following schedule θ and placement π were determined: $\theta(k, i) = 2 * k + i$ and $\pi(k, i) = k$.

For obtaining the task dependence graph, tiling is applied on the transformed target program. Fig. 6 shows the representation of the transformed program after tiling is applied using the same color tone for tiles that can be executed independently. The final model is derived by joining each tile as a node into a graph with every inter-tile dependence as a directed edge in that graph. From the

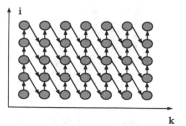
Figure 5. Input program (M=7, N=5)

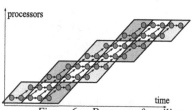
Figure 6. Program after tiling

task graph model representation, the LooPo-HOC generates three Java classes as output which are stored in the Code Service [17]: SORMaster, SORData and SORTask. The SORMaster holds the dependence graph (it implements the interface SchTaskDependence from the mwDependenceService package) and provides the join-method (required for distributing data to task groups; see Section 2.2). SORData objects are used for buffering application data and the SORTask class describes a single task (as an implementation of the execute method from the interface mwDependenceService.UserTask).

Since these files comply with the interface definitions in the HOC-SA [15], the user can directly load the three output files for parallel processing as code parameters of the farm described in Section 2.1.

4. Experiments

Fig. 8 shows the computation times for matrices of different sizes using from 1 to 10 workers running on common 1.7 GHz PCs. We also experimented in a more heterogeneous environment (and observed promising speedups), but here, we only report the most regular results (for homogeneous workers), since these results are the most comprehensible ones.

The experimental environment was set up in a high-performing network reaching a data throughput of approximately $3.4MBit/s$. The strong time decay in the left of Fig. 8 (from 1 to 3 workers) shows that especially the adding of the first 2 workers leads to a strong performance improvement, as compared to the sequential computation time. The corresponding efficiency values support this assumption: for 3 workers, the efficiency was above 80% and for 2 workers even around 90% in multiple measurements.

The decline of the plane along the z axis (matrix size) shows that using more than 5 workers is only profitable for large matrices, while, for the $100K \times 200K$ matrix there are not enough tasks (using a 5×5 tiling [18]) to take advantage of more than 4 workers.

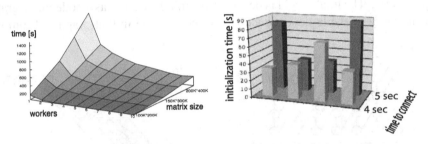

Figure 7.   Computation Times   *Figure 8.*   Initialization Times

The eight bars in Fig. 9 represent the initialization times for 10 workers (i. e. the time that passes by after the client sends a request, until the remote computations in the farm start). The time required to establish an ssh connection between the master and all workers varied between 4 and 5 seconds. As can be observed by comparing the bars in the front row and the back row, there is no correspondence between the time required to connect and the full initialization time (including the remote code loading), which exhibits strong variations between 30 and 90 seconds (the standard deviation σ from the mean value of 50 seconds was 22). This is due to the connection between the farm and the database: as explained in Section 2.1, the farm workers load the code for processing the single tasks from the Code Service using OGSA-DAI [25], which is known to deliver unreliable performance under certain conditions, especially when it is deployed on a single server together with other Web services [14]. In relation to the much longer computation times of the SOR application (from several minutes to several hours for large matrices), the initialization time can, thus, be disregarded. It should also be noted that the initialization is only performed once per worker and application. After the first set of input data (a matrix in the SOR example) has been processed, the same parallel code is used to process any number of successive inputs without repeating its generation (using LooPo) and its transfer from the Code Service to the workers.

The transformation of the single loop nest used in the SOR example in Section 3 takes approximately 1 min on a contemporary dual-core PC, utilizing 50% of its overall CPU capacity. From this quick increase of computational load, we conclude that, if only one server is used to run the code transformations in multiple different applications of the LooPo-HOC, this machine should be a powerful multiprocessor server.

5. Conclusion

The idea of using LooPo for transforming the code parameters of a HOC was suggested in an earlier paper [13] and a prototype of such a component was tested for local area networks [5]. By now, the implementation of a Grid-aware version, called LooPo-HOC, has been completed and extended on the server side: instead of a farm, that supports only dependence-free applications, the distributed master/worker implementation, described in Section 2.1, now provides a distributed environment for Java programs that is capable of processing dependent tasks using a task graph scheduler. Using the LooPo-HOC, the treatment of dependences becomes fully transparent, i. e., the Grid application programmer is no more responsible for scheduling independent task groups [13], but there is an internal scheduler in the master.

Using the SOR program from Section 3 as an example, we have shown that the LooPo-HOC provides a promising scalability and the time needed for the initial code transformations does not critically impact the overall application performance.

Another approach to automating the generation of parallel code was developed within the recent research on OpenMP programs and *reparallelizing* them for the Grid [8]. This work also covers Java programs and the use of *distributed shared memory* (DSM) for data exchange among tasks, but still requires from programmers dependence-free input and the explicit declaration of parallel loops via OpenMP directives. The LooPo-HOC, on the contrary, offers a fully transparent programming interface that requires only sequential code. The required data sharing could have been implemented using Sun's standardized DSM implementation in *JavaSpaces* [4]. However, the LooPo-HOC requires only the joining of single tasks and no support for distributed transactions, and, thus, relies on a more light-weight implementation [5], which provides much better performance.

The LooPo-HOC (including the source code) can be downloaded from the Internet as a part of the HOC-SA Globus incubator project [15]. It is interoperable with any other Globus-based Grid software. For integrating the presented parallelization technique into the GCM, the task graph may also be included into an automatic manager in the membrane of a GCM component [16]. The suggested combination of components with loop parallelization is not only useful for the GCM, but also for other popular component models, such as CCA [23] and CCM [21]. Beside the code transfer mechanism used by HOCs [12], no other special features of this component technology are required.

References

[1] Institut National de Recherche en Informatique (INRIA), *The Fractal Web Site*, 2007. http://fractal.objectweb.org.

[2] Marco Danelutto, *Task Farm Computations in Java*, International Conference on High-Performance Computing and Networking, Amsterdam, NL, 2000, pp. 385–394.

[3] INRIA, *The ProActive Web Site*, 2007. http://www-sop.inria.fr/oasis/ProActive.

[4] 1994–2007 Sun Microsystems, *The JavaSpaces Specification*. www.sun.com/software/jini.

[5] Eduardo Argollo, Michael Claßen, Philipp Claßen, and Martin Griebl, *Loop Parallelization for a Grid Master-Worker Framework*, CG Integration Workshop Heraklion, Greece, 2007, pp. 516–527.

[6] Yousef Saad, *Iterative Methods for Sparse Linear Systems*, SIAM U.S.A., 2003.

[7] University of Passau, *The Polyhedral Loop Parallelizer: LooPo*, 1997. http://www.infosun.fim.uni-passau.de/cl/loopo.

[8] Michael Klemm, Matthias Bezold, Ronald Veldema, and Michael Philippsen, *Reparallelization and Migration of OpenMP Programs*, International Symposium on Cluster Computing and the Grid, Rio de Janeiro, Brazil, 2007, pp. 529–540.

[9] James Clark and Steve DeRose, *XML Path Language*, W3C Recommendations, 1999–2007.

[10] Ian Foster, *Globus Toolkit Version 4: Software for Service-Oriented Systems*, International Conference on Network and Parallel Computing, 2006, pp. 2–13.

[11] Cătălin L. Dumitrescu, Dick H.J. Epema, Jan Dünnweber, and Sergei Gorlatch, *User-transparant Scheduling of Structured Parallel Applications in Grid Environments*, Workshop on Grid programming Environments and Components, Paris, France, 2006, pp. 85–92.

[12] Cătălin L. Dumitrescu, Jan Dünnweber, Philipp Lüdeking, Sergei Gorlatch, Ioan Raicu, and Ian Foster, *Simplifying Grid Application Programming Using Web-enabled Code Transfer Tools*, in Toward Next Generation Grids, *Springer 2007*, pp. 225–235.

[13] Jan Dünnweber, Sergei Gorlatch, Martin Griebl, Eduardo Argollo, and Christian Lengauer, *Making a Task Farm Component Parallelize Loops for the Grid*, CG Integration Workshop (CYFRONET), 2006, pp. 93–104.

[14] William Hoarau, Sébastien Tixeuil, Nuno Rodrigues, Décio Sousa, and Luis Silva, *Benchmarking the OGSA-DAI Middleware*, CG Integration Workshop (CYFRONET), 2006, pp. 357–368.

[15] Jan Dünnweber, Philipp Lüdeking, Cătălin L. Dumitrescu, Eduardo Argollo, and Sergei Gorlatch, *The HOC-SA Globus Incubator Project*, 2006. http://dev.globus.org/incubator/hoc-sa.

[16] CoreGRID Network of Excellence www.coregrid.net, *Basic Features of the Grid Component Model (GCM)*, Technical Report D.PM.04, Institute on Component-based Programming, 2005.

[17] Sergei Gorlatch and Jan Dünnweber, *From Grid Middleware to Grid Applications: Bridging the Gap with HOCs*, in *Future Generation Grids*, Springer Verlag, 2005, pp. 241–261.

[18] Martin Griebl, Peter Faber, and Christian Lengauer, *Space-time Mapping and Tiling – A Helpful Combination*, Concurrency and Computation: Practice and Experience **16** (March 2004), no. 3, 221–246.

[19] Jarek Gawor, Ian Foster, and Stephen Pickles et al., *State and Events for Web Services*, Intl' Conference on High-Performance and Distributed Computing, 2005, pp. 3–13.

[20] Christian Lengauer, *Loop Parallelization in the Polytope Model*, CONCUR, 1993, pp. 398–416.

[21] Object Management Group, *The Corba Component Model*, 1997. http://www.omg.org.

[22] C. Szyperski, *Component Software: Beyond Object-Oriented Programming*, Addison Weseley, 1998.

[23] The CCA Forum, *CCA Glossary*. http://www.cca-forum.org/glossary.

[24] European Research Network on Foundations, Software Infrastructures and Applications for large scale distributed, GRID and Peer-to-Peer Technologies, *CoreGRID*. http://www.coregrid.net.

[25] UK Grid Database Task Force, *OGSA Data Access and Integration*. http://www.ogsadai.org.

Acknowledgement

This research work is carried out under the FP6 Network of Excellence CoreGRID funded by the European Commission (Contract IST-2002-004265) and has received financial support from the German Research Foundation (DFG) for project CompSpread.

IMPLEMENTING DYNAMIC QUERYING SEARCH IN K-ARY DHT-BASED OVERLAYS*

Paolo Trunfio and Domenico Talia
DEIS, University of Calabria
Via P. Bucci 41C, 87036 Rende (CS), Italy
trunfio@deis.unical.it
talia@deis.unical.it

Ali Ghodsi and Seif Haridi
Swedish Institute of Computer Science
P.O. Box 1263, 164 29 Kista, Sweden
ali@sics.se
seif@sics.se

Abstract   Distributed Hash Tables (DHTs) provide scalable mechanisms for implementing resource discovery services in structured Peer-to-Peer (P2P) networks. However, DHT-based lookups do not support some types of queries that are fundamental in several classes of applications. A way to support arbitrary queries in structured P2P networks is implementing unstructured search techniques on top of DHT-based overlays. This approach has been exploited in the design of DQ-DHT, a P2P search algorithm that combines the Dynamic Querying (DQ) technique used in unstructured networks with an algorithm for efficient broadcast over a DHT. Similarly to DQ, DQ-DHT dynamically adapts the search extent on the basis of the desired number of results and the popularity of the resource to be found. Differently from DQ, DQ-DHT exploits the structural constraints of the DHT to avoid message duplications. The original DQ-DHT algorithm has been implemented using Chord as basic overlay. In this paper we focus on extending DQ-DHT to work in k-ary DHT-based overlays. In a k-ary DHT, broadcast takes only $O(\log_k N)$ hops using $O(\log_k N)$ pointers per node. We exploit this "k-ary principle" in DQ-DHT to improve the search time with respect to the original Chord-based implementation. This paper describes the implementation of DQ-DHT over a k-ary DHT and analyzes its performance in terms of search time and generated number of messages in different configuration scenarios.

Keywords: Peer-to-Peer, resource discovery, dynamic querying, distributed hash tables.

*This research work is carried out under the FP6 Network of Excellence CoreGRID funded by the European Commission (Contract IST-2002-004265).

1. Introduction

Distributed Hash Tables (DHTs) provide scalable mechanisms for implementing resource discovery services in structured Peer-to-Peer (P2P) networks. Structured P2P systems like Chord [1] use a DHT to assign to each node the responsibility for a specific part of the resources in the network. When a peer wishes to find a resource with a given key, the DHT allows to locate the node responsible for that key typically in $O(\log N)$ hops using only $O(\log N)$ neighbors per node.

As compared to unstructured search techniques like flooding or random walks, DHT-based lookups have significant scalability advantages in terms of both search time and network traffic [2]. However, DHT-based lookups do not support arbitrary types of queries (e.g., regular expressions [3]) since it is infeasible to generate and store keys for every query expression. On the other hand, unstructured systems can do it effortless since all queries are processed locally on a node-by-node basis [4].

A way to support arbitrary queries in structured P2P networks is implementing unstructured search techniques on top of DHT-based overlays. Following this approach, an unstructured search method can be implemented over the DHT to distribute the query to as many nodes as needed. The query can then be processed on a node-by-node basis as in unstructured systems. In this way, the DHT can be used for both key-based lookups and arbitrary queries, combining the efficiency of structured networks with the flexibility of unstructured search.

The approach above has been exploited in the design of DQ-DHT [5], a P2P search algorithm that combines the Dynamic Querying (DQ) technique used in unstructured networks [6], with an algorithm for efficient broadcast over a DHT [7].

The goal of DQ is to reduce the traffic generated by the search process in unstructured P2P networks. The query initiator starts the search by sending the query to a few of its neighbors and with a small Time-to-Live (TTL). The main goal of this first phase (referred to as "probe query") is to estimate the popularity of the resource to be found. If such an attempt does not produce a sufficient number of results, the search initiator sends the query towards the next neighbor with a new TTL. Such TTL is calculated taking into account both the desired number of results, and the resource popularity estimated during the previous phase. This process is repeated until the expected number of results is received or all the neighbors have already been queried.

Similarly to DQ, DQ-DHT dynamically adapts the search extent on the basis of the desired number of results and the popularity of the resource to be located. Differently from DQ, DQ-DHT exploits the structural constraints of the DHT to avoid message duplications. Performance results presented in [5] show that

DQ-DHT generates much less network overhead than the enhanced DQ algorithm proposed in [8], with a comparable - and in some cases better - search time, and with a higher success rate.

The original DQ-DHT algorithm has been implemented using Chord as basic overlay. In this paper we focus on extending DQ-DHT to work in k-ary DHT-based overlays [9]. In a k-ary DHT, broadcast (as well as lookup) takes only $O(\log_k N)$ hops using $O(\log_k N)$ pointers per node. We exploit this "k-ary principle" in DQ-DHT to improve he search time with respect to the original Chord-based implementation. This paper describes the implementation of DQ-DHT over a k-ary DHT and analyzes its performance in terms of search time and number of messages in different configuration scenarios.

The remainder of the paper is organized as follows. Section 2 briefly describes the original DQ-DHT algorithm. Section 3 describes the implementation of DQ-DHT on top of k-ary DHT-based overlays. Section 4 discusses the algorithm performance. Finally, Section 5 concludes the paper.

2.   Dynamic Querying over a DHT

Dynamic Querying over a DHT (DQ-DHT) uses a combination of the DQ technique described above with an algorithm for efficient broadcast over DHTs proposed in [7]. In this section we first describe how the algorithm of broadcast over a DHT works, and then we briefly describe the original DQ-DHT algorithm.

2.1   Broadcast over a DHT

We describe the Chord-based implementation of the broadcast algorithm, as it is presented in [7]. Chord assigns to each node an m-bit identifier that represents the position of the node in a circular identifier space, ranging from 0 and $2^m - 1$. Each node, x, maintains a *finger table* with m entries. The jth entry in the finger table at node x contains the identity of the first node, s, that succeeds x by at least 2^{j-1} positions on the identifier circle, where $1 \leq j \leq m$. Node s is called the jth *finger* of node x.

If the identifier space is not fully populated (i.e., the number of nodes, N, is lower than 2^m), the finger table contains redundant fingers. In a Chord network of N nodes, the number u of unique (i.e., distinct) fingers of a generic node x is likely to be $\log_2 N$ [1]. In the following, we will use the notation F_i to indicate the ith *unique finger* of node x, where $1 \leq i \leq u$.

To perform the broadcast of a data item D, a node x sends a BROADCAST message to all its unique fingers. The BROADCAST message contains D and a *limit* argument, which is used to restrict the forwarding space of a receiving node. The *limit* sent to F_i is set to F_{i+1}, for $1 \leq i \leq u - 1$. The *limit* sent to the last unique finger, F_u, is set to the identifier of the sender, x.

When a nodes y receives a BROADCAST message with a data item D and a given *limit*, it is responsible for forwarding D to all its unique fingers in the interval $]y$, *limit*$[$. When forwarding the message to F_i, for $1 \leq i \leq u - 1$, y supplies it a new *limit*, which is set to F_{i+1} if it does not exceed the old *limit*, to the old *limit* otherwise. As before, the new *limit* sent to F_u is set to y.

As shown in [7], in a network of N nodes, a broadcast message originating at an arbitrary node reaches all other nodes after exactly $N - 1$ messages, with $\log_2 N$ steps. The overall broadcast procedure can be viewed as the process of passing the data item through a spanning tree that covers all nodes in the network. As an example, Figure 1 shows the spanning tree corresponding to the broadcast initiated by Node 0 in a fully populated Chord network with $N = 64$ nodes.

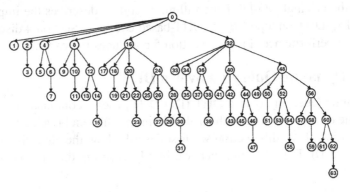

Figure 1.   Spanning trees corresponding to the broadcast initiated by Node 0 in a fully populated Chord network with $N = 64$.

2.2   DQ-DHT algorithm

The DQ-DHT algorithm works as follows. Let x be the node that initiates the search, U the set of unique fingers not yet visited, and R_d the desired number of results. Initially U includes all unique fingers of x. Node x starts by choosing a subset V of U and sending the query to all fingers in V (this phase corresponds to the "probe query" of DQ). These fingers will in turn forward the query to all nodes in the portions of the spanning tree they are responsible for, following the broadcast algorithm described above. When a node receives a query, it checks for local items matching the query criteria and, for each matching item, sends a query hit directly to x. The fingers in V are removed from U to indicate that they have already been visited.

After sending the query to all nodes in V, x waits for an amount of time T_L, which is the estimated time needed by the query to reach all nodes, up to a given level L, of the subtrees rooted at the unique fingers in V, plus the time needed to receive a query hit from those nodes. Then, if the current number of received query hits R_c is equal or greater than R_d, x terminates. Otherwise, an iterative procedure takes place.

At each iteration, node x: 1) calculates the item popularity P as the ratio between R_c and the number of nodes already theoretically queried; 2) calculates the number H_q of hosts in the network that should be queried to hit R_d query hits based on P; 3) chooses, among the nodes in U, a new subset V' of unique fingers whose associated subtrees contain at least H_q nodes; 4) sends the query to all nodes in V'; 5) waits for an amount of time needed to propagate the query to all nodes in the subtrees associated to V'.

The iterative procedure above is repeated until the desired number of query hits is reached, or there are no more fingers to contact. Note that, if the item popularity is properly estimated after the probe query, only one additional iteration may be sufficient to obtain the desired number of query hits.

A key point in the implementation of DQ-DHT is estimating the properties of the spanning tree associated to the broadcast process. This can be done easily by observing that the spanning tree associated to the broadcast over a Chord network is - in the ideal case - a binomial tree [10] (see Figure 1). The basic properties of binomial trees can therefore be used to calculate with good approximation the number of nodes present in the different subtrees, and at different levels, of the spanning tree associated to the broadcast process, as shown in [5]. These values can be in turn used to calculate the number of nodes already theoretically queried, or to be queried, during the iterative DQ process described above.

3. Dynamic Querying over a k-ary DHT

In a k-ary DHT, pointers are placed to achieve a time complexity of $O(\log_k N)$, where N is the number of nodes in the network and k is some predefined constant. This is referred to as doing k-ary lookup or placing pointers according to the "k-ary principle" [9].

Let $M = k^m$ be the size of the identifier space, for some positive integer m. To achieve k-ary lookup, each node x keeps $n_p = (k-1) \times m$ pointers (or fingers) in its finger table. Each of these fingers can be chosen to be the first node that succeeds the start of every interval $f(j)$, where $f(j) = (x+c) \bmod M$, and $c = (1 + ((j-1) \bmod (k-1))) \times k^{\lfloor \frac{j-1}{k-1} \rfloor}$, for $1 \le j \le n_p$. For $k = 2$, it is easy to prove that intervals coincide with those of Chord. If the identifier space is not fully populated (i.e., $N < M$), the finger table contains redundant fingers. In a network of N nodes, the number u of unique fingers of a generic node x is likely to be $(k-1) \times \log_k N$.

The broadcast algorithm described in Section 2.1, which is exploited by DQ-DHT as described in Section 2.2, can also be used in a k-ary DHT. In such case, the whole broadcast process takes only $O(\log_k N)$ hops.

This can be illustrated as in Section 2.1 using a spanning tree view to represent the broadcast process over a k-ary DHT. As an example, Figure 2 shows the spanning tree corresponding to the broadcast initiated by Node 0 in a fully populated k-ary DHT with $k = 4$ and $N = 64$.

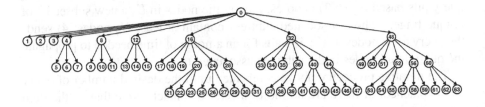

Figure 2.   Spanning trees corresponding to the broadcast initiated by Node 0 in a fully populated k-ary DHT with $k = 4$ and $N = 64$.

By comparing Figure 1 with Figure 2, it can be noted that the number of hops (that is, the depth of the spanning tree) needed to complete the broadcast in a k-ary DHT with $N = 64$ nodes passes from 5 with $k = 2$ (i.e., with Chord), to 3 with $k = 4$. We exploit this principle by extending DQ-DHT to improve the search time with respect to the original Chord-based implementation.

3.1   Properties of the spanning tree associated to the broadcast over a k-ary DHT

As DQ-DHT iteratively calculates the number of nodes already theoretically queried, as well as the number of nodes that must be queried to reach the desired number of results, we need to estimate the number of nodes in the different subtrees, and at different levels, of the spanning tree associated to the broadcast process.

Since for $k \neq 2$ the resulting spanning tree is no more a binomial tree, we experimentally generalized the formulas presented in [5] to be applicable to the broadcast over a k-ary DHT, for any fixed k. Table 1, in particular, shows how we calculate the properties of the spanning tree associated to the broadcast process in case of fully populated identifier space.

To verify the validity of the formulas in case of not fully populated identifier spaces, we employed a network simulator (the same used for the performance evaluation presented in Section 4). Through the simulator we built several random k-ary DHT overlays with different values of k, and compared the real properties of the broadcast spanning tree with the values computed using the formulas in Table 1. The results of such experiments are summarized in Figure 3.

Table 1.   Properties of the spanning tree rooted at a node with u unique fingers $F_1..F_u$ in a fully populated k-ary DHT.

Notation	Description	Value
N_i	Number of nodes in the subtree rooted at F_i, for $1 \leq i \leq u$	$N/(k^{(\lfloor \frac{u-i}{k-1} \rfloor + 1)})$
D_i	Depth of the subtree rooted at F_i, for $1 \leq i \leq u$	$\log_k N_i$
N_i^l	Number of nodes at level l of the subtree rooted at F_i, for $1 \leq i \leq u$ and $0 \leq l \leq D_i$	$\binom{D_i}{l} \times (k-1)^l$

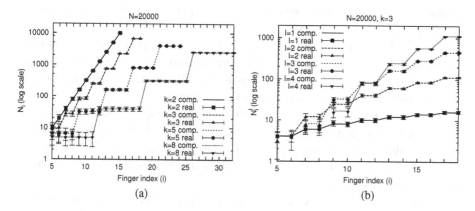

(a)   (b)

Figure 3.   Comparison between computed and real values of N_i and N_i^l for different values of k, i and l, in a simulated k-ary DHT with $N = 20000$ and $m = 20$. Lines represent the computed values. Single points with error bars represent the real values. The error bars of the real values represent the standard deviations from the mean, obtained from 100 simulation runs. All values of N_i and N_i^l are computed or measured from nodes with the following values of u: 15 for networks with $k = 2$; 18 for $k = 3$; 24 for $k = 5$; 32 for $k = 8$.

Figure 3a compares computed and real (i.e., measured) values of N_i for different values of i, in a k-ary DHT with 20000 nodes and $m = 20$, considering the following values of k: 2, 3, 5, and 8. As shown by the graph, the means of the real values (represented as points) are very close to the computed values (represented as lines) for any value of i and k.

The graph in Figure 3b considers again a k-ary DHT with $N = 20000$ and $m = 20$, but with k fixed to 3, and compares computed and real values of N_i^l for different values of i, with l ranging from 1 to 4. As before, the mean of the real values resulted very close to the computed values for any value of i and l.

In summary, the experimental results demonstrate that the formulas in Table 1 can also be used to estimate - with high accuracy - the properties of the spanning tree associated to the broadcast process in not fully populated k-ary DHTs.

3.2   Minor modifications to the original DQ-DHT algorithm

The original DQ-DHT algorithm [5] works correctly over a k-ary DHT using the formulas defined in Section 3.1. In particular: i) the N_i^l formula is used during the probe query to calculate the number of nodes theoretically queried after a predefined amount of time (which corresponds to the number of nodes up to a given depth in the subtrees rooted at the fingers queried during the probe phase); ii) the N_i formula is used both to calculate the number of nodes already theoretically queried (given the set of unique fingers already contacted), and to choose a new subset of unique fingers to contact based on the theoretical number of nodes to query.

Even if the original DQ-DHT algorithm works properly for any value of k, we slightly modified it to obtain a more uniform comparison of its performance when different values of k are used. The difference between the original version and the new one is explained in the following.

As discussed in Section 2.2, to perform the probe query the original algorithm needs two parameters : 1) the initial value of V, which is the first subset of unique fingers to which the query has to be sent to; and 2) L, the last level of the subtrees associated to V from which to wait a response before to estimate the resource popularity.

In the k-ary version, we replaced the two parameters above with the following: 1) H_P, defined as the number of hosts that will receive the query as a result of the probe phase; 2) H_E, the number of hosts to query before to estimate the resource popularity.

Given H_P and the set U of unique fingers of the querying node, the algorithm calculates the initial set V of unique fingers to contact as the subset of U whose associated subtrees have the minimum number of nodes greater or equal to H_P. In other terms, in the original algorithm the fingers to contact during the probe query are chosen explicitly, whereas in the k-ary version they are selected automatically based on the value of H_P.

While H_P indicates the total number of nodes in the subtrees that will be flooded as a result of the probe phase, H_E is the minimum number of nodes that must have received the query before to estimate the resource popularity ($H_E \leq H_P$). Given H_E and the initial set V (calculated through H_P), the algorithm calculates the minimum number L of levels of the subtrees associated to V that contain a number of nodes greater or equal to H_E. Therefore, H_E is used in the k-ary version as an indirect way of specifying the value of L.

Since H_P and H_E are independent from the actual number of unique fingers and from the depth of the corresponding subtrees, their use allows to compare the algorithm performance using different values of k, independently from the number of pointers per node they produce in the resulting overlay.

4. Performance evaluation

We evaluated the performance of the algorithm using a discrete-event simulator. Two performance parameters have been evaluated: the *number of messages* and the *search time*. The first parameter is the total number of messages generated during the search process, while the second parameter is the time needed to receive the desired number of results.

The network parameters are: the number of nodes in the network, N, and the resource replication rate, r, defined as the ratio between the total number of resources satisfying the query criteria and N. The algorithm parameters are: H_P and H_E, introduced in the previous section, and R_d, which is the desired number of results.

We performed all the tests in a random network with $N = 50000$ nodes and a value of r ranging from 0.25 % to 32 %. Different combinations of the H_P and H_E have been experimented, while R_d was fixed to 100. All the results presented in the following have been calculated as an average of 100 independent simulation runs, where at each run the search is initiated by a randomly chosen node.

We run a first set of simulations in a k-ary DHT with $k = 2$ (i.e., a Chord network), with H_P fixed to 2000, and H_E ranging from 250 to 2000. The goal of these first experiments was evaluating the behavior of the algorithm (i.e., number of messages and search time) varying the number H_E of nodes that have received the query before to estimate the resource popularity.

The graphs in Figure 4 show number of messages and search time in function of the replication rate. The search time is expressed in time units, where one time unit corresponds to the average time to pass a message from node to node.

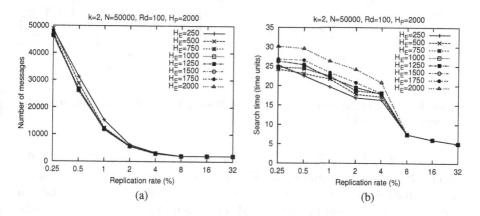

Figure 4. Effect of varying the value of H_E, with $H_P = 2000$ and $k = 2$: (a) number of messages; (b) search time.

As expected, Figure 4a shows that the number of messages decreases as the replication rate increases, for any value of H_E. In general, the number of messages is lower for higher values of H_E. In fact, the generated number of messages depends on the accuracy of the popularity estimation, which is better when H_E is higher. This is particularly true in presence of low replication rates. For example, the number of messages for $r = 0.5$ % passes from 25889 with $H_E = 2000$, to 31209 with $H_E = 250$.

As shown by Figure 4b, also the search time decreases as the replication rate increases. Moreover, the search time decreases as the value of H_E decreases, since lower values of H_E correspond to a lower duration of the probe query. For instance, the search time for $r = 0.5$ % passes from 29.58 with $H_E = 2000$, to 22.53 with $H_E = 250$. However, since lower values of H_E generate more messages, an intermediate value of H_E should be preferred. For example, $H_E = 1000$ represents a good compromise since it generates the same number of messages of $H_E = 2000$, but with a search time close to that of $H_E = 250$.

Then, we compared the performance of the algorithm with different values of k. Based on the first set of simulations, we chosen the following algorithm parameters: $H_P = 2000$ and $H_E = 1000$. Figure 5 shows how number of messages and response time vary in this configuration with k ranging from 2 to 8.

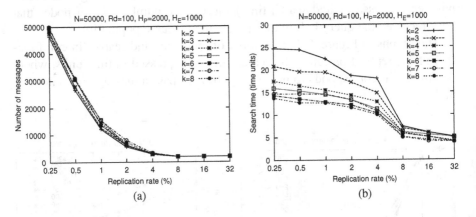

Figure 5.   Effect of varying the value of k, with $H_P = 2000$ and $H_E = 1000$: (a) number of messages; (b) search time.

As shown by Figure 5b, the search time strongly depends on the arity of the DHT. The maximum gain (nearly 48 %) is obtained for $r = 0.5$ %, with the search time passing from 24.46 with $k = 2$, to 12.74 with $k = 8$. The minimum gain (20 %) is obtained for the highest replication rate ($r = 32$ %), when the search time passes from 5.02 with $k = 2$, to 4.0 with $k = 8$. The number of messages is less related to the value of k than the search time (see Figure 5a), but - in general - lower values of k generate lower number of messages. The maximum difference between $k = 2$ and $k = 8$ is reached with $r = 0.5\ \%$ (about 14 %), but it is counterbalanced by a search time gain of 48 %, as shown in Figure 5b.

We repeated the comparison above using the following configuration: $H_P = 4000$ and $H_E = 2000$. Since H_P is the minimum number of messages that will be generated during the search process, a so high value should be used when it is fundamental to minimize the search time. The simulation results are reported in Figure 6.

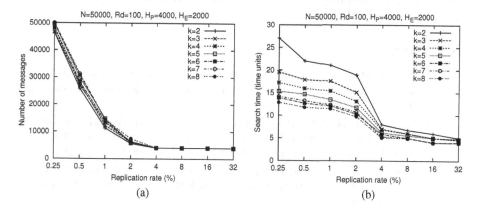

Figure 6. Effect of varying the value of k, with $H_P = 4000$ and $H_E = 2000$: (a) number of messages; (b) search time.

The trends are similar to those shown in Figure 6. In general, the search time is lower of 1-2 units w.r.t. that measured for $H_P = 2000$ and $H_E = 1000$. For $r = 4\ \%$, the search time is significantly improved because the probe query, with $H_P = 4000$, resulted in most cases sufficient to obtain the desired number of results.

In summary, the simulation results presented above demonstrate that implementing DQ over a k-ary DHT allows to achieve a significant improvement of the search time with respect to a Chord-based implementation.

5. Conclusions

Implementing unstructured search techniques on top of DHT-based overlays is an efficient way to support arbitrary queries in structured P2P networks. This approach has been followed in the design of DQ-DHT [5], a P2P search algorithm that combines the DQ technique used in unstructured networks with an algorithm for efficient broadcast over DHTs.

The original DQ-DHT algorithm has been implemented using Chord as basic overlay. This paper focused on extending DQ-DHT to work in k-ary DHT-based overlays [9]. As demonstrated by the experimental results presented in this paper, the "k-ary principle" allowed DQ-DHT to achieve a significant improvement of the search time with respect to the original Chord-based implementation.

DQ over a DHT can be effectively used to implement resource discovery services in large distributed environments, as demonstrated by the DQ-based Grid resource discovery system proposed in [11]. The k-ary DQ-DHT algorithm proposed in this paper could be therefore used to implement a more efficient version of that Grid system. Another application of this work could be adding the capability to perform DQ search to existing distributed k-ary systems like DKS [12].

References

[1] I. Stoica, R. Morris, D. R. Karger, M. F. Kaashoek, H. Balakrishnan. Chord: A Scalable Peer-to-Peer Lookup Service for Internet Applications. ACM SIGCOMM'01, San Diego, USA, 2001.

[2] P. Trunfio, D. Talia, H. Papadakis, P. Fragopoulou, M. Mordacchini, M. Pennanen, K. Popov, V. Vlassov, S. Haridi. Peer-to-Peer Resource Discovery in Grids: Models and Systems, Future Generation Computer Systems, vol. 23 n. 7, pp. 864-878, 2007.

[3] M. Castro, M. Costa, A. Rowstron. Debunking Some Myths About Structured and Unstructured Overlays. 2nd Symp. on Networked Systems Design and Implementation (NSDI'05), Boston, USA, 2005.

[4] Y. Chawathe, S. Ratnasamy, L. Breslau, N. Lanham, S. Shenker. Making Gnutella-like P2P Systems Scalable. ACM SIGCOMM'03, Karlsruhe, Germany, 2003.

[5] D. Talia, P. Trunfio. Dynamic Querying in Structured Peer-to-Peer Networks. Submitted for publication. Available at: http://grid.deis.unical.it/papers/pdf/DQ-DHT.pdf.

[6] A. Fisk. Gnutella Dynamic Query Protocol v0.1, May 2003. Available at: http://www9.limewire.com/developer/dynamic_query.html.

[7] S. El-Ansary, L. Onana Alima, P. Brand, S. Haridi. Efficient Broadcast in Structured P2P Networks. 2nd Int. Workshop on Peer-to-Peer Systems (IPTPS'03), Berkeley, USA, 2003.

[8] H. Jiang, S. Jin. Exploiting Dynamic Querying like Flooding Techniques in Unstructured Peer-to-Peer Networks. 13th IEEE Int. Conf. on Network Protocols (ICNP 2005), Boston, USA, 2005.

[9] A. Ghodsi. Distributed k-ary System: Algorithms for Distributed Hash Tables. Ph.D. Thesis, ECS Dept., The Royal Institute of Technology (KTH), Stockholm, Sweden, 2006.

[10] T. H. Cormen, C. E. Leiserson, R. L. Rivest. Introduction to Algorithms. MIT Press, 1990.

[11] H. Papadakis, P. Trunfio, D. Talia, P. Fragopoulou. Design and Implementation of a Hybrid P2P-based Grid Resource Discovery System. In: Making Grids Work, M. Danelutto, P. Fragopoulou, V. Getov (Eds.), Springer, USA, 2008.

[12] L. O. Alima, S. El-Ansary, P. Brand, S. Haridi. DKS (N, k, f): A Family of Low Communication, Scalable and Fault-Tolerant Infrastructures for P2P Applications. 3rd Int. Symp. on Cluster Computing and the Grid (CCGrid 2003), Tokyo, Japan, 2003.

Author Index